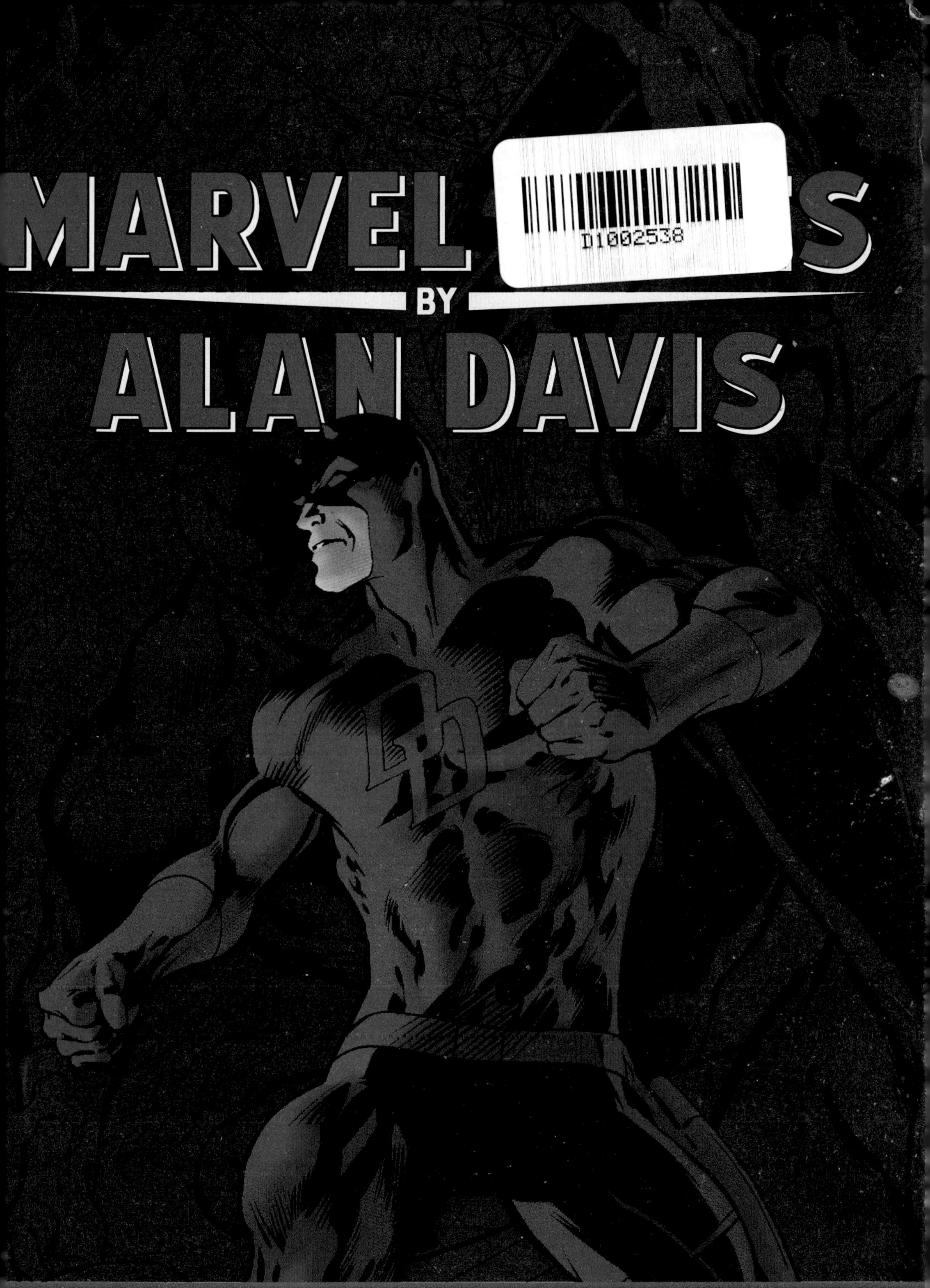
MARVEL
BY
ALAN DAVIS



**ARVEL TALES BY ALAN DAVIS.** Contains material originally published in magazine form as FANTASTIC FOUR ANNUAL #33, DAREDEVIL ANNUAL #1, WOLVERINE ANNUAL #1 and THOR: TRUTH OF HISTORY #1. rst printing 2012. ISBN# 978-0-7851-4032-0. Published by MARVEL WORLDWIDE, INC., a subsidiary of MARVEL ENTERTAINMENT, LLC. OFFICE OF PUBLICATION: 135 West 50th Street, New York, NY 10020.

**Printed in the U.S.A.** ALAN FINE, EVP - Office of the President, Marvel orldwide, Inc. and EVP & CMO Marvel Characters B.V.; DAN BUCKLEY, Publisher & President - Print, Animation & Digital Divisions; JOE QUESADA, Chief Creative Officer; TOM BREVOORT, SVP of Publishing; DAVID OGART, SVP of Operations & Procurement, Publishing; RUWAN JAYATILLEKE, SVP & Associate Publisher, Publishing; C.B. CEBULSKI, SVP of Creator & Content Development; DAVID GABRIEL, SVP of Publishing ales & Circulation; MICHAEL PASCIULLO, SVP of Brand Planning & Communications; JIM O'KEEFE, VP of Operations & Logistics; DAN CARR, Executive Director of Publishing Technology; SUSAN CRESPI, Editorial perations Manager; ALEX MORALES, Publishing Operations Manager; STAN LEE, Chairman Emeritus. For information regarding advertising in Marvel Comics or on Marvel.com, please contact Niza Disla, Director f Marvel Partnerships, at ndisla@marvel.com. For Marvel subscription inquiries, please call 800-217-9158. **Manufactured between 9/6/2012 and 10/9/2012 by QUAD/GRAPHICS, DUBUQUE, IA, USA.**

0 9 8 7 6 5 4 3 2 1

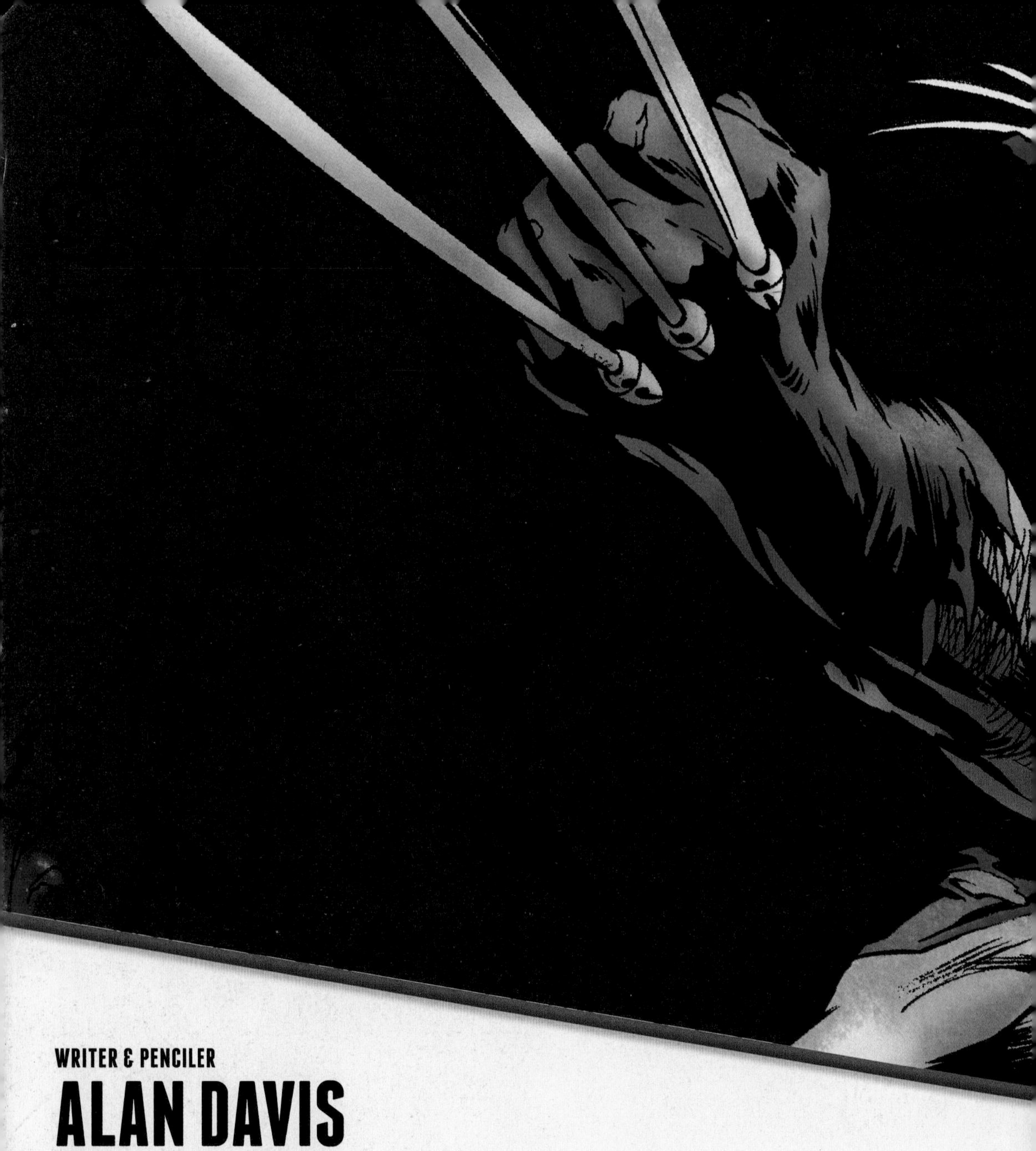

WRITER & PENCILER
**ALAN DAVIS**
INKER
**MARK FARMER**
COLORIST
**JAVIER RODRIGUEZ**
WITH **ROB SCHWAGER** (*THOR: TRUTH OF HISTORY*)
LETTERER
**VC'S CLAYTON COWLES**
WITH **JOE CARAMAGNA** (*THOR: TRUTH OF HISTORY*)
COVER ART
**ALAN DAVIS, MARK FARMER & JAVIER RODRIGUEZ**

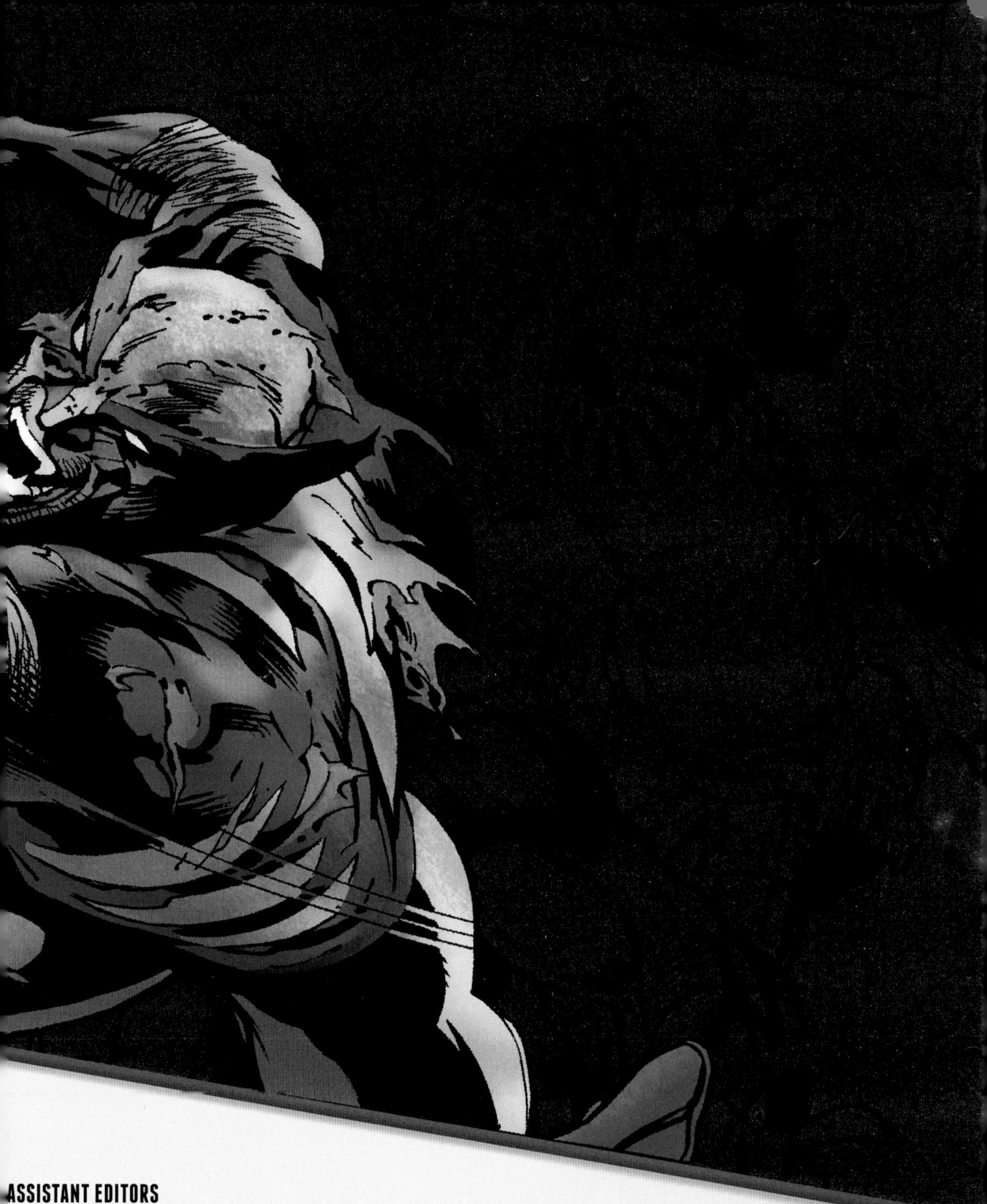


ASSISTANT EDITORS

**JOHN DENNING, JAKE THOMAS & ALEJANDRO ARBONA**

ASSOCIATE EDITOR

**LAUREN SANKOVITCH**

EDITORS

**TOM BREVOORT & WARREN SIMONS**

COLLECTION EDITOR: CORY LEVINE • ASSISTANT EDITORS: ALEX STARBUCK & NELSON RIBEIRO
EDITORS, SPECIAL PROJECTS: JENNIFER GRÜNWALD & MARK D. BEAZLEY • SENIOR EDITOR, SPECIAL PROJECTS: JEFF YOUNGQUIST
SENIOR VICE PRESIDENT OF SALES: DAVID GABRIEL • SVP OF BRAND PLANNING & COMMUNICATIONS: MICHAEL PASCIULLO • COVER DESIGN: JEFF POWELL
EDITOR IN CHIEF: AXEL ALONSO • CHIEF CREATIVE OFFICER: JOE QUESADA • PUBLISHER: DAN BUCKLEY • EXECUTIVE PRODUCER: ALAN FINE

# CLANDESTINE

When Adam Destine fell in love with the djinn Elalyth, the mystical Clan Destine was born! Ancient and mysterious, the Destine family spent centuries carefully secreted away from humanity. Now, with an increasingly interconnected world, the Clan Destine finds itself drawn out of hiding...but will they be heroes or villains?

# FANTASTIC FOUR

Reed Richards, Sue Storm Richards, Johnny Storm and Ben Grimm are the Fantastic Four. A team — and a family — of adventurers, explorers and imaginauts.

# DAREDEVIL

Lawyer Matt Murdock was blinded in a tragic toxic chemical spill as a child, but his senses became dramatically heightened, giving him the power and dexterity to patrol the streets as Daredevil — The Man Without Fear!

# WOLVERINE

Many years ago, a secret government organization abducted the man called Logan, a mutant possessing razor-sharp bone claws and the ability to heal from any wound. In their attempt to create the perfect living weapon, the organization bonded the unbreakable metal Adamantium to his skeleton. The process was excruciating and by the end, there was little left of the man known as Logan. He had become Wolverine!

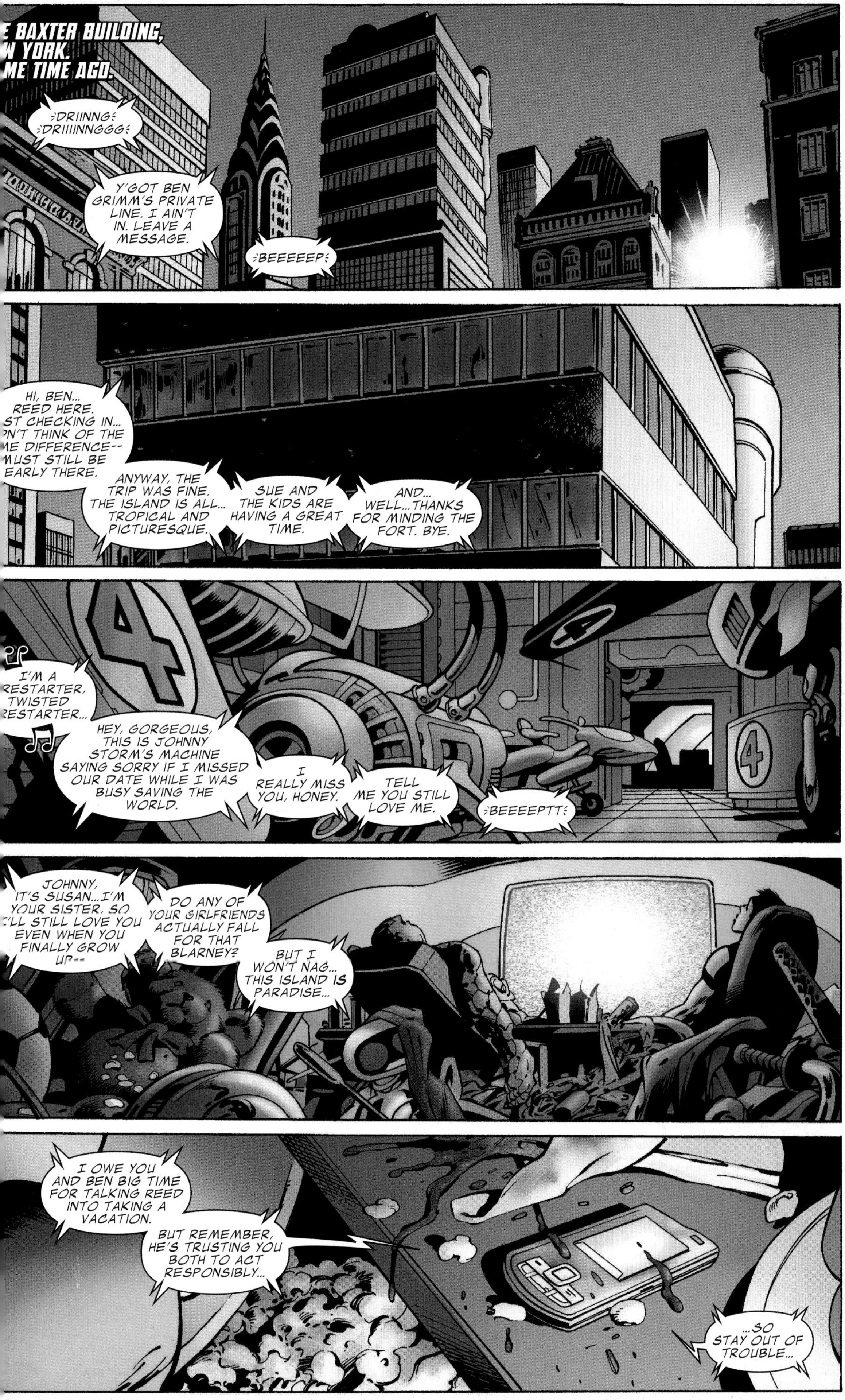
E BAXTER BUILDING,
W YORK.
ME TIME AGO.
DRIINNG
DRIIIINNGGG
Y'GOT BEN GRIMM'S PRIVATE LINE. I AIN'T IN. LEAVE A MESSAGE.
BEEEEEP
HI, BEN... REED HERE. ST CHECKING IN... N'T THINK OF THE ME DIFFERENCE-- MUST STILL BE EARLY THERE.
ANYWAY, THE TRIP WAS FINE. THE ISLAND IS ALL... TROPICAL AND PICTURESQUE.
SUE AND THE KIDS ARE HAVING A GREAT TIME.
AND... WELL...THANKS FOR MINDING THE FORT. BYE.
I'M A RESTARTER, TWISTED RESTARTER...
HEY, GORGEOUS, THIS IS JOHNNY STORM'S MACHINE SAYING SORRY IF I MISSED OUR DATE WHILE I WAS BUSY SAVING THE WORLD.
I REALLY MISS YOU, HONEY.
TELL ME YOU STILL LOVE ME.
BEEEEPTT
JOHNNY, IT'S SUSAN...I'M YOUR SISTER, SO 'LL STILL LOVE YOU EVEN WHEN YOU FINALLY GROW UP--
DO ANY OF YOUR GIRLFRIENDS ACTUALLY FALL FOR THAT BLARNEY?
BUT I WON'T NAG... THIS ISLAND IS PARADISE...
I OWE YOU AND BEN BIG TIME FOR TALKING REED INTO TAKING A VACATION.
BUT REMEMBER, HE'S TRUSTING YOU BOTH TO ACT RESPONSIBLY...
...SO STAY OUT OF TROUBLE...

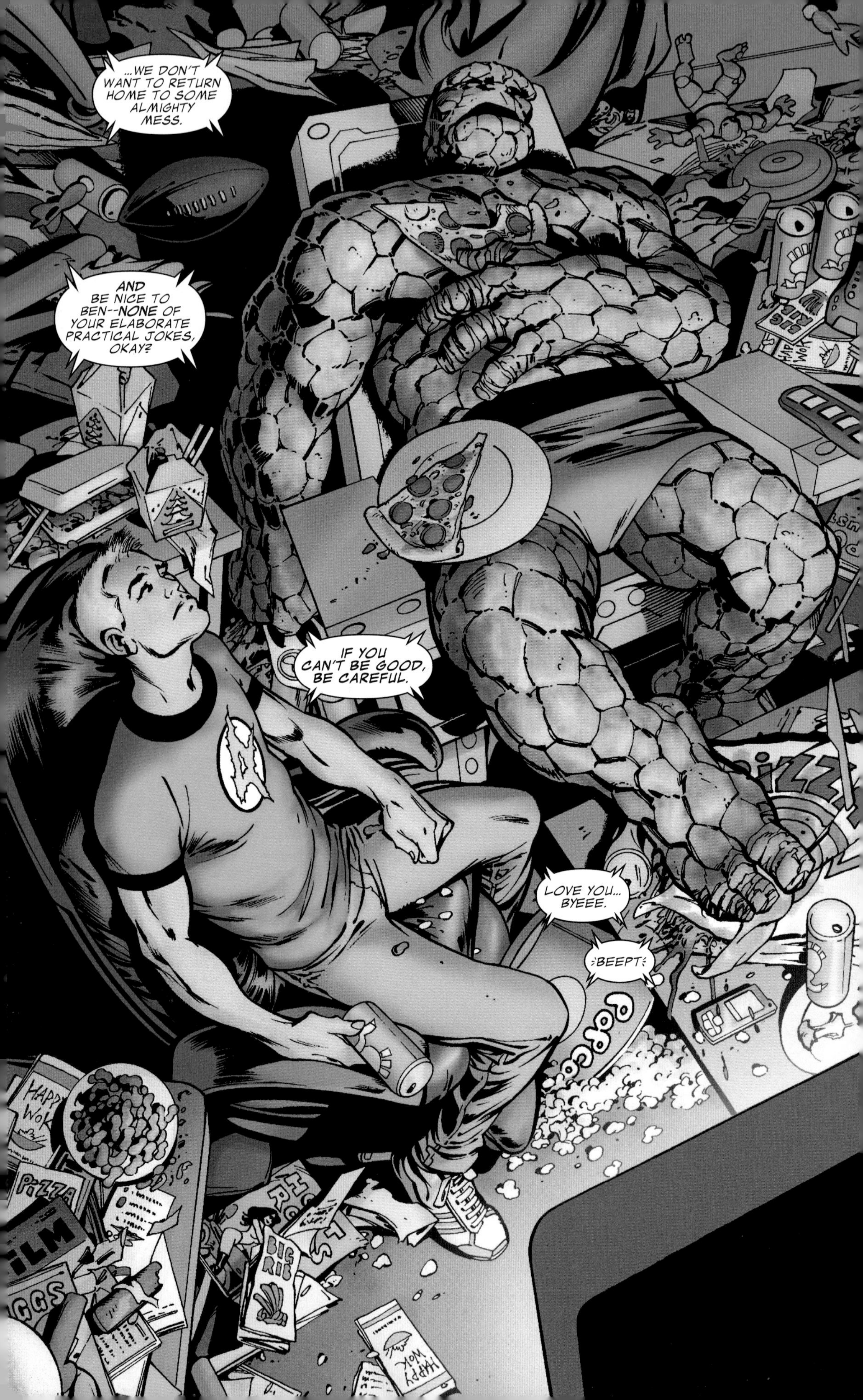
...WE DON'T WANT TO RETURN HOME TO SOME ALMIGHTY MESS.
AND BE NICE TO BEN--NONE OF YOUR ELABORATE PRACTICAL JOKES, OKAY?
IF YOU CAN'T BE GOOD, BE CAREFUL.
LOVE YOU... BYEEE.
BEEPT
HAPPY WOK
PIZZA
FILM
BIG RIB
HAPPY WOK

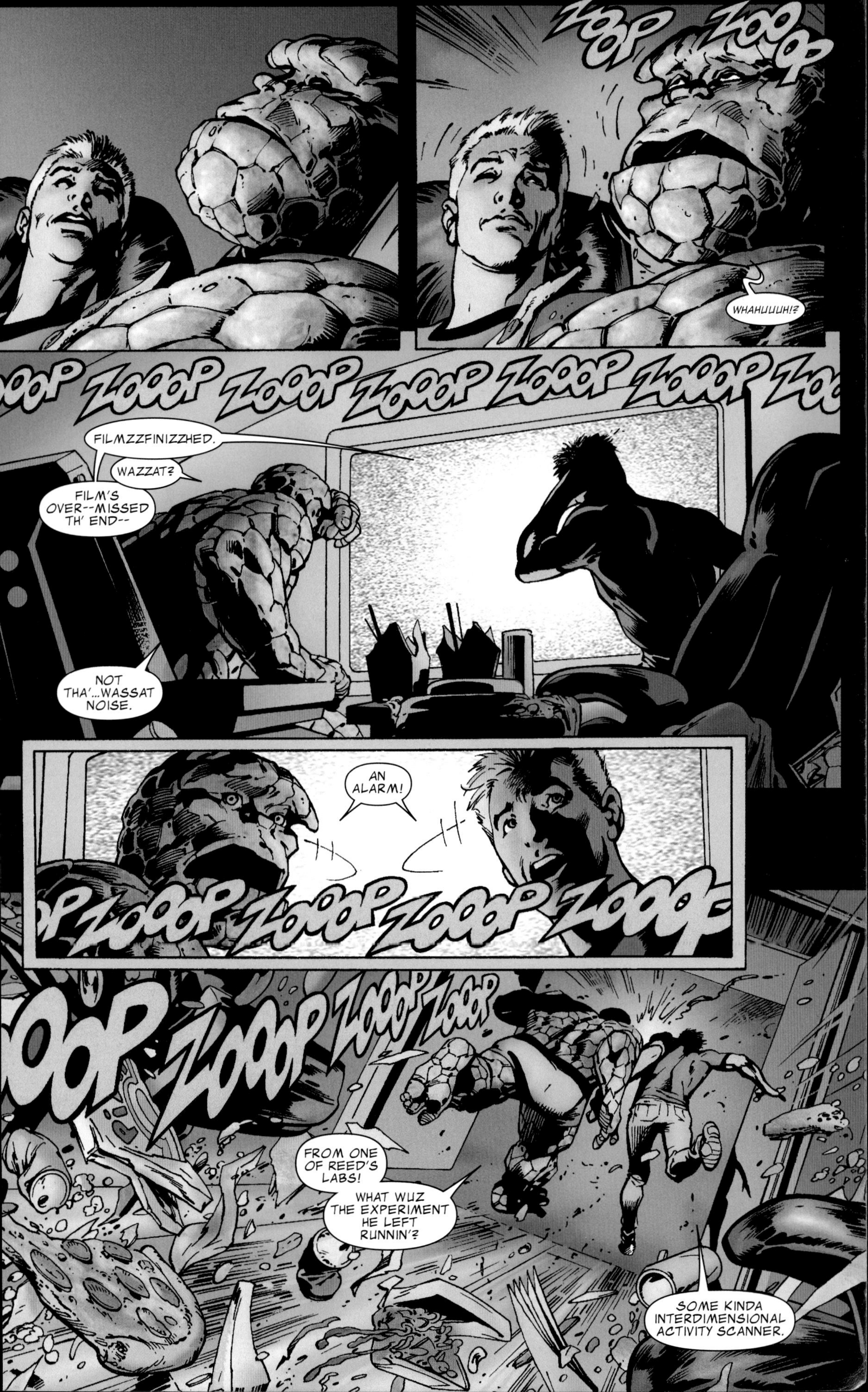
ZOOP ZOOOP
WHAHUUUH!?
ZOOOP ZOOOP ZOOOP ZOOOP ZOOOP ZOOOP
FILMZZFINIZZHED.
WAZZAT?
FILM'S OVER--MISSED TH' END--
NOT THA'...WASSAT NOISE.
AN ALARM!
ZOOOP ZOOOP ZOOOP ZOOO-
ZOOOP ZOOOP ZOOOP ZOOOP
FROM ONE OF REED'S LABS!
WHAT WUZ THE EXPERIMENT HE LEFT RUNNIN'?
SOME KINDA INTERDIMENSIONAL ACTIVITY SCANNER.

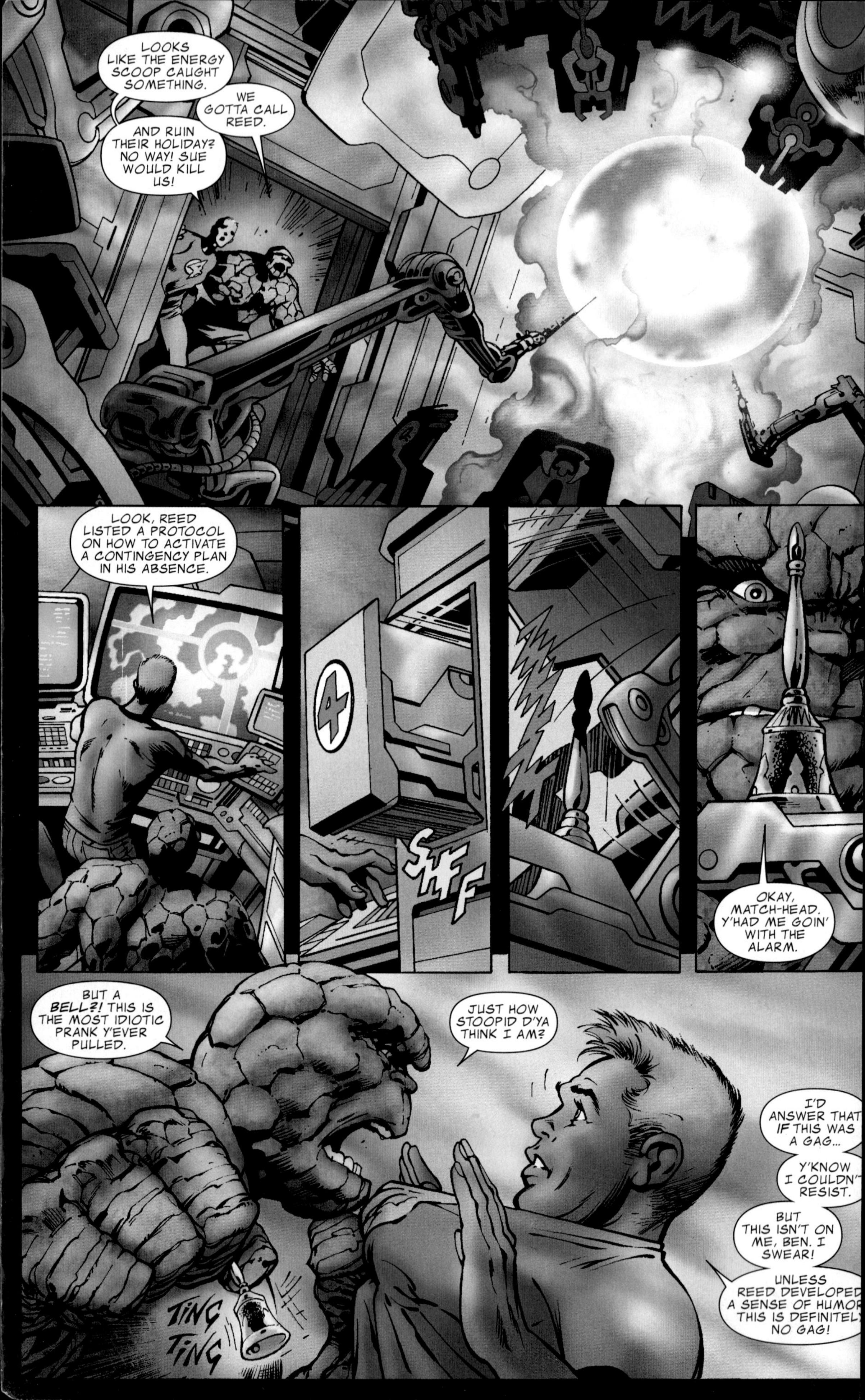
LOOKS LIKE THE ENERGY SCOOP CAUGHT SOMETHING.
WE GOTTA CALL REED.
AND RUIN THEIR HOLIDAY? NO WAY! SUE WOULD KILL US!
LOOK, REED LISTED A PROTOCOL ON HOW TO ACTIVATE A CONTINGENCY PLAN IN HIS ABSENCE.
SHFF
OKAY, MATCH-HEAD. Y'HAD ME GOIN' WITH THE ALARM.
BUT A BELL?! THIS IS THE MOST IDIOTIC PRANK Y'EVER PULLED.
JUST HOW STOOPID D'YA THINK I AM?
I'D ANSWER THAT IF THIS WAS A GAG...
Y'KNOW I COULDN'T RESIST.
BUT THIS ISN'T ON ME, BEN. I SWEAR!
UNLESS REED DEVELOPED A SENSE OF HUMOR THIS IS DEFINITELY NO GAG!
TING TING

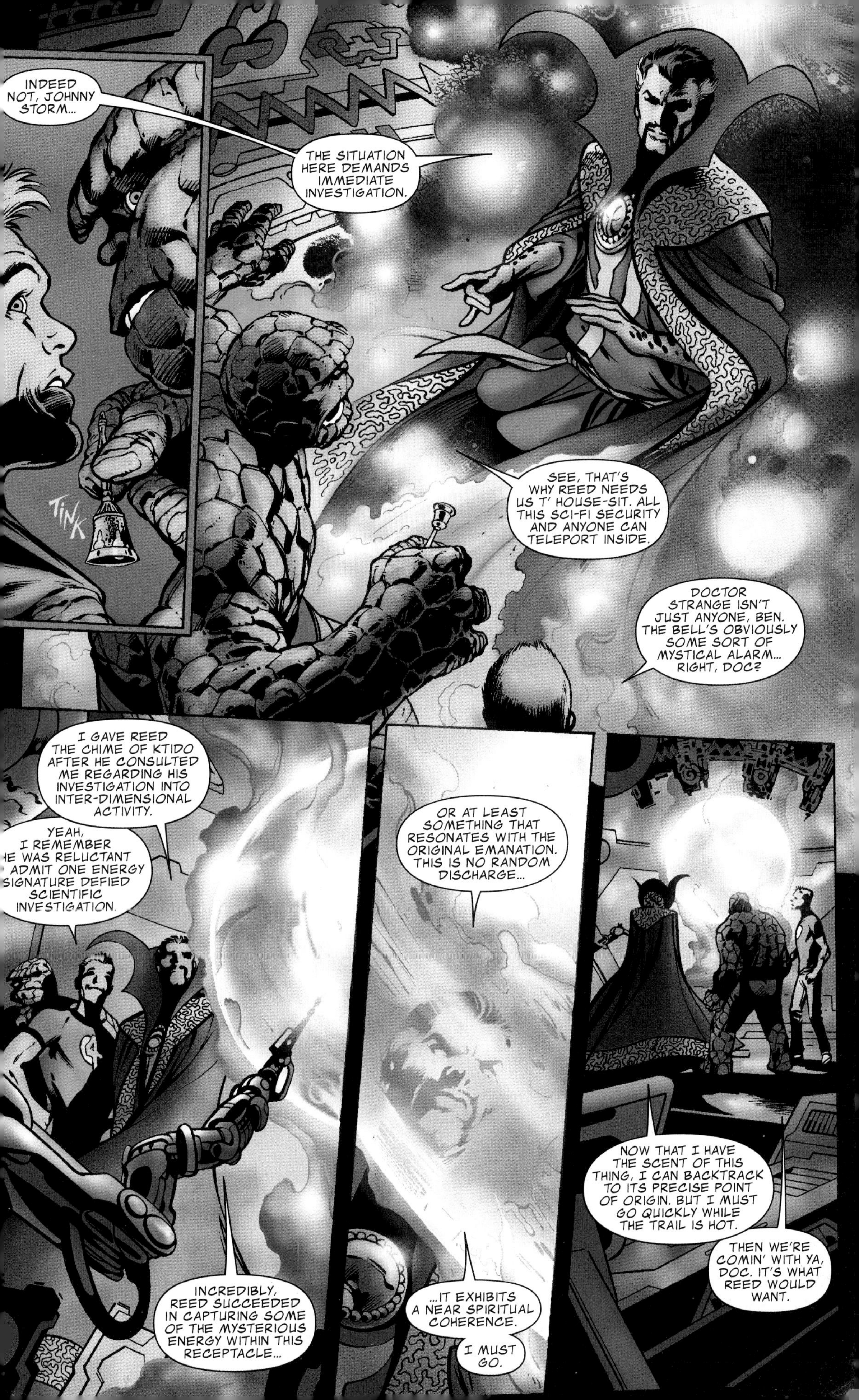
INDEED NOT, JOHNNY STORM...
THE SITUATION HERE DEMANDS IMMEDIATE INVESTIGATION.
TINK
SEE, THAT'S WHY REED NEEDS US T' HOUSE-SIT. ALL THIS SCI-FI SECURITY AND ANYONE CAN TELEPORT INSIDE.
DOCTOR STRANGE ISN'T JUST ANYONE, BEN. THE BELL'S OBVIOUSLY SOME SORT OF MYSTICAL ALARM... RIGHT, DOC?
I GAVE REED THE CHIME OF KTIDO AFTER HE CONSULTED ME REGARDING HIS INVESTIGATION INTO INTER-DIMENSIONAL ACTIVITY.
YEAH, I REMEMBER HE WAS RELUCTANT ADMIT ONE ENERGY SIGNATURE DEFIED SCIENTIFIC INVESTIGATION.
INCREDIBLY, REED SUCCEEDED IN CAPTURING SOME OF THE MYSTERIOUS ENERGY WITHIN THIS RECEPTACLE...
OR AT LEAST SOMETHING THAT RESONATES WITH THE ORIGINAL EMANATION. THIS IS NO RANDOM DISCHARGE...
...IT EXHIBITS A NEAR SPIRITUAL COHERENCE.
I MUST GO.
NOW THAT I HAVE THE SCENT OF THIS THING, I CAN BACKTRACK TO ITS PRECISE POINT OF ORIGIN. BUT I MUST GO QUICKLY WHILE THE TRAIL IS HOT.
THEN WE'RE COMIN' WITH YA, DOC. IT'S WHAT REED WOULD WANT.

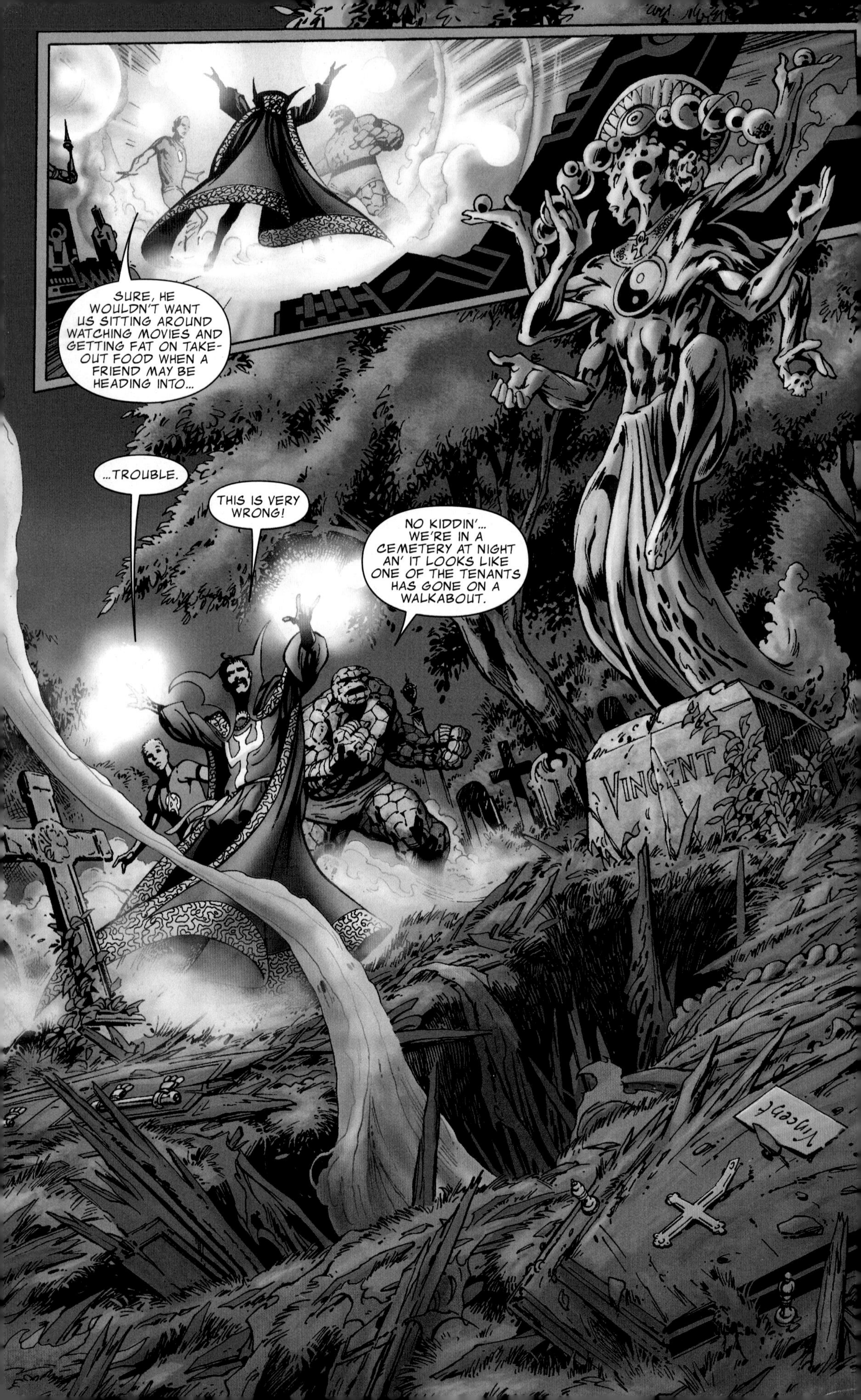
SURE, HE WOULDN'T WANT US SITTING AROUND WATCHING MOVIES AND GETTING FAT ON TAKE-OUT FOOD WHEN A FRIEND MAY BE HEADING INTO...
...TROUBLE.
THIS IS VERY WRONG!
NO KIDDIN'... WE'RE IN A CEMETERY AT NIGHT AN' IT LOOKS LIKE ONE OF THE TENANTS HAS GONE ON A WALKABOUT.
VINCENT
Vincent

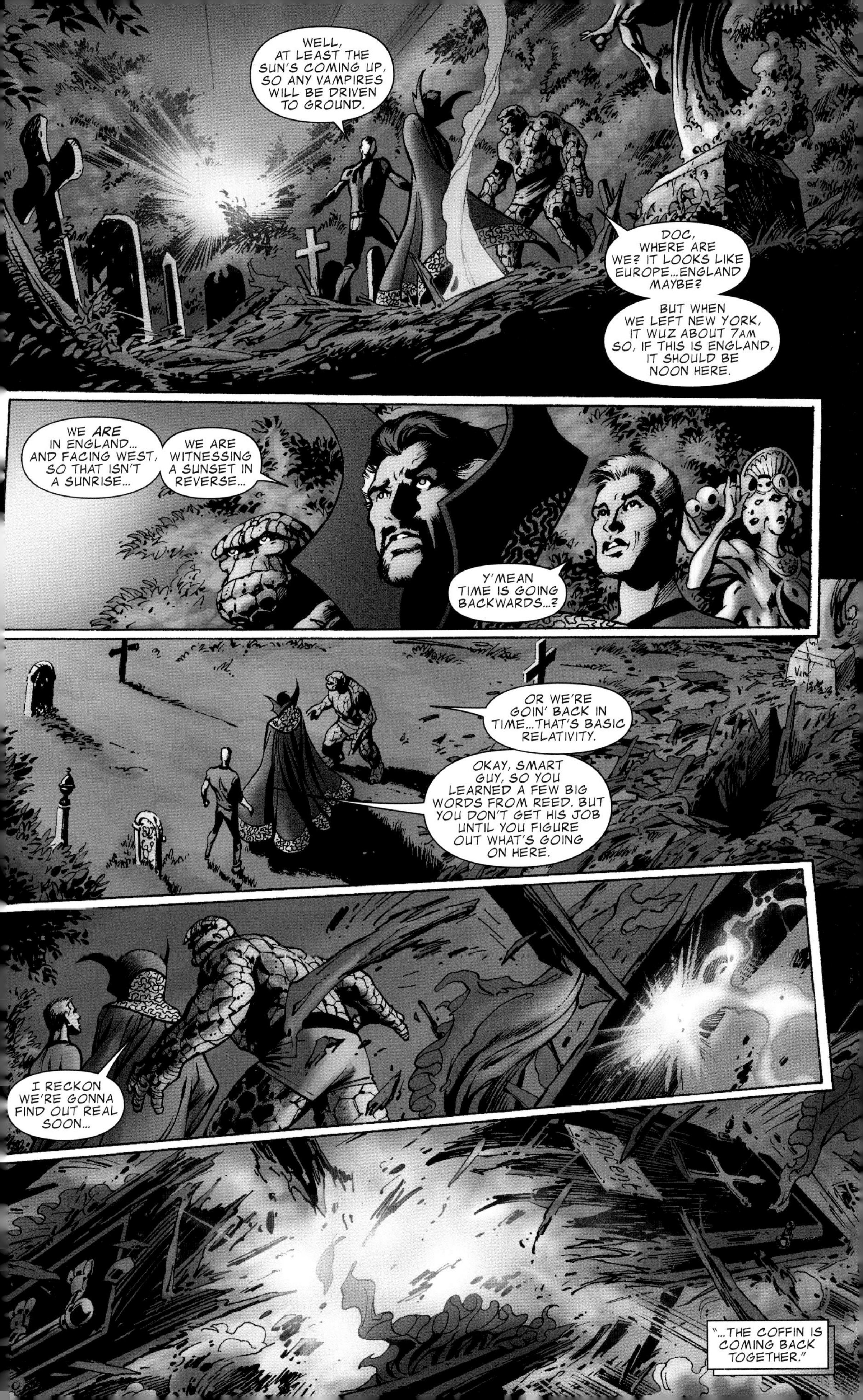
WELL, AT LEAST THE SUN'S COMING UP, SO ANY VAMPIRES WILL BE DRIVEN TO GROUND.
DOC, WHERE ARE WE? IT LOOKS LIKE EUROPE...ENGLAND MAYBE?
BUT WHEN WE LEFT NEW YORK, IT WUZ ABOUT 7AM SO, IF THIS IS ENGLAND, IT SHOULD BE NOON HERE.
WE ARE IN ENGLAND... AND FACING WEST, SO THAT ISN'T A SUNRISE...
WE ARE WITNESSING A SUNSET IN REVERSE...
Y'MEAN TIME IS GOING BACKWARDS...?
OR WE'RE GOIN' BACK IN TIME...THAT'S BASIC RELATIVITY.
OKAY, SMART GUY, SO YOU LEARNED A FEW BIG WORDS FROM REED. BUT YOU DON'T GET HIS JOB UNTIL YOU FIGURE OUT WHAT'S GOING ON HERE.
I RECKON WE'RE GONNA FIND OUT REAL SOON...
"...THE COFFIN IS COMING BACK TOGETHER."

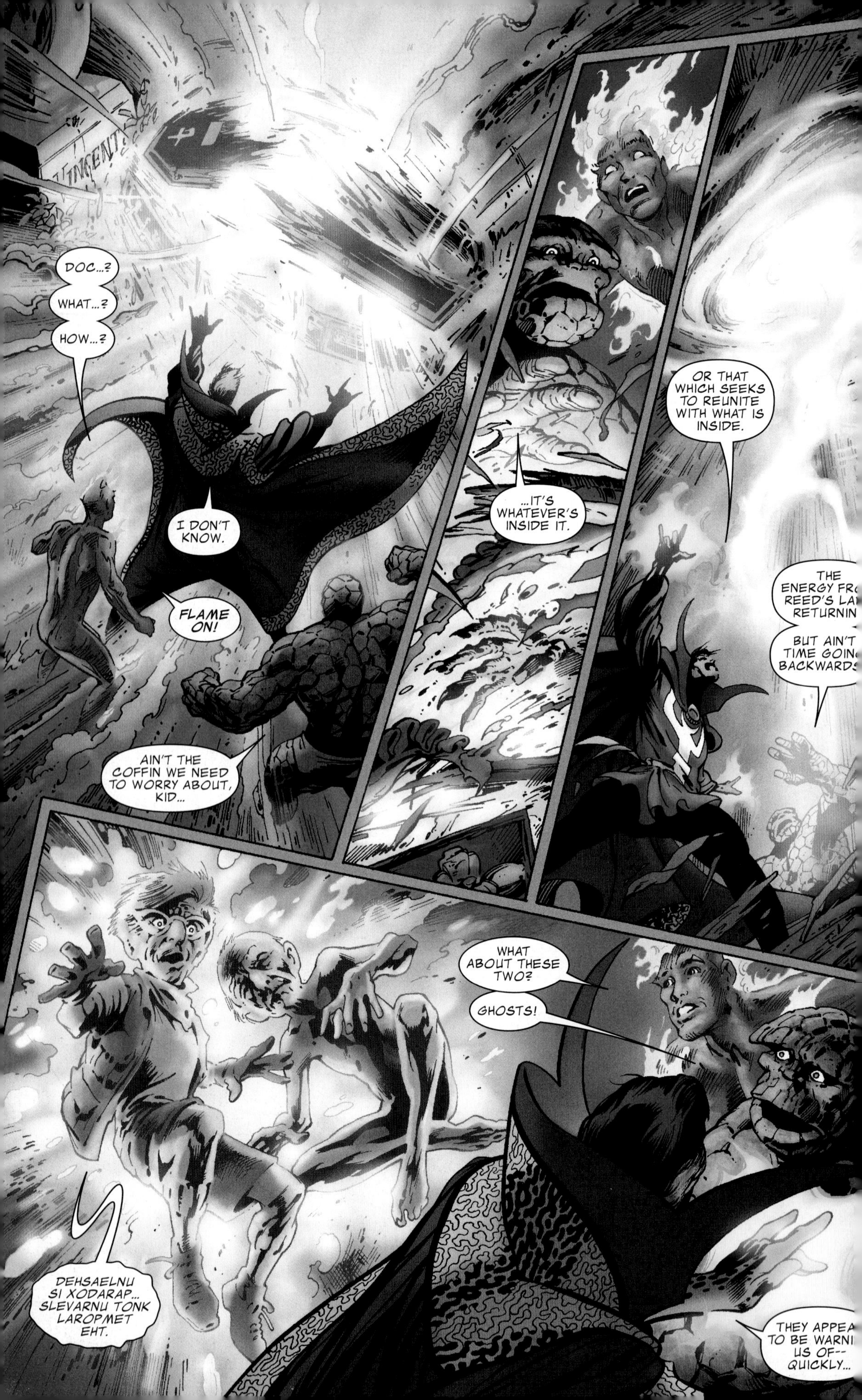
VINCENT
DOC...?
WHAT...?
HOW...?
I DON'T KNOW.
FLAME ON!
AIN'T THE COFFIN WE NEED TO WORRY ABOUT, KID...
...IT'S WHATEVER'S INSIDE IT.
OR THAT WHICH SEEKS TO REUNITE WITH WHAT IS INSIDE.
THE ENERGY FR REED'S LA RETURNIN
BUT AIN'T TIME GOIN BACKWARDS
WHAT ABOUT THESE TWO?
GHOSTS!
DEHSAELNU SI XODARAP... SLEVARNU TONK LAROPMET EHT.
THEY APPEA TO BE WARNI US OF-- QUICKLY...

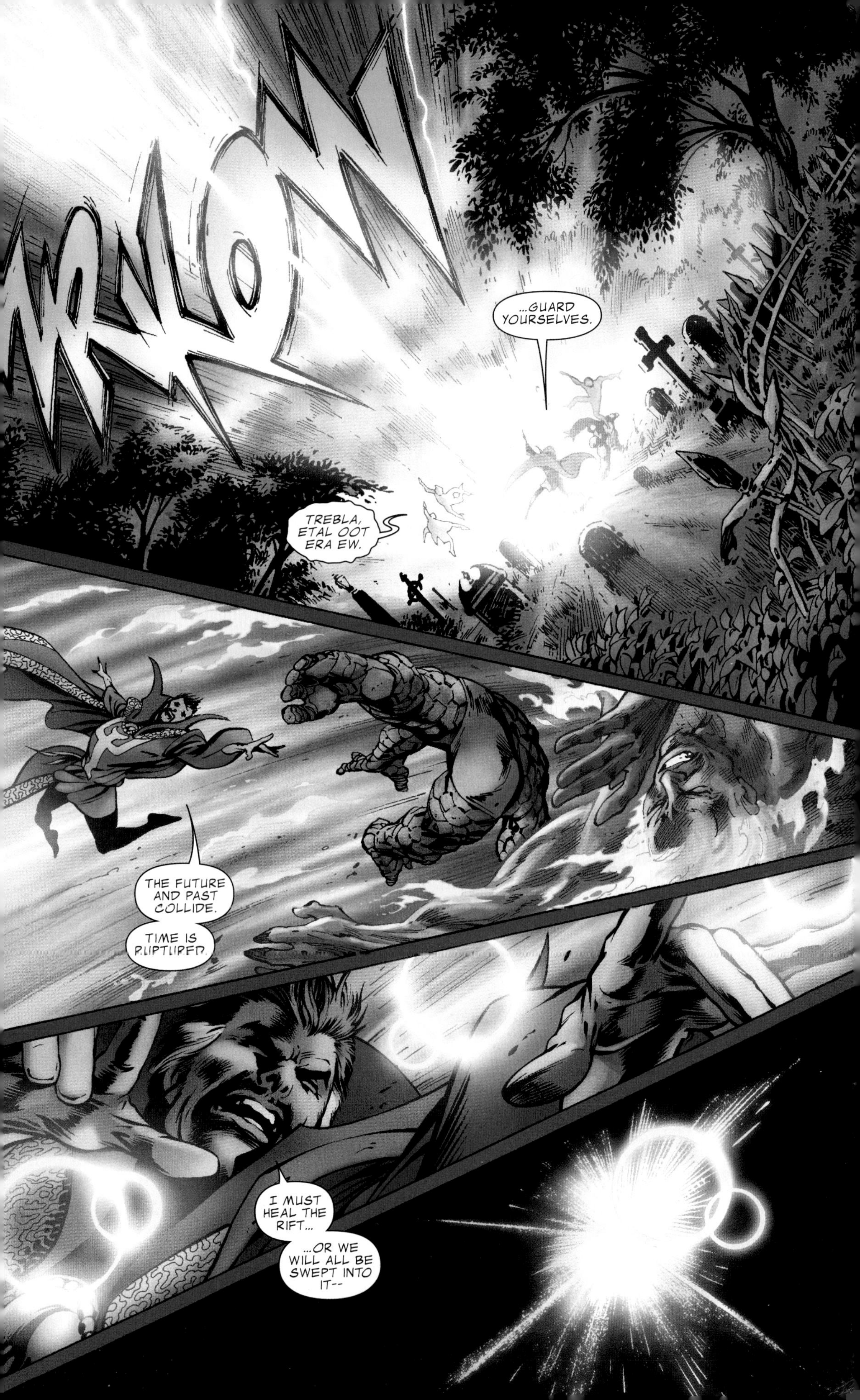

...GUARD YOURSELVES.
TREBLA, ETAL OOT ERA EW.
THE FUTURE AND PAST COLLIDE.
TIME IS RUPTURED.
I MUST HEAL THE RIFT...
...OR WE WILL ALL BE SWEPT INTO IT--

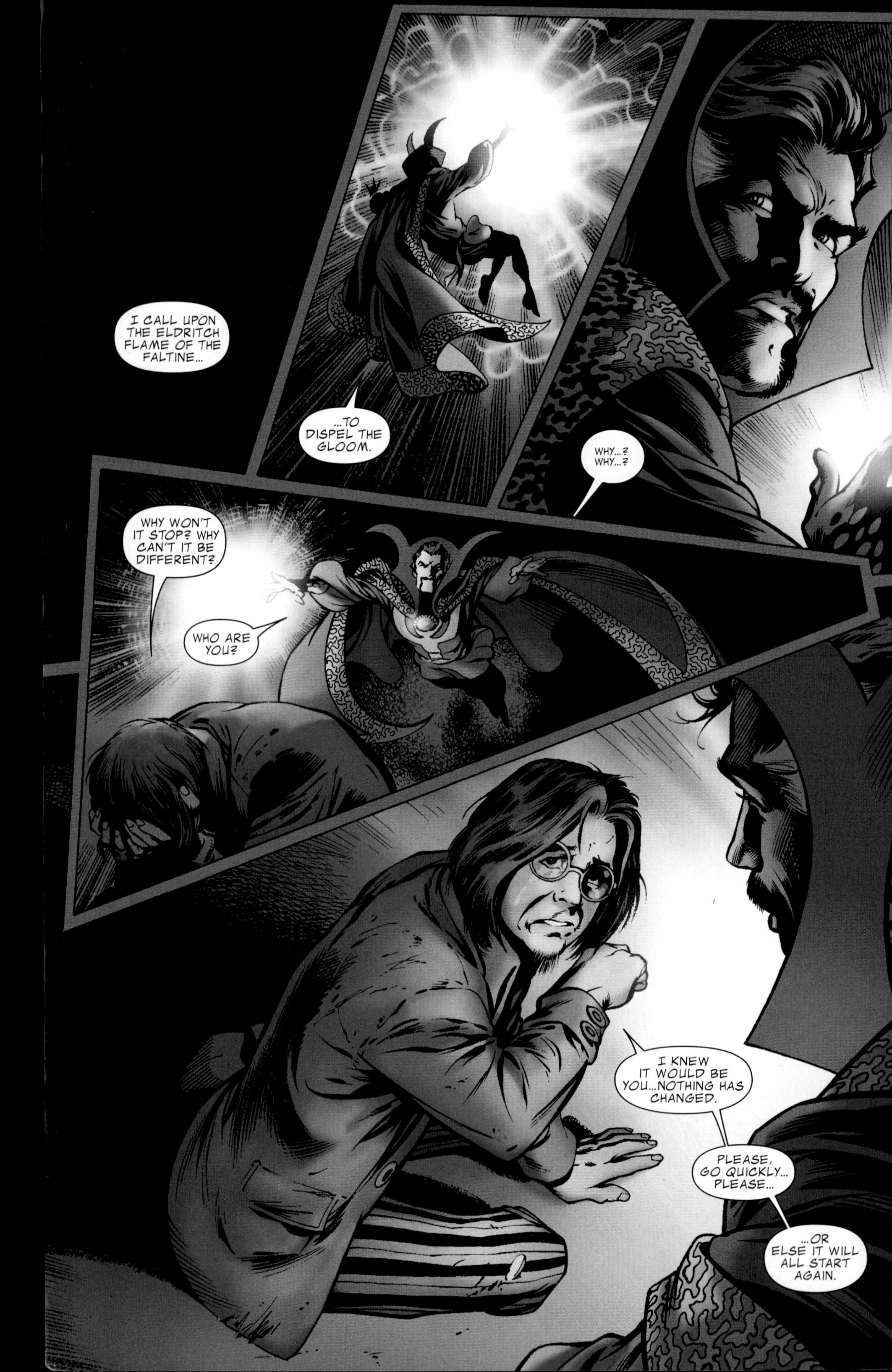

I CALL UPON THE ELDRITCH FLAME OF THE FALTINE...
...TO DISPEL THE GLOOM.
WHY...? WHY...?
WHY WON'T IT STOP? WHY CAN'T IT BE DIFFERENT?
WHO ARE YOU?
I KNEW IT WOULD BE YOU...NOTHING HAS CHANGED.
PLEASE, GO QUICKLY... PLEASE...
...OR ELSE IT WILL ALL START AGAIN.

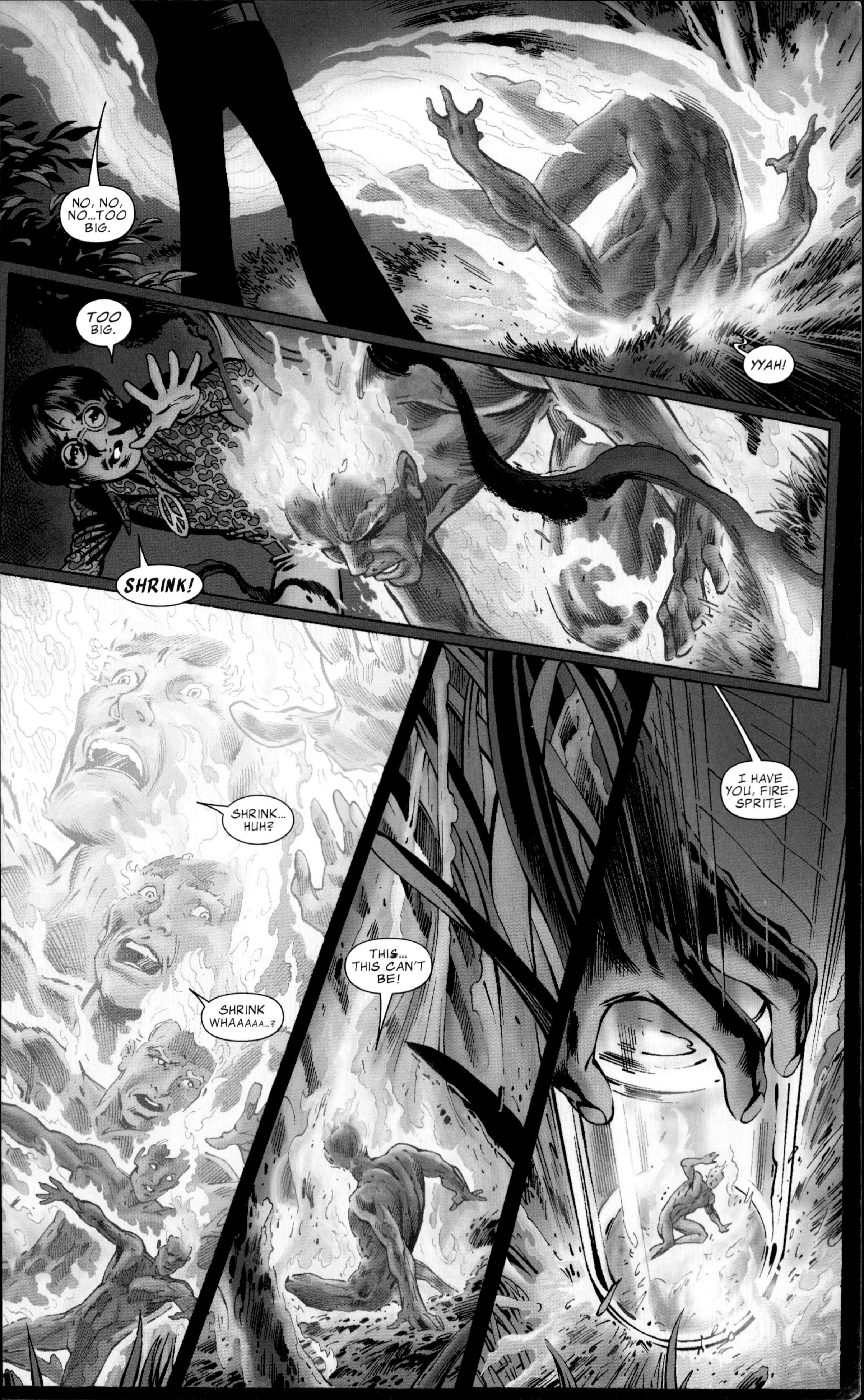
NO, NO, NO...TOO BIG.
TOO BIG.
YYAH!
SHRINK!
SHRINK... HUH?
SHRINK WHAAAAA...?
THIS... THIS CAN'T BE!
I HAVE YOU, FIRE-SPRITE.

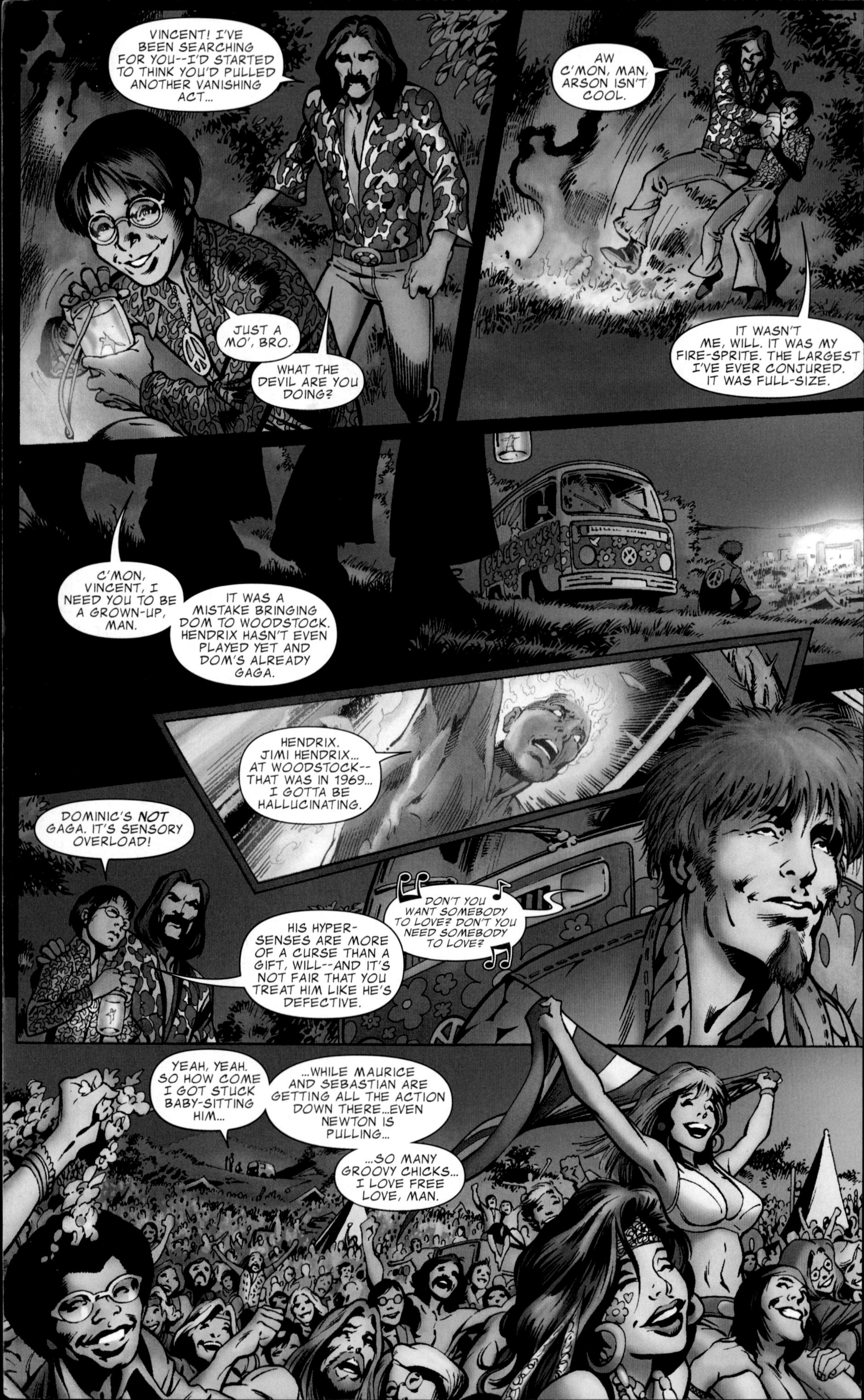
VINCENT! I'VE BEEN SEARCHING FOR YOU--I'D STARTED TO THINK YOU'D PULLED ANOTHER VANISHING ACT...
JUST A MO', BRO.
WHAT THE DEVIL ARE YOU DOING?
AW C'MON, MAN, ARSON ISN'T COOL.
IT WASN'T ME, WILL. IT WAS MY FIRE-SPRITE. THE LARGEST I'VE EVER CONJURED. IT WAS FULL-SIZE.
C'MON, VINCENT, I NEED YOU TO BE A GROWN-UP, MAN.
IT WAS A MISTAKE BRINGING DOM TO WOODSTOCK. HENDRIX HASN'T EVEN PLAYED YET AND DOM'S ALREADY GAGA.
HENDRIX. JIMI HENDRIX... AT WOODSTOCK--THAT WAS IN 1969... I GOTTA BE HALLUCINATING.
DOMINIC'S **NOT** GAGA. IT'S SENSORY OVERLOAD!
HIS HYPER-SENSES ARE MORE OF A CURSE THAN A GIFT, WILL--AND IT'S NOT FAIR THAT YOU TREAT HIM LIKE HE'S DEFECTIVE.
DON'T YOU WANT SOMEBODY TO LOVE? DON'T YOU NEED SOMEBODY TO LOVE?
YEAH, YEAH. SO HOW COME I GOT STUCK BABY-SITTING HIM...
...WHILE MAURICE AND SEBASTIAN ARE GETTING ALL THE ACTION DOWN THERE...EVEN NEWTON IS PULLING...
...SO MANY GROOVY CHICKS... I LOVE FREE LOVE, MAN.

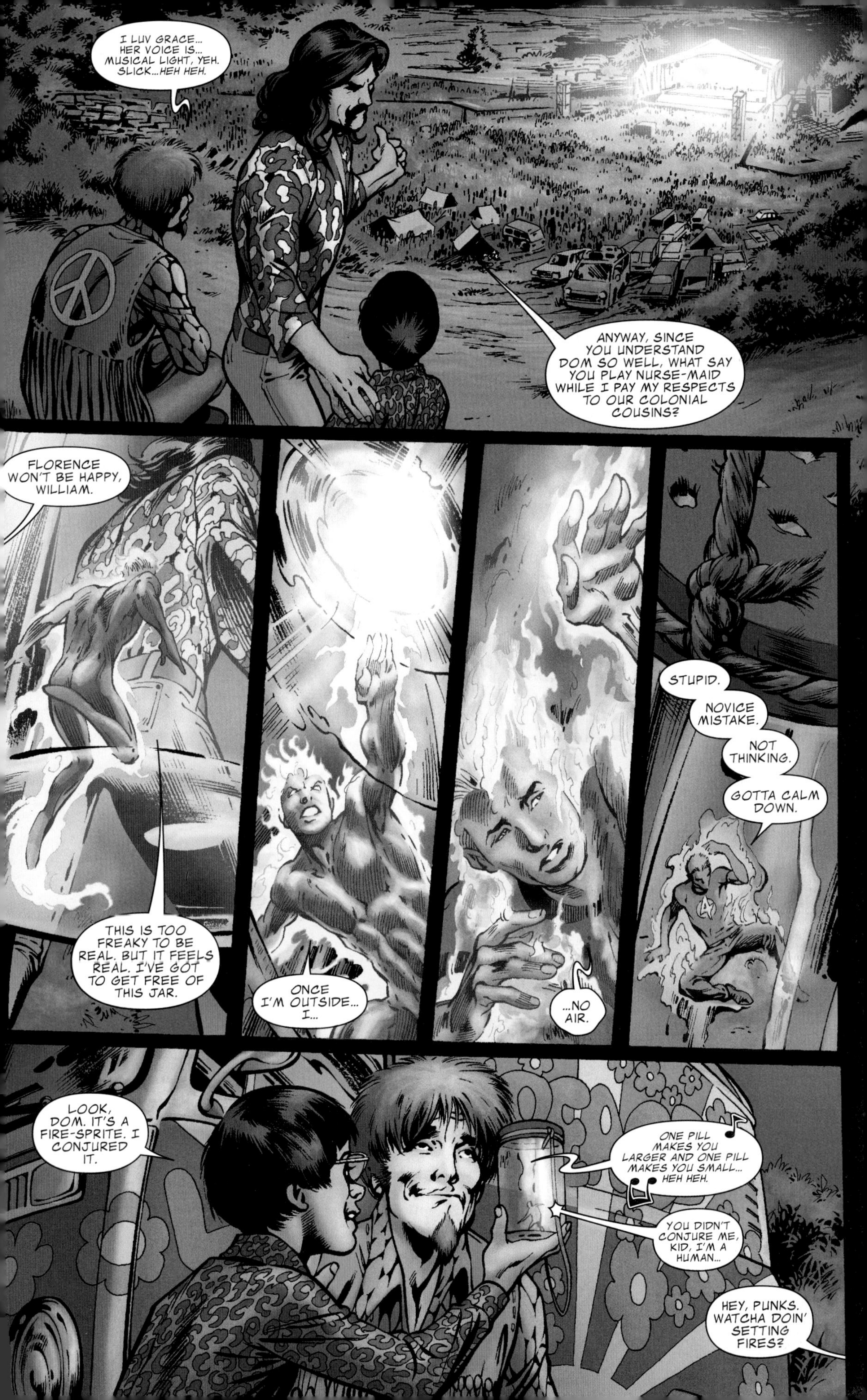
I LUV GRACE... HER VOICE IS... MUSICAL LIGHT, YEH. SLICK...HEH HEH.
ANYWAY, SINCE YOU UNDERSTAND DOM SO WELL, WHAT SAY YOU PLAY NURSE-MAID WHILE I PAY MY RESPECTS TO OUR COLONIAL COUSINS?
FLORENCE WON'T BE HAPPY, WILLIAM.
THIS IS TOO FREAKY TO BE REAL. BUT IT FEELS REAL. I'VE GOT TO GET FREE OF THIS JAR.
ONCE I'M OUTSIDE... I...
...NO AIR.
STUPID.
NOVICE MISTAKE.
NOT THINKING.
GOTTA CALM DOWN.
LOOK, DOM. IT'S A FIRE-SPRITE. I CONJURED IT.
ONE PILL MAKES YOU LARGER AND ONE PILL MAKES YOU SMALL... HEH HEH.
YOU DIDN'T CONJURE ME, KID, I'M A HUMAN...
HEY, PUNKS. WATCHA DOIN' SETTING FIRES?

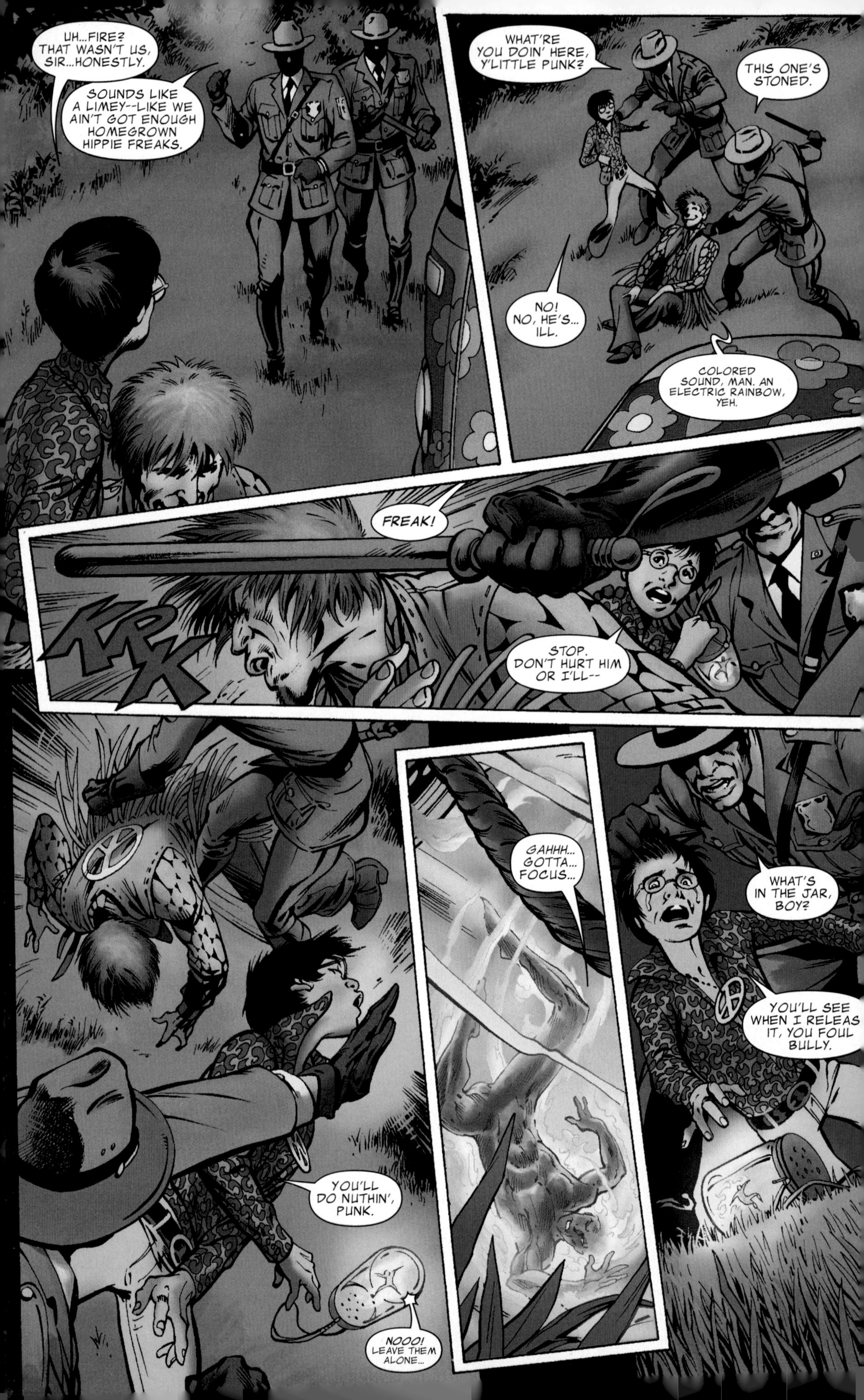
UH...FIRE? THAT WASN'T US, SIR...HONESTLY.
SOUNDS LIKE A LIMEY--LIKE WE AIN'T GOT ENOUGH HOMEGROWN HIPPIE FREAKS.
WHAT'RE YOU DOIN' HERE, Y'LITTLE PUNK?
THIS ONE'S STONED.
NO! NO, HE'S... ILL.
COLORED SOUND, MAN. AN ELECTRIC RAINBOW, YEH.
FREAK!
KRAK
STOP. DON'T HURT HIM OR I'LL--
GAHHH... GOTTA... FOCUS...
WHAT'S IN THE JAR, BOY?
YOU'LL SEE WHEN I RELEAS IT, YOU FOUL BULLY.
YOU'LL DO NUTHIN', PUNK.
NOOO! LEAVE THEM ALONE...

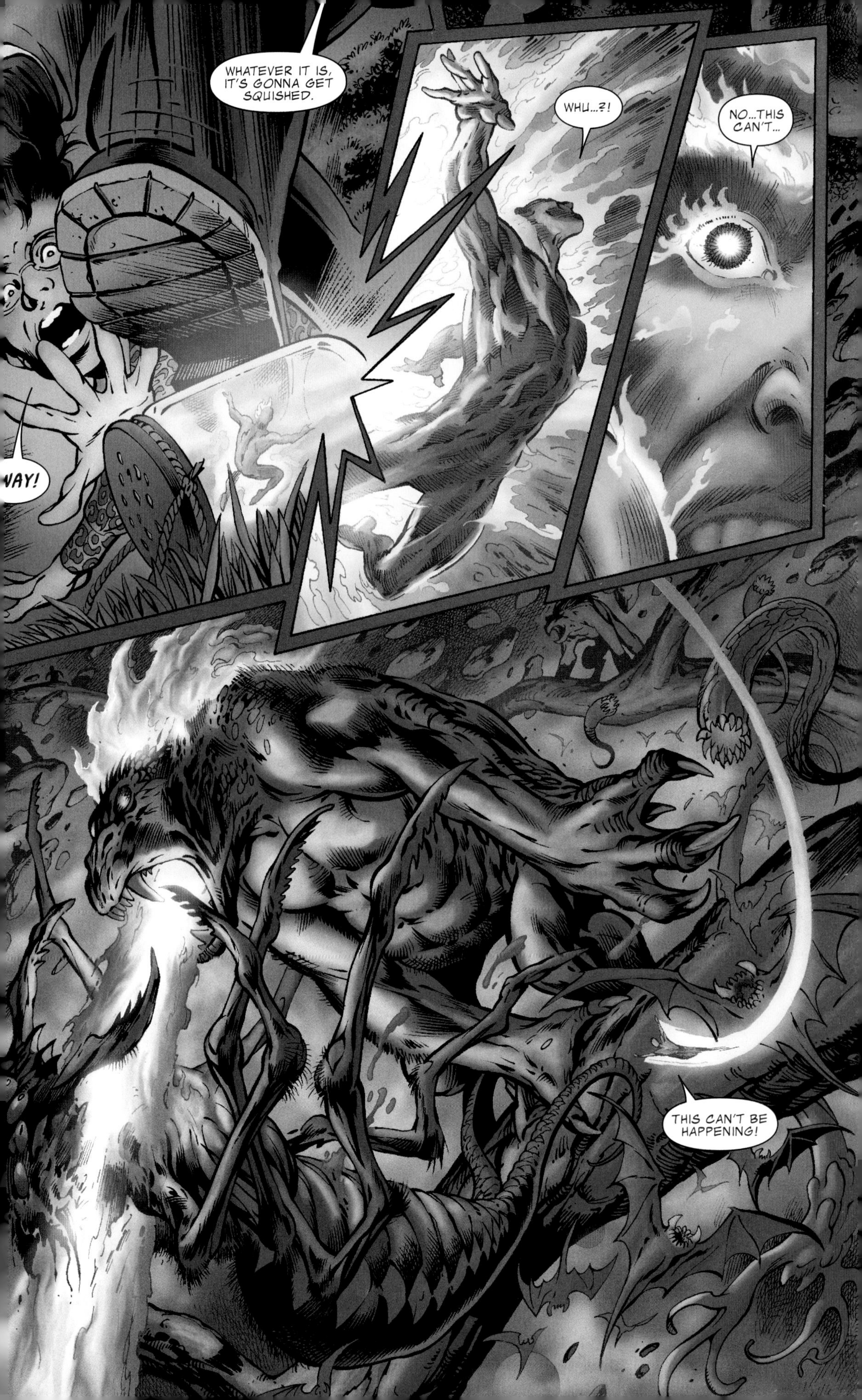
WHATEVER IT IS, IT'S GONNA GET SQUISHED.
WAY!
WHU...?!
NO...THIS CAN'T...
THIS CAN'T BE HAPPENING!

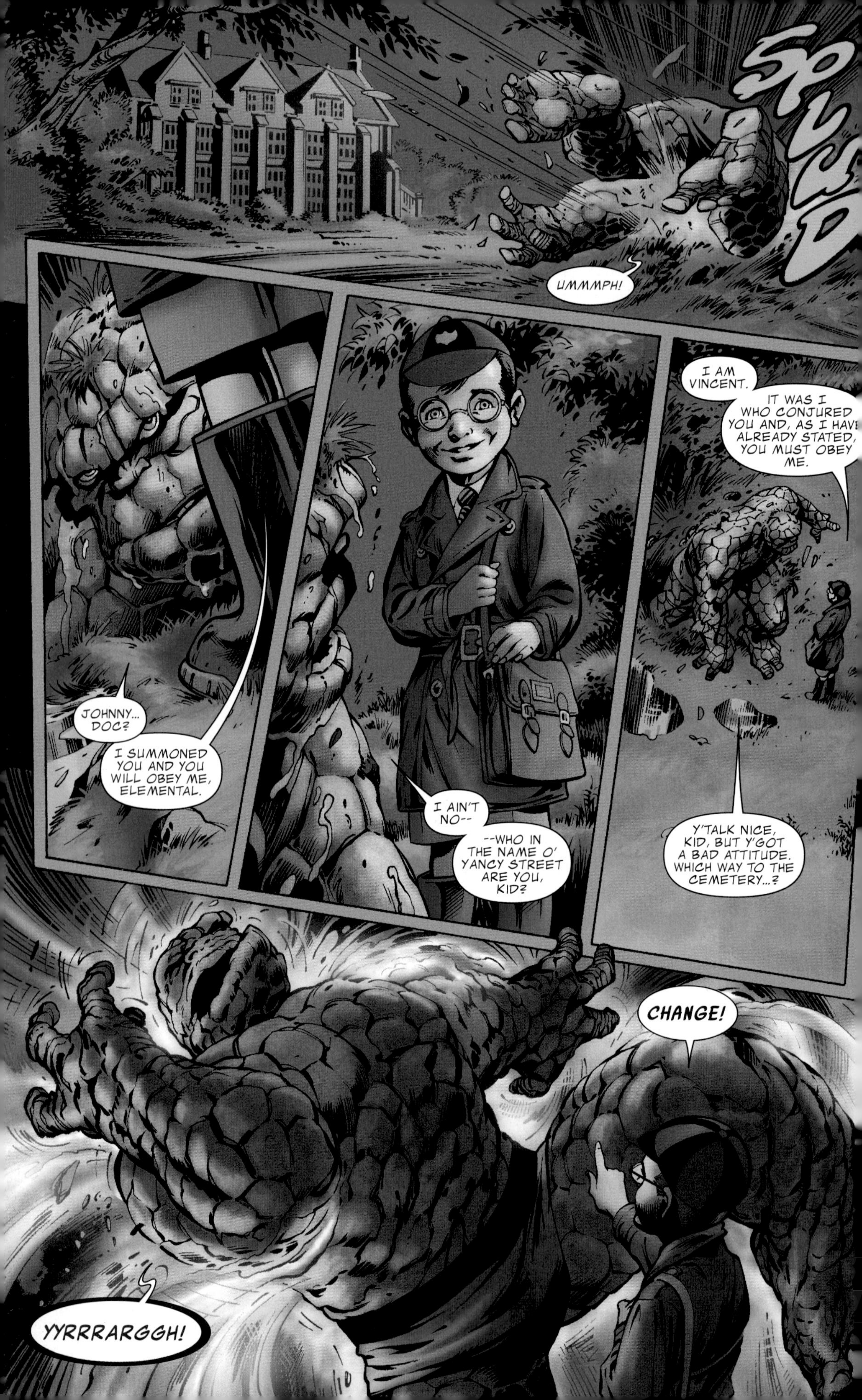
SPUUD
UMMMPH!
JOHNNY... DOC?
I SUMMONED YOU AND YOU WILL OBEY ME, ELEMENTAL.
I AIN'T NO--
--WHO IN THE NAME O' YANCY STREET ARE YOU, KID?
I AM VINCENT.
IT WAS I WHO CONJURED YOU AND, AS I HAVE ALREADY STATED, YOU MUST OBEY ME.
Y'TALK NICE, KID, BUT Y'GOT A BAD ATTITUDE. WHICH WAY TO THE CEMETERY...?
CHANGE!
YYRRRARGGH!

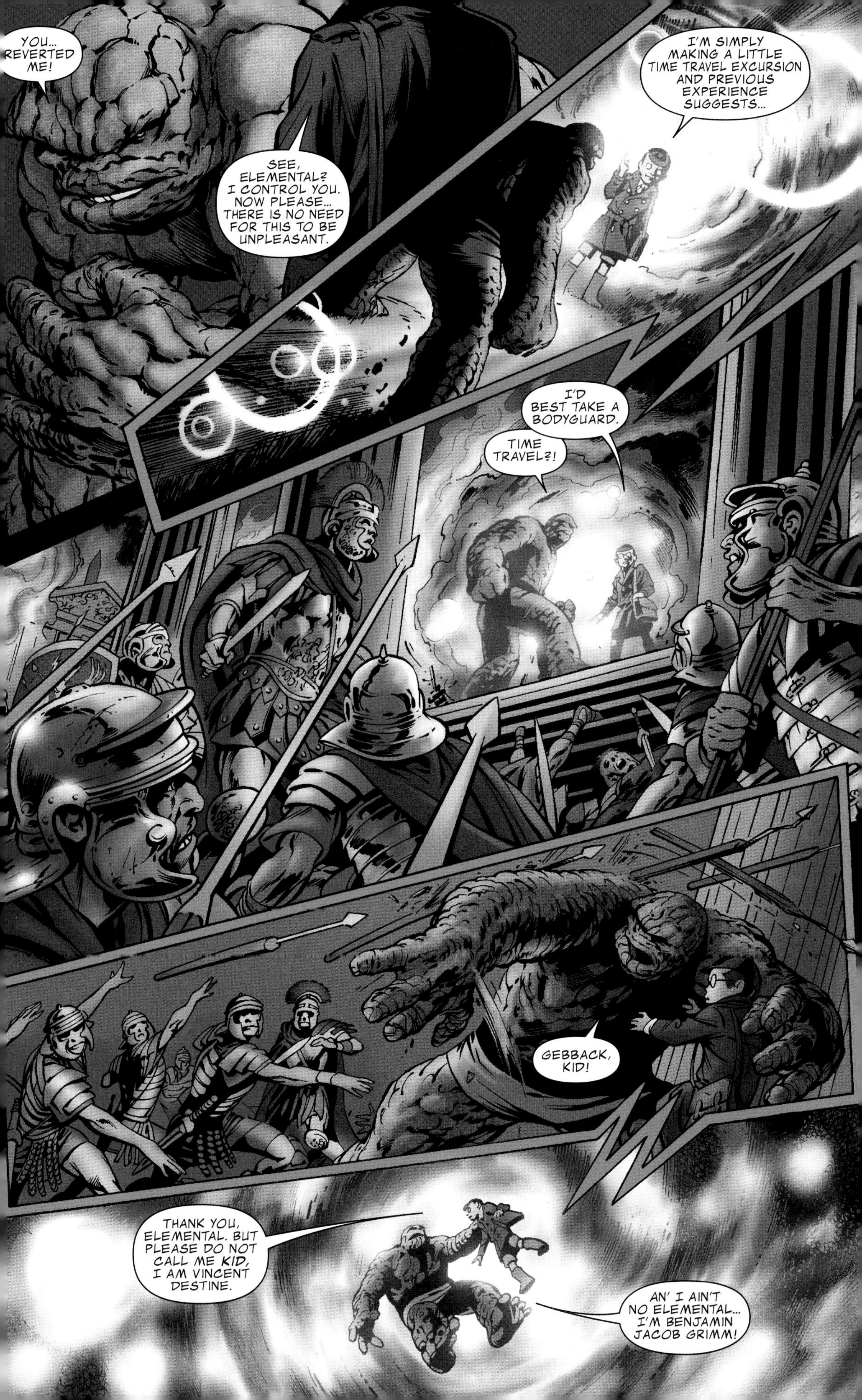

YOU... REVERTED ME!
SEE, ELEMENTAL? I CONTROL YOU. NOW PLEASE... THERE IS NO NEED FOR THIS TO BE UNPLEASANT.
I'M SIMPLY MAKING A LITTLE TIME TRAVEL EXCURSION AND PREVIOUS EXPERIENCE SUGGESTS...
I'D BEST TAKE A BODYGUARD.
TIME TRAVEL?!
GEBBACK, KID!
THANK YOU, ELEMENTAL. BUT PLEASE DO NOT CALL ME KID, I AM VINCENT DESTINE.
AN' I AIN'T NO ELEMENTAL... I'M BENJAMIN JACOB GRIMM!

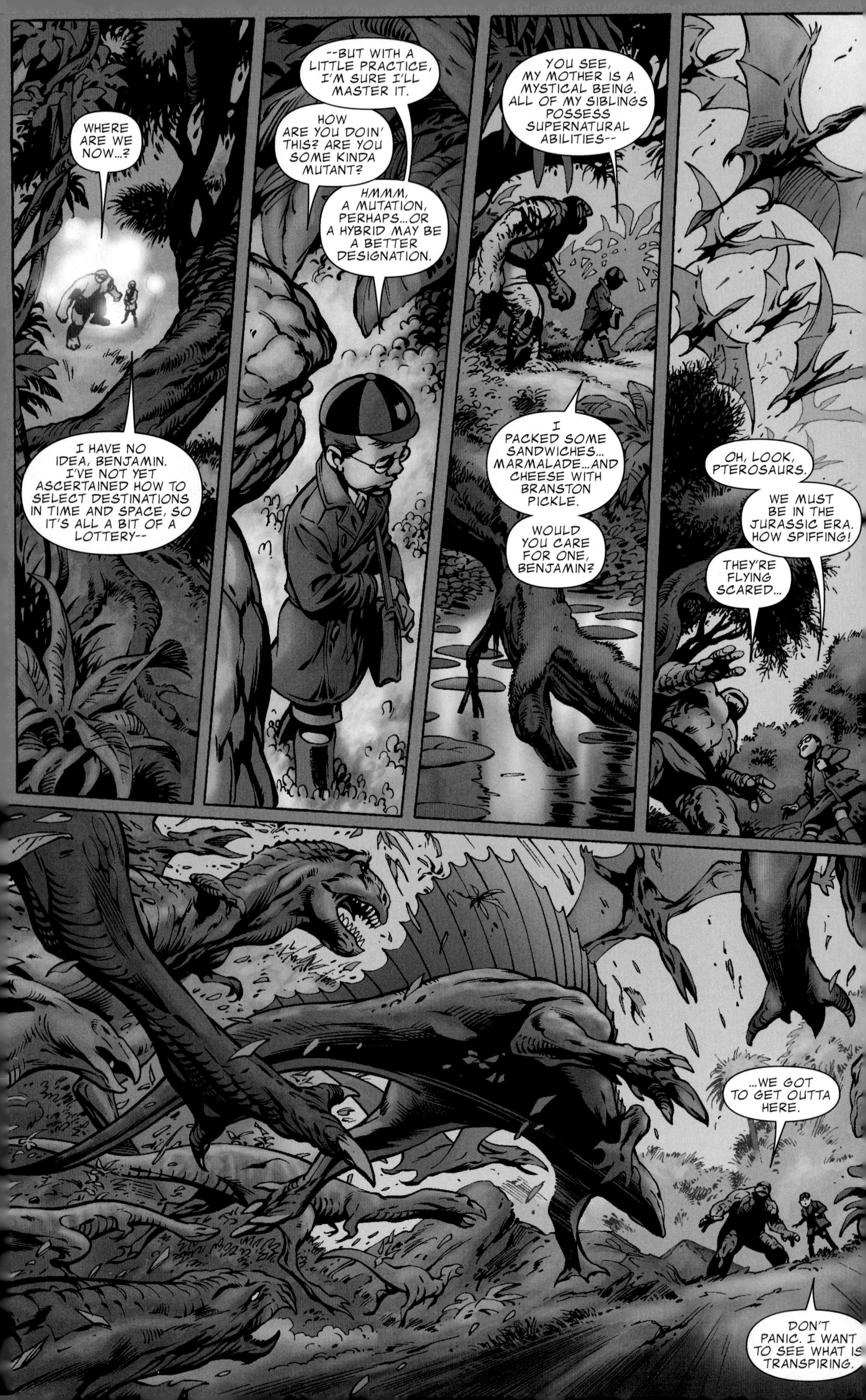
WHERE ARE WE NOW...?
I HAVE NO IDEA, BENJAMIN. I'VE NOT YET ASCERTAINED HOW TO SELECT DESTINATIONS IN TIME AND SPACE, SO IT'S ALL A BIT OF A LOTTERY--
--BUT WITH A LITTLE PRACTICE, I'M SURE I'LL MASTER IT.
HOW ARE YOU DOIN' THIS? ARE YOU SOME KINDA MUTANT?
HMMM, A MUTATION, PERHAPS...OR A HYBRID MAY BE A BETTER DESIGNATION.
YOU SEE, MY MOTHER IS A MYSTICAL BEING. ALL OF MY SIBLINGS POSSESS SUPERNATURAL ABILITIES--
I PACKED SOME SANDWICHES... MARMALADE...AND CHEESE WITH BRANSTON PICKLE.
WOULD YOU CARE FOR ONE, BENJAMIN?
OH, LOOK, PTEROSAURS.
WE MUST BE IN THE JURASSIC ERA. HOW SPIFFING!
THEY'RE FLYING SCARED...
...WE GOT TO GET OUTTA HERE.
DON'T PANIC. I WANT TO SEE WHAT IS TRANSPIRING.

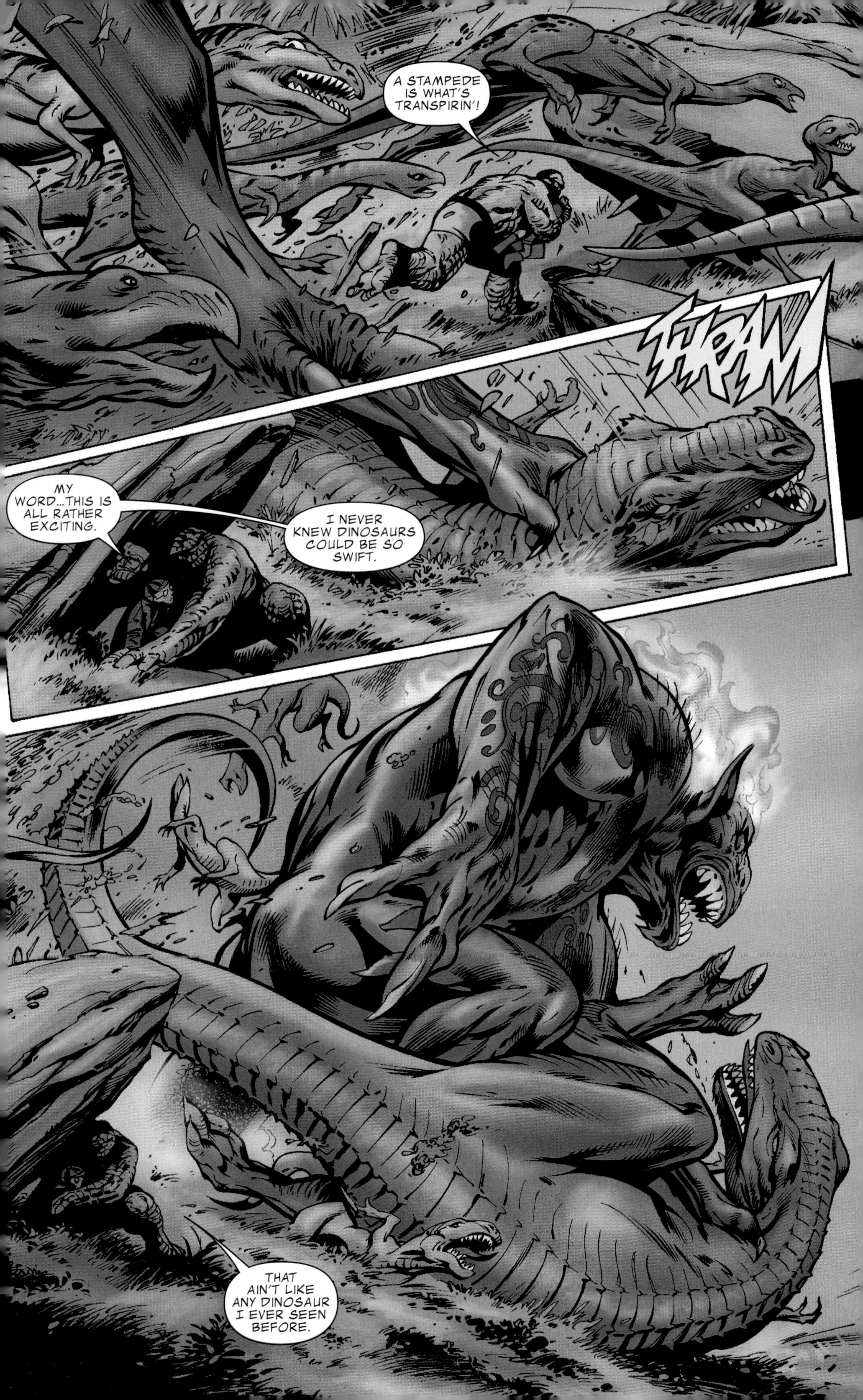
A STAMPEDE IS WHAT'S TRANSPIRIN'!
THRAM
MY WORD...THIS IS ALL RATHER EXCITING.
I NEVER KNEW DINOSAURS COULD BE SO SWIFT.
THAT AIN'T LIKE ANY DINOSAUR I EVER SEEN BEFORE.

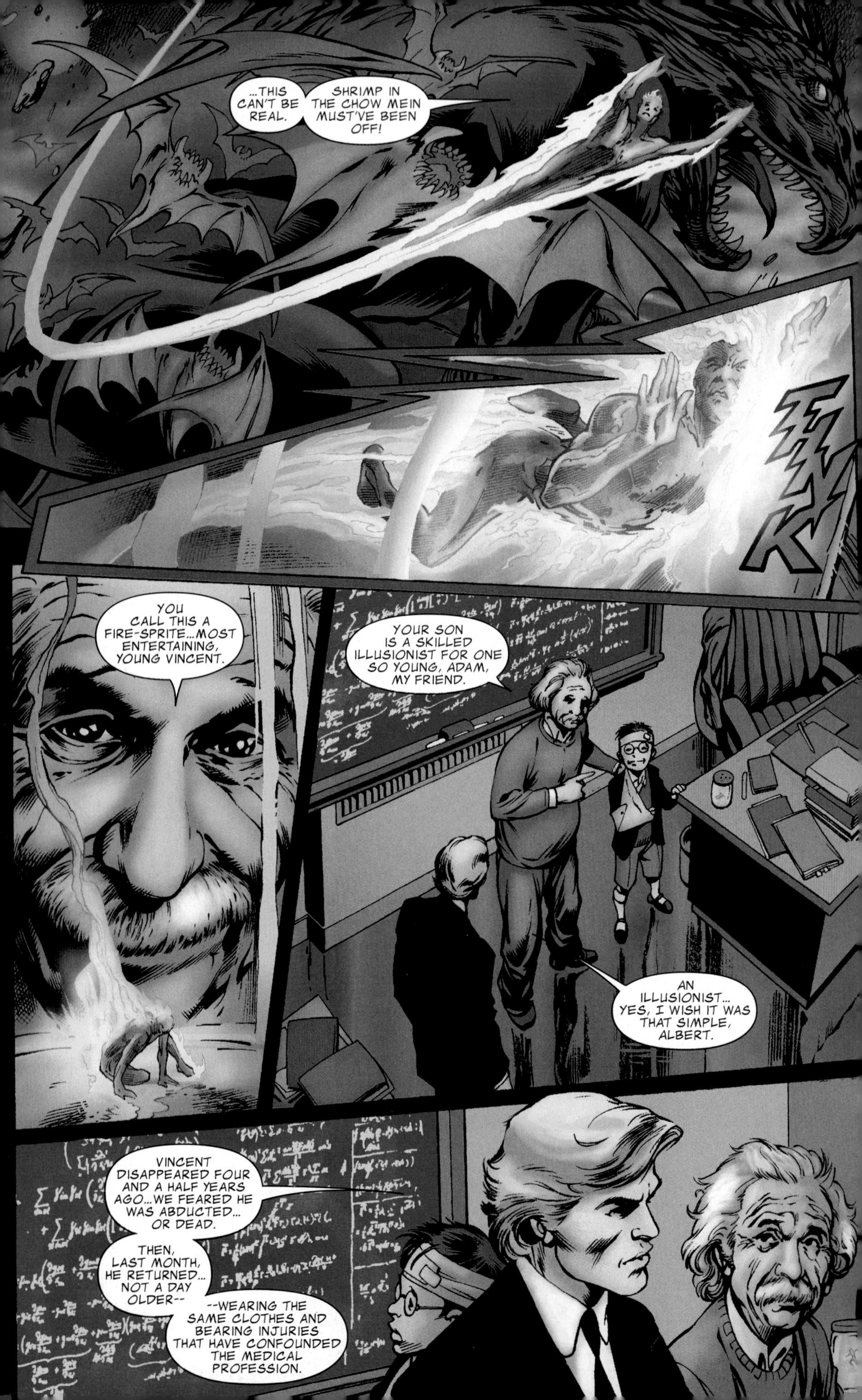
...THIS CAN'T BE REAL.
SHRIMP IN THE CHOW MEIN MUST'VE BEEN OFF!
TINK
YOU CALL THIS A FIRE-SPRITE...MOST ENTERTAINING, YOUNG VINCENT.
YOUR SON IS A SKILLED ILLUSIONIST FOR ONE SO YOUNG, ADAM, MY FRIEND.
AN ILLUSIONIST... YES, I WISH IT WAS THAT SIMPLE, ALBERT.
VINCENT DISAPPEARED FOUR AND A HALF YEARS AGO...WE FEARED HE WAS ABDUCTED... OR DEAD.
THEN, LAST MONTH, HE RETURNED... NOT A DAY OLDER--
--WEARING THE SAME CLOTHES AND BEARING INJURIES THAT HAVE CONFOUNDED THE MEDICAL PROFESSION.

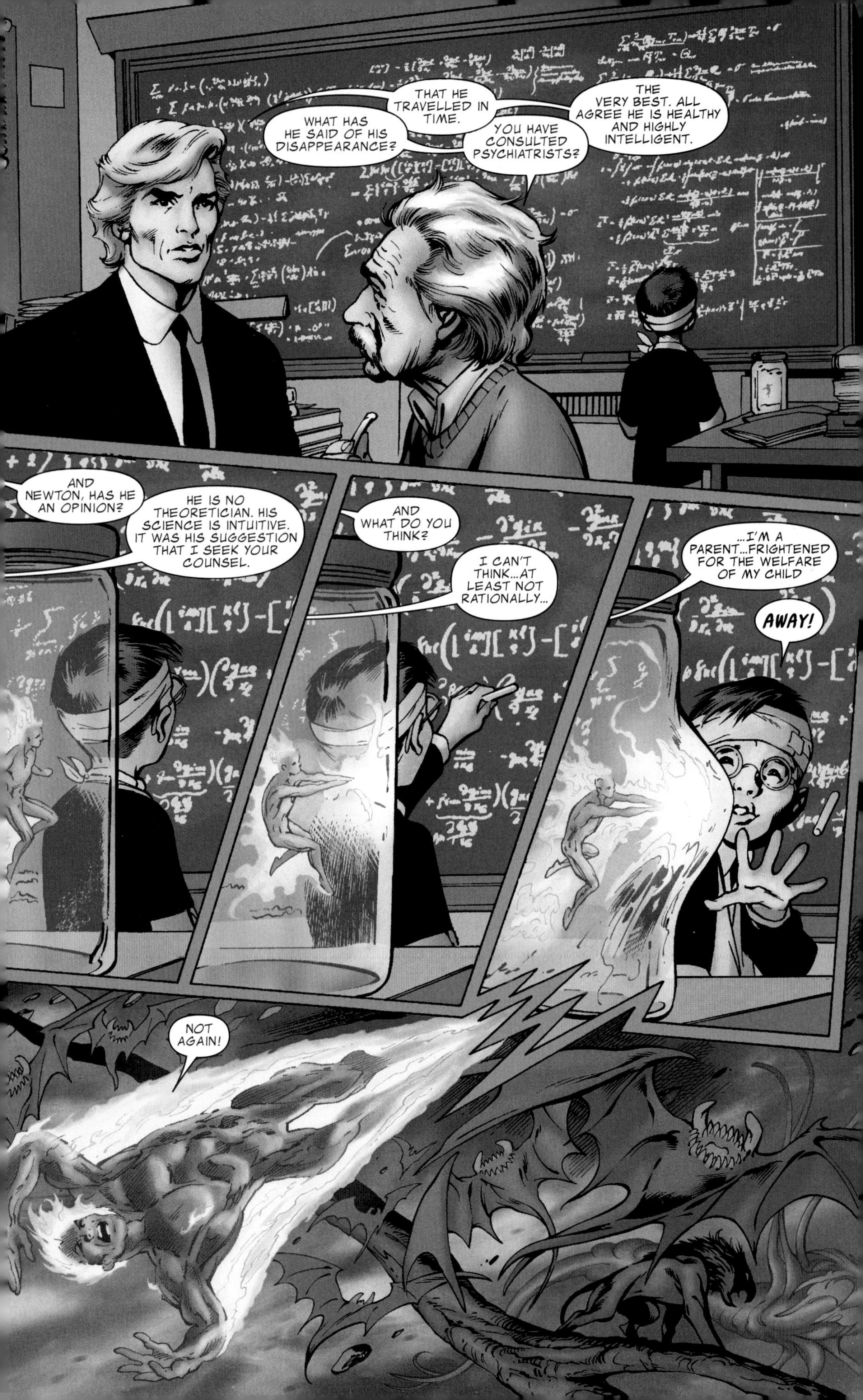
WHAT HAS HE SAID OF HIS DISAPPEARANCE?
THAT HE TRAVELLED IN TIME.
YOU HAVE CONSULTED PSYCHIATRISTS?
THE VERY BEST. ALL AGREE HE IS HEALTHY AND HIGHLY INTELLIGENT.
AND NEWTON, HAS HE AN OPINION?
HE IS NO THEORETICIAN. HIS SCIENCE IS INTUITIVE. IT WAS HIS SUGGESTION THAT I SEEK YOUR COUNSEL.
AND WHAT DO YOU THINK?
I CAN'T THINK...AT LEAST NOT RATIONALLY...
...I'M A PARENT...FRIGHTENED FOR THE WELFARE OF MY CHILD
AWAY!
NOT AGAIN!

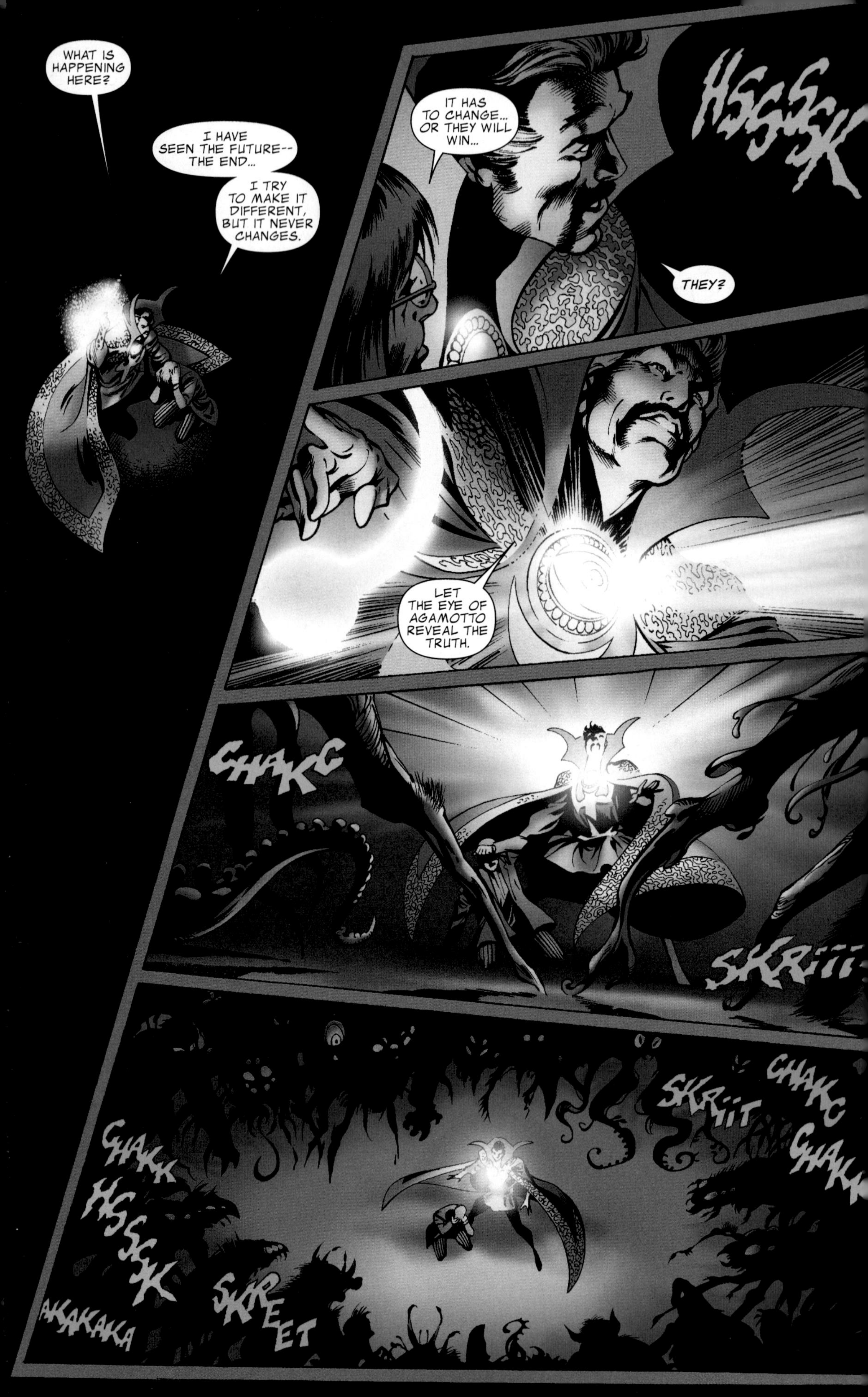
WHAT IS HAPPENING HERE?
I HAVE SEEN THE FUTURE-- THE END...
I TRY TO MAKE IT DIFFERENT, BUT IT NEVER CHANGES.
HSSSSK
IT HAS TO CHANGE... OR THEY WILL WIN...
THEY?
LET THE EYE OF AGAMOTTO REVEAL THE TRUTH.
CHAKC
SKRIIT
CHAKC
SKRIIT
CHAKK
CHAKK
HSSSK
SKREET
AKAKAKA

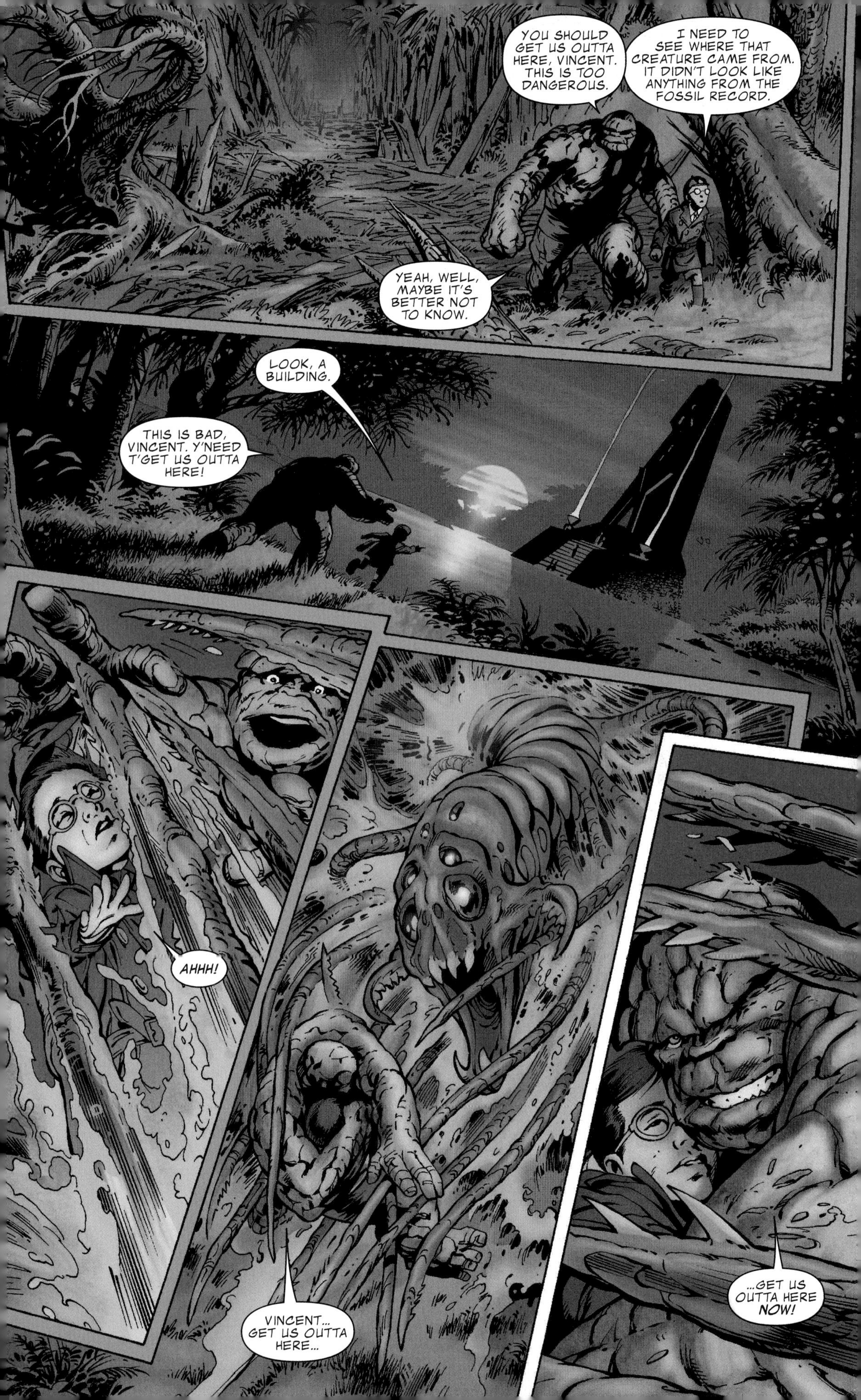
YOU SHOULD GET US OUTTA HERE, VINCENT. THIS IS TOO DANGEROUS.
I NEED TO SEE WHERE THAT CREATURE CAME FROM. IT DIDN'T LOOK LIKE ANYTHING FROM THE FOSSIL RECORD.
YEAH, WELL, MAYBE IT'S BETTER NOT TO KNOW.
LOOK, A BUILDING.
THIS IS BAD, VINCENT. Y'NEED T'GET US OUTTA HERE!
AHHH!
VINCENT... GET US OUTTA HERE...
...GET US OUTTA HERE NOW!

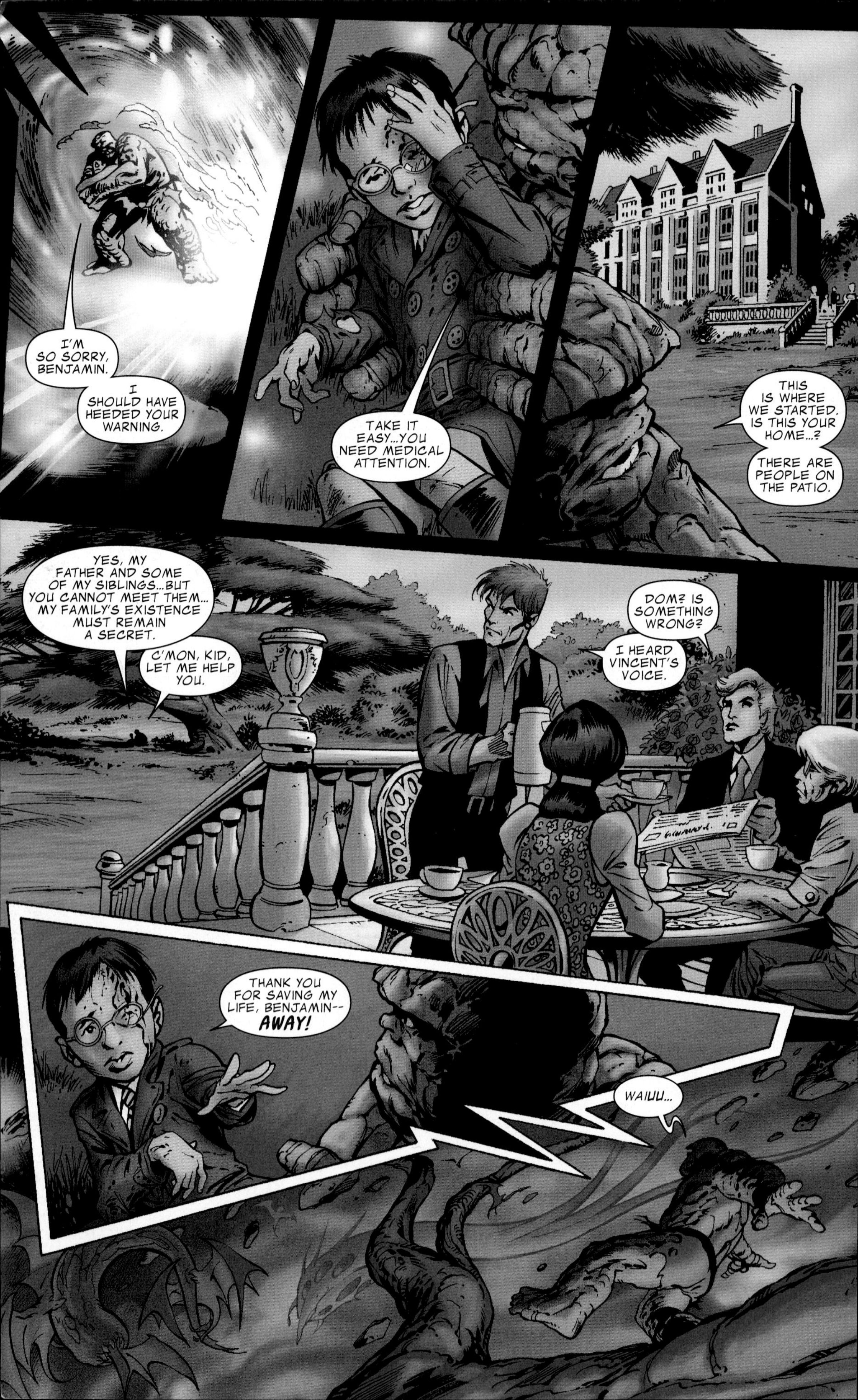
I'M SO SORRY, BENJAMIN.
I SHOULD HAVE HEEDED YOUR WARNING.
TAKE IT EASY...YOU NEED MEDICAL ATTENTION.
THIS IS WHERE WE STARTED. IS THIS YOUR HOME...?
THERE ARE PEOPLE ON THE PATIO.
YES, MY FATHER AND SOME OF MY SIBLINGS...BUT YOU CANNOT MEET THEM... MY FAMILY'S EXISTENCE MUST REMAIN A SECRET.
C'MON, KID, LET ME HELP YOU.
DOM? IS SOMETHING WRONG?
I HEARD VINCENT'S VOICE.
THANK YOU FOR SAVING MY LIFE, BENJAMIN-- AWAY!
WAIUU...

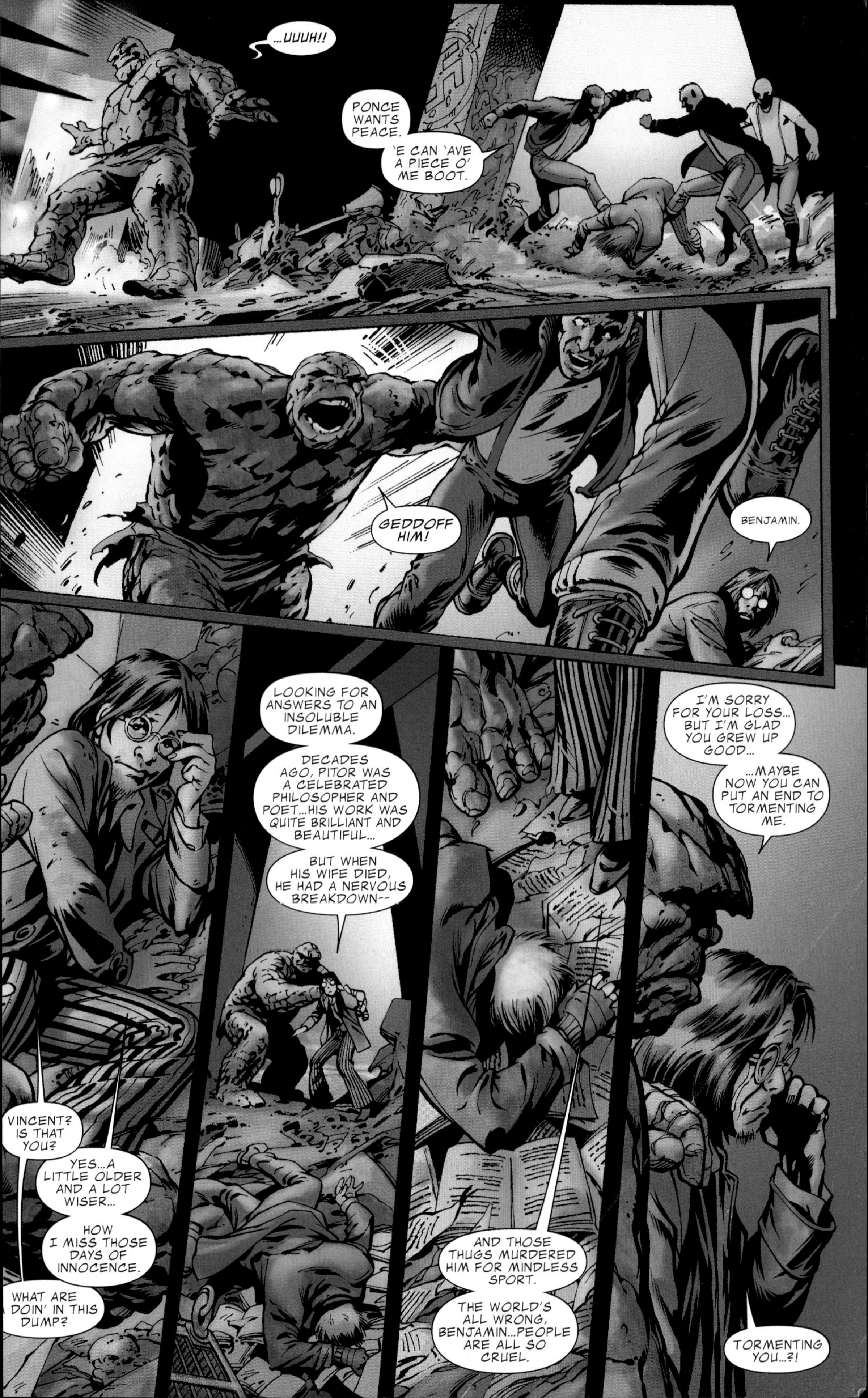
...UUUH!!
PONCE WANTS PEACE.
'E CAN 'AVE A PIECE O' ME BOOT.
GEDDOFF HIM!
BENJAMIN.
VINCENT? IS THAT YOU?
YES...A LITTLE OLDER AND A LOT WISER...
HOW I MISS THOSE DAYS OF INNOCENCE.
WHAT ARE DOIN' IN THIS DUMP?
LOOKING FOR ANSWERS TO AN INSOLUBLE DILEMMA.
DECADES AGO, PITOR WAS A CELEBRATED PHILOSOPHER AND POET...HIS WORK WAS QUITE BRILLIANT AND BEAUTIFUL...
BUT WHEN HIS WIFE DIED, HE HAD A NERVOUS BREAKDOWN--
AND THOSE THUGS MURDERED HIM FOR MINDLESS SPORT.
THE WORLD'S ALL WRONG, BENJAMIN...PEOPLE ARE ALL SO CRUEL.
I'M SORRY FOR YOUR LOSS... BUT I'M GLAD YOU GREW UP GOOD...
...MAYBE NOW YOU CAN PUT AN END TO TORMENTING ME.
TORMENTING YOU...?!

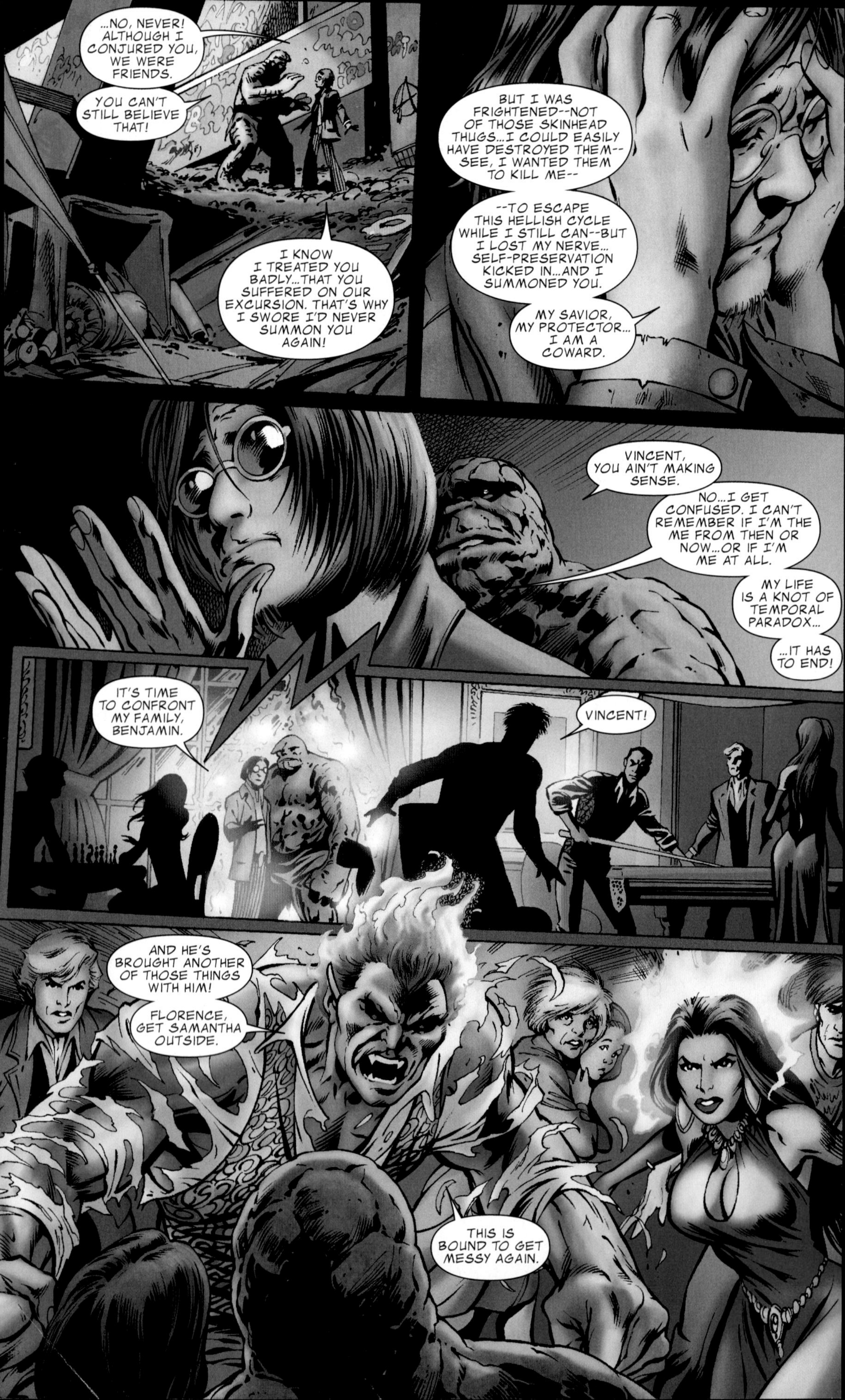
...NO, NEVER! ALTHOUGH I CONJURED YOU, WE WERE FRIENDS.
YOU CAN'T STILL BELIEVE THAT!
I KNOW I TREATED YOU BADLY...THAT YOU SUFFERED ON OUR EXCURSION. THAT'S WHY I SWORE I'D NEVER SUMMON YOU AGAIN!
BUT I WAS FRIGHTENED--NOT OF THOSE SKINHEAD THUGS...I COULD EASILY HAVE DESTROYED THEM--SEE, I WANTED THEM TO KILL ME--
--TO ESCAPE THIS HELLISH CYCLE WHILE I STILL CAN--BUT I LOST MY NERVE... SELF-PRESERVATION KICKED IN...AND I SUMMONED YOU.
MY SAVIOR, MY PROTECTOR... I AM A COWARD.
VINCENT, YOU AIN'T MAKING SENSE.
NO...I GET CONFUSED. I CAN'T REMEMBER IF I'M THE ME FROM THEN OR NOW...OR IF I'M ME AT ALL.
MY LIFE IS A KNOT OF TEMPORAL PARADOX...
...IT HAS TO END!
IT'S TIME TO CONFRONT MY FAMILY, BENJAMIN.
VINCENT!
AND HE'S BROUGHT ANOTHER OF THOSE THINGS WITH HIM!
FLORENCE, GET SAMANTHA OUTSIDE.
THIS IS BOUND TO GET MESSY AGAIN.

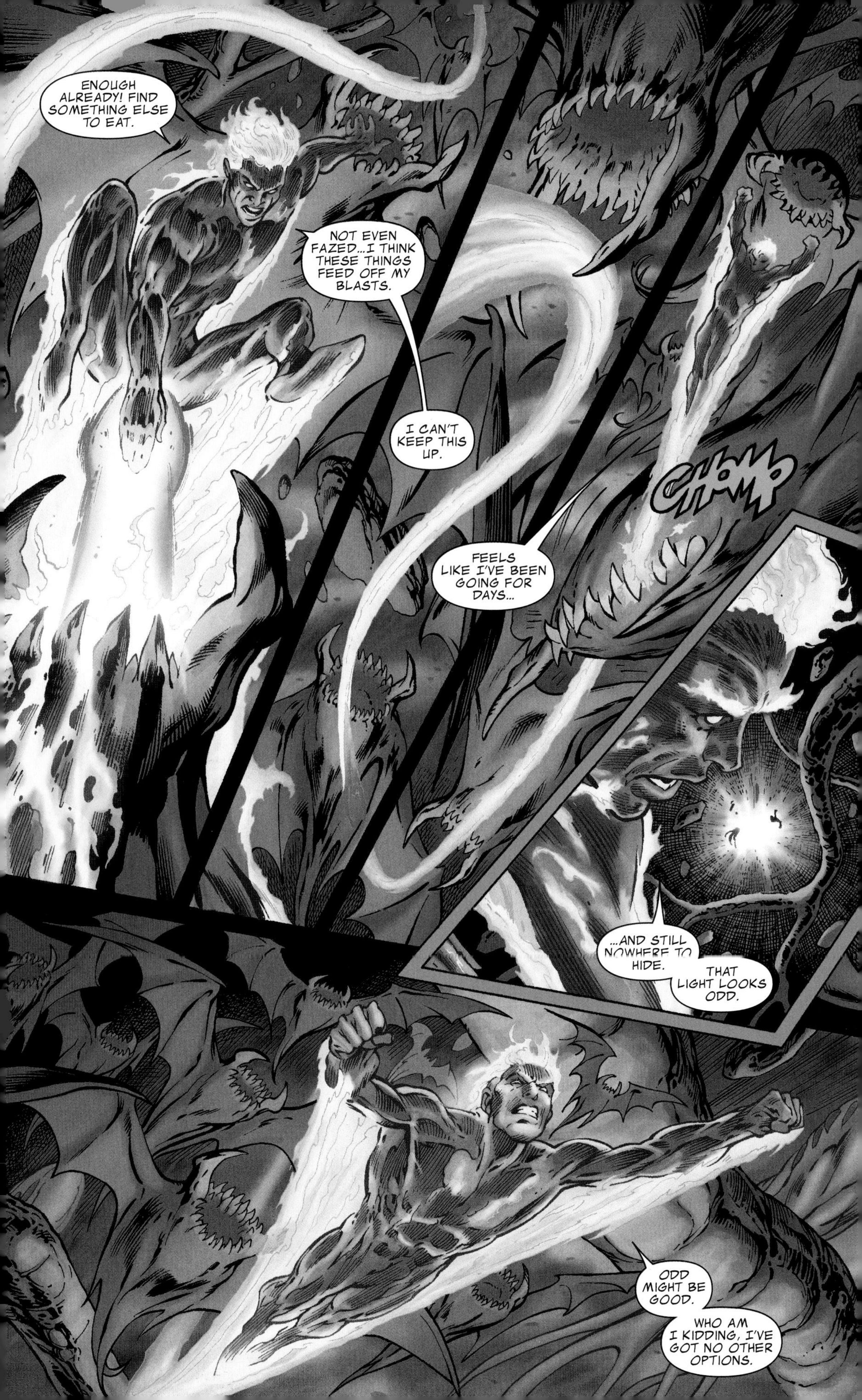
ENOUGH ALREADY! FIND SOMETHING ELSE TO EAT.
NOT EVEN FAZED...I THINK THESE THINGS FEED OFF MY BLASTS.
I CAN'T KEEP THIS UP.
CHOMP
FEELS LIKE I'VE BEEN GOING FOR DAYS...
...AND STILL NOWHERE TO HIDE.
THAT LIGHT LOOKS ODD.
ODD MIGHT BE GOOD.
WHO AM I KIDDING, I'VE GOT NO OTHER OPTIONS.

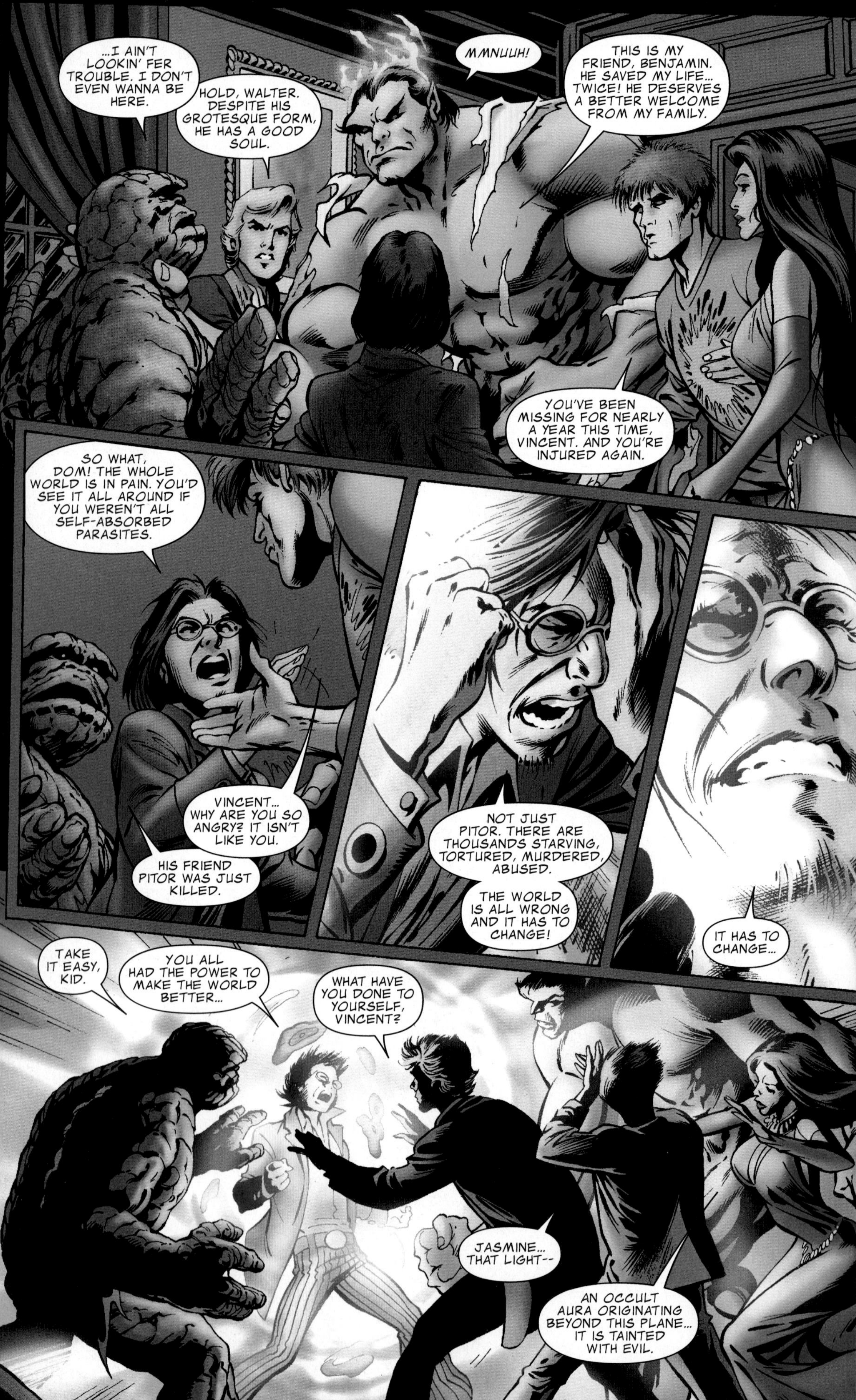
...I AIN'T LOOKIN' FER TROUBLE. I DON'T EVEN WANNA BE HERE.
HOLD, WALTER. DESPITE HIS GROTESQUE FORM, HE HAS A GOOD SOUL.
MMNUUH!
THIS IS MY FRIEND, BENJAMIN. HE SAVED MY LIFE... TWICE! HE DESERVES A BETTER WELCOME FROM MY FAMILY.
YOU'VE BEEN MISSING FOR NEARLY A YEAR THIS TIME, VINCENT. AND YOU'RE INJURED AGAIN.
SO WHAT, DOM! THE WHOLE WORLD IS IN PAIN. YOU'D SEE IT ALL AROUND IF YOU WEREN'T ALL SELF-ABSORBED PARASITES.
VINCENT... WHY ARE YOU SO ANGRY? IT ISN'T LIKE YOU.
HIS FRIEND PITOR WAS JUST KILLED.
NOT JUST PITOR. THERE ARE THOUSANDS STARVING, TORTURED, MURDERED, ABUSED.
THE WORLD IS ALL WRONG AND IT HAS TO CHANGE!
IT HAS TO CHANGE...
TAKE IT EASY, KID.
YOU ALL HAD THE POWER TO MAKE THE WORLD BETTER...
WHAT HAVE YOU DONE TO YOURSELF, VINCENT?
JASMINE... THAT LIGHT--
AN OCCULT AURA ORIGINATING BEYOND THIS PLANE... IT IS TAINTED WITH EVIL.

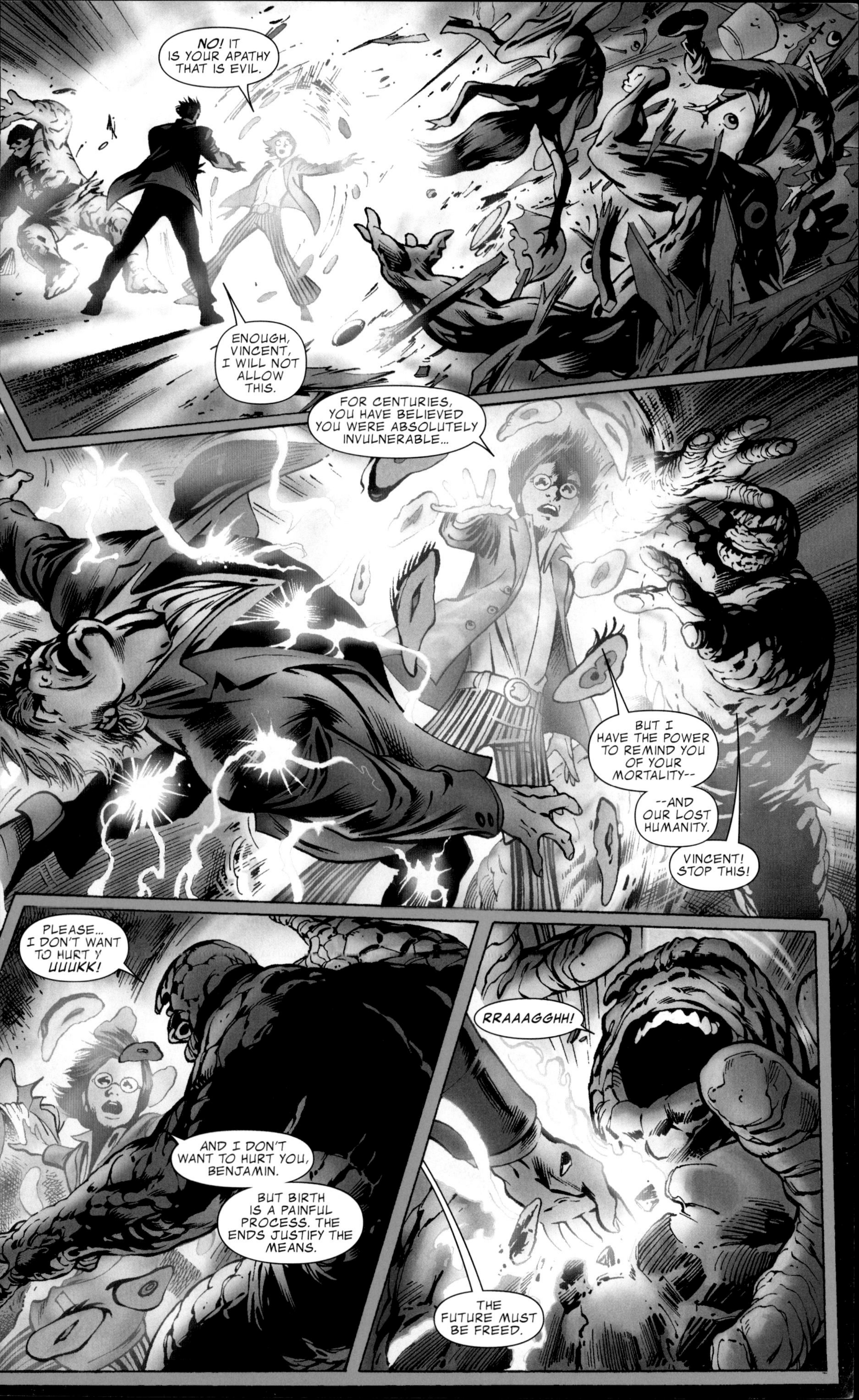
NO! IT IS YOUR APATHY THAT IS EVIL.
ENOUGH, VINCENT, I WILL NOT ALLOW THIS.
FOR CENTURIES, YOU HAVE BELIEVED YOU WERE ABSOLUTELY INVULNERABLE...
BUT I HAVE THE POWER TO REMIND YOU OF YOUR MORTALITY--
--AND OUR LOST HUMANITY.
VINCENT! STOP THIS!
PLEASE... I DON'T WANT TO HURT Y UUUKK!
AND I DON'T WANT TO HURT YOU, BENJAMIN.
BUT BIRTH IS A PAINFUL PROCESS. THE ENDS JUSTIFY THE MEANS.
RRAAAGGHH!
THE FUTURE MUST BE FREED.

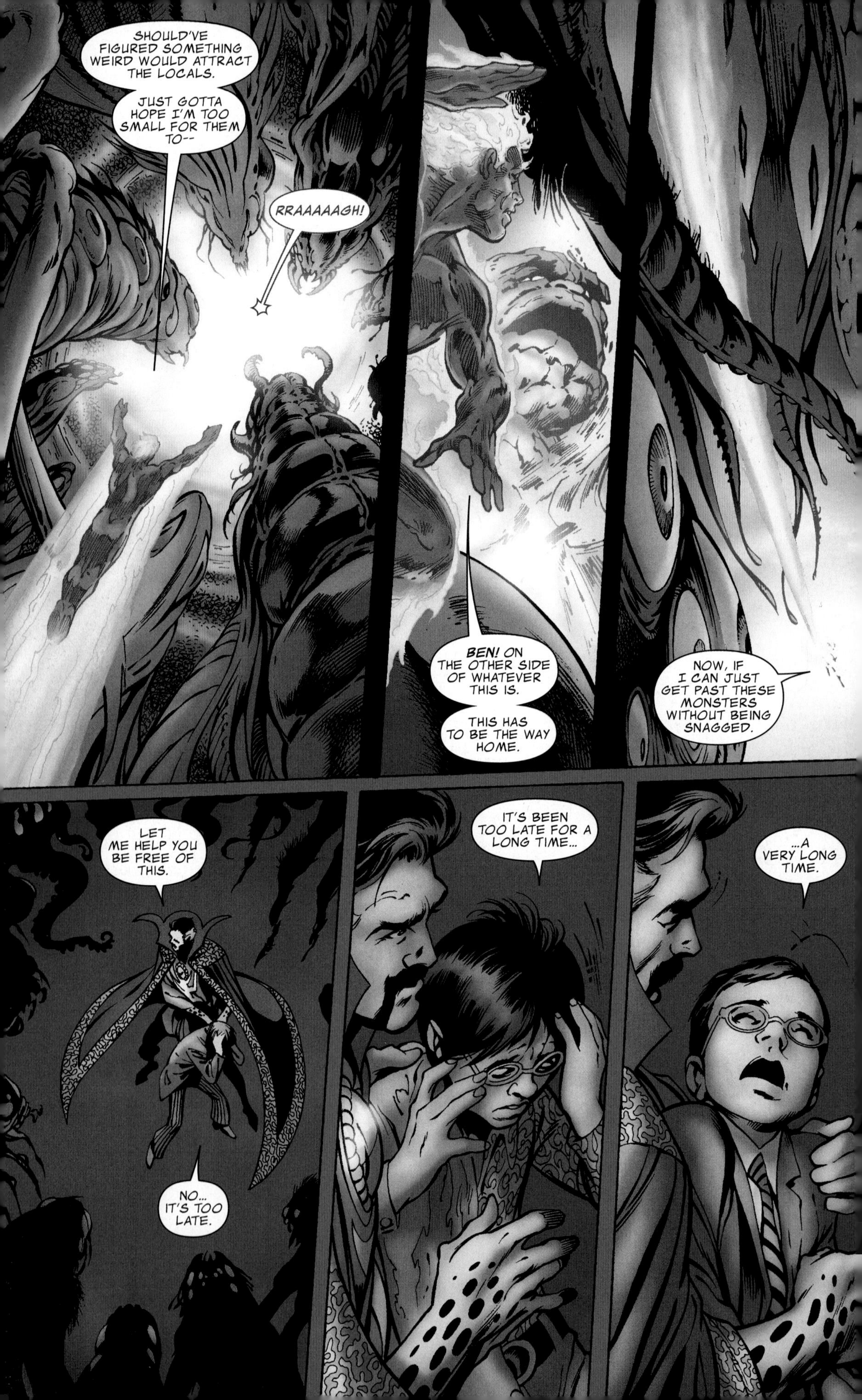
SHOULD'VE FIGURED SOMETHING WEIRD WOULD ATTRACT THE LOCALS.
JUST GOTTA HOPE I'M TOO SMALL FOR THEM TO--
RRAAAAAAGH!
BEN! ON THE OTHER SIDE OF WHATEVER THIS IS.
THIS HAS TO BE THE WAY HOME.
NOW, IF I CAN JUST GET PAST THESE MONSTERS WITHOUT BEING SNAGGED.
LET ME HELP YOU BE FREE OF THIS.
NO... IT'S TOO LATE.
IT'S BEEN TOO LATE FOR A LONG TIME...
...A VERY LONG TIME.

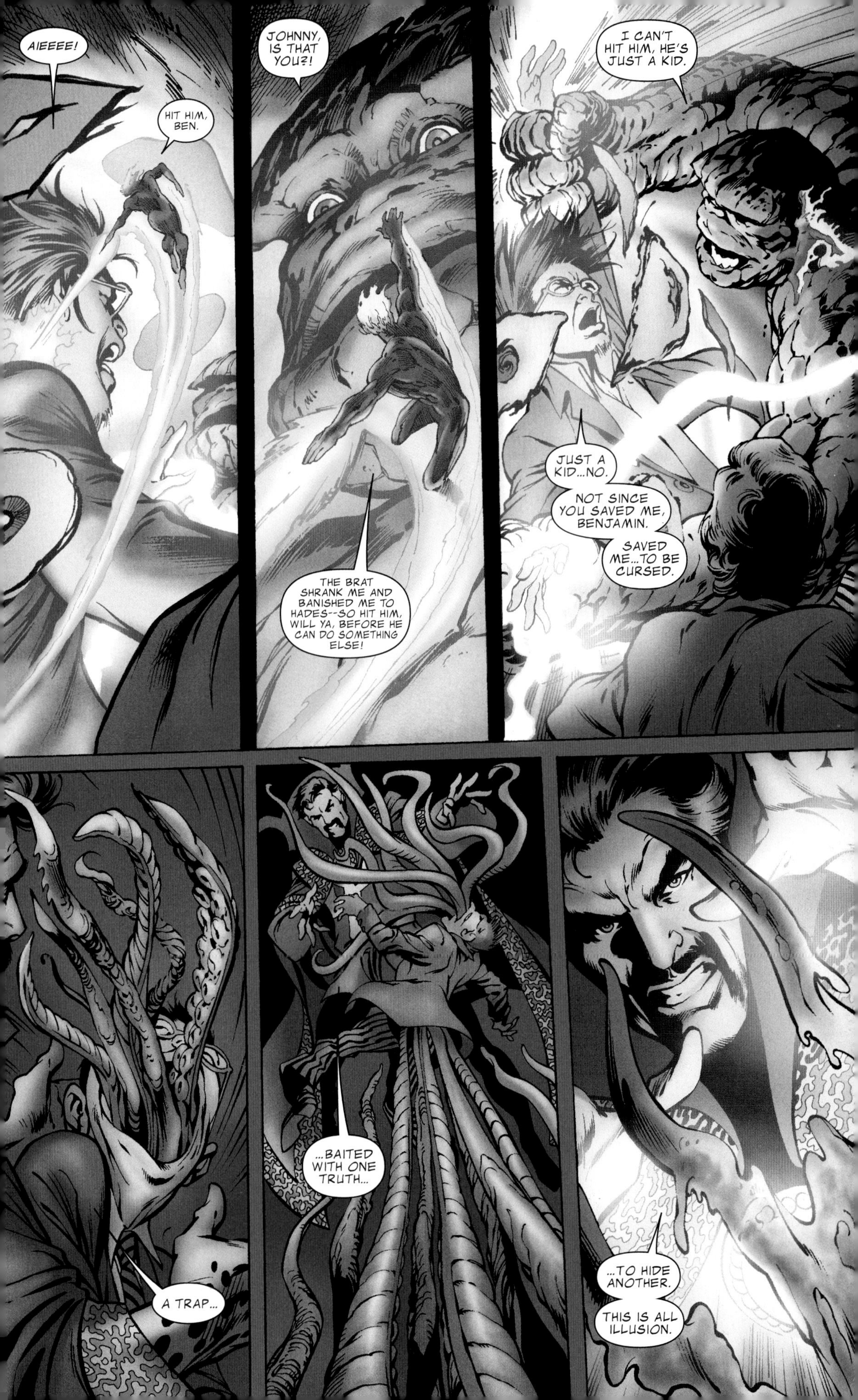
AIEEEE!
HIT HIM, BEN.
JOHNNY, IS THAT YOU?!
THE BRAT SHRANK ME AND BANISHED ME TO HADES--SO HIT HIM, WILL YA, BEFORE HE CAN DO SOMETHING ELSE!
I CAN'T HIT HIM, HE'S JUST A KID.
JUST A KID...NO.
NOT SINCE YOU SAVED ME, BENJAMIN.
SAVED ME...TO BE CURSED.
A TRAP...
...BAITED WITH ONE TRUTH...
...TO HIDE ANOTHER.
THIS IS ALL ILLUSION.

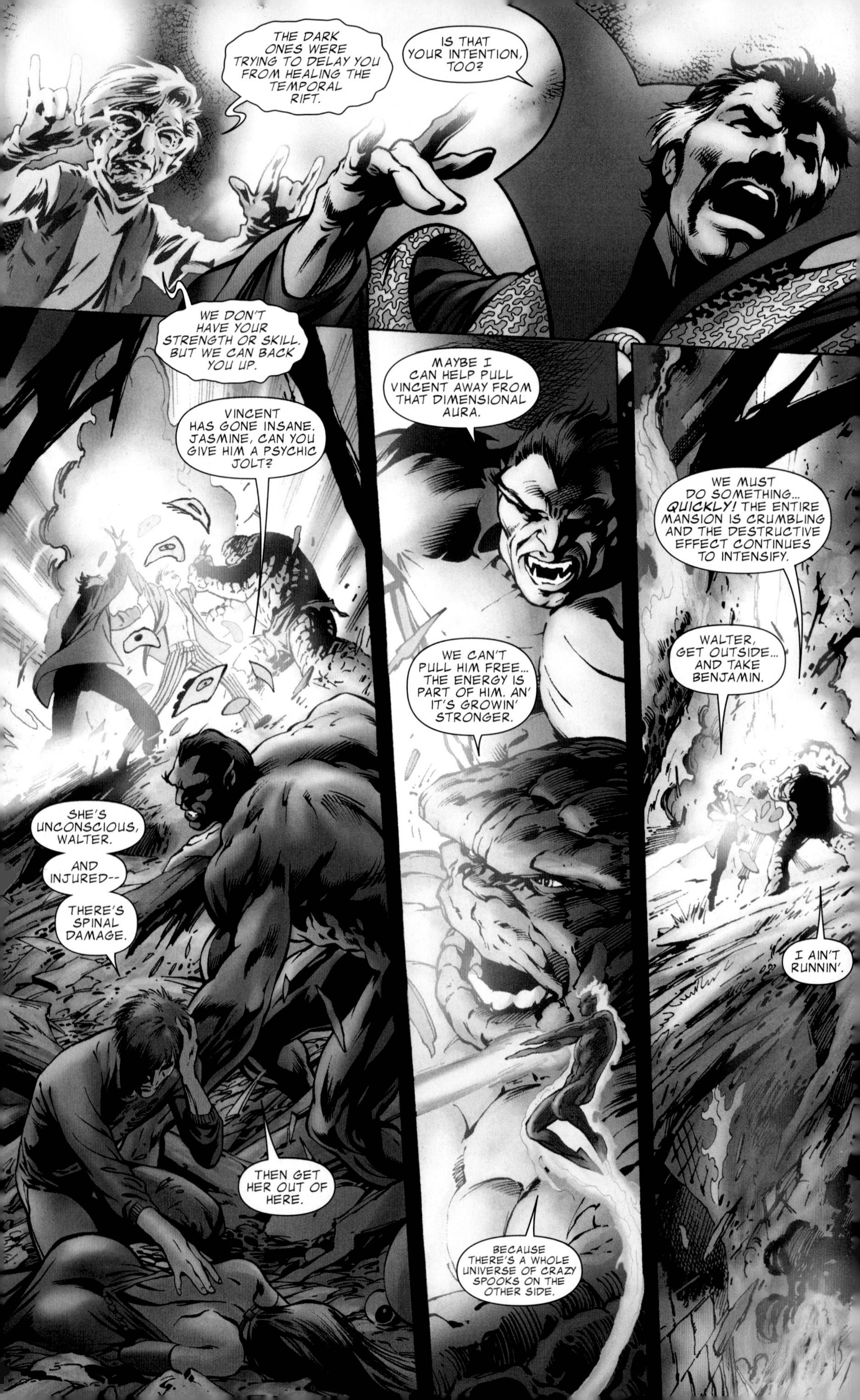
THE DARK ONES WERE TRYING TO DELAY YOU FROM HEALING THE TEMPORAL RIFT.
IS THAT YOUR INTENTION, TOO?
WE DON'T HAVE YOUR STRENGTH OR SKILL. BUT WE CAN BACK YOU UP.
VINCENT HAS GONE INSANE. JASMINE, CAN YOU GIVE HIM A PSYCHIC JOLT?
SHE'S UNCONSCIOUS, WALTER.
AND INJURED--
THERE'S SPINAL DAMAGE.
THEN GET HER OUT OF HERE.
MAYBE I CAN HELP PULL VINCENT AWAY FROM THAT DIMENSIONAL AURA.
WE CAN'T PULL HIM FREE... THE ENERGY IS PART OF HIM. AN' IT'S GROWIN' STRONGER.
BECAUSE THERE'S A WHOLE UNIVERSE OF CRAZY SPOOKS ON THE OTHER SIDE.
WE MUST DO SOMETHING... QUICKLY! THE ENTIRE MANSION IS CRUMBLING AND THE DESTRUCTIVE EFFECT CONTINUES TO INTENSIFY.
WALTER, GET OUTSIDE... AND TAKE BENJAMIN.
I AIN'T RUNNIN'.

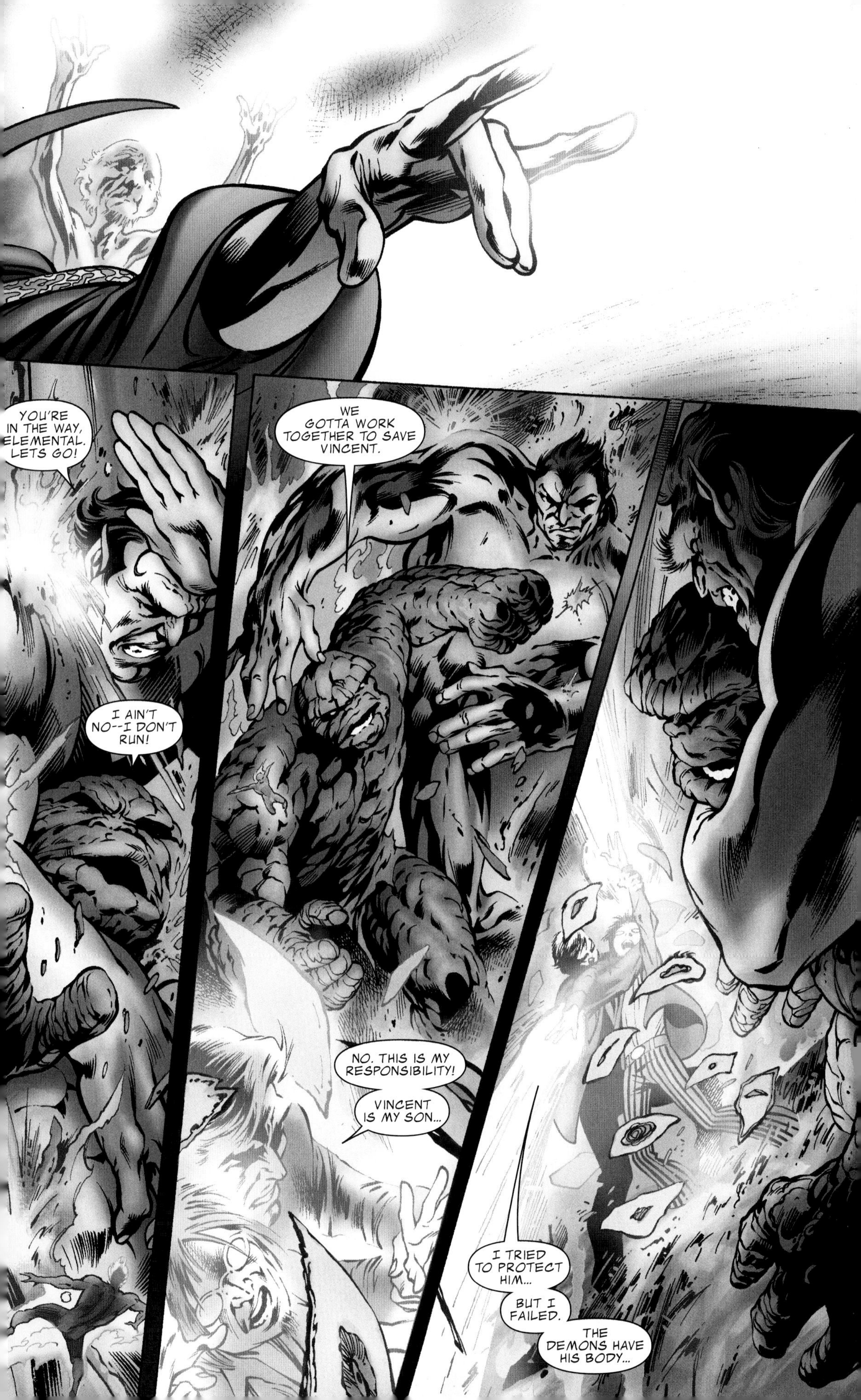
YOU'RE IN THE WAY, ELEMENTAL. LETS GO!
I AIN'T NO--I DON'T RUN!
WE GOTTA WORK TOGETHER TO SAVE VINCENT.
NO. THIS IS MY RESPONSIBILITY!
VINCENT IS MY SON...
I TRIED TO PROTECT HIM...
BUT I FAILED.
THE DEMONS HAVE HIS BODY...

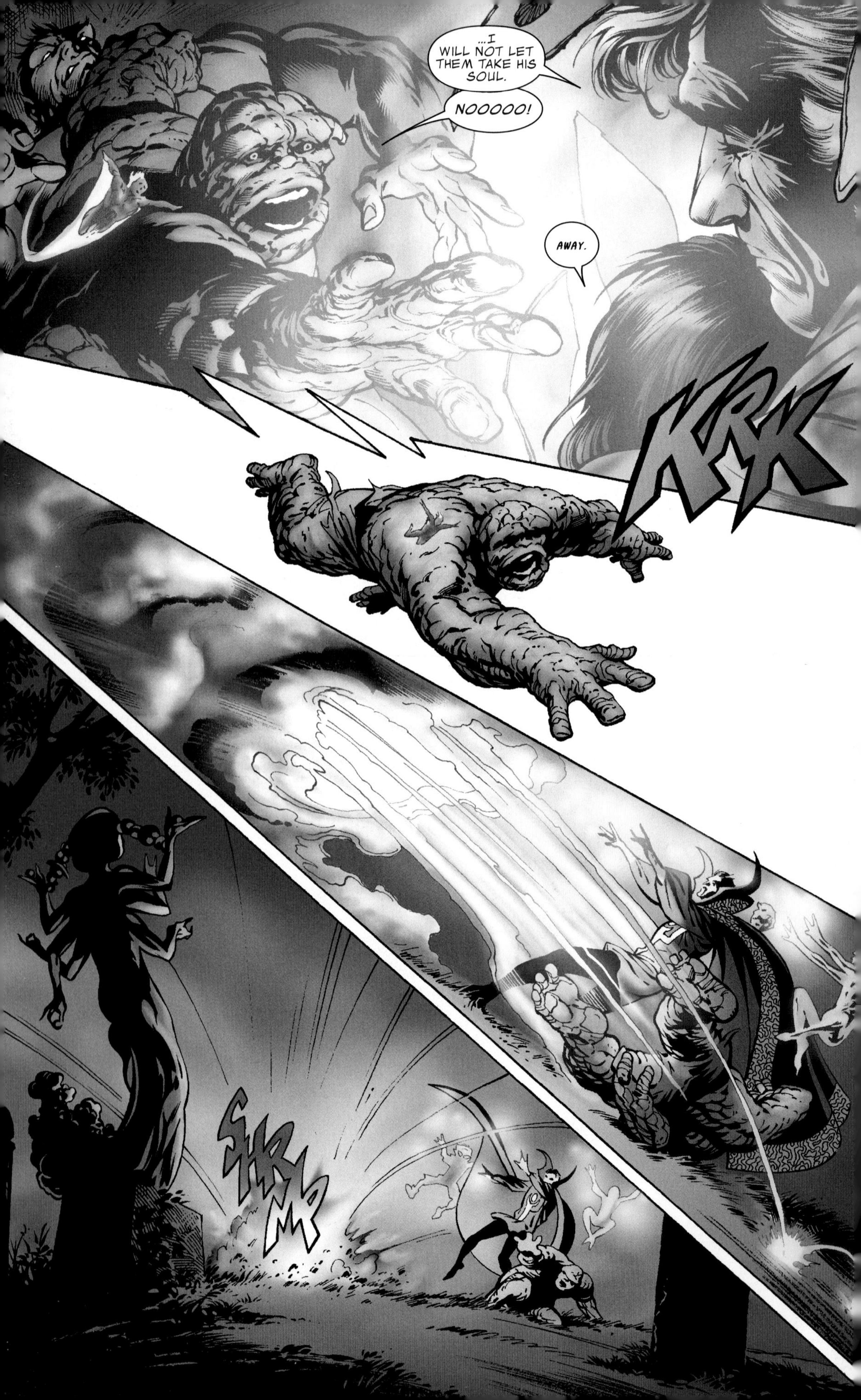
...I WILL NOT LET THEM TAKE HIS SOUL.
NOOOOO!
AWAY.
KRK
SHRAKOOM

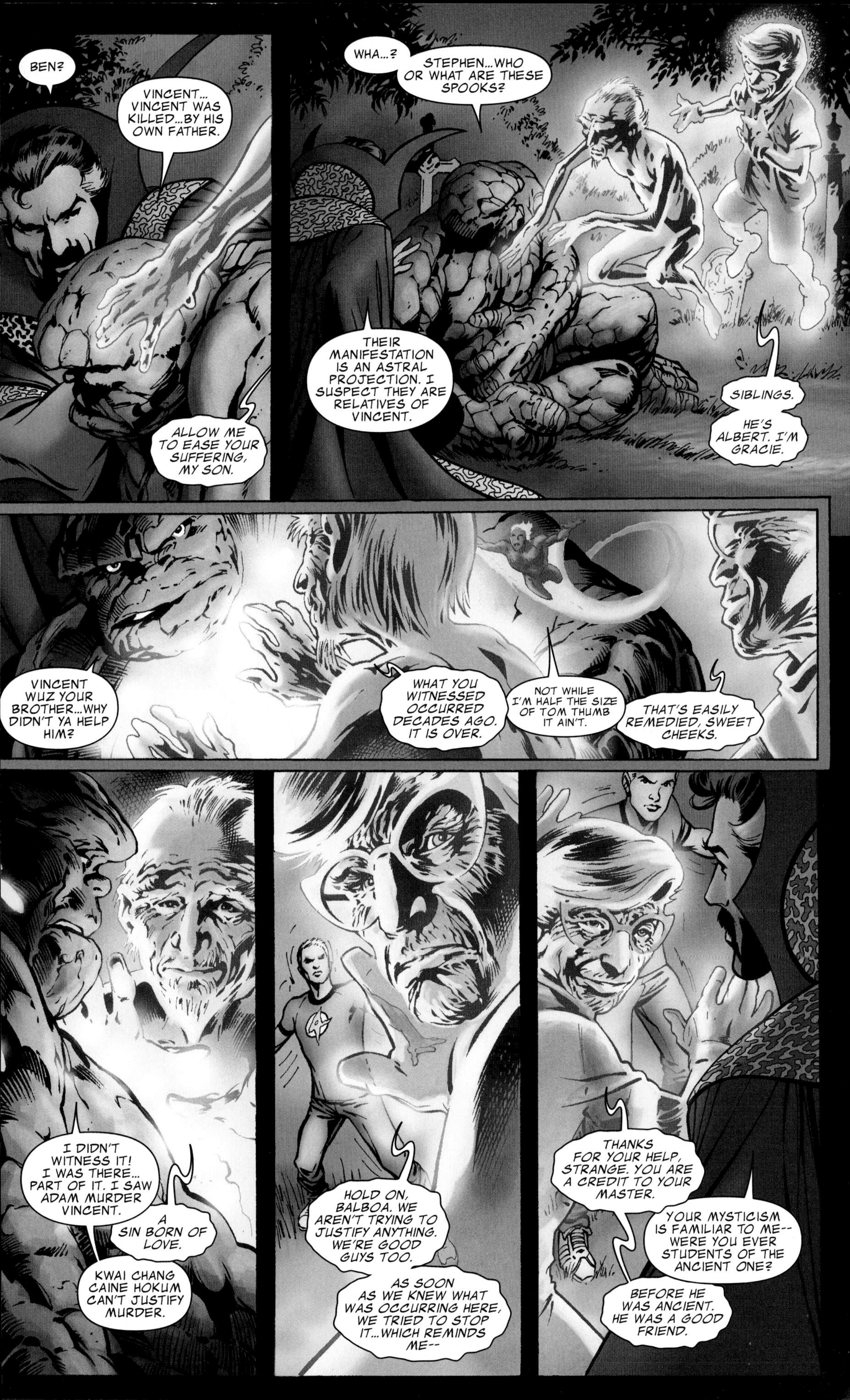
BEN?
VINCENT... VINCENT WAS KILLED...BY HIS OWN FATHER.
ALLOW ME TO EASE YOUR SUFFERING, MY SON.
WHA...?
STEPHEN...WHO OR WHAT ARE THESE SPOOKS?
THEIR MANIFESTATION IS AN ASTRAL PROJECTION. I SUSPECT THEY ARE RELATIVES OF VINCENT.
SIBLINGS.
HE'S ALBERT. I'M GRACIE.
VINCENT WUZ YOUR BROTHER...WHY DIDN'T YA HELP HIM?
WHAT YOU WITNESSED OCCURRED DECADES AGO. IT IS OVER.
NOT WHILE I'M HALF THE SIZE OF TOM THUMB IT AIN'T.
THAT'S EASILY REMEDIED, SWEET CHEEKS.
I DIDN'T WITNESS IT! I WAS THERE... PART OF IT. I SAW ADAM MURDER VINCENT.
A SIN BORN OF LOVE.
KWAI CHANG CAINE HOKUM CAN'T JUSTIFY MURDER.
HOLD ON, BALBOA. WE AREN'T TRYING TO JUSTIFY ANYTHING. WE'RE GOOD GUYS TOO.
AS SOON AS WE KNEW WHAT WAS OCCURRING HERE, WE TRIED TO STOP IT...WHICH REMINDS ME--
THANKS FOR YOUR HELP, STRANGE. YOU ARE A CREDIT TO YOUR MASTER.
YOUR MYSTICISM IS FAMILIAR TO ME-- WERE YOU EVER STUDENTS OF THE ANCIENT ONE?
BEFORE HE WAS ANCIENT. HE WAS A GOOD FRIEND.

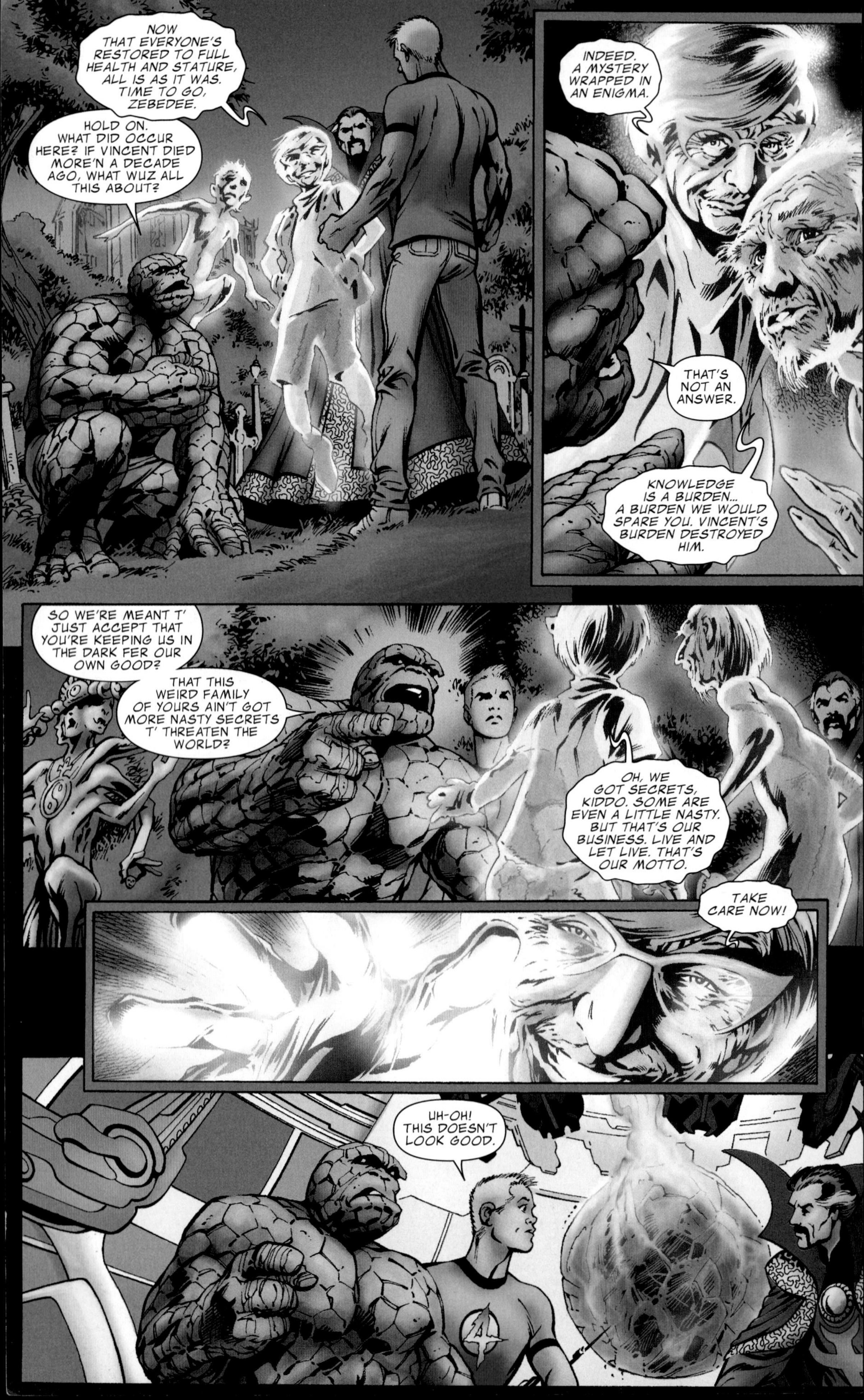
NOW THAT EVERYONE'S RESTORED TO FULL HEALTH AND STATURE, ALL IS AS IT WAS. TIME TO GO, ZEBEDEE.
HOLD ON. WHAT DID OCCUR HERE? IF VINCENT DIED MORE'N A DECADE AGO, WHAT WUZ ALL THIS ABOUT?
INDEED. A MYSTERY WRAPPED IN AN ENIGMA.
THAT'S NOT AN ANSWER.
KNOWLEDGE IS A BURDEN... A BURDEN WE WOULD SPARE YOU. VINCENT'S BURDEN DESTROYED HIM.
SO WE'RE MEANT T' JUST ACCEPT THAT YOU'RE KEEPING US IN THE DARK FER OUR OWN GOOD?
THAT THIS WEIRD FAMILY OF YOURS AIN'T GOT MORE NASTY SECRETS T' THREATEN THE WORLD?
OH, WE GOT SECRETS, KIDDO. SOME ARE EVEN A LITTLE NASTY. BUT THAT'S OUR BUSINESS. LIVE AND LET LIVE. THAT'S OUR MOTTO.
TAKE CARE NOW!
UH-OH! THIS DOESN'T LOOK GOOD.

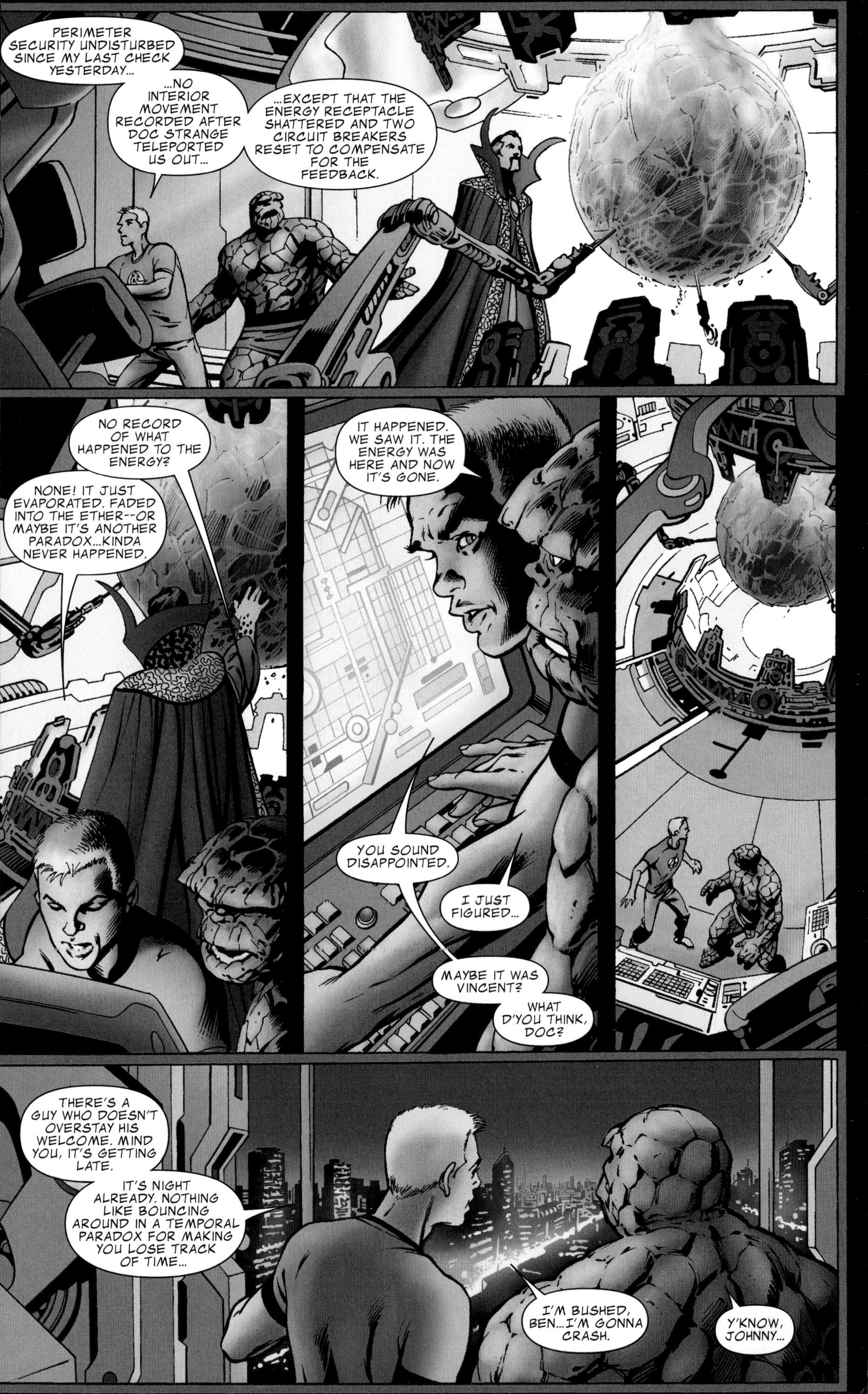
PERIMETER SECURITY UNDISTURBED SINCE MY LAST CHECK YESTERDAY...
...NO INTERIOR MOVEMENT RECORDED AFTER DOC STRANGE TELEPORTED US OUT...
...EXCEPT THAT THE ENERGY RECEPTACLE SHATTERED AND TWO CIRCUIT BREAKERS RESET TO COMPENSATE FOR THE FEEDBACK.
NO RECORD OF WHAT HAPPENED TO THE ENERGY?
NONE! IT JUST EVAPORATED. FADED INTO THE ETHER--OR MAYBE IT'S ANOTHER PARADOX...KINDA NEVER HAPPENED.
IT HAPPENED. WE SAW IT. THE ENERGY WAS HERE AND NOW IT'S GONE.
YOU SOUND DISAPPOINTED.
I JUST FIGURED...
MAYBE IT WAS VINCENT?
WHAT D'YOU THINK, DOC?
THERE'S A GUY WHO DOESN'T OVERSTAY HIS WELCOME. MIND YOU, IT'S GETTING LATE.
IT'S NIGHT ALREADY. NOTHING LIKE BOUNCING AROUND IN A TEMPORAL PARADOX FOR MAKING YOU LOSE TRACK OF TIME...
I'M BUSHED, BEN...I'M GONNA CRASH.
Y'KNOW, JOHNNY...

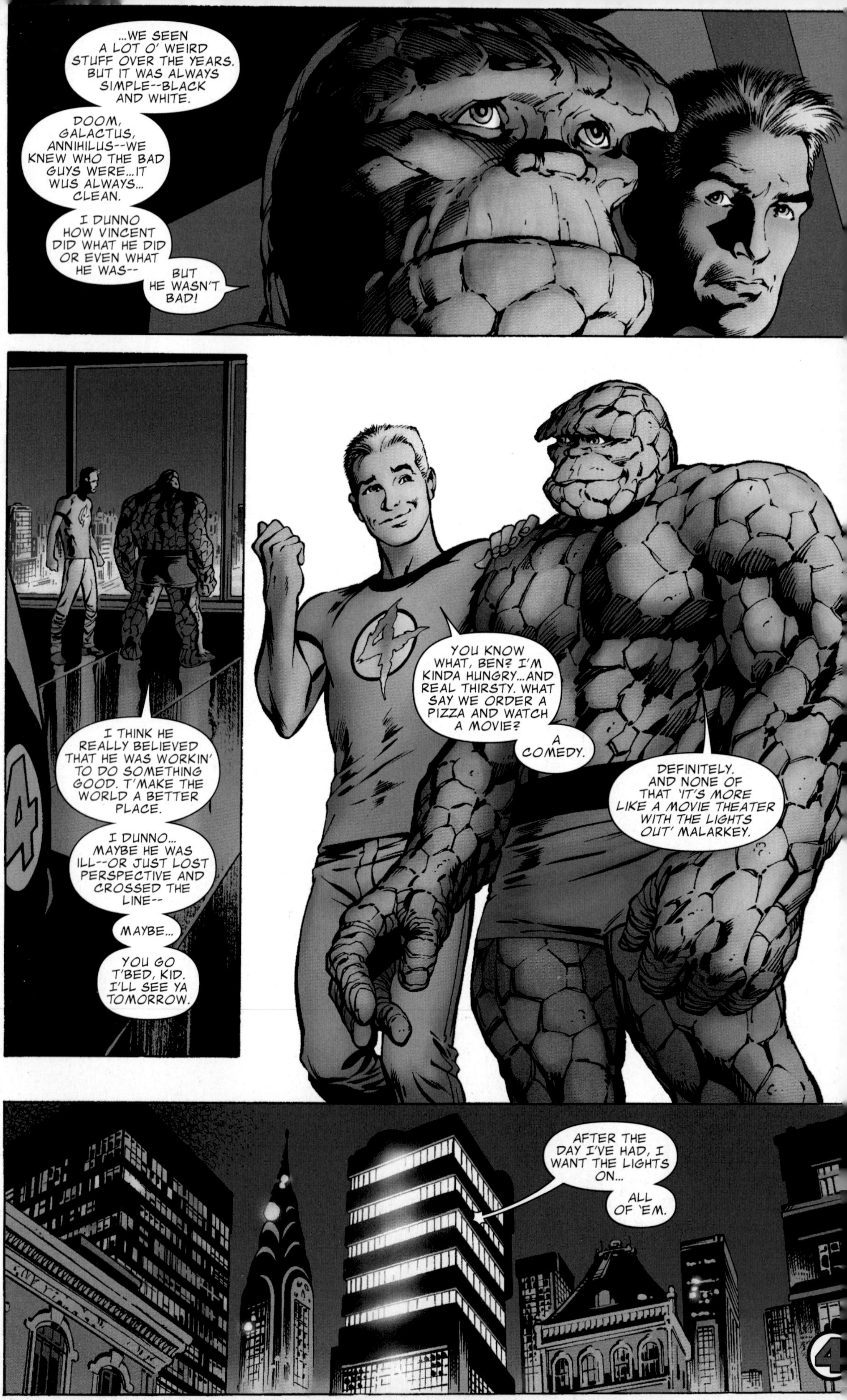
...WE SEEN A LOT O' WEIRD STUFF OVER THE YEARS. BUT IT WAS ALWAYS SIMPLE--BLACK AND WHITE.
DOOM, GALACTUS, ANNIHILUS--WE KNEW WHO THE BAD GUYS WERE...IT WUS ALWAYS... CLEAN.
I DUNNO HOW VINCENT DID WHAT HE DID OR EVEN WHAT HE WAS--
BUT HE WASN'T BAD!
I THINK HE REALLY BELIEVED THAT HE WAS WORKIN' TO DO SOMETHING GOOD. T'MAKE THE WORLD A BETTER PLACE.
I DUNNO... MAYBE HE WAS ILL--OR JUST LOST PERSPECTIVE AND CROSSED THE LINE--
MAYBE...
YOU GO T'BED, KID. I'LL SEE YA TOMORROW.
YOU KNOW WHAT, BEN? I'M KINDA HUNGRY...AND REAL THIRSTY. WHAT SAY WE ORDER A PIZZA AND WATCH A MOVIE?
A COMEDY.
DEFINITELY. AND NONE OF THAT 'IT'S MORE LIKE A MOVIE THEATER WITH THE LIGHTS OUT' MALARKEY.
AFTER THE DAY I'VE HAD, I WANT THE LIGHTS ON...
ALL OF 'EM.

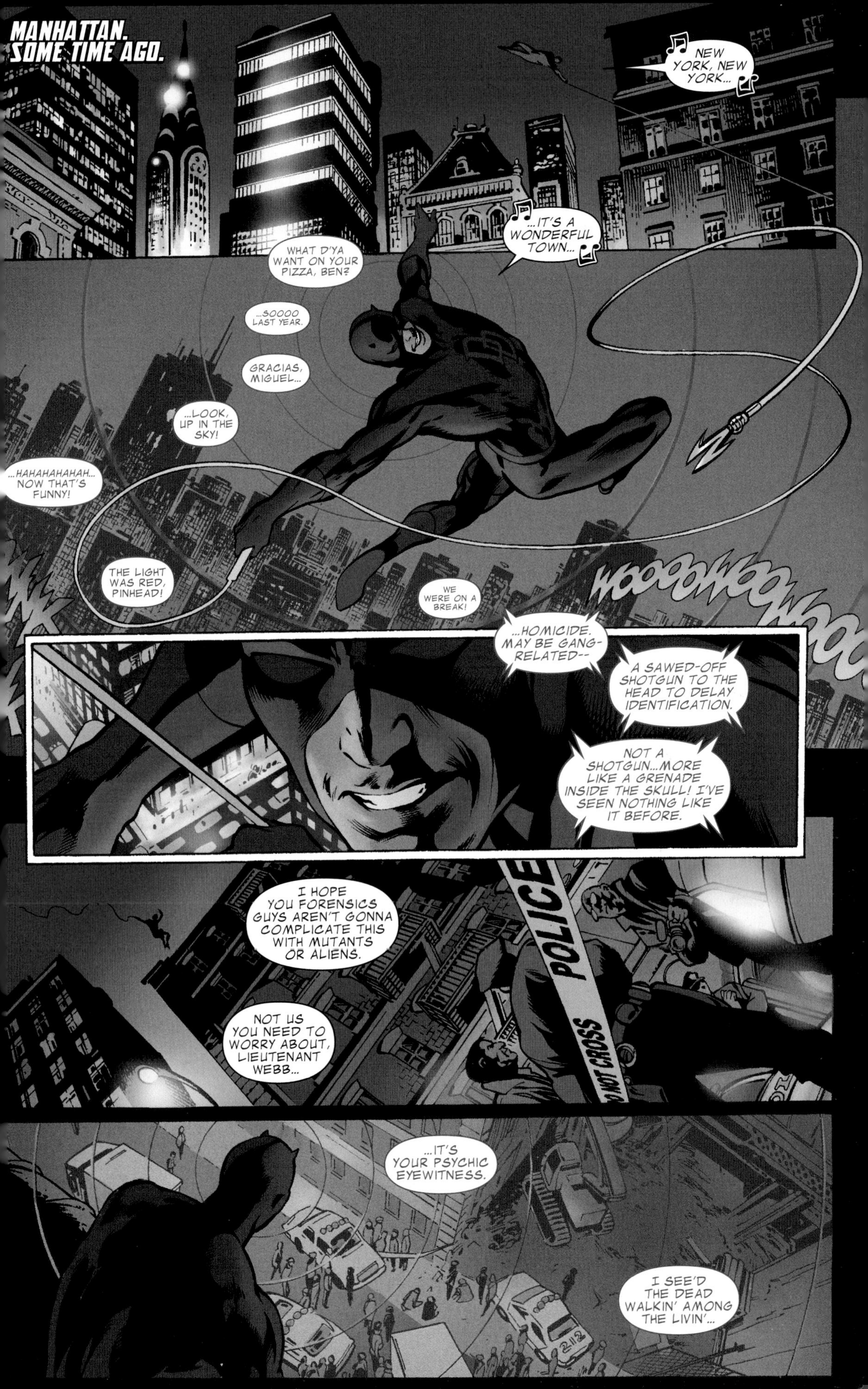
MANHATTAN. SOME TIME AGO.
NEW YORK, NEW YORK...
...IT'S A WONDERFUL TOWN...
WHAT D'YA WANT ON YOUR PIZZA, BEN?
...SOOOO LAST YEAR.
GRACIAS, MIGUEL...
...LOOK, UP IN THE SKY!
...HAHAHAHAHAH... NOW THAT'S FUNNY!
THE LIGHT WAS RED, PINHEAD!
WE WERE ON A BREAK!
WOOOOWOOOWOOOO
...HOMICIDE. MAY BE GANG-RELATED--
A SAWED-OFF SHOTGUN TO THE HEAD TO DELAY IDENTIFICATION.
NOT A SHOTGUN...MORE LIKE A GRENADE INSIDE THE SKULL! I'VE SEEN NOTHING LIKE IT BEFORE.
POLICE
DO NOT CROSS
I HOPE YOU FORENSICS GUYS AREN'T GONNA COMPLICATE THIS WITH MUTANTS OR ALIENS.
NOT US YOU NEED TO WORRY ABOUT, LIEUTENANT WEBB...
...IT'S YOUR PSYCHIC EYEWITNESS.
I SEE'D THE DEAD WALKIN' AMONG THE LIVIN'...

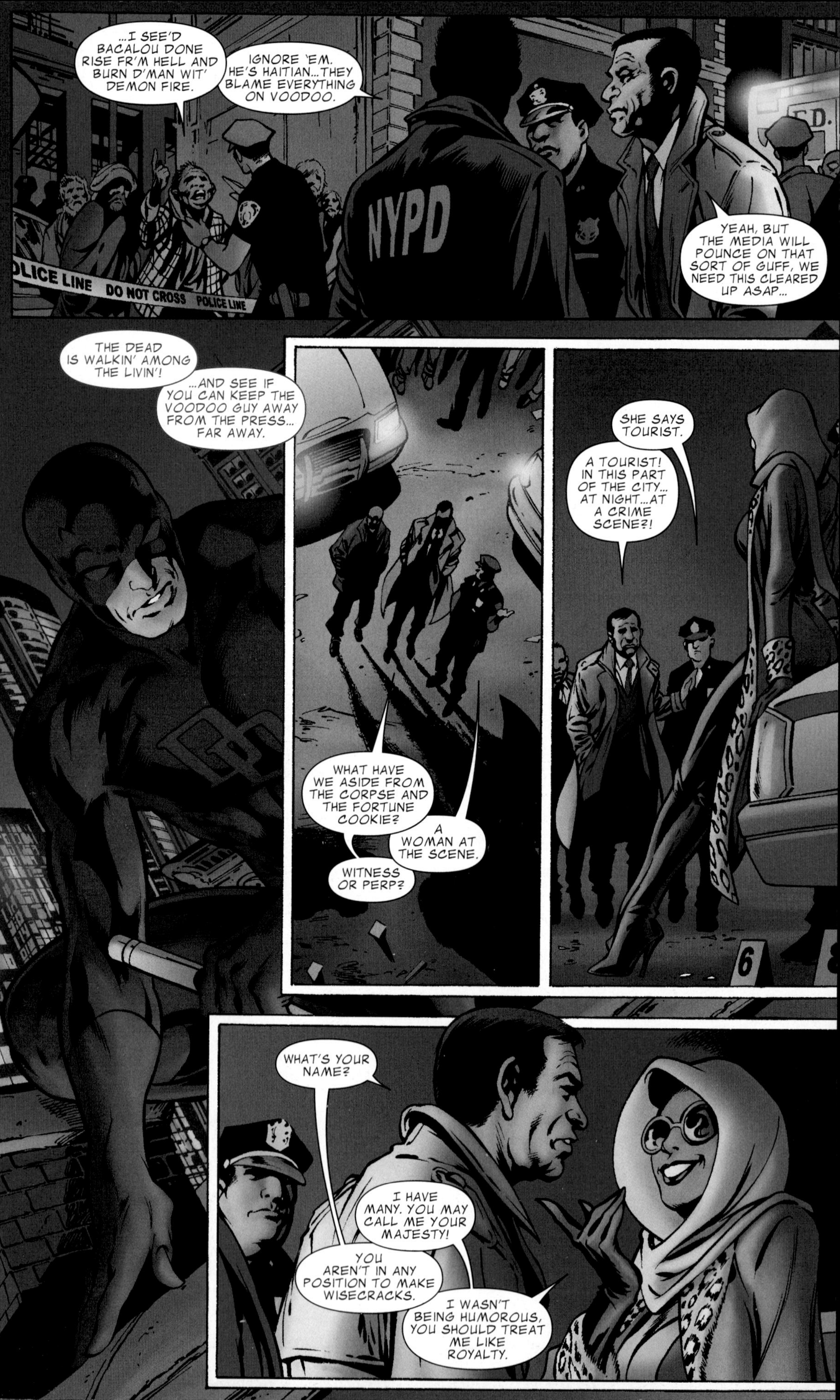

...I SEE'D BACALOU DONE RISE FR'M HELL AND BURN D'MAN WIT' DEMON FIRE.
IGNORE 'EM. HE'S HAITIAN...THEY BLAME EVERYTHING ON VOODOO.
YEAH, BUT THE MEDIA WILL POUNCE ON THAT SORT OF GUFF, WE NEED THIS CLEARED UP ASAP...
POLICE LINE DO NOT CROSS POLICE LINE
NYPD
THE DEAD IS WALKIN' AMONG THE LIVIN'!
...AND SEE IF YOU CAN KEEP THE VOODOO GUY AWAY FROM THE PRESS... FAR AWAY.
WHAT HAVE WE ASIDE FROM THE CORPSE AND THE FORTUNE COOKIE?
A WOMAN AT THE SCENE.
WITNESS OR PERP?
SHE SAYS TOURIST.
A TOURIST! IN THIS PART OF THE CITY... AT NIGHT...AT A CRIME SCENE?!
WHAT'S YOUR NAME?
I HAVE MANY. YOU MAY CALL ME YOUR MAJESTY!
YOU AREN'T IN ANY POSITION TO MAKE WISECRACKS.
I WASN'T BEING HUMOROUS, YOU SHOULD TREAT ME LIKE ROYALTY.

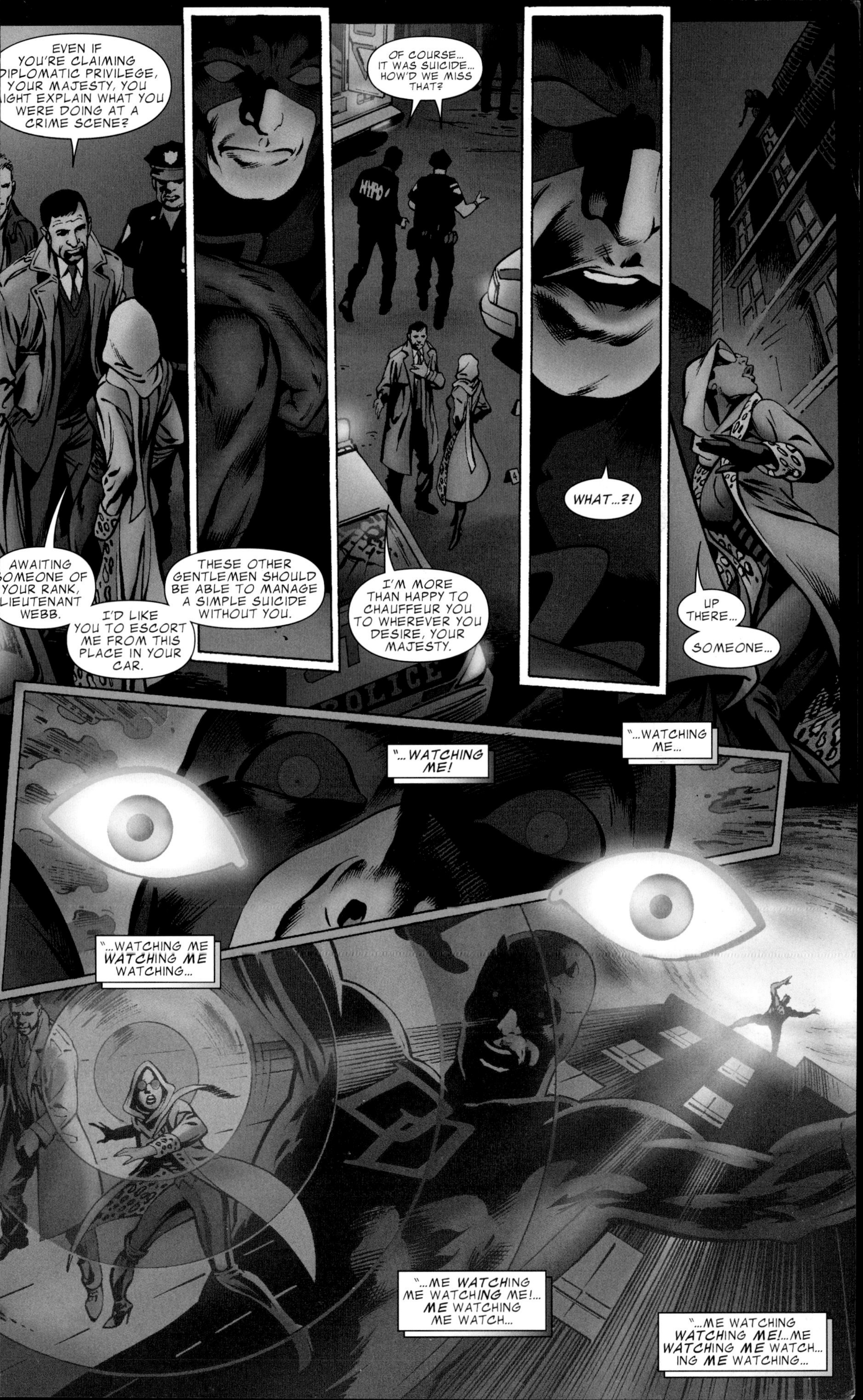
EVEN IF YOU'RE CLAIMING DIPLOMATIC PRIVILEGE, YOUR MAJESTY, YOU MIGHT EXPLAIN WHAT YOU WERE DOING AT A CRIME SCENE?
AWAITING SOMEONE OF YOUR RANK, LIEUTENANT WEBB.
I'D LIKE YOU TO ESCORT ME FROM THIS PLACE IN YOUR CAR.
THESE OTHER GENTLEMEN SHOULD BE ABLE TO MANAGE A SIMPLE SUICIDE WITHOUT YOU.
OF COURSE... IT WAS SUICIDE... HOW'D WE MISS THAT?
I'M MORE THAN HAPPY TO CHAUFFEUR YOU TO WHEREVER YOU DESIRE, YOUR MAJESTY.
POLICE
WHAT...?!
UP THERE...
SOMEONE...
"...WATCHING ME...
"...WATCHING ME!
"...WATCHING ME WATCHING ME WATCHING...
"...ME WATCHING ME WATCHING ME!... ME WATCHING ME WATCH...
"...ME WATCHING WATCHING ME!...ME WATCHING ME WATCH... ING ME WATCHING...

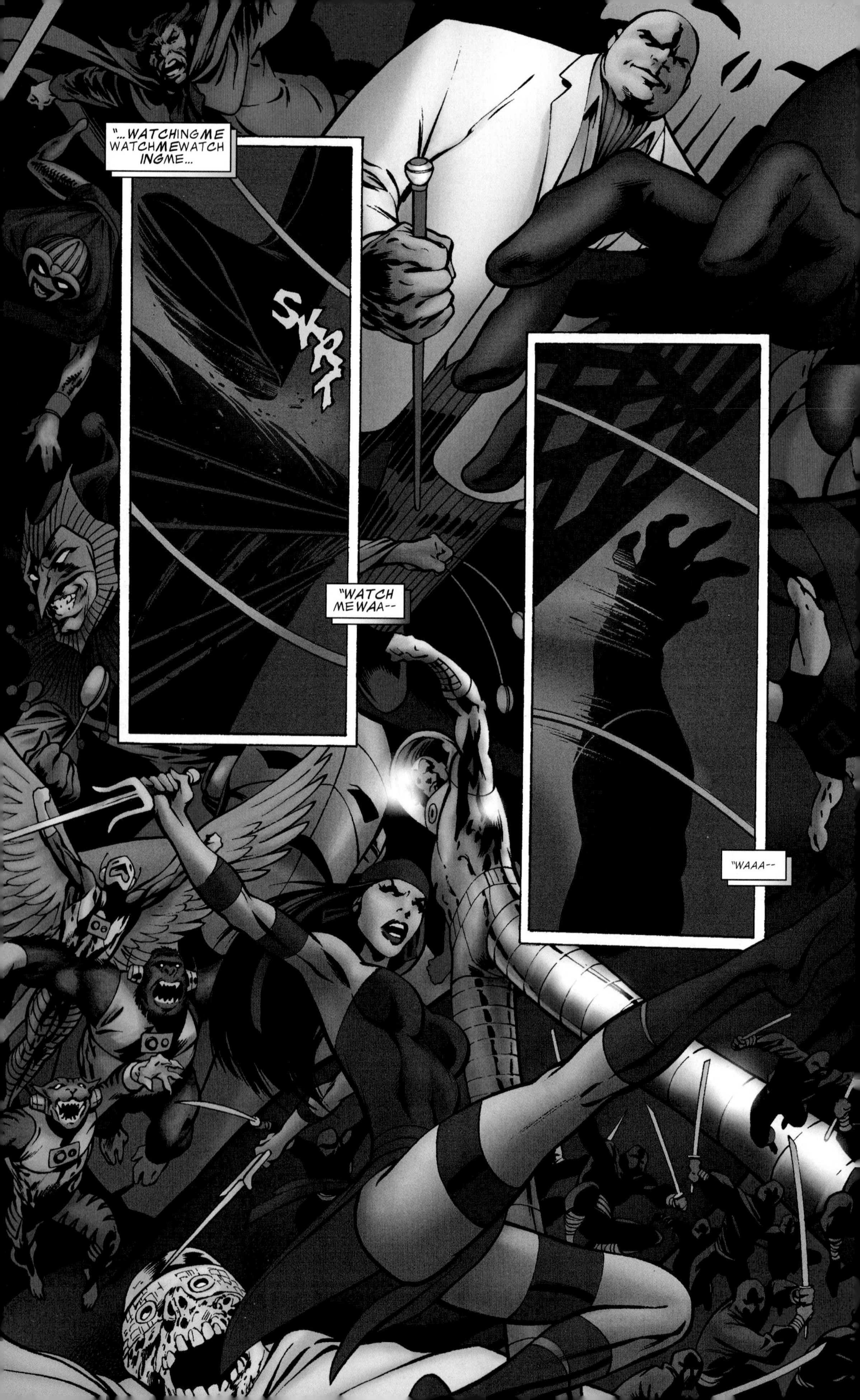
"...WATCHINGME WATCHMEWATCH INGME...
SKRT
"WATCH MEWAA--
"WAAA--

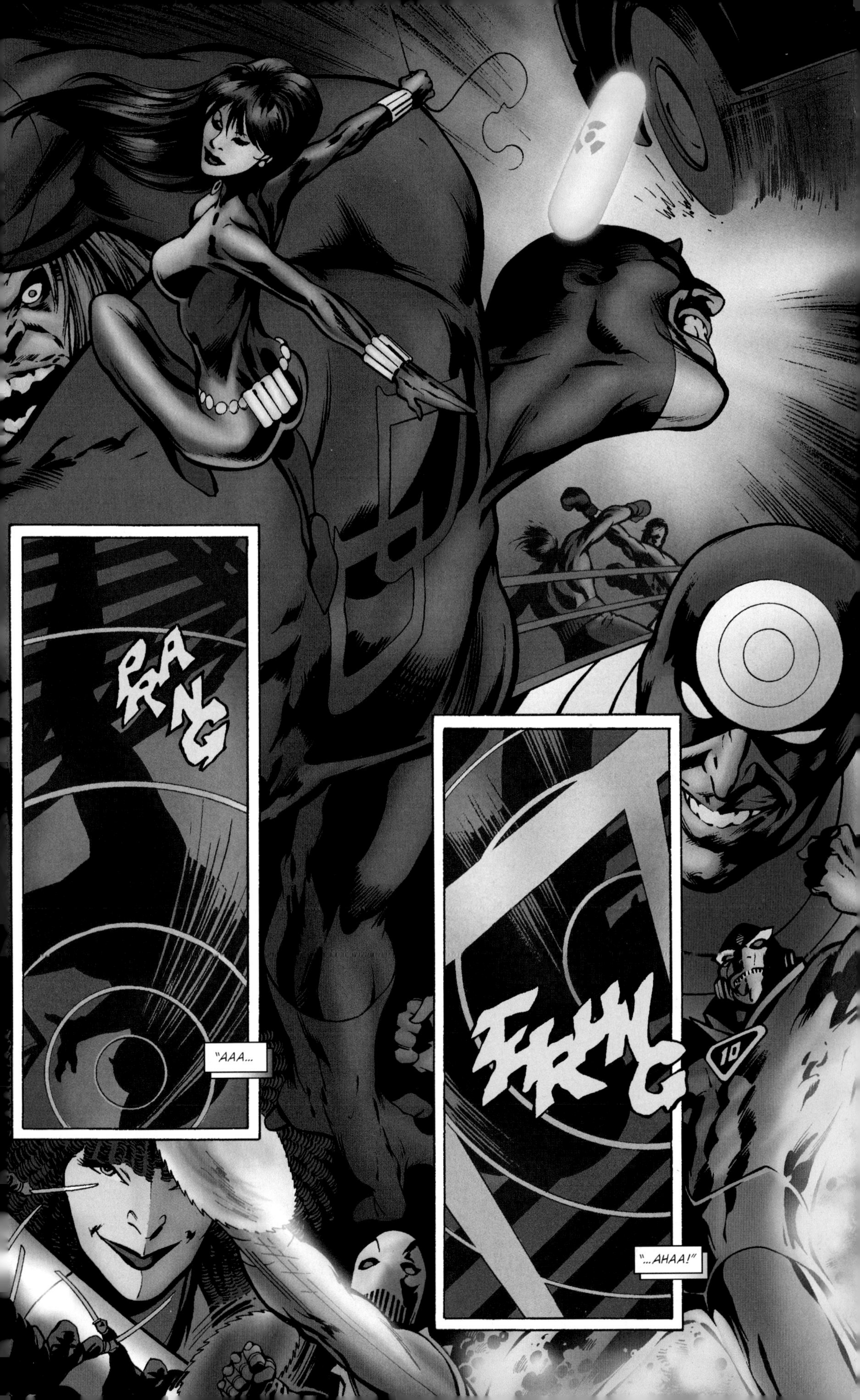
PRANG
"AAA...
FRUNG
"...AHAA!"

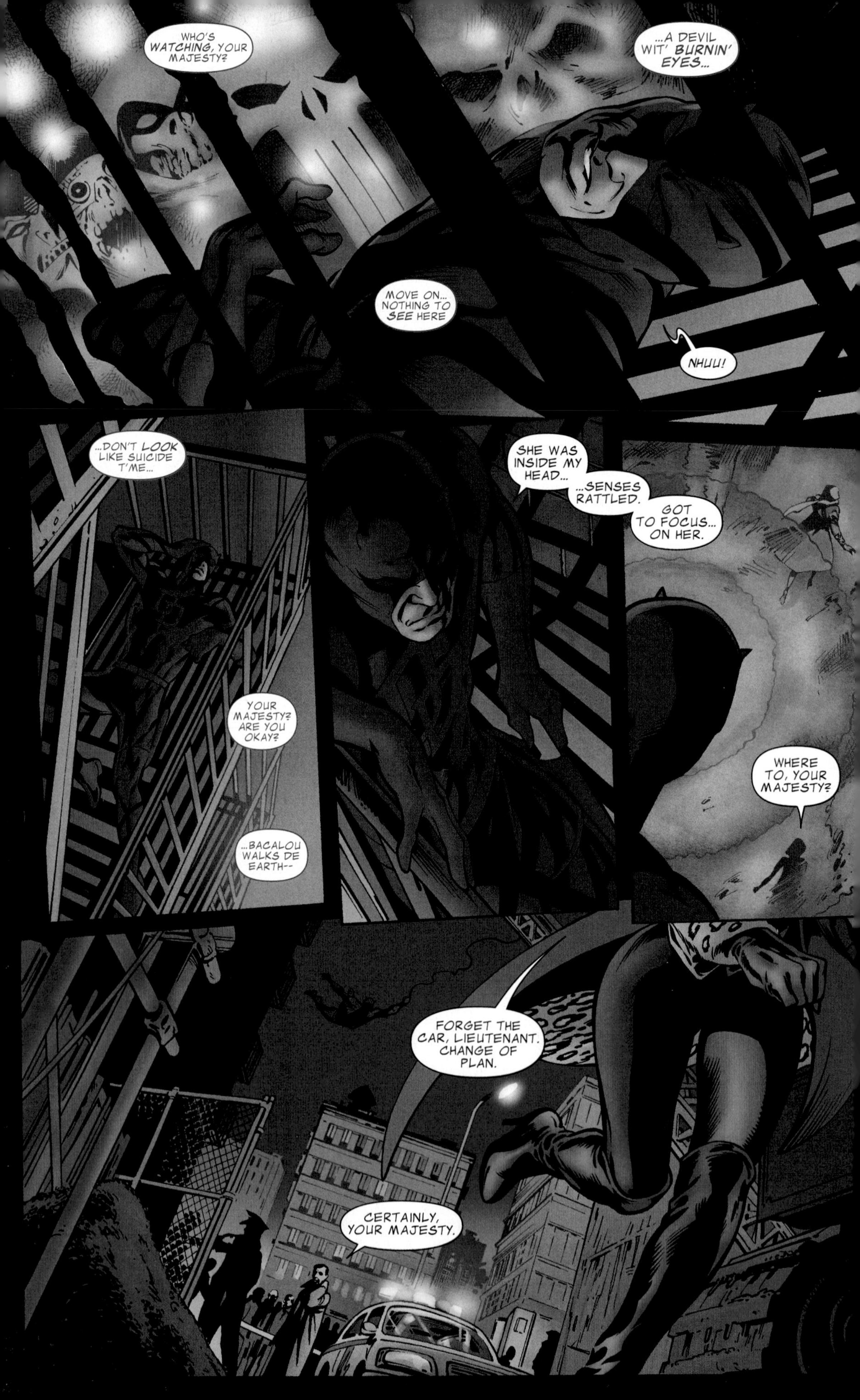
WHO'S WATCHING, YOUR MAJESTY?
...A DEVIL WIT' BURNIN' EYES...
MOVE ON... NOTHING TO SEE HERE
NHUU!
...DON'T LOOK LIKE SUICIDE T'ME...
YOUR MAJESTY? ARE YOU OKAY?
...BACALOU WALKS DE EARTH--
SHE WAS INSIDE MY HEAD...
...SENSES RATTLED.
GOT TO FOCUS... ON HER.
WHERE TO, YOUR MAJESTY?
FORGET THE CAR, LIEUTENANT. CHANGE OF PLAN.
CERTAINLY, YOUR MAJESTY.

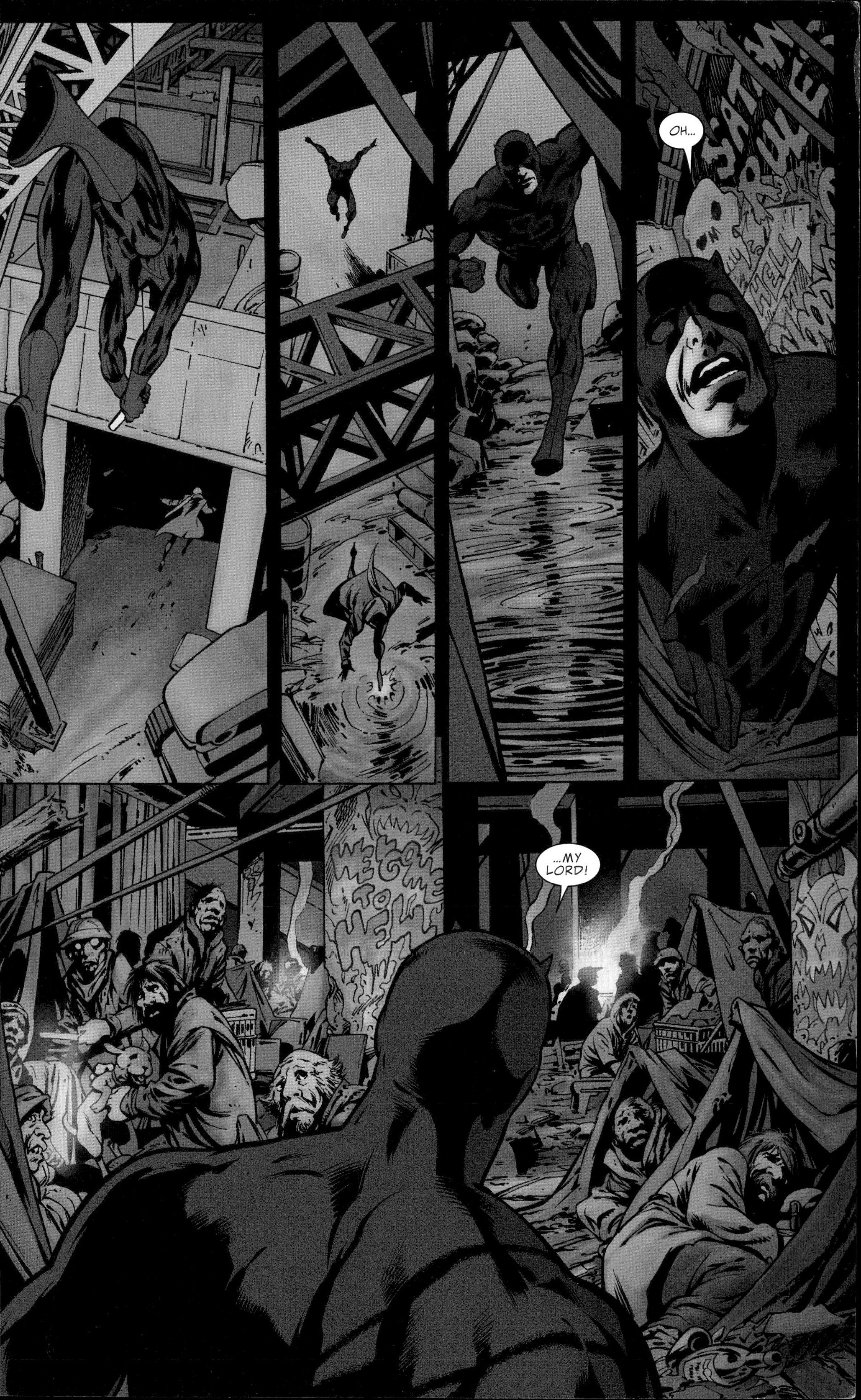
OH...
...MY LORD!

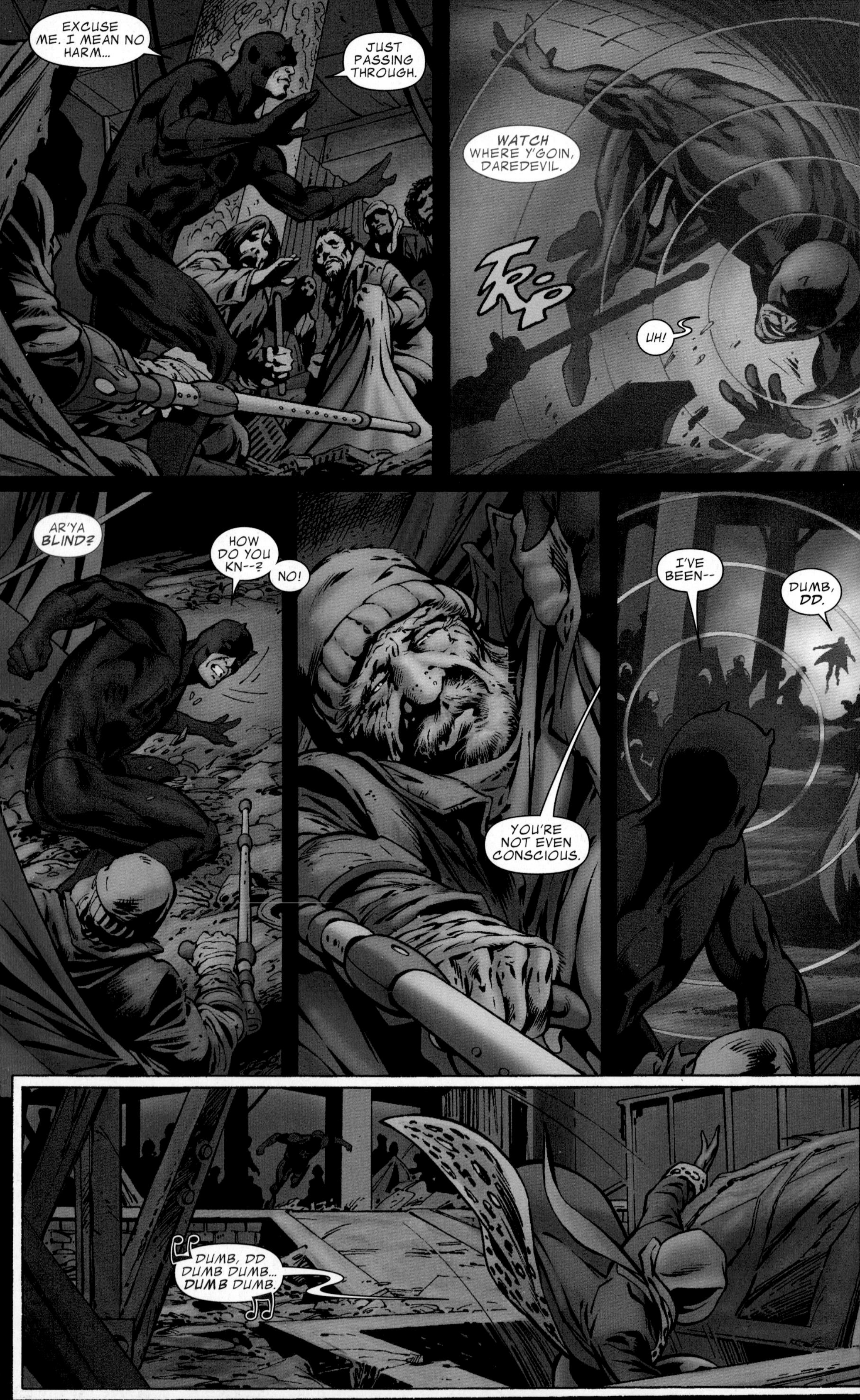
EXCUSE ME. I MEAN NO HARM...
JUST PASSING THROUGH.
WATCH WHERE Y'GOIN, DAREDEVIL.
UH!
AR'YA BLIND?
HOW DO YOU KN--?
NO!
YOU'RE NOT EVEN CONSCIOUS.
I'VE BEEN--
DUMB, DD.
DUMB, DD DUMB DUMB... DUMB DUMB.

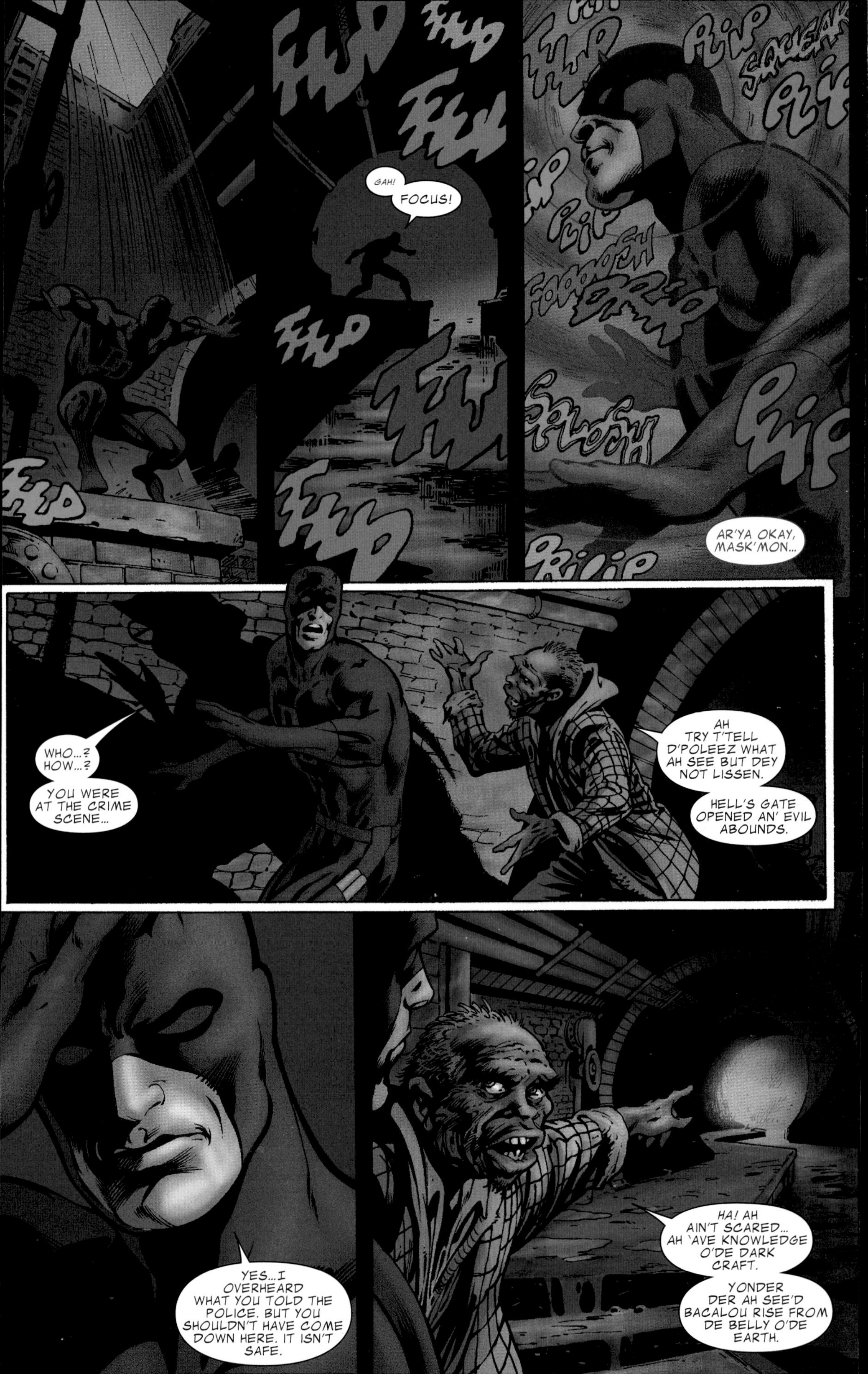
FLIP FLIP
FLIP
GAH!
FOCUS!
FLIP
FLIP
RIP
SQUEAK
RIP
FOOOOFSH
SPLOOSH
RIP
AR'YA OKAY, MASK'MON...
WHO...? HOW...?
YOU WERE AT THE CRIME SCENE...
AH TRY T'TELL D'POLEEZ WHAT AH SEE BUT DEY NOT LISSEN.
HELL'S GATE OPENED AN' EVIL ABOUNDS.
YES...I OVERHEARD WHAT YOU TOLD THE POLICE. BUT YOU SHOULDN'T HAVE COME DOWN HERE. IT ISN'T SAFE.
HA! AH AIN'T SCARED... AH 'AVE KNOWLEDGE O'DE DARK CRAFT.
YONDER DER AH SEE'D BACALOU RISE FROM DE BELLY O'DE EARTH.

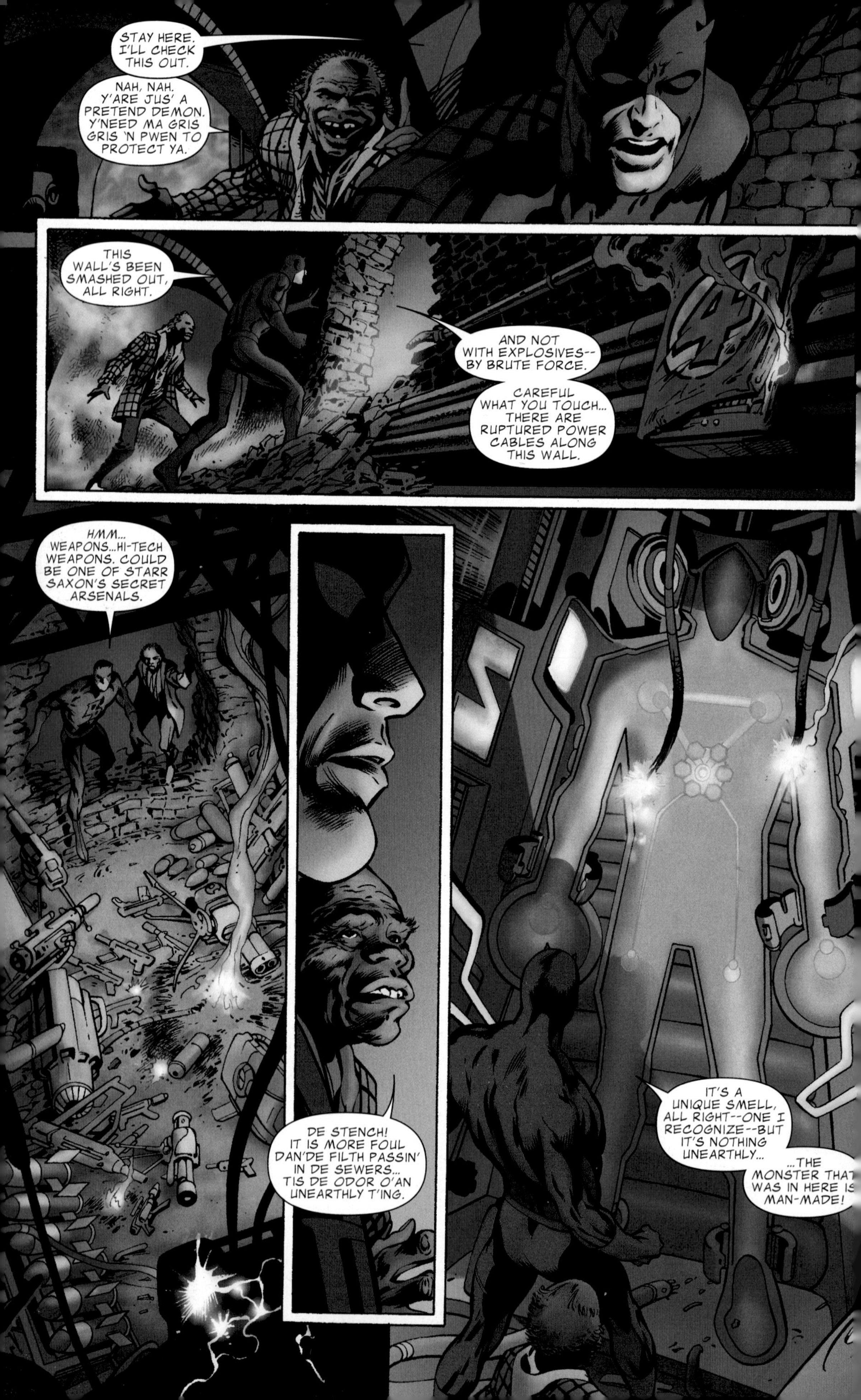
STAY HERE. I'LL CHECK THIS OUT.
NAH, NAH. Y'ARE JUS' A PRETEND DEMON. Y'NEED MA GRIS GRIS 'N PWEN TO PROTECT YA.
THIS WALL'S BEEN SMASHED OUT, ALL RIGHT.
AND NOT WITH EXPLOSIVES-- BY BRUTE FORCE.
CAREFUL WHAT YOU TOUCH... THERE ARE RUPTURED POWER CABLES ALONG THIS WALL.
HMM... WEAPONS...HI-TECH WEAPONS. COULD BE ONE OF STARR SAXON'S SECRET ARSENALS.
DE STENCH! IT IS MORE FOUL DAN'DE FILTH PASSIN' IN DE SEWERS... TIS DE ODOR O'AN UNEARTHLY T'ING.
IT'S A UNIQUE SMELL, ALL RIGHT--ONE I RECOGNIZE--BUT IT'S NOTHING UNEARTHLY...
...THE MONSTER THAT WAS IN HERE IS MAN-MADE!

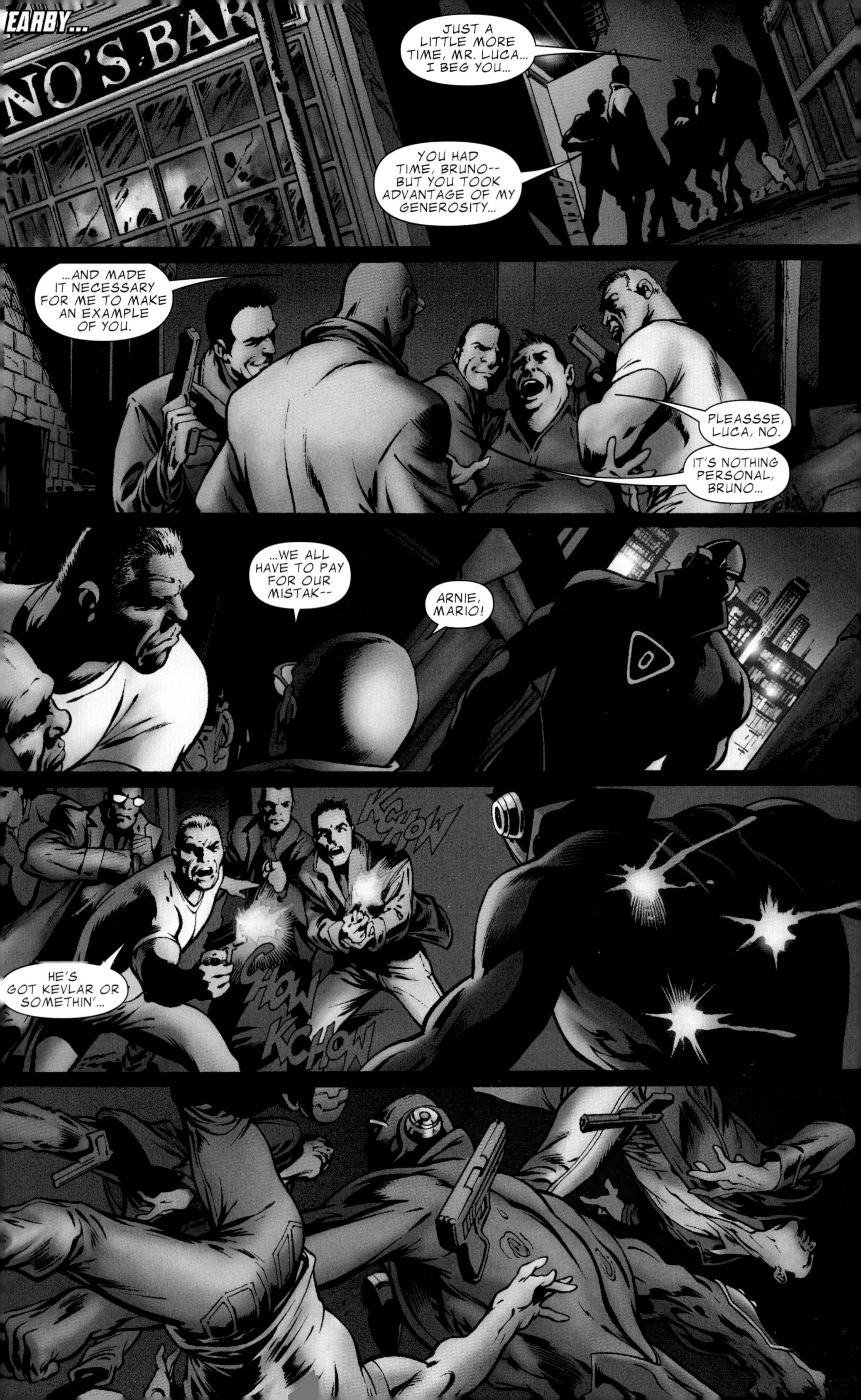
EARBY...
NO'S BAR
JUST A LITTLE MORE TIME, MR. LUCA... I BEG YOU...
YOU HAD TIME, BRUNO-- BUT YOU TOOK ADVANTAGE OF MY GENEROSITY...
...AND MADE IT NECESSARY FOR ME TO MAKE AN EXAMPLE OF YOU.
PLEASSSE, LUCA, NO.
IT'S NOTHING PERSONAL, BRUNO...
...WE ALL HAVE TO PAY FOR OUR MISTAK--
ARNIE, MARIO!
KCHOW
HE'S GOT KEVLAR OR SOMETHIN'...
CHOW
KCHOW

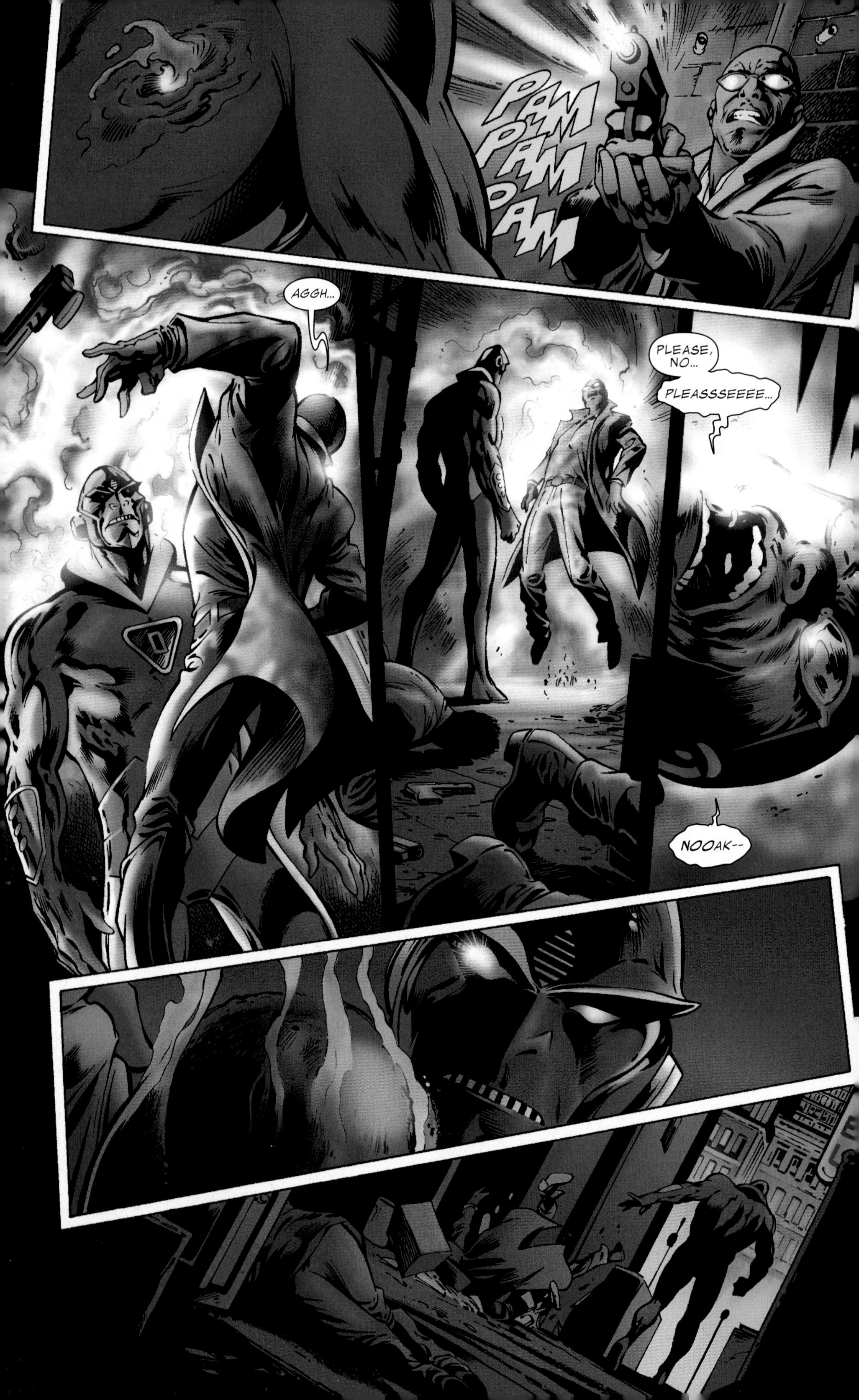
PAM
PAM
PAM
PAM
AGGH...
PLEASE, NO...
PLEASSSEEEE...
NOOAK--

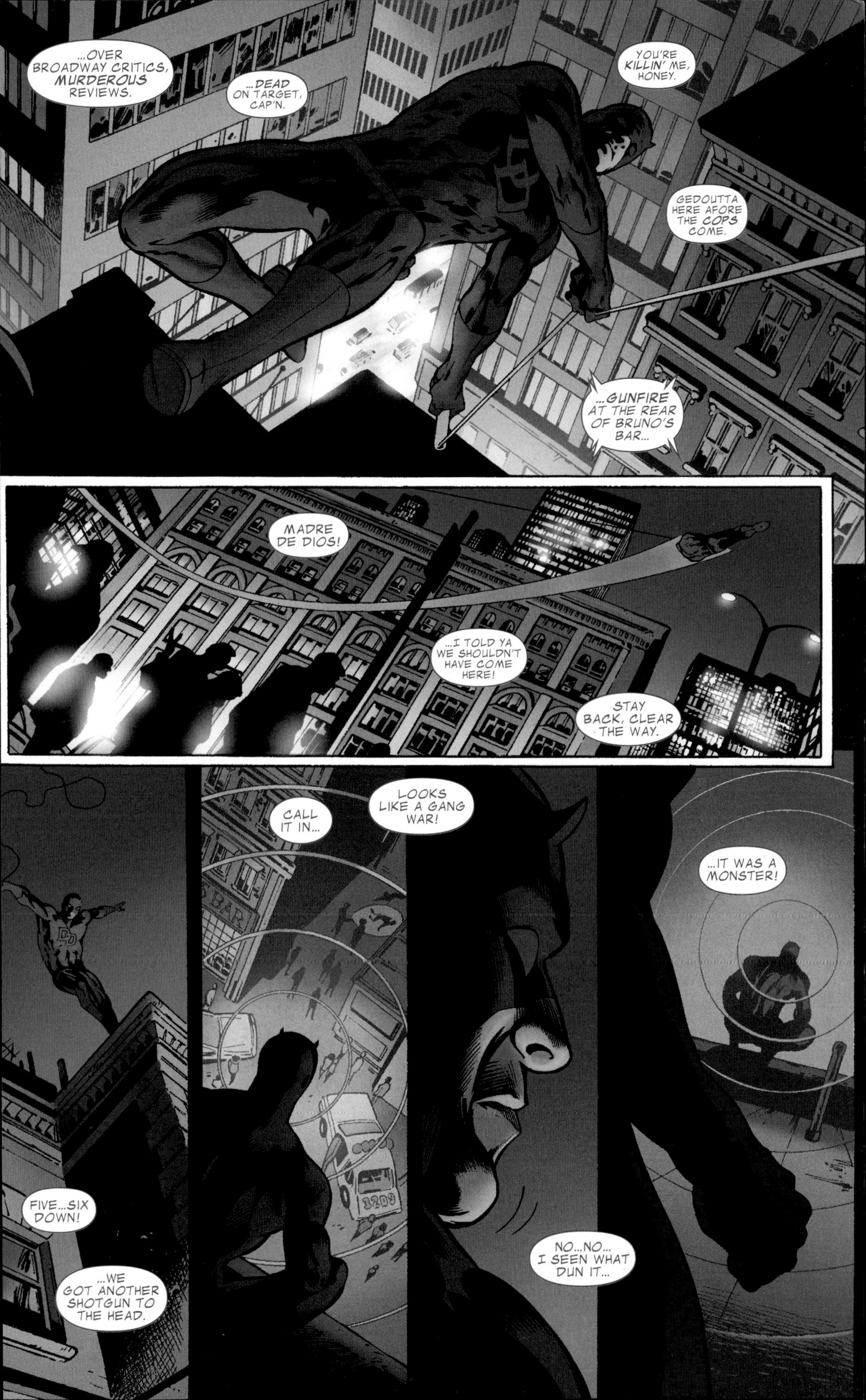
...OVER BROADWAY CRITICS, MURDEROUS REVIEWS.
...DEAD ON TARGET, CAP'N.
YOU'RE KILLIN' ME, HONEY.
GEDOUTTA HERE AFORE THE COPS COME.
...GUNFIRE AT THE REAR OF BRUNO'S BAR...
MADRE DE DIOS!
...I TOLD YA WE SHOULDN'T HAVE COME HERE!
STAY BACK, CLEAR THE WAY.
FIVE...SIX DOWN!
...WE GOT ANOTHER SHOTGUN TO THE HEAD.
CALL IT IN...
LOOKS LIKE A GANG WAR!
NO...NO... I SEEN WHAT DUN IT...
...IT WAS A MONSTER!

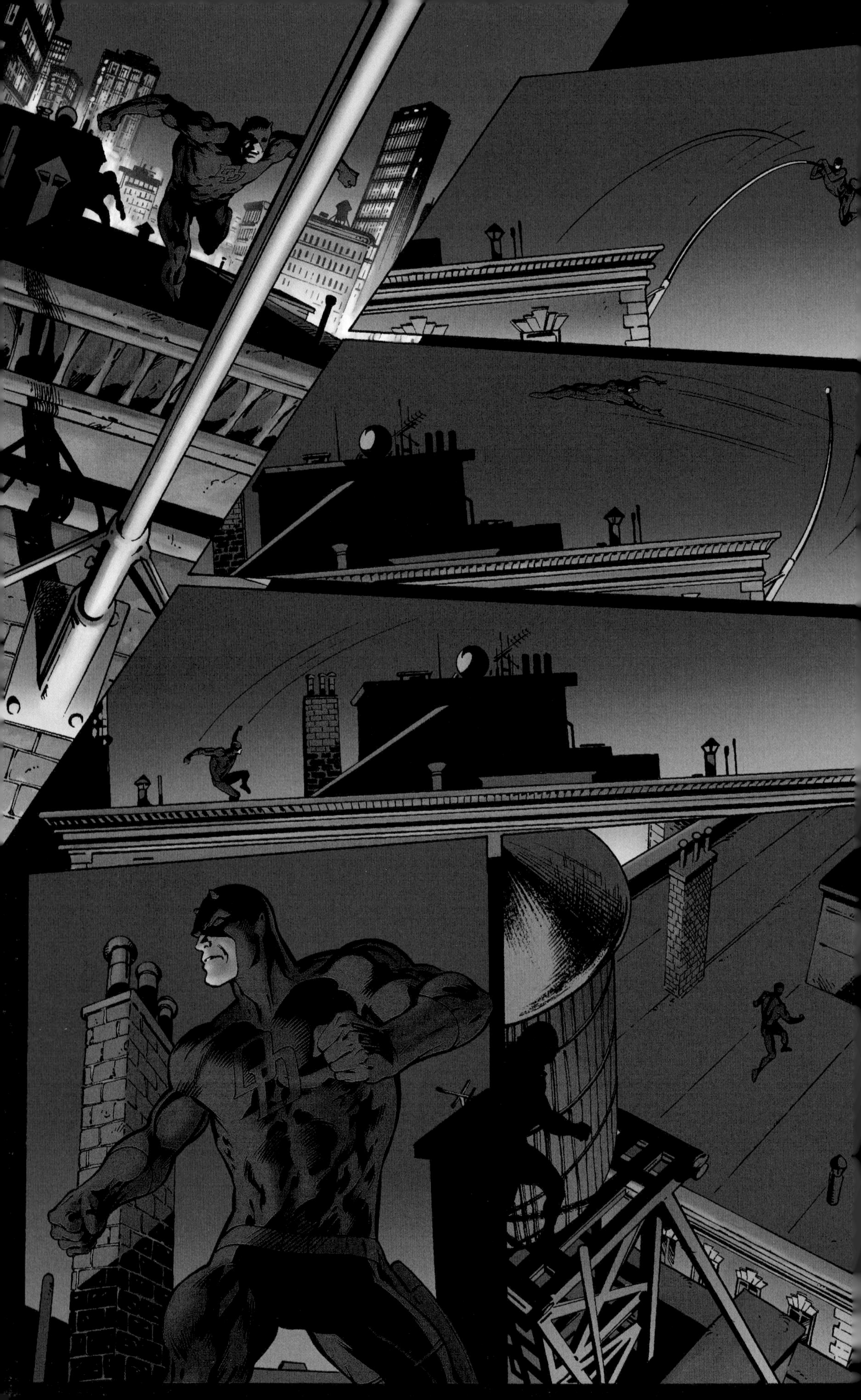

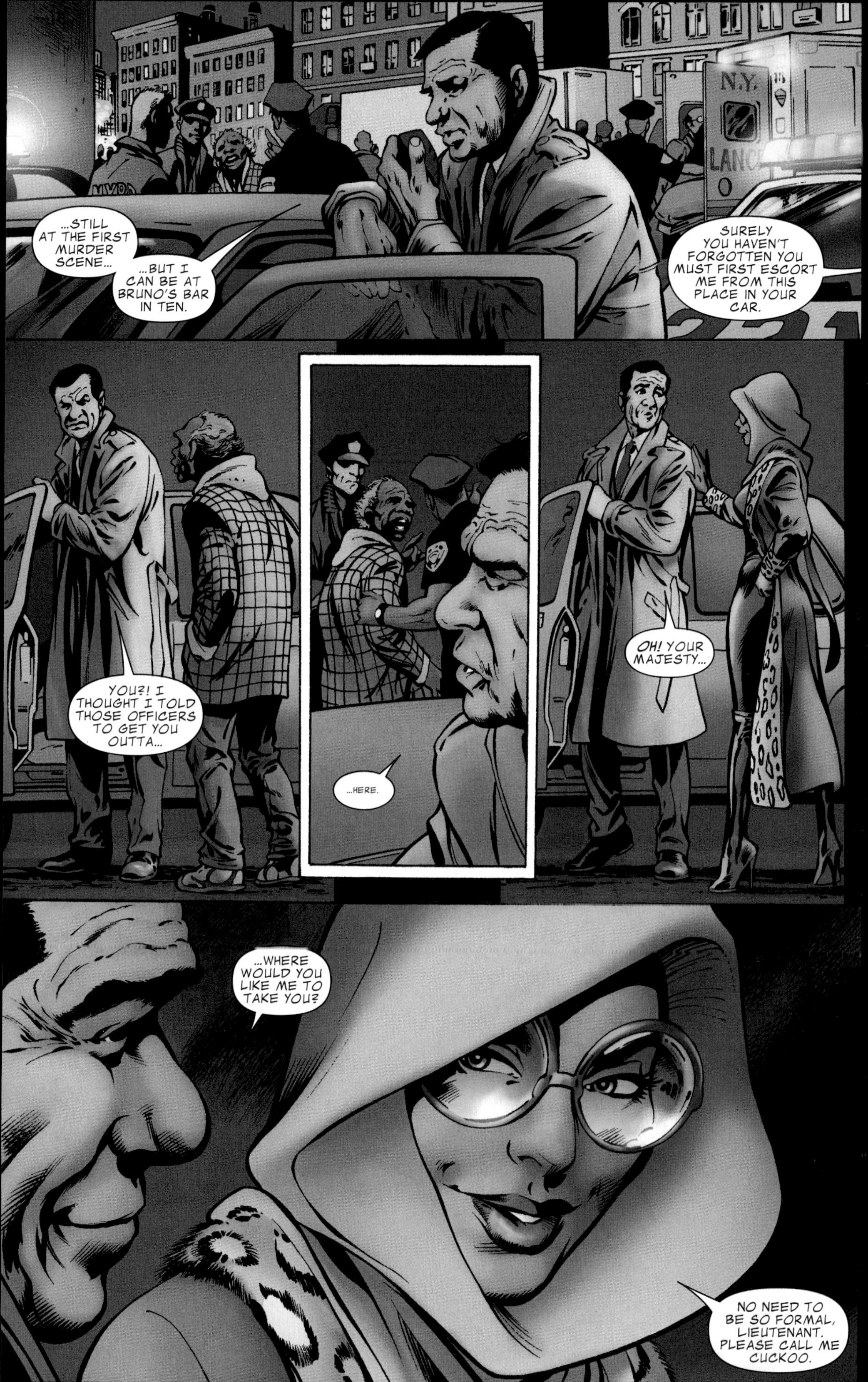
...STILL AT THE FIRST MURDER SCENE...
...BUT I CAN BE AT BRUNO'S BAR IN TEN.
SURELY YOU HAVEN'T FORGOTTEN YOU MUST FIRST ESCORT ME FROM THIS PLACE IN YOUR CAR.
YOU?! I THOUGHT I TOLD THOSE OFFICERS TO GET YOU OUTTA...
...HERE.
OH! YOUR MAJESTY...
...WHERE WOULD YOU LIKE ME TO TAKE YOU?
NO NEED TO BE SO FORMAL, LIEUTENANT. PLEASE CALL ME CUCKOO.

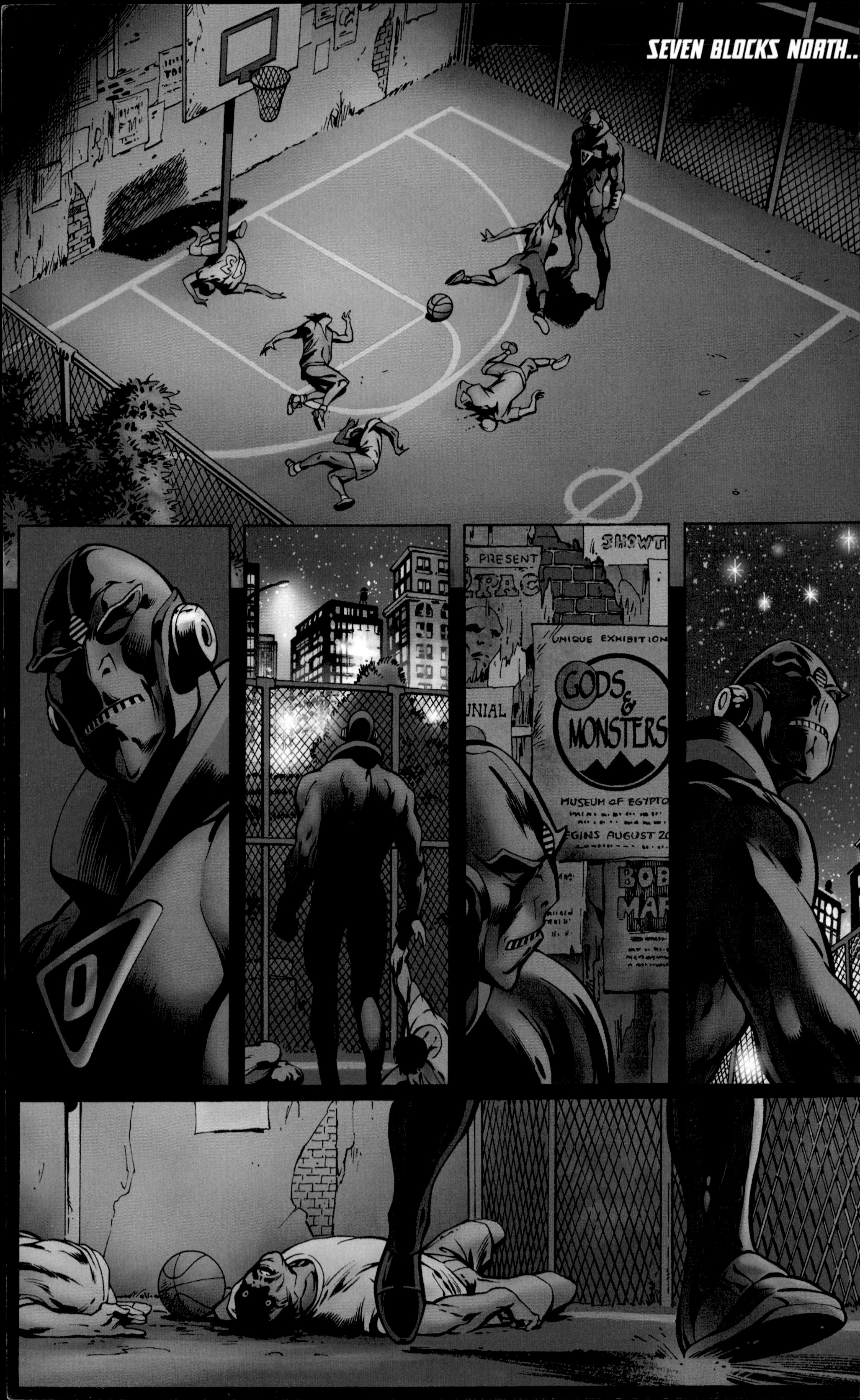
SEVEN BLOCKS NORTH..
UNIQUE EXHIBITION
GODS & MONSTERS
MUSEUM OF EGYPTO
EGINS AUGUST 20

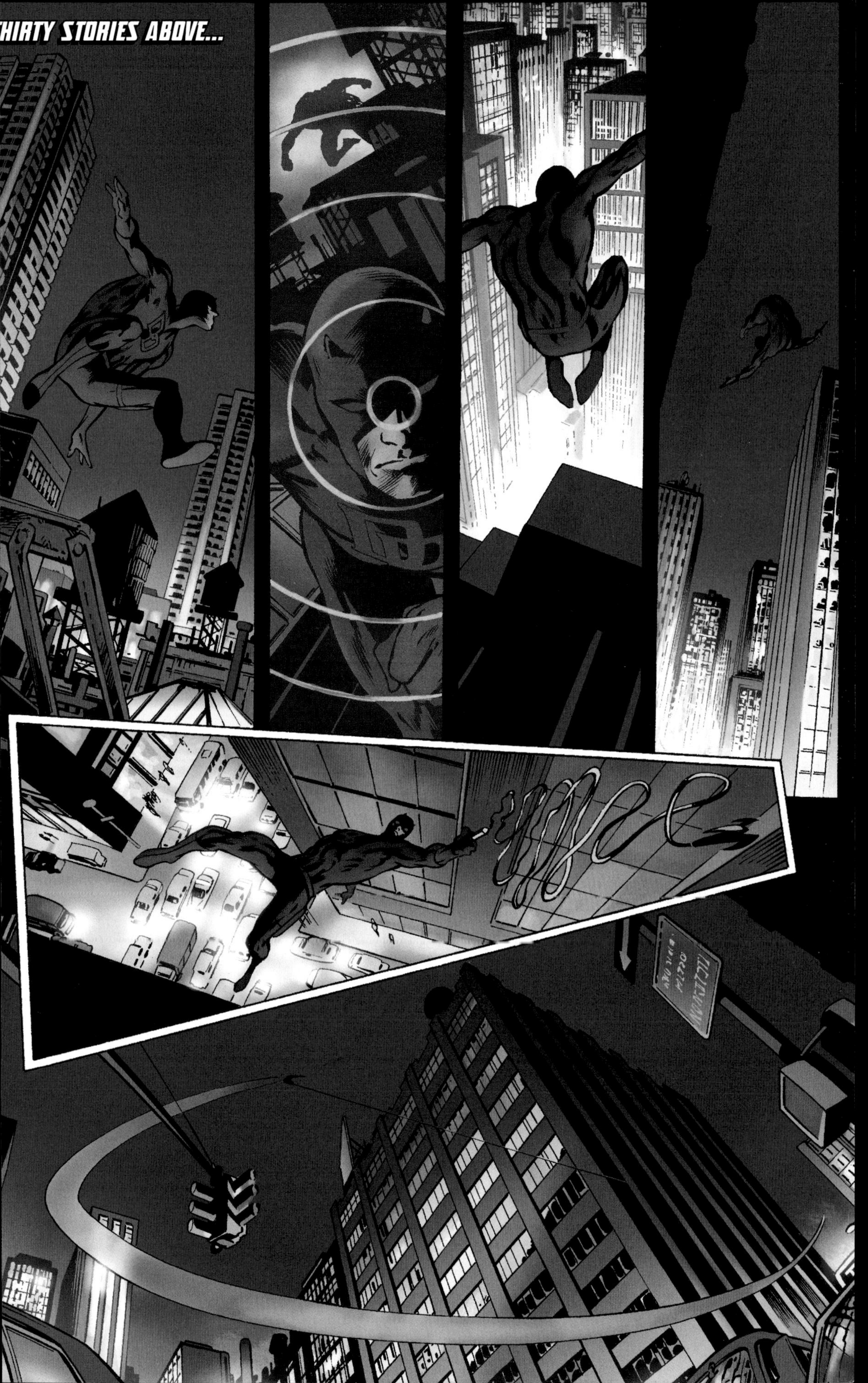
THIRTY STORIES ABOVE...

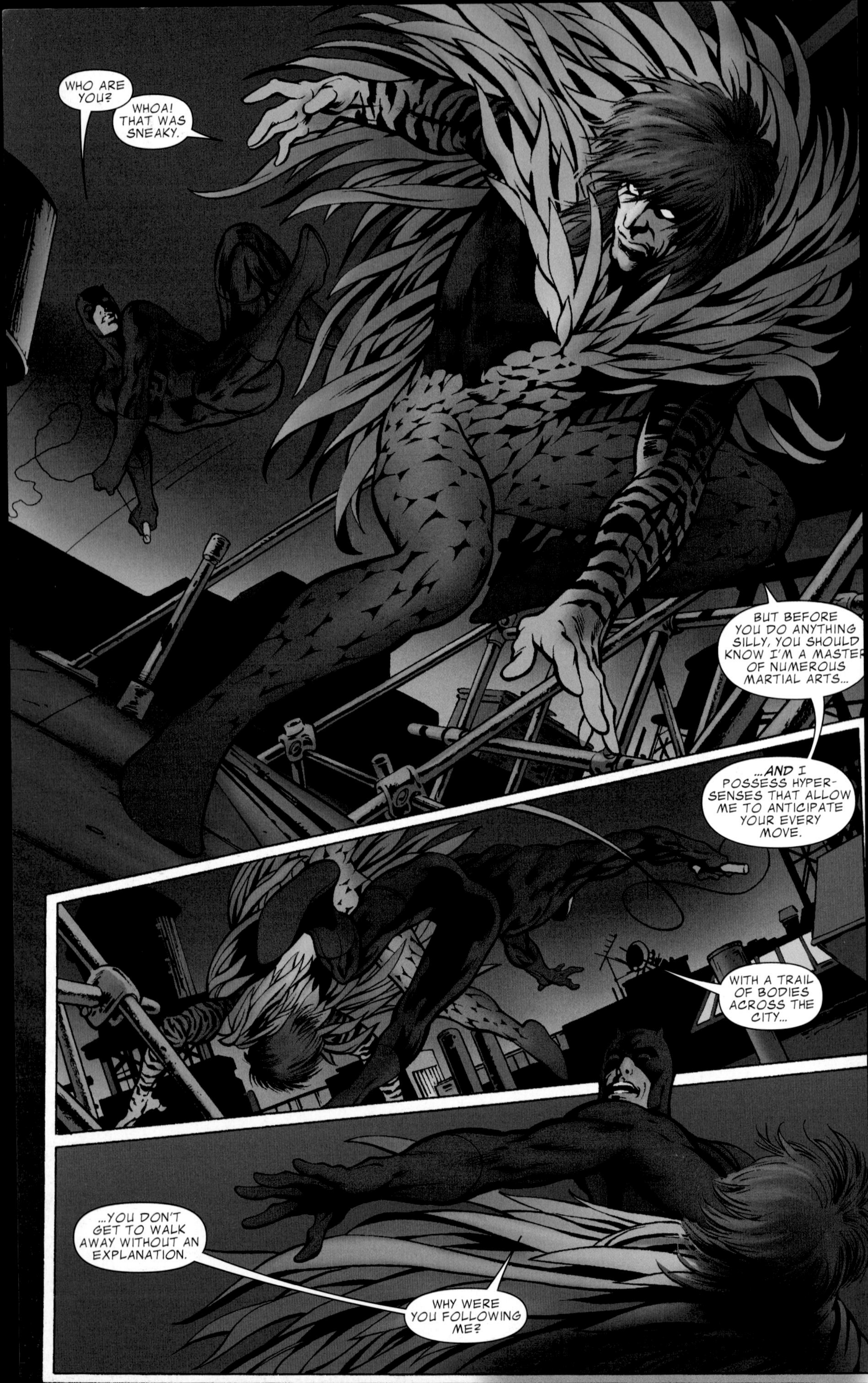
WHO ARE YOU?
WHOA! THAT WAS SNEAKY.
BUT BEFORE YOU DO ANYTHING SILLY, YOU SHOULD KNOW I'M A MASTER OF NUMEROUS MARTIAL ARTS...
...AND I POSSESS HYPER-SENSES THAT ALLOW ME TO ANTICIPATE YOUR EVERY MOVE.
WITH A TRAIL OF BODIES ACROSS THE CITY...
...YOU DON'T GET TO WALK AWAY WITHOUT AN EXPLANATION.
WHY WERE YOU FOLLOWING ME?

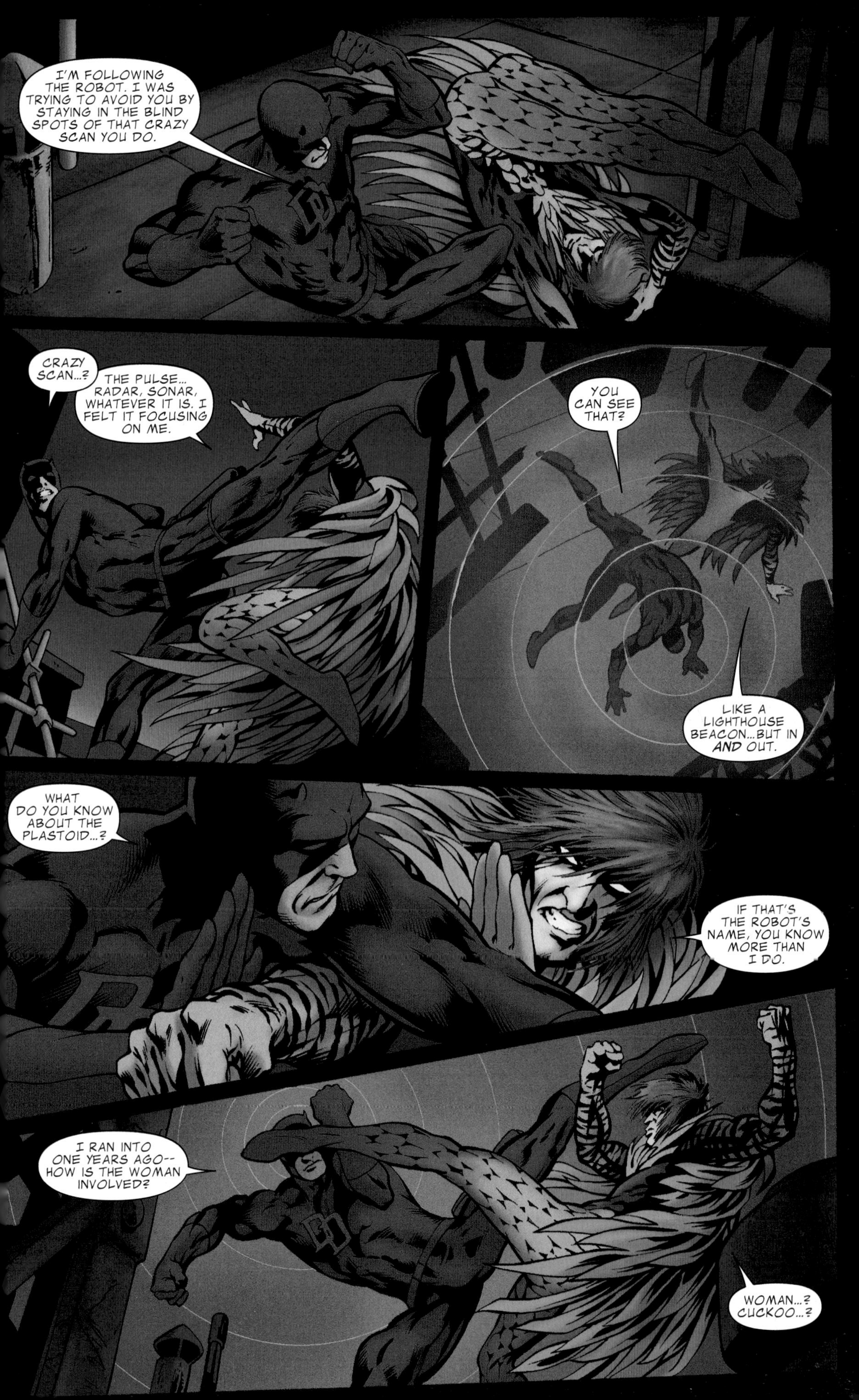
I'M FOLLOWING THE ROBOT. I WAS TRYING TO AVOID YOU BY STAYING IN THE BLIND SPOTS OF THAT CRAZY SCAN YOU DO.
CRAZY SCAN...?
THE PULSE... RADAR, SONAR, WHATEVER IT IS. I FELT IT FOCUSING ON ME.
YOU CAN SEE THAT?
LIKE A LIGHTHOUSE BEACON...BUT IN AND OUT.
WHAT DO YOU KNOW ABOUT THE PLASTOID...?
IF THAT'S THE ROBOT'S NAME, YOU KNOW MORE THAN I DO.
I RAN INTO ONE YEARS AGO-- HOW IS THE WOMAN INVOLVED?
WOMAN...? CUCKOO...?

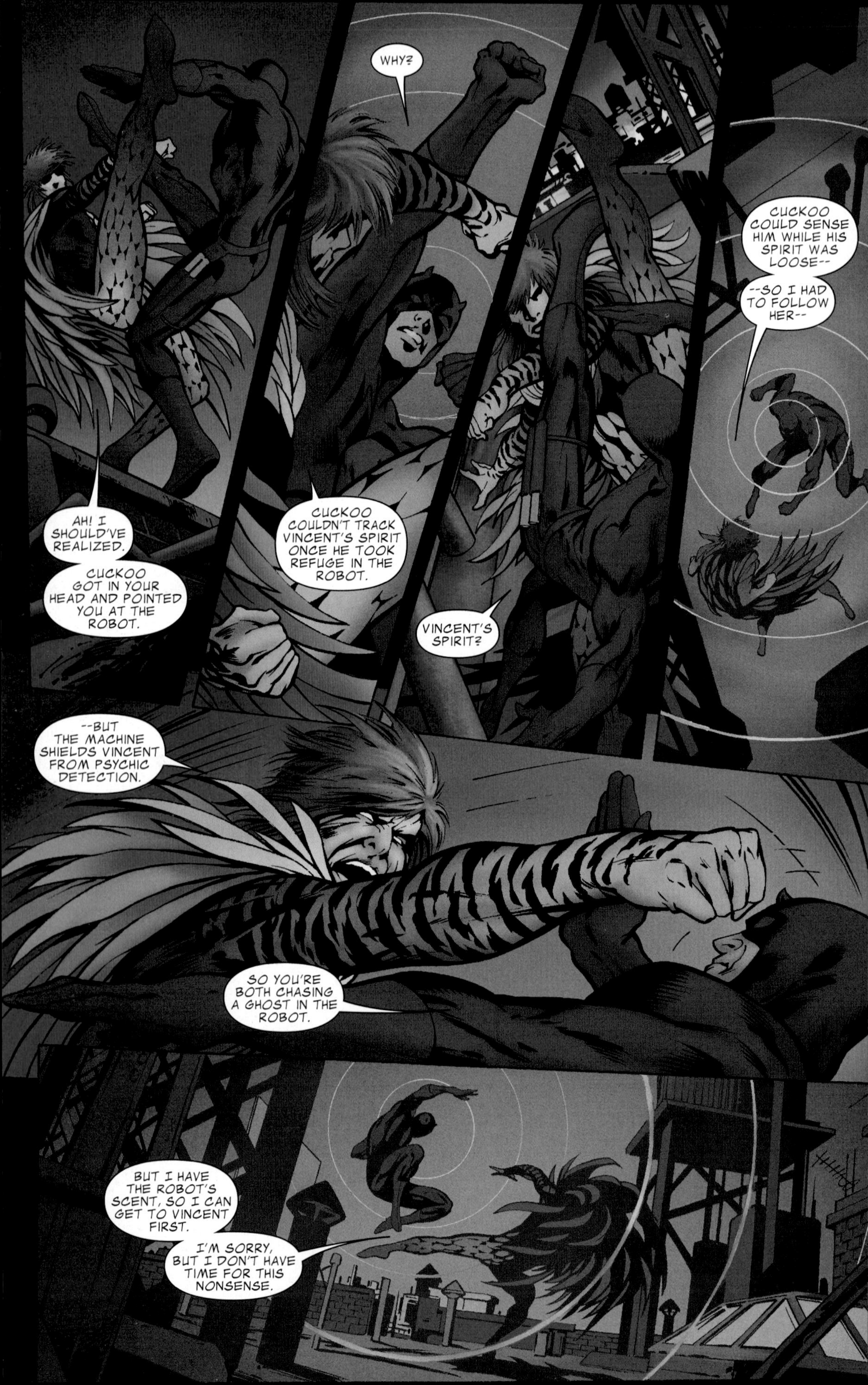
AH! I SHOULD'VE REALIZED.
CUCKOO GOT IN YOUR HEAD AND POINTED YOU AT THE ROBOT.
WHY?
CUCKOO COULDN'T TRACK VINCENT'S SPIRIT ONCE HE TOOK REFUGE IN THE ROBOT.
VINCENT'S SPIRIT?
CUCKOO COULD SENSE HIM WHILE HIS SPIRIT WAS LOOSE--
--SO I HAD TO FOLLOW HER--
--BUT THE MACHINE SHIELDS VINCENT FROM PSYCHIC DETECTION.
SO YOU'RE BOTH CHASING A GHOST IN THE ROBOT.
BUT I HAVE THE ROBOT'S SCENT, SO I CAN GET TO VINCENT FIRST.
I'M SORRY, BUT I DON'T HAVE TIME FOR THIS NONSENSE.

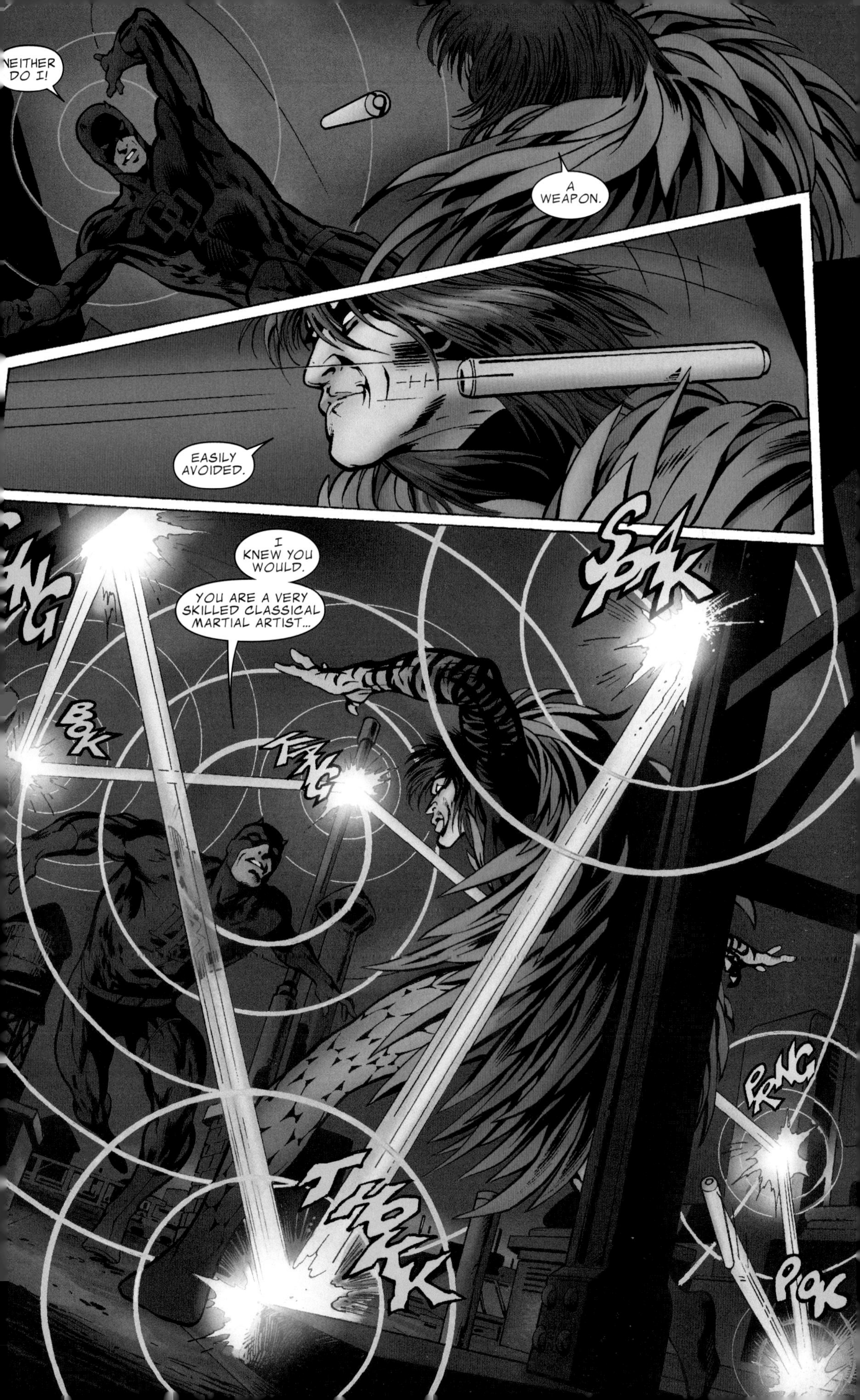
NEITHER DO I!
A WEAPON.
EASILY AVOIDED.
I KNEW YOU WOULD.
YOU ARE A VERY SKILLED CLASSICAL MARTIAL ARTIST...
BOK

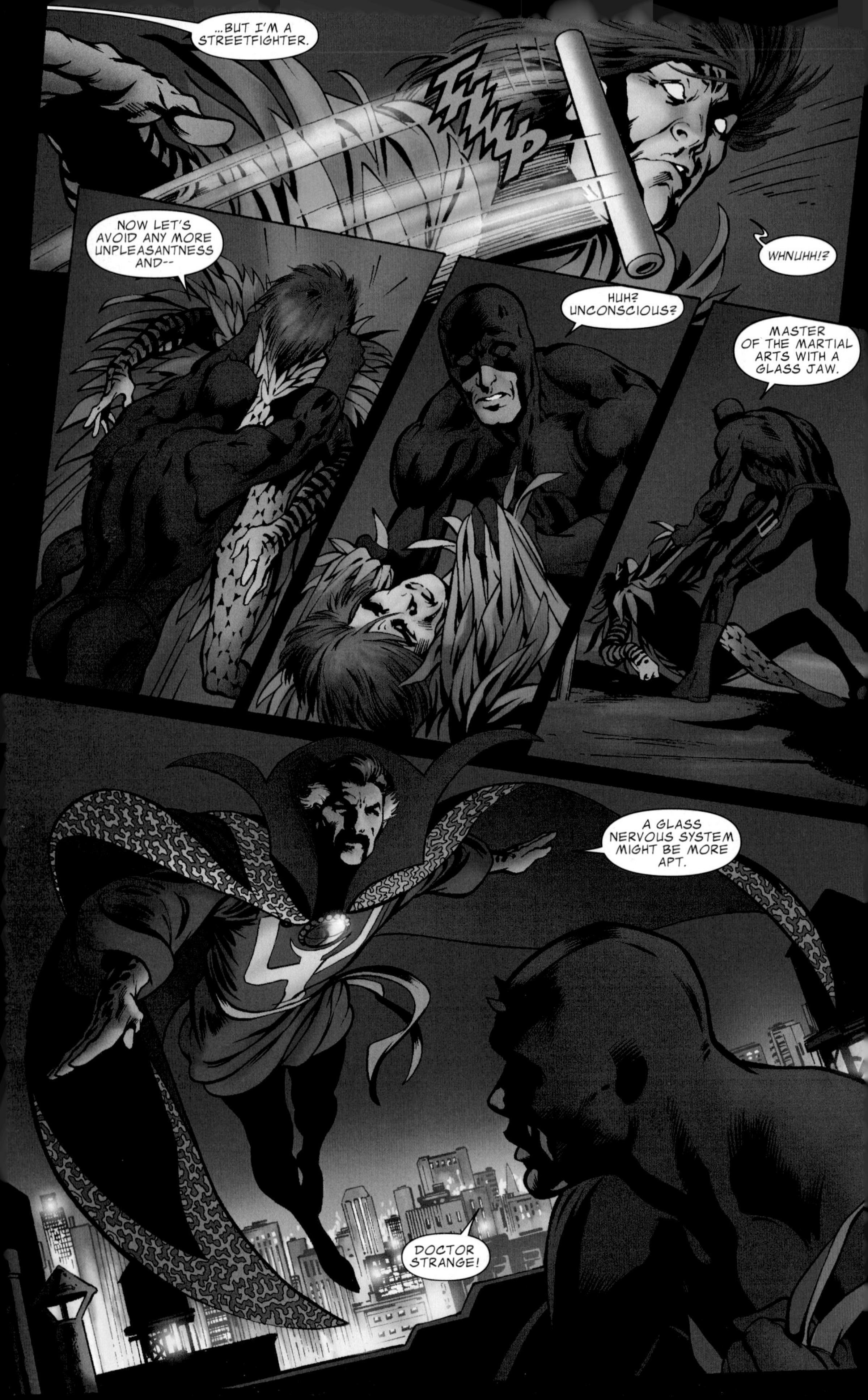
...BUT I'M A STREETFIGHTER.
THWP
WHNUHH!?
NOW LET'S AVOID ANY MORE UNPLEASANTNESS AND--
HUH? UNCONSCIOUS?
MASTER OF THE MARTIAL ARTS WITH A GLASS JAW.
A GLASS NERVOUS SYSTEM MIGHT BE MORE APT.
DOCTOR STRANGE!

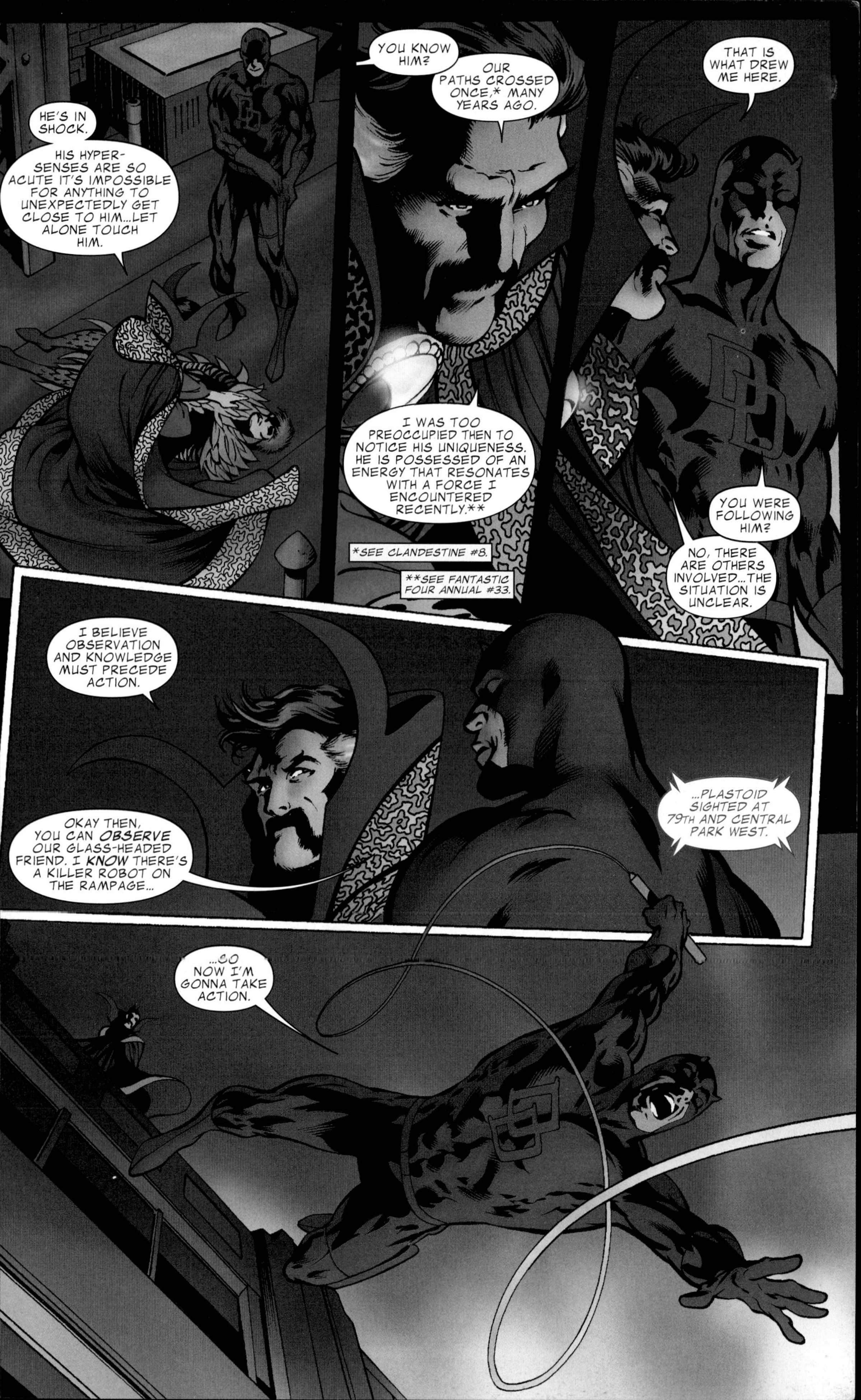
HE'S IN SHOCK.
HIS HYPER-SENSES ARE SO ACUTE IT'S IMPOSSIBLE FOR ANYTHING TO UNEXPECTEDLY GET CLOSE TO HIM...LET ALONE TOUCH HIM.
YOU KNOW HIM?
OUR PATHS CROSSED ONCE,* MANY YEARS AGO.
I WAS TOO PREOCCUPIED THEN TO NOTICE HIS UNIQUENESS. HE IS POSSESSED OF AN ENERGY THAT RESONATES WITH A FORCE I ENCOUNTERED RECENTLY.**
*SEE CLANDESTINE #8.
**SEE FANTASTIC FOUR ANNUAL #33.
THAT IS WHAT DREW ME HERE.
YOU WERE FOLLOWING HIM?
NO, THERE ARE OTHERS INVOLVED...THE SITUATION IS UNCLEAR.
I BELIEVE OBSERVATION AND KNOWLEDGE MUST PRECEDE ACTION.
OKAY THEN, YOU CAN OBSERVE OUR GLASS-HEADED FRIEND. I KNOW THERE'S A KILLER ROBOT ON THE RAMPAGE...
...PLASTOID SIGHTED AT 79TH AND CENTRAL PARK WEST.
...SO NOW I'M GONNA TAKE ACTION.

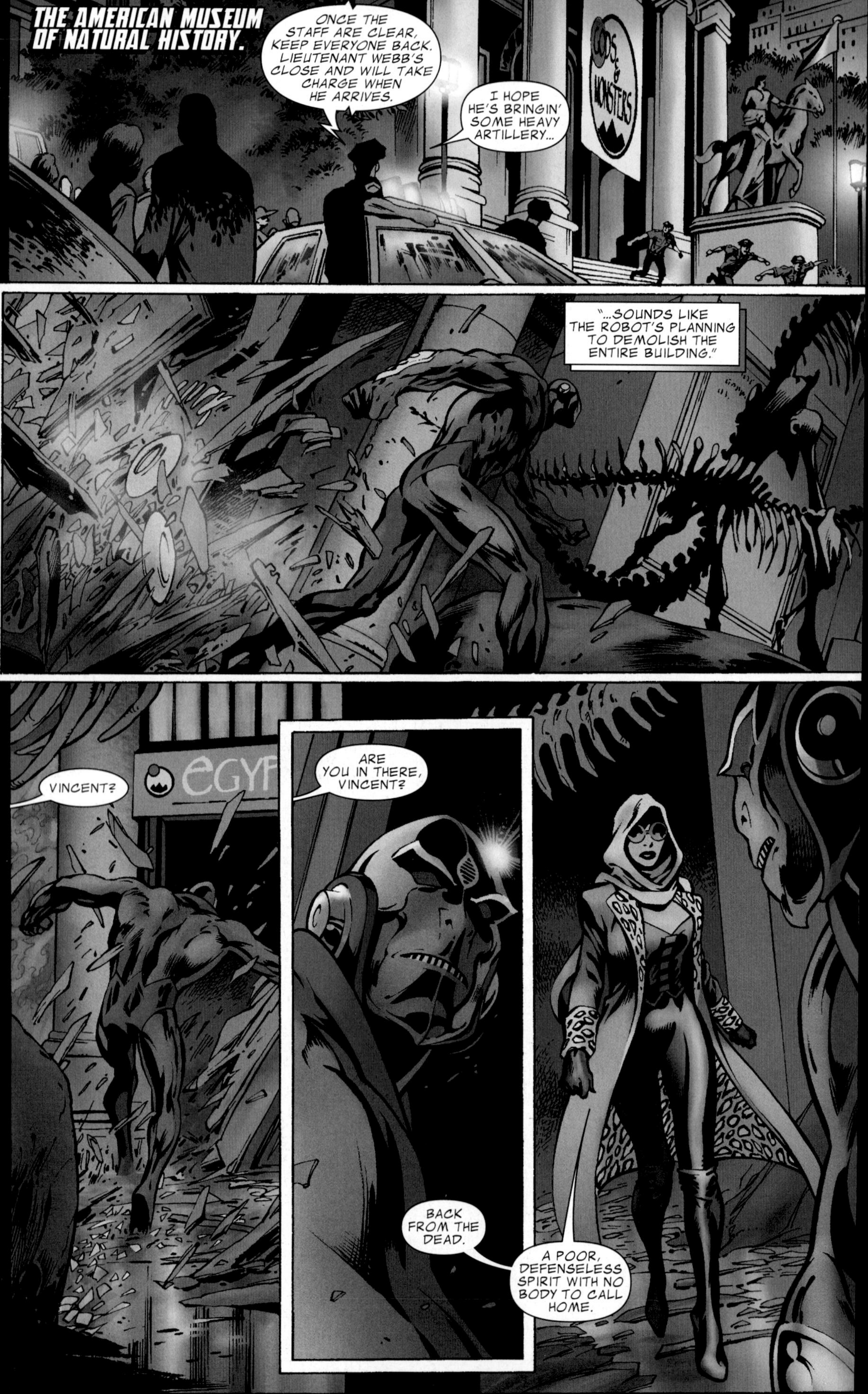
THE AMERICAN MUSEUM OF NATURAL HISTORY.
ONCE THE STAFF ARE CLEAR, KEEP EVERYONE BACK. LIEUTENANT WEBB'S CLOSE AND WILL TAKE CHARGE WHEN HE ARRIVES.
I HOPE HE'S BRINGIN' SOME HEAVY ARTILLERY...
GODS & MONSTERS
"...SOUNDS LIKE THE ROBOT'S PLANNING TO DEMOLISH THE ENTIRE BUILDING."
EGYP
VINCENT?
ARE YOU IN THERE, VINCENT?
BACK FROM THE DEAD.
A POOR, DEFENSELESS SPIRIT WITH NO BODY TO CALL HOME.

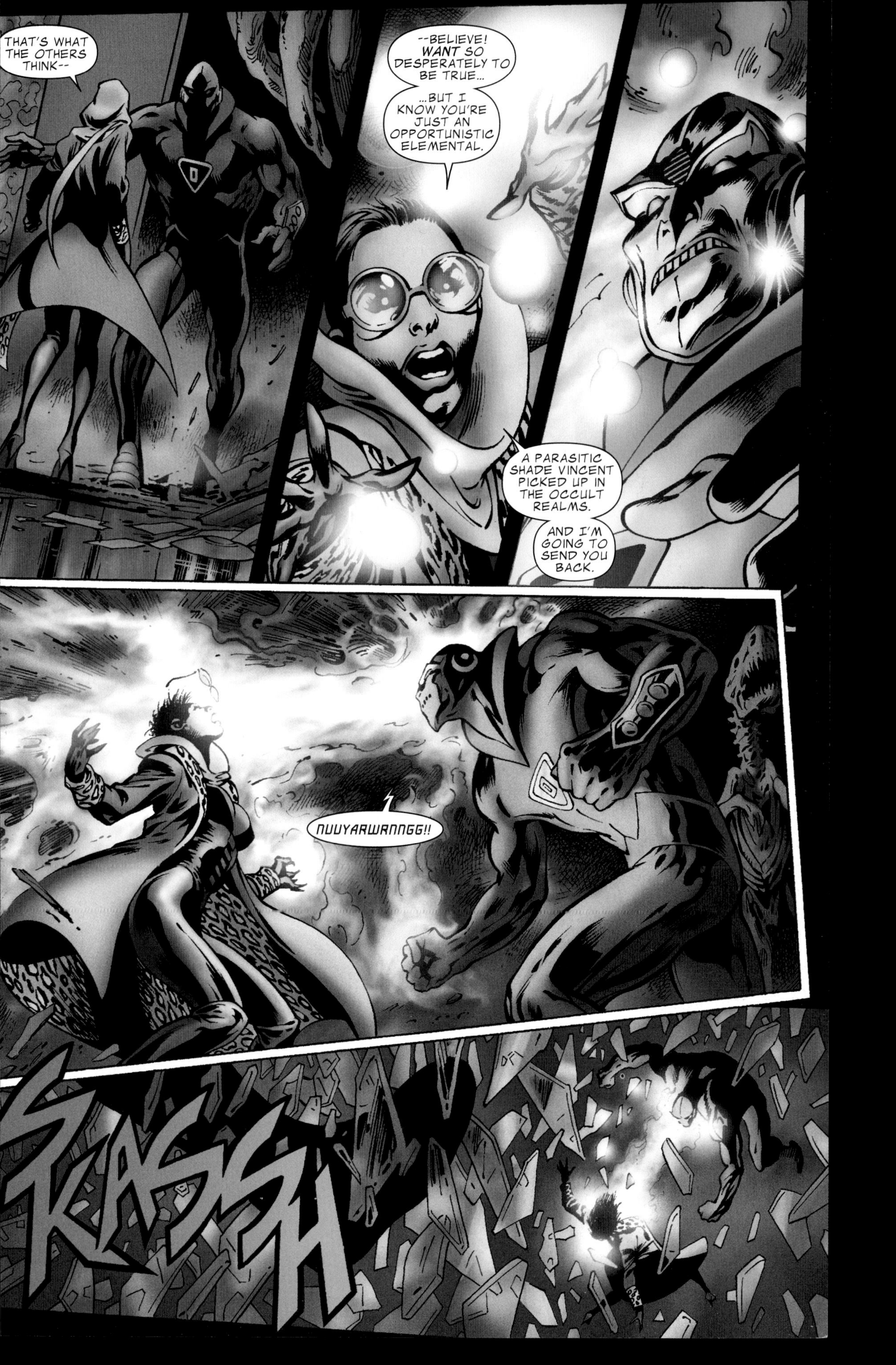
THAT'S WHAT THE OTHERS THINK--
--BELIEVE! WANT SO DESPERATELY TO BE TRUE...
...BUT I KNOW YOU'RE JUST AN OPPORTUNISTIC ELEMENTAL.
A PARASITIC SHADE VINCENT PICKED UP IN THE OCCULT REALMS.
AND I'M GOING TO SEND YOU BACK.
NUUYARWRNNGG!!
KASSH

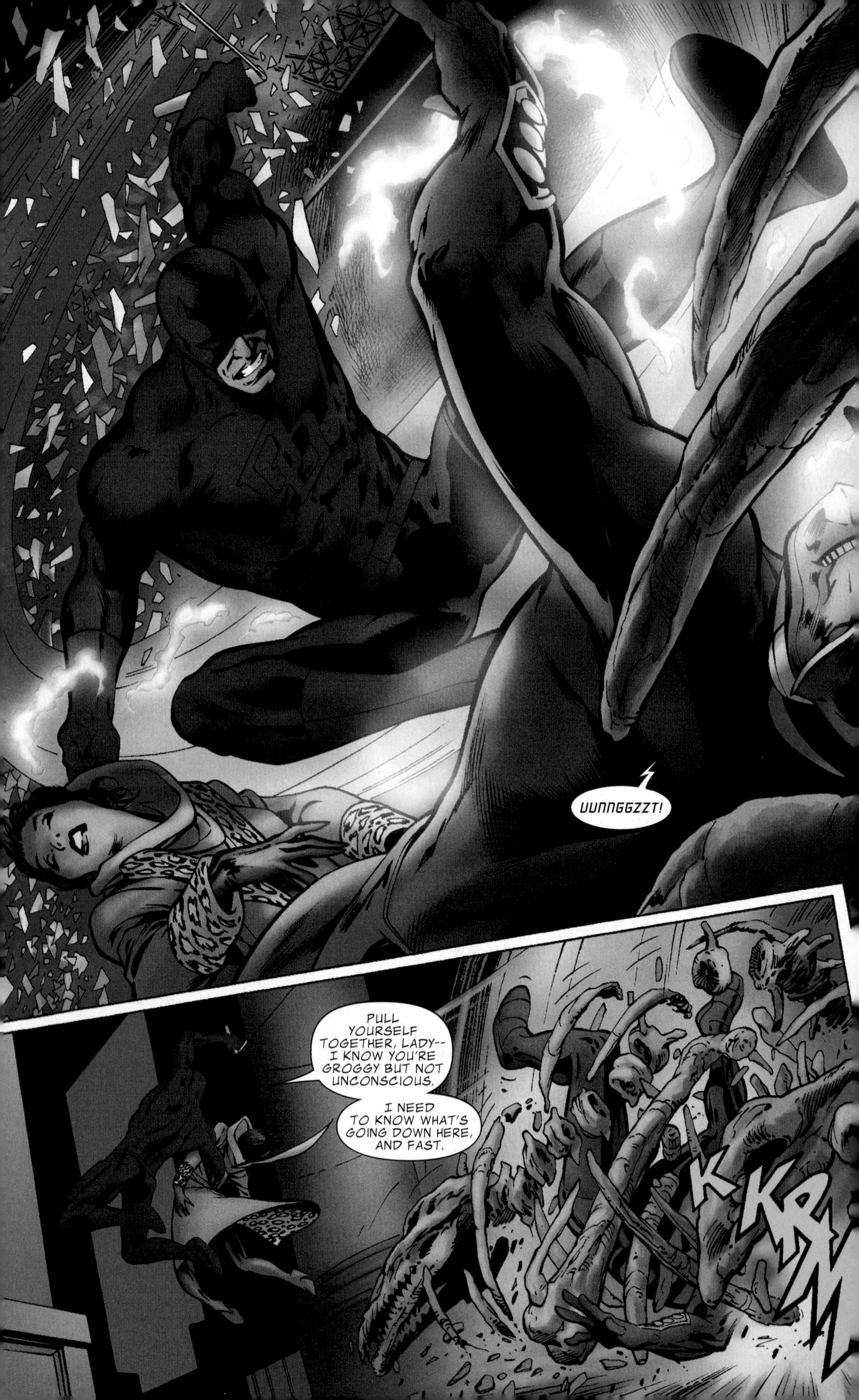
UUNNGGZZT!
PULL YOURSELF TOGETHER, LADY-- I KNOW YOU'RE GROGGY BUT NOT UNCONSCIOUS.
I NEED TO KNOW WHAT'S GOING DOWN HERE, AND FAST.
KKR

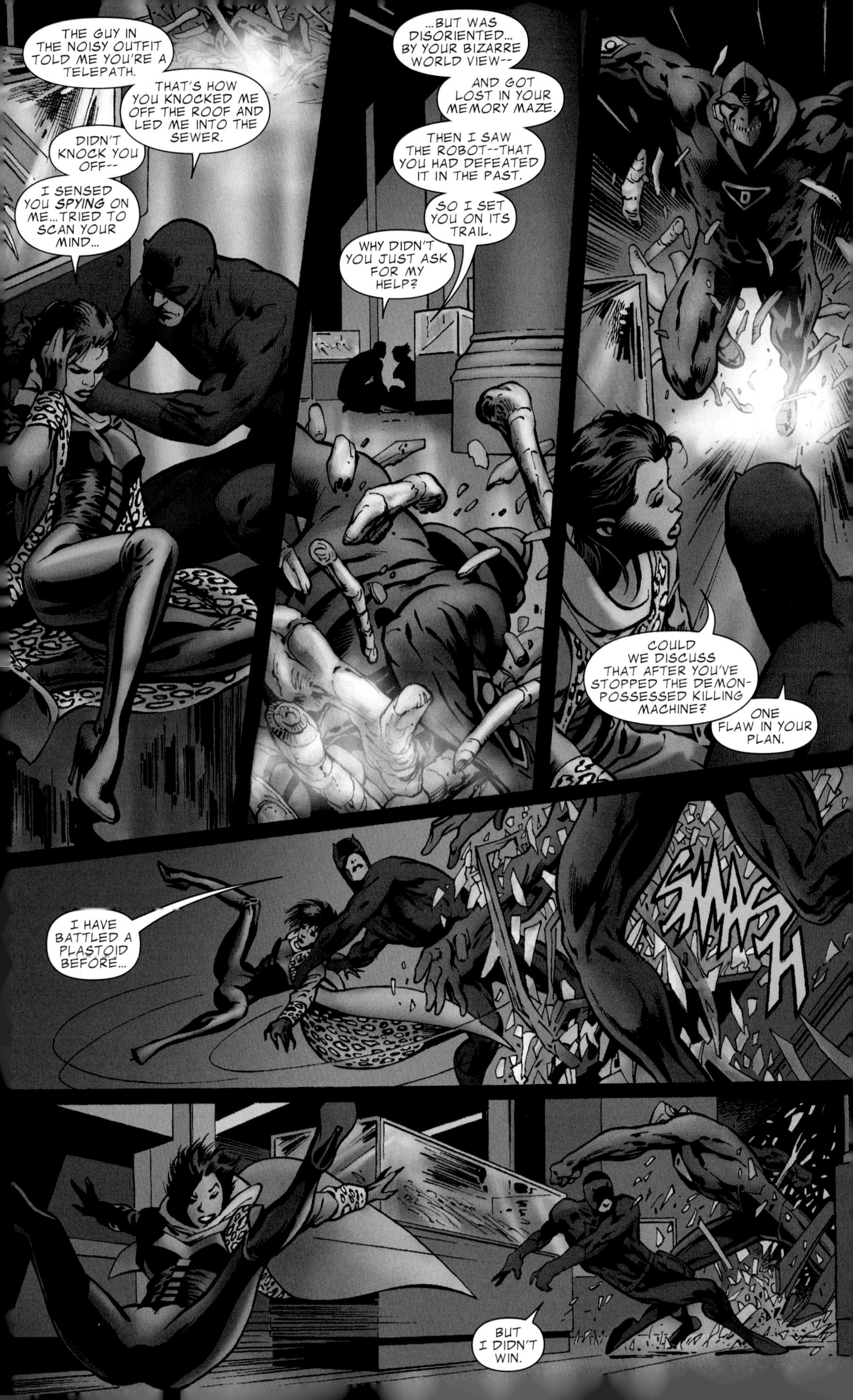
THE GUY IN THE NOISY OUTFIT TOLD ME YOU'RE A TELEPATH.
THAT'S HOW YOU KNOCKED ME OFF THE ROOF AND LED ME INTO THE SEWER.
DIDN'T KNOCK YOU OFF--
I SENSED YOU **SPYING** ON ME...TRIED TO SCAN YOUR MIND...
...BUT WAS DISORIENTED... BY YOUR BIZARRE WORLD VIEW--
AND GOT LOST IN YOUR MEMORY MAZE.
THEN I SAW THE ROBOT--THAT YOU HAD DEFEATED IT IN THE PAST.
SO I SET YOU ON ITS TRAIL.
WHY DIDN'T YOU JUST ASK FOR MY HELP?
COULD WE DISCUSS THAT AFTER YOU'VE STOPPED THE DEMON-POSSESSED KILLING MACHINE?
ONE FLAW IN YOUR PLAN.
SMASH
I HAVE BATTLED A PLASTOID BEFORE...
BUT I DIDN'T WIN.

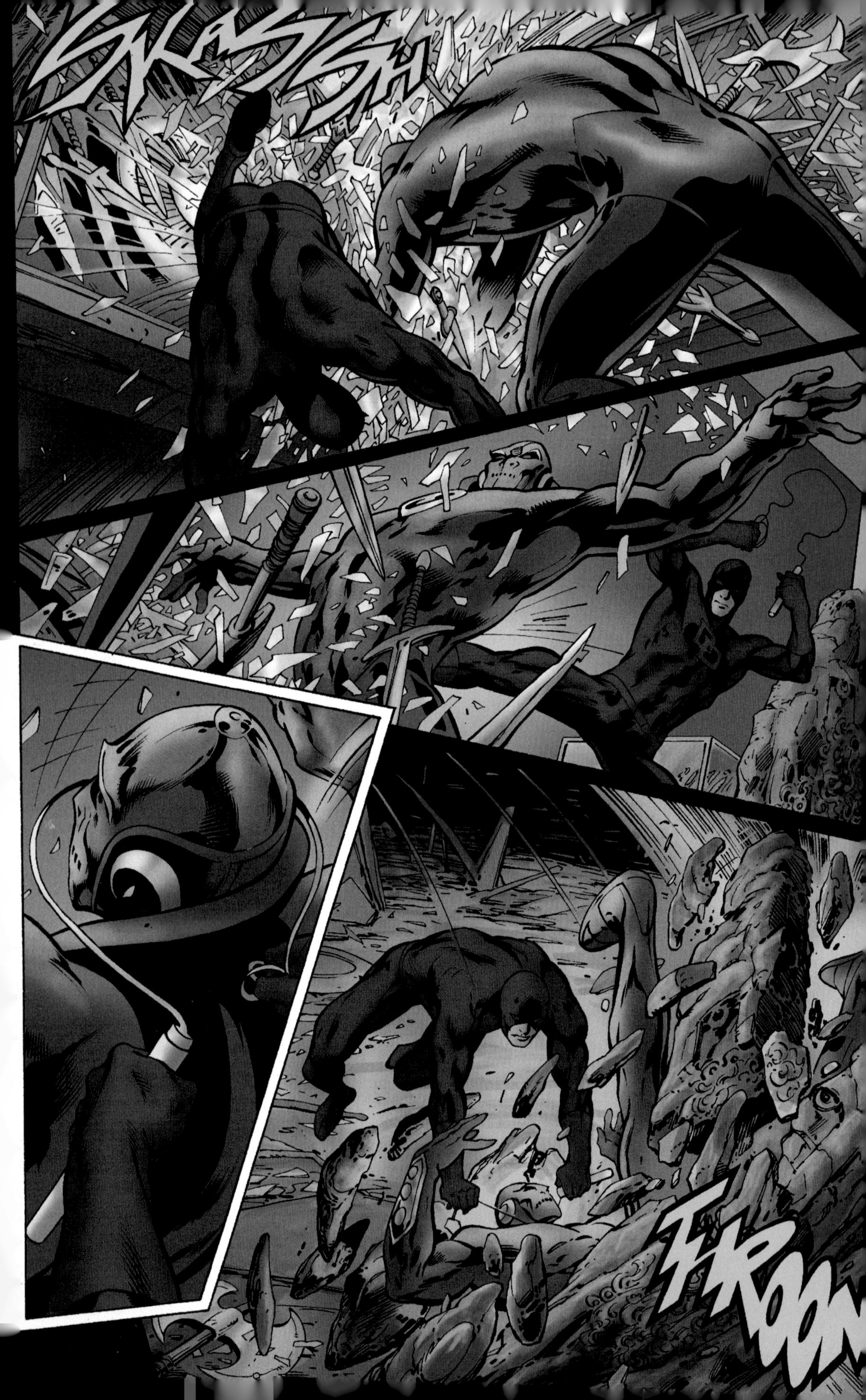
SKASSH
FROOM

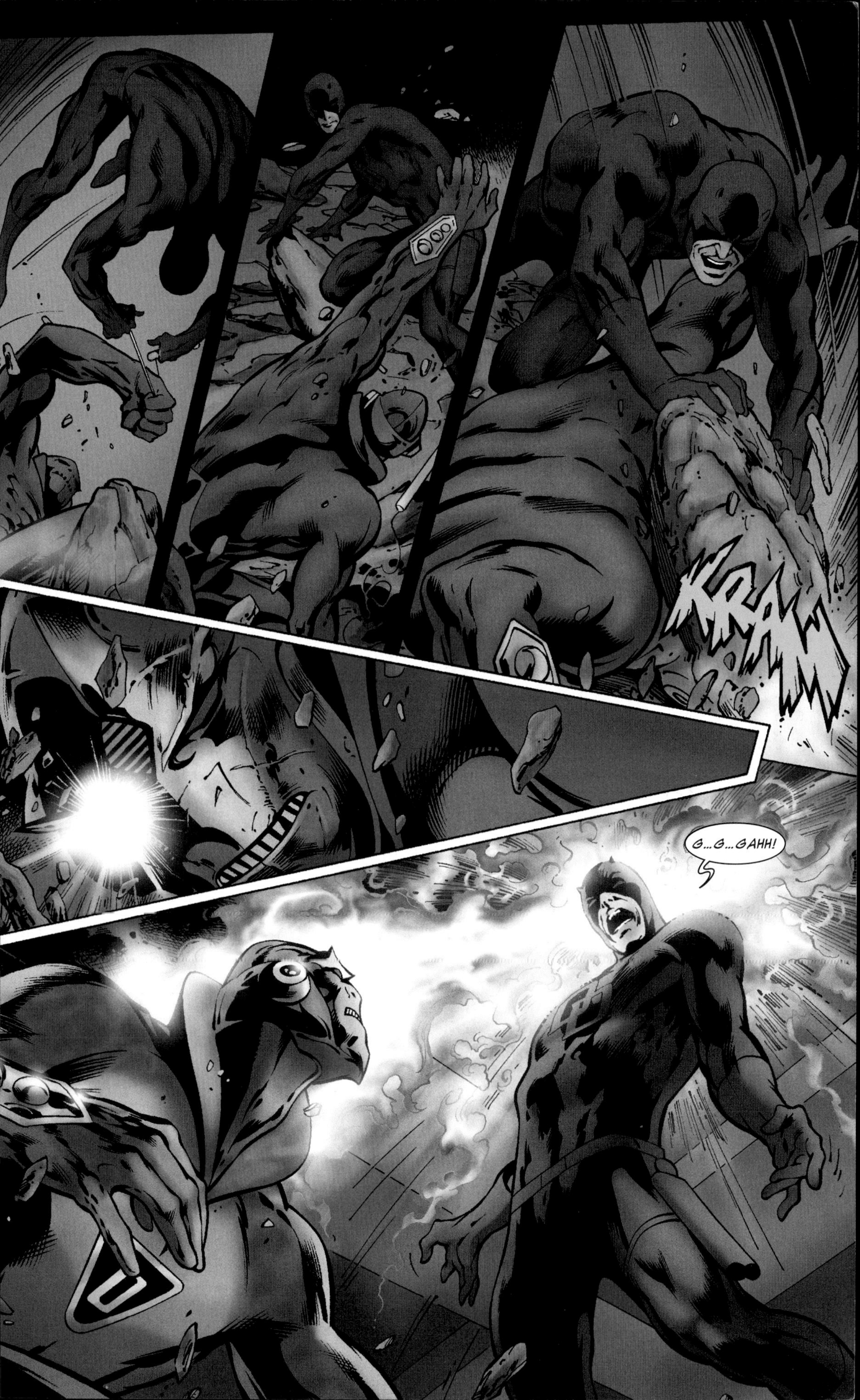
KRAW
G...G...GAHH!

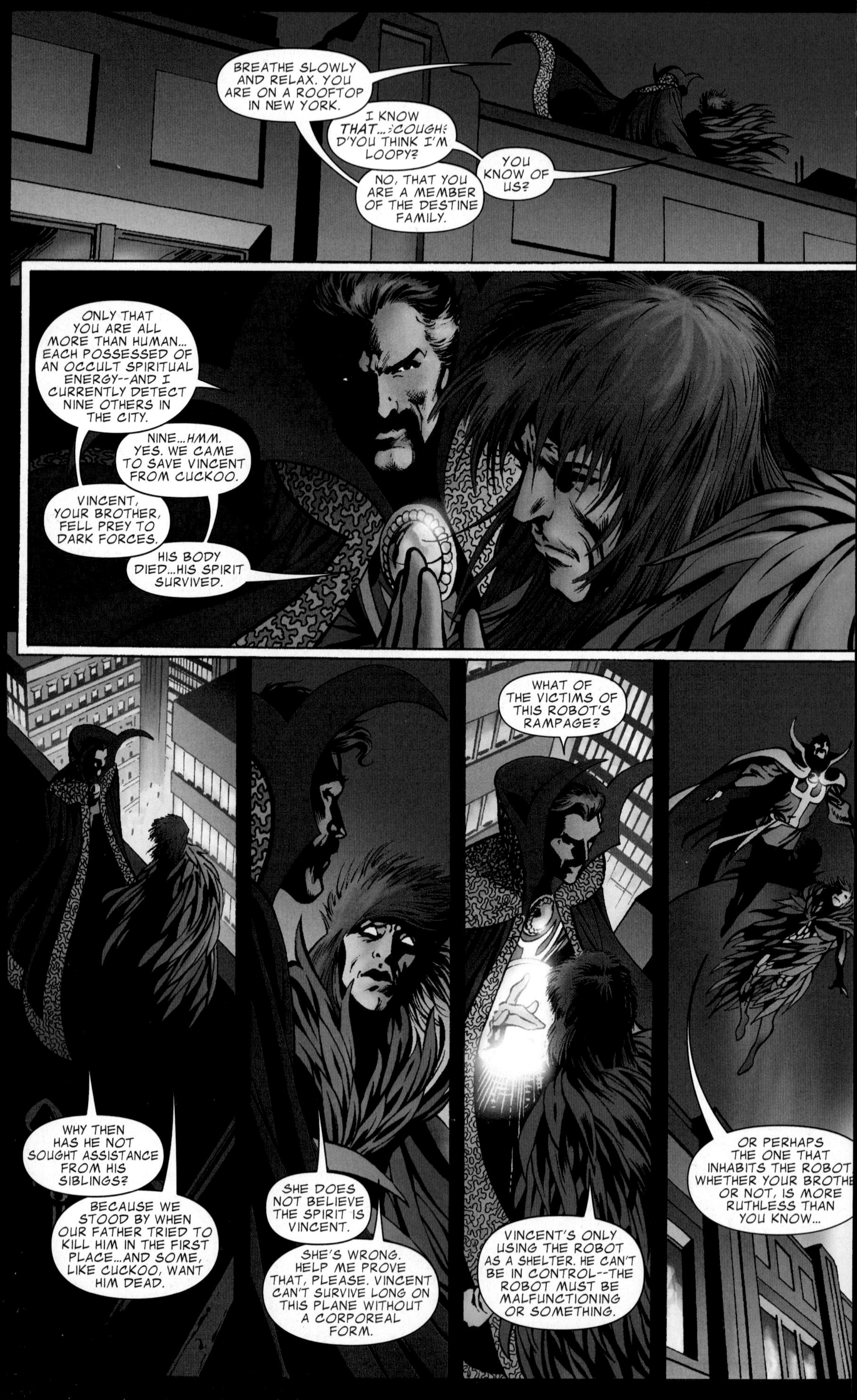
BREATHE SLOWLY AND RELAX. YOU ARE ON A ROOFTOP IN NEW YORK.
I KNOW THAT... *COUGH* D'YOU THINK I'M LOOPY?
NO, THAT YOU ARE A MEMBER OF THE DESTINE FAMILY.
YOU KNOW OF US?
ONLY THAT YOU ARE ALL MORE THAN HUMAN... EACH POSSESSED OF AN OCCULT SPIRITUAL ENERGY--AND I CURRENTLY DETECT NINE OTHERS IN THE CITY.
NINE... HMM. YES. WE CAME TO SAVE VINCENT FROM CUCKOO.
VINCENT, YOUR BROTHER, FELL PREY TO DARK FORCES.
HIS BODY DIED... HIS SPIRIT SURVIVED.
WHY THEN HAS HE NOT SOUGHT ASSISTANCE FROM HIS SIBLINGS?
BECAUSE WE STOOD BY WHEN OUR FATHER TRIED TO KILL HIM IN THE FIRST PLACE... AND SOME, LIKE CUCKOO, WANT HIM DEAD.
SHE DOES NOT BELIEVE THE SPIRIT IS VINCENT.
SHE'S WRONG. HELP ME PROVE THAT, PLEASE. VINCENT CAN'T SURVIVE LONG ON THIS PLANE WITHOUT A CORPOREAL FORM.
WHAT OF THE VICTIMS OF THIS ROBOT'S RAMPAGE?
VINCENT'S ONLY USING THE ROBOT AS A SHELTER. HE CAN'T BE IN CONTROL--THE ROBOT MUST BE MALFUNCTIONING OR SOMETHING.
OR PERHAPS THE ONE THAT INHABITS THE ROBOT, WHETHER YOUR BROTHER OR NOT, IS MORE RUTHLESS THAN YOU KNOW...

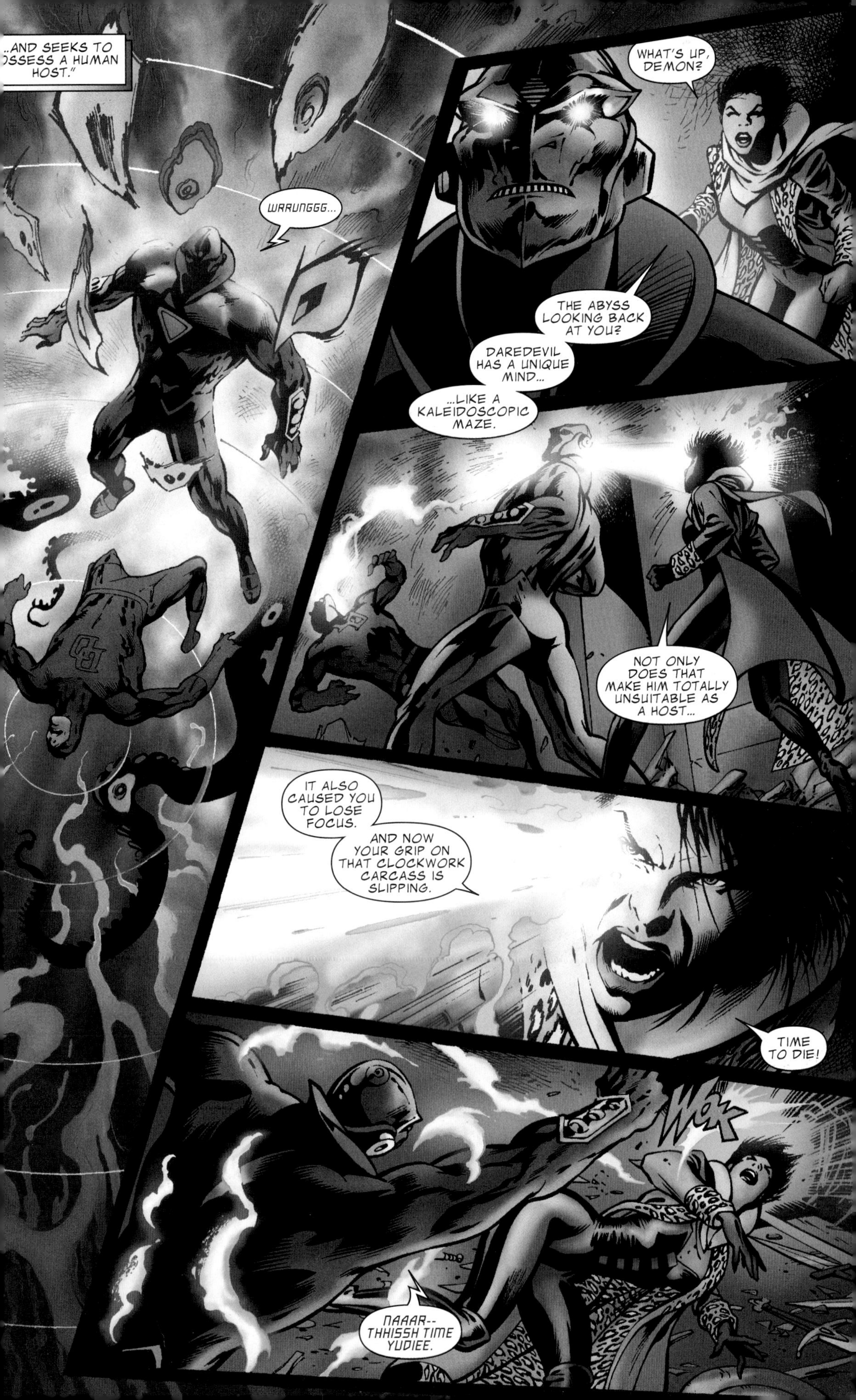
..AND SEEKS TO
OSSESS A HUMAN
HOST."
WRRUNGGG...
WHAT'S UP, DEMON?
THE ABYSS LOOKING BACK AT YOU?
DAREDEVIL HAS A UNIQUE MIND...
...LIKE A KALEIDOSCOPIC MAZE.
NOT ONLY DOES THAT MAKE HIM TOTALLY UNSUITABLE AS A HOST...
IT ALSO CAUSED YOU TO LOSE FOCUS.
AND NOW YOUR GRIP ON THAT CLOCKWORK CARCASS IS SLIPPING.
TIME TO DIE!
WOK
NAAAR-- THHISSH TIME YUDIEE.

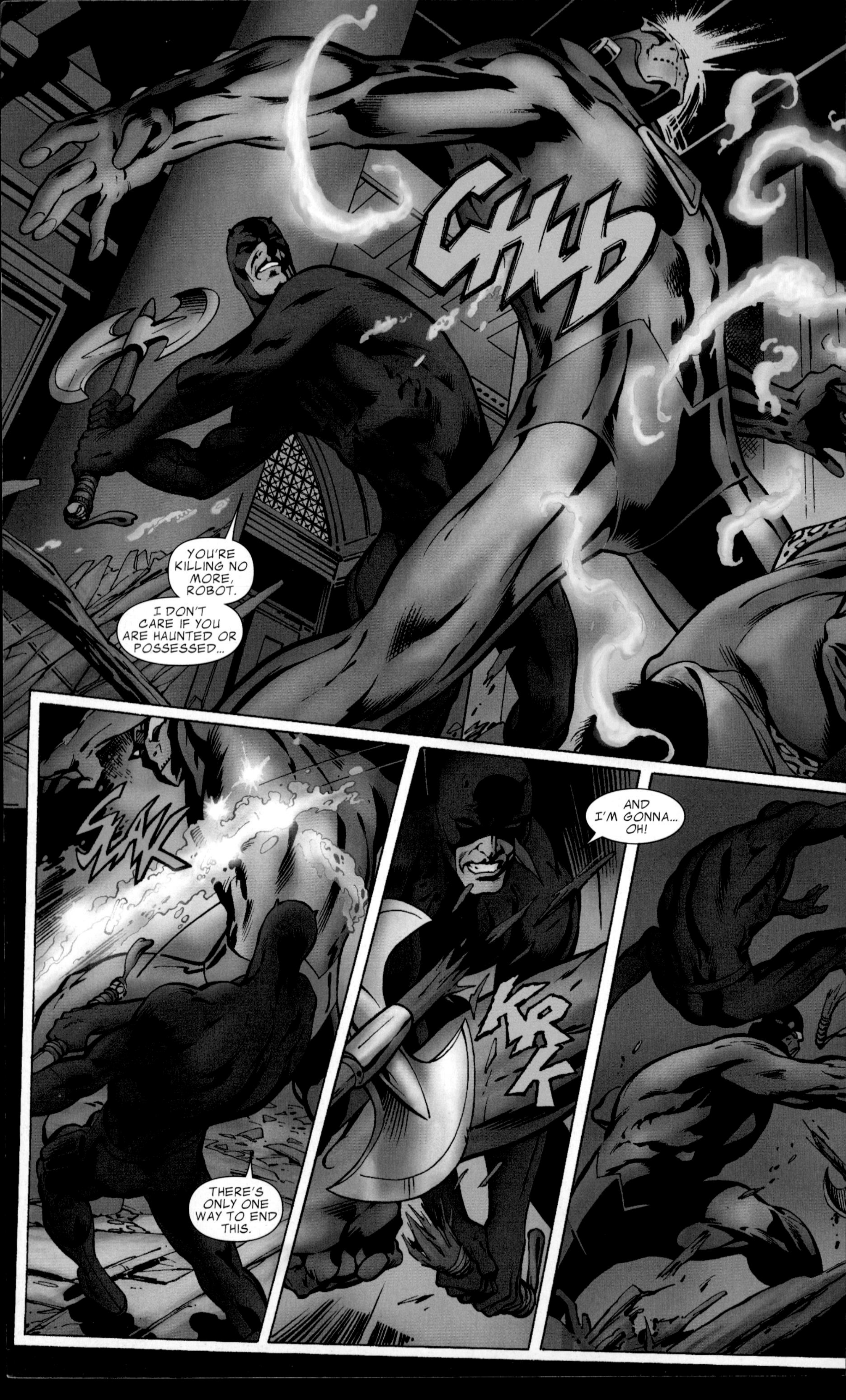
CHUD
YOU'RE KILLING NO MORE, ROBOT.
I DON'T CARE IF YOU ARE HAUNTED OR POSSESSED...
SLAK
THERE'S ONLY ONE WAY TO END THIS.
AND I'M GONNA... OH!
KRAK

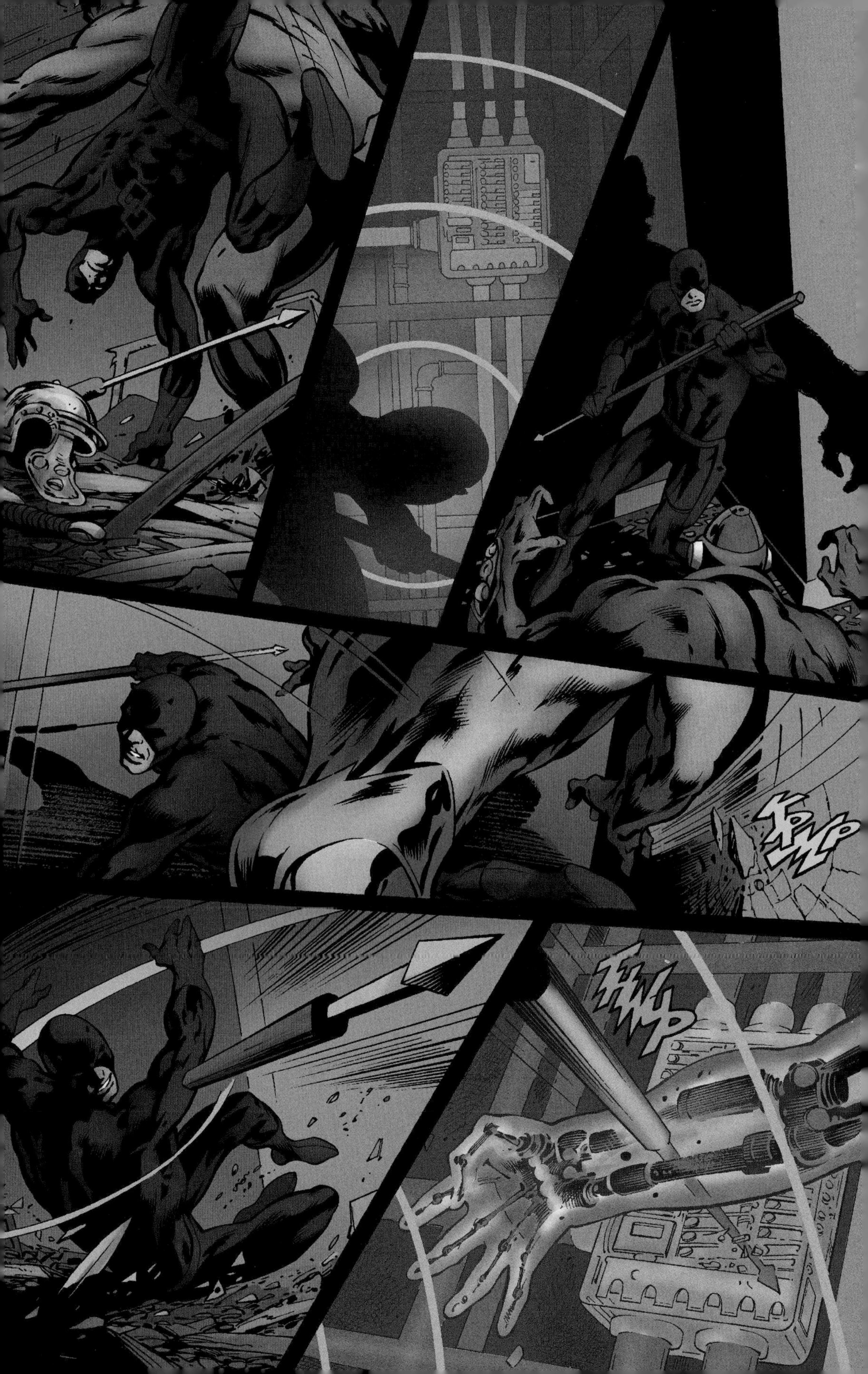
THWP

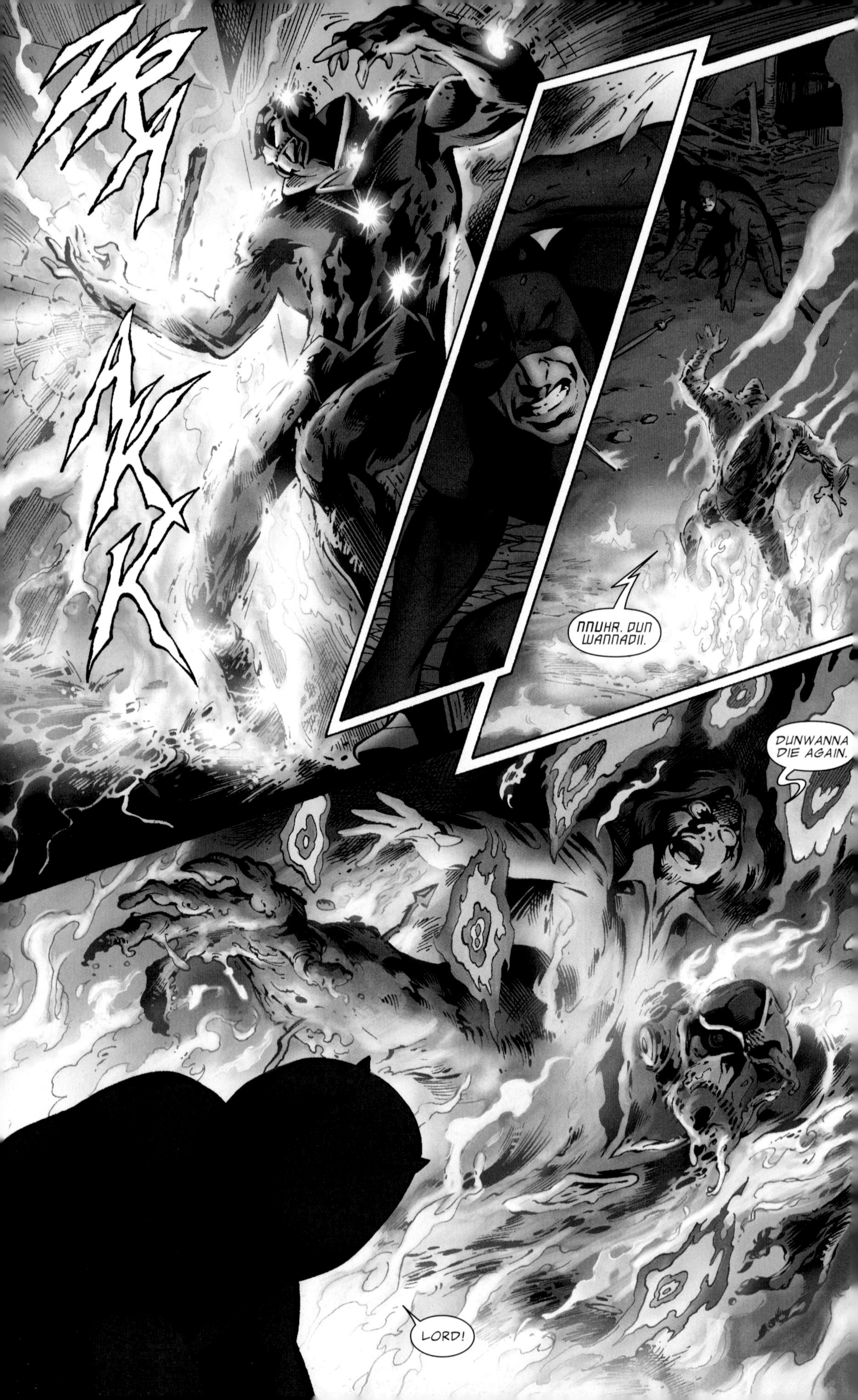
ZRAAKK
NNUHR. DUN WANNADII.
DUNWANNA DIE AGAIN.
LORD!

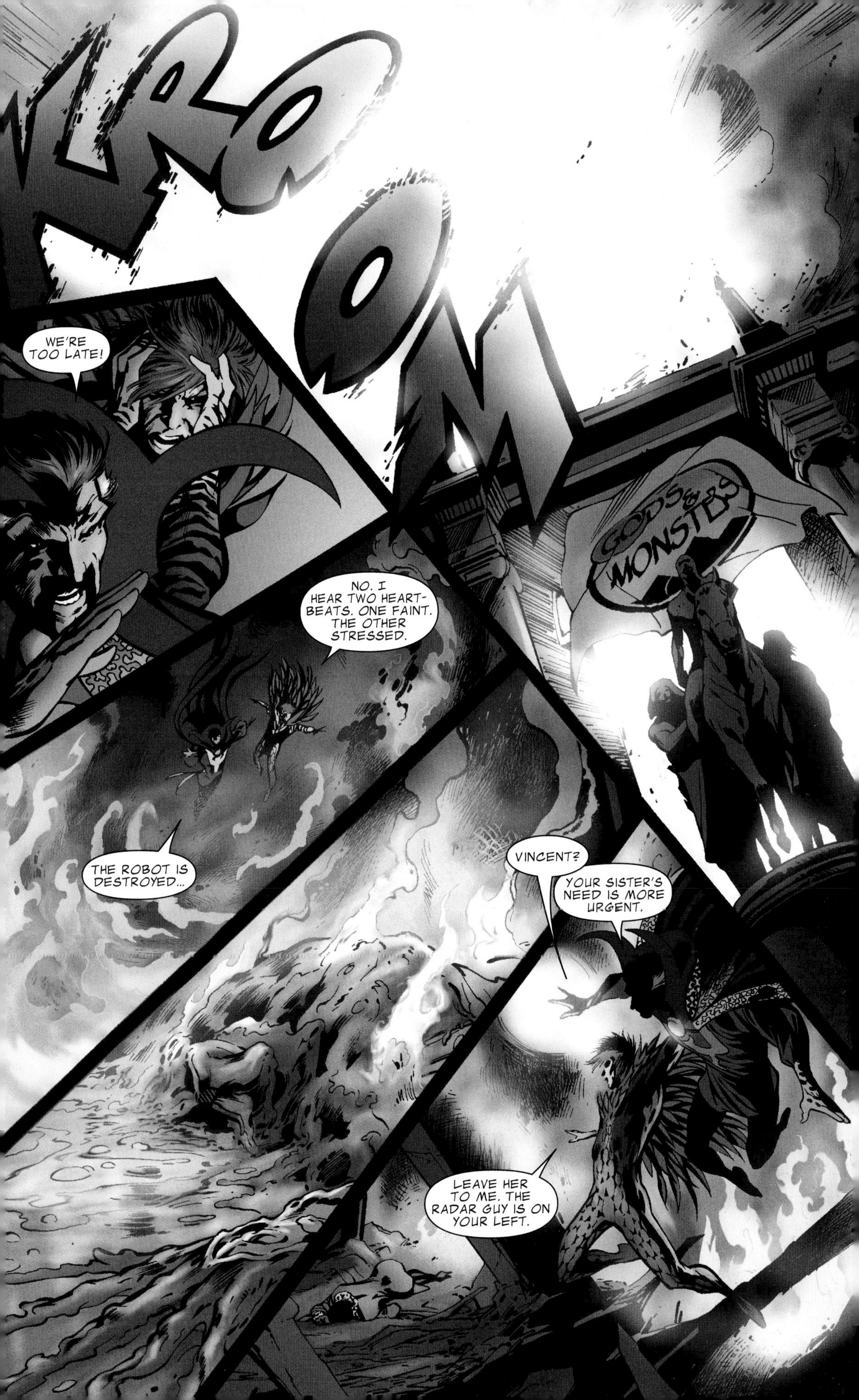

VRROOM
WE'RE TOO LATE!
NO. I HEAR TWO HEART-BEATS. ONE FAINT. THE OTHER STRESSED.
GODS & MONSTERS
THE ROBOT IS DESTROYED...
VINCENT?
YOUR SISTER'S NEED IS MORE URGENT.
LEAVE HER TO ME. THE RADAR GUY IS ON YOUR LEFT.

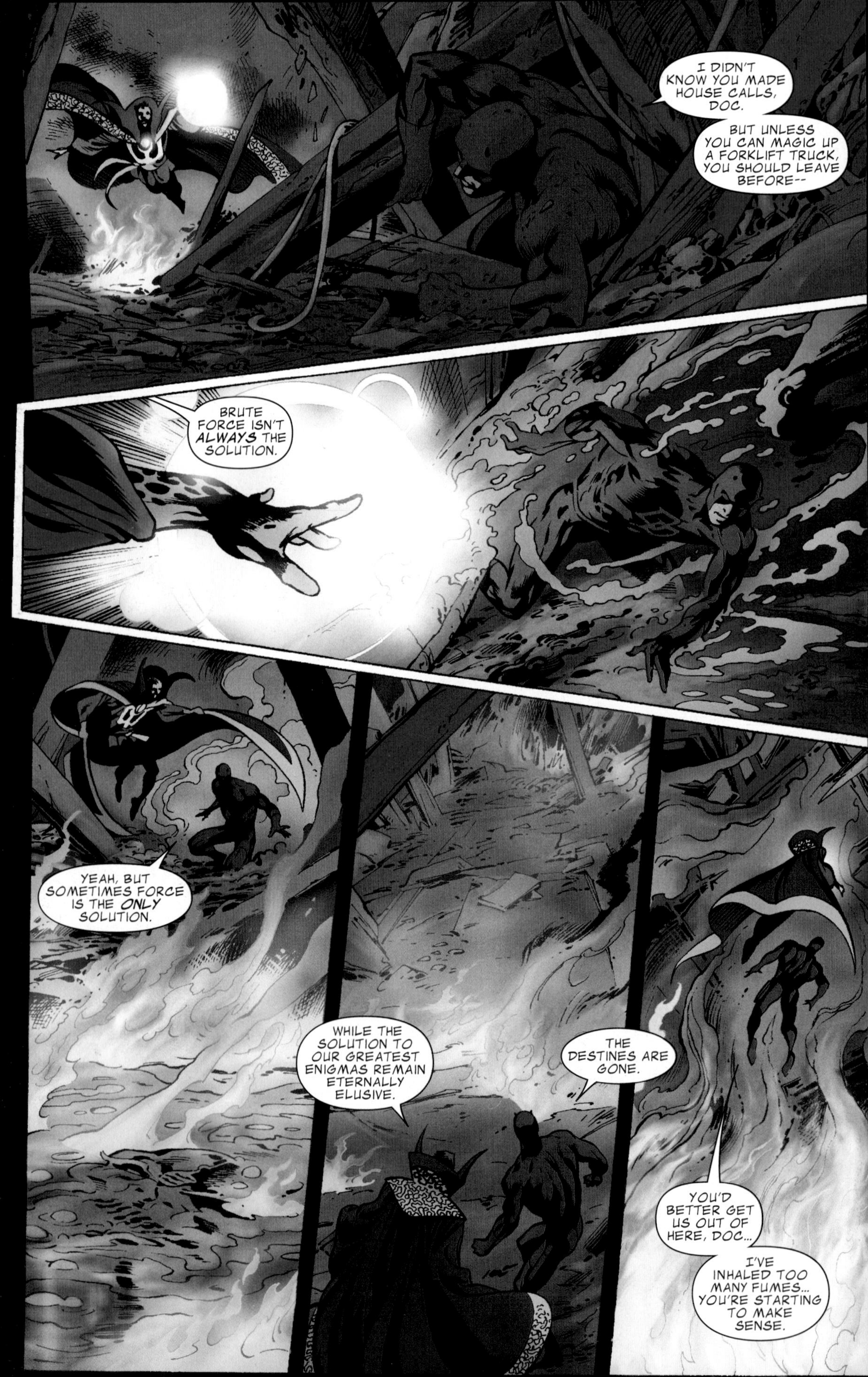
I DIDN'T KNOW YOU MADE HOUSE CALLS, DOC.
BUT UNLESS YOU CAN MAGIC UP A FORKLIFT TRUCK, YOU SHOULD LEAVE BEFORE--
BRUTE FORCE ISN'T ALWAYS THE SOLUTION.
YEAH, BUT SOMETIMES FORCE IS THE ONLY SOLUTION.
WHILE THE SOLUTION TO OUR GREATEST ENIGMAS REMAIN ETERNALLY ELUSIVE.
THE DESTINES ARE GONE.
YOU'D BETTER GET US OUT OF HERE, DOC...
I'VE INHALED TOO MANY FUMES... YOU'RE STARTING TO MAKE SENSE.

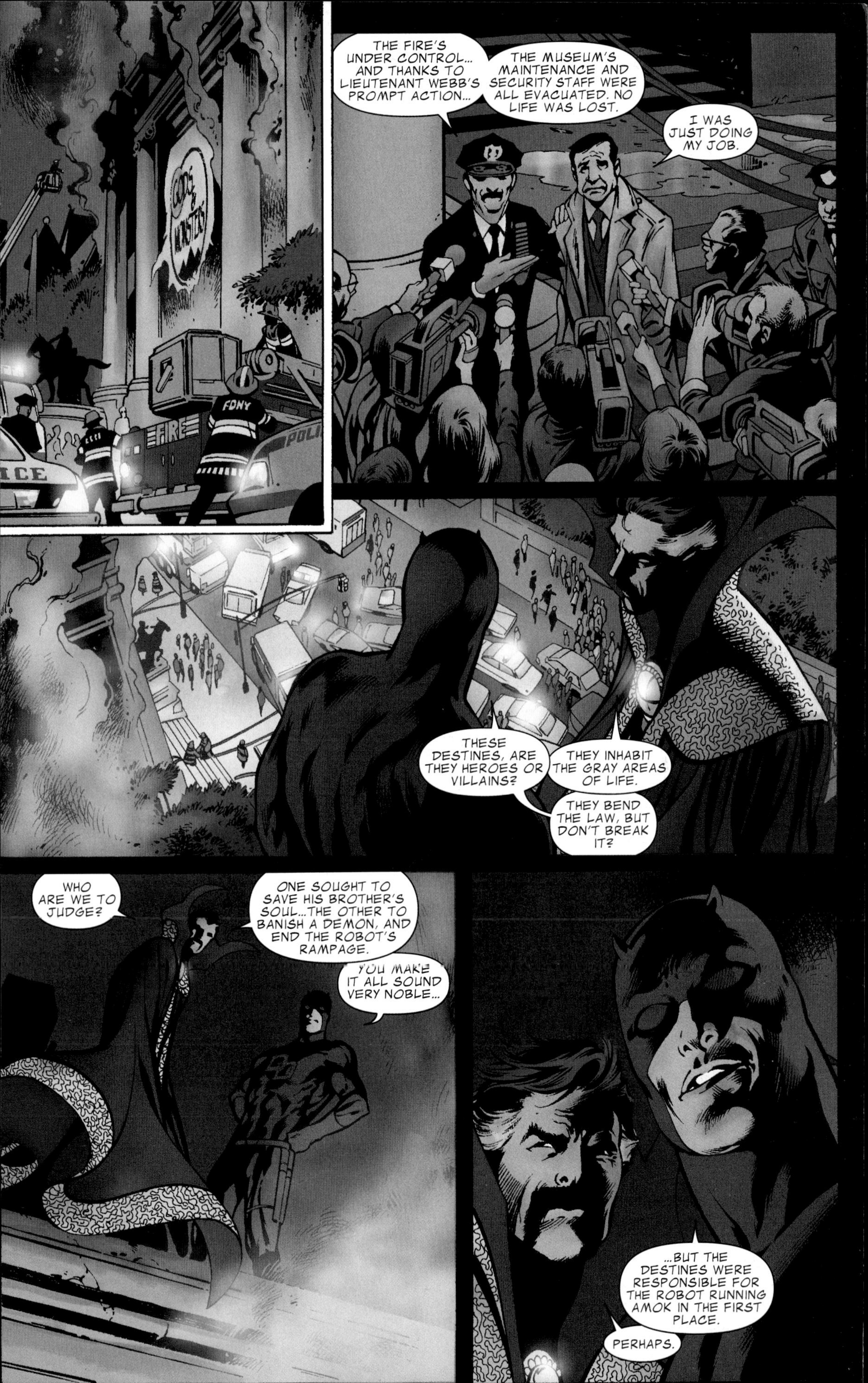
GODS & MONSTERS
FDNY
FIRE
POLICE
THE FIRE'S UNDER CONTROL... AND THANKS TO LIEUTENANT WEBB'S PROMPT ACTION...
THE MUSEUM'S MAINTENANCE AND SECURITY STAFF WERE ALL EVACUATED. NO LIFE WAS LOST.
I WAS JUST DOING MY JOB.
THESE DESTINES, ARE THEY HEROES OR VILLAINS?
THEY INHABIT THE GRAY AREAS OF LIFE.
THEY BEND THE LAW, BUT DON'T BREAK IT?
WHO ARE WE TO JUDGE?
ONE SOUGHT TO SAVE HIS BROTHER'S SOUL...THE OTHER TO BANISH A DEMON, AND END THE ROBOT'S RAMPAGE.
YOU MAKE IT ALL SOUND VERY NOBLE...
...BUT THE DESTINES WERE RESPONSIBLE FOR THE ROBOT RUNNING AMOK IN THE FIRST PLACE.
PERHAPS.

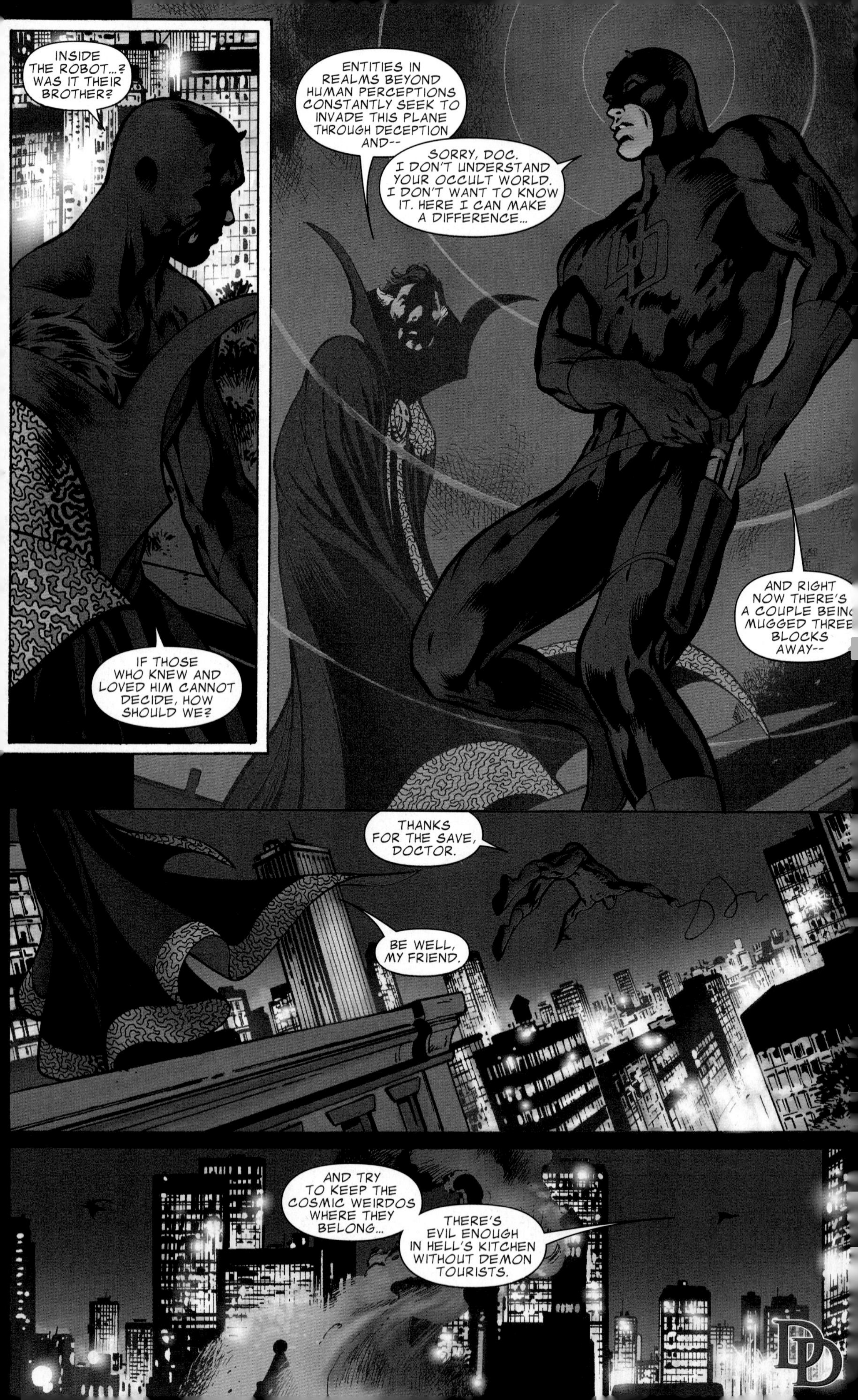
INSIDE THE ROBOT...? WAS IT THEIR BROTHER?
ENTITIES IN REALMS BEYOND HUMAN PERCEPTIONS CONSTANTLY SEEK TO INVADE THIS PLANE THROUGH DECEPTION AND--
SORRY, DOC. I DON'T UNDERSTAND YOUR OCCULT WORLD. I DON'T WANT TO KNOW IT. HERE I CAN MAKE A DIFFERENCE...
AND RIGHT NOW THERE'S A COUPLE BEING MUGGED THREE BLOCKS AWAY--
IF THOSE WHO KNEW AND LOVED HIM CANNOT DECIDE, HOW SHOULD WE?
THANKS FOR THE SAVE, DOCTOR.
BE WELL, MY FRIEND.
AND TRY TO KEEP THE COSMIC WEIRDOS WHERE THEY BELONG...
THERE'S EVIL ENOUGH IN HELL'S KITCHEN WITHOUT DEMON TOURISTS.
DD

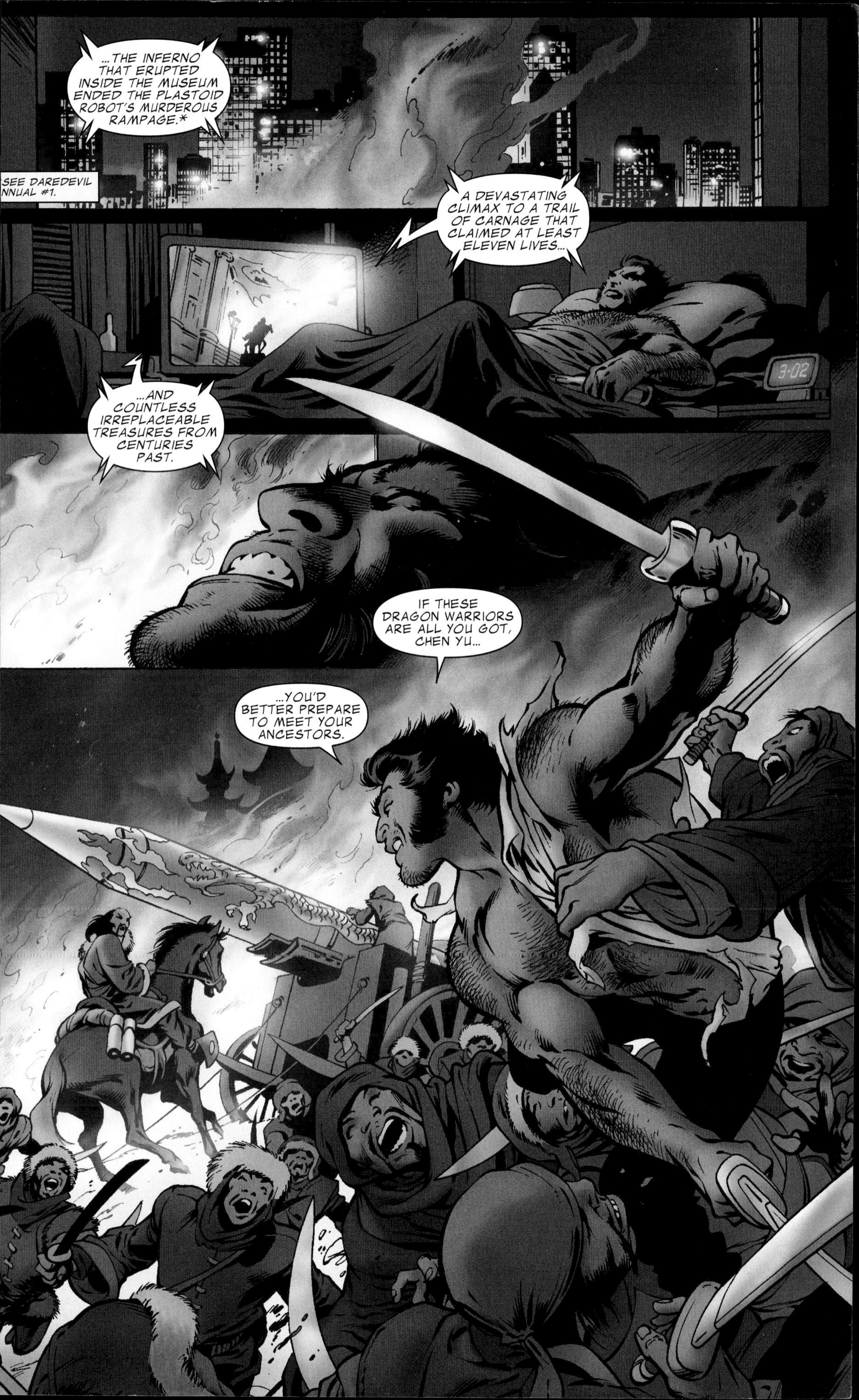
...THE INFERNO THAT ERUPTED INSIDE THE MUSEUM ENDED THE PLASTOID ROBOT'S MURDEROUS RAMPAGE.*
*SEE DAREDEVIL ANNUAL #1.
A DEVASTATING CLIMAX TO A TRAIL OF CARNAGE THAT CLAIMED AT LEAST ELEVEN LIVES...
3:02
...AND COUNTLESS IRREPLACEABLE TREASURES FROM CENTURIES PAST.
IF THESE DRAGON WARRIORS ARE ALL YOU GOT, CHEN YU...
...YOU'D BETTER PREPARE TO MEET YOUR ANCESTORS.

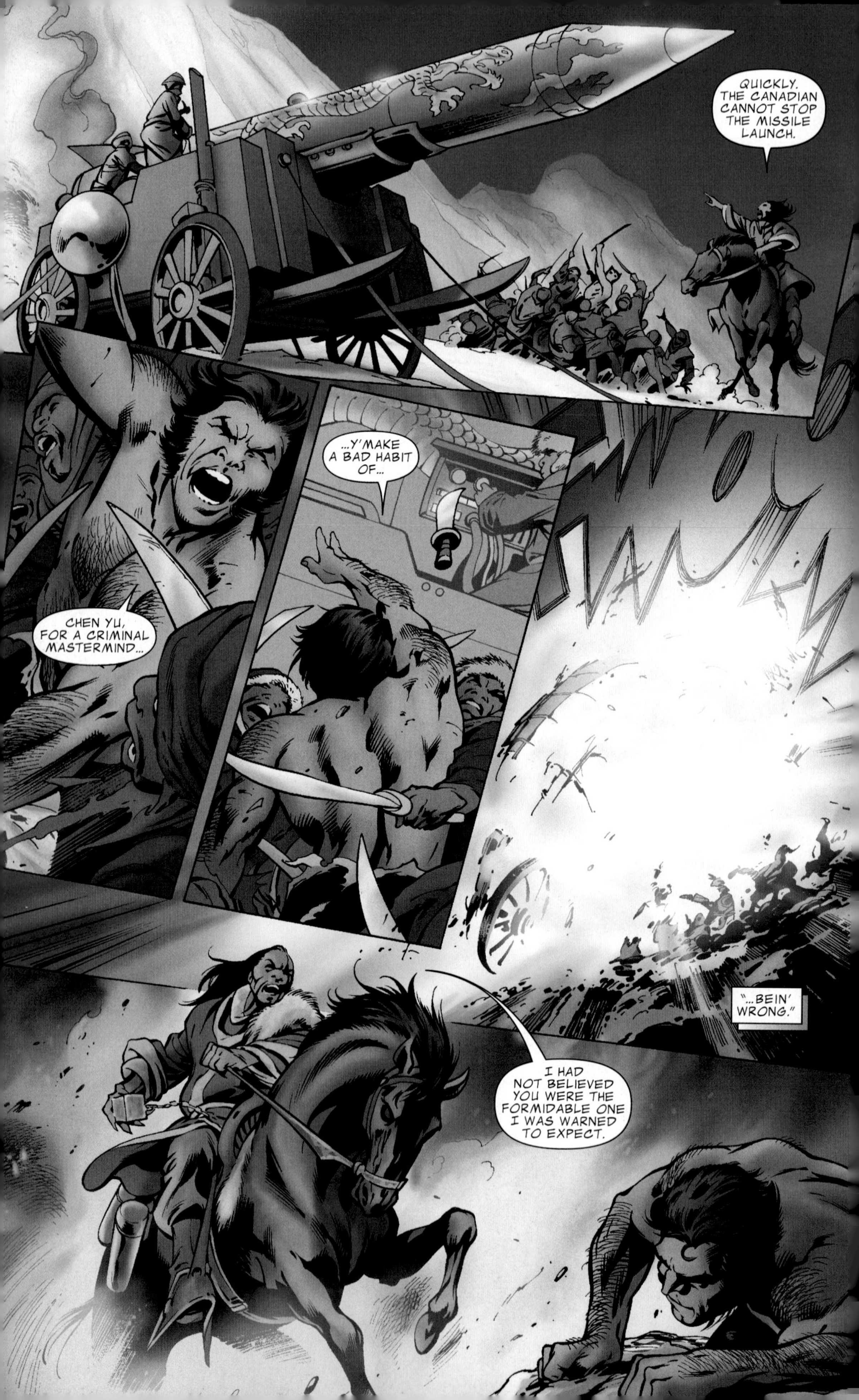
QUICKLY. THE CANADIAN CANNOT STOP THE MISSILE LAUNCH.
CHEN YU, FOR A CRIMINAL MASTERMIND...
...Y'MAKE A BAD HABIT OF...
"...BEIN' WRONG."
I HAD NOT BELIEVED YOU WERE THE FORMIDABLE ONE I WAS WARNED TO EXPECT.

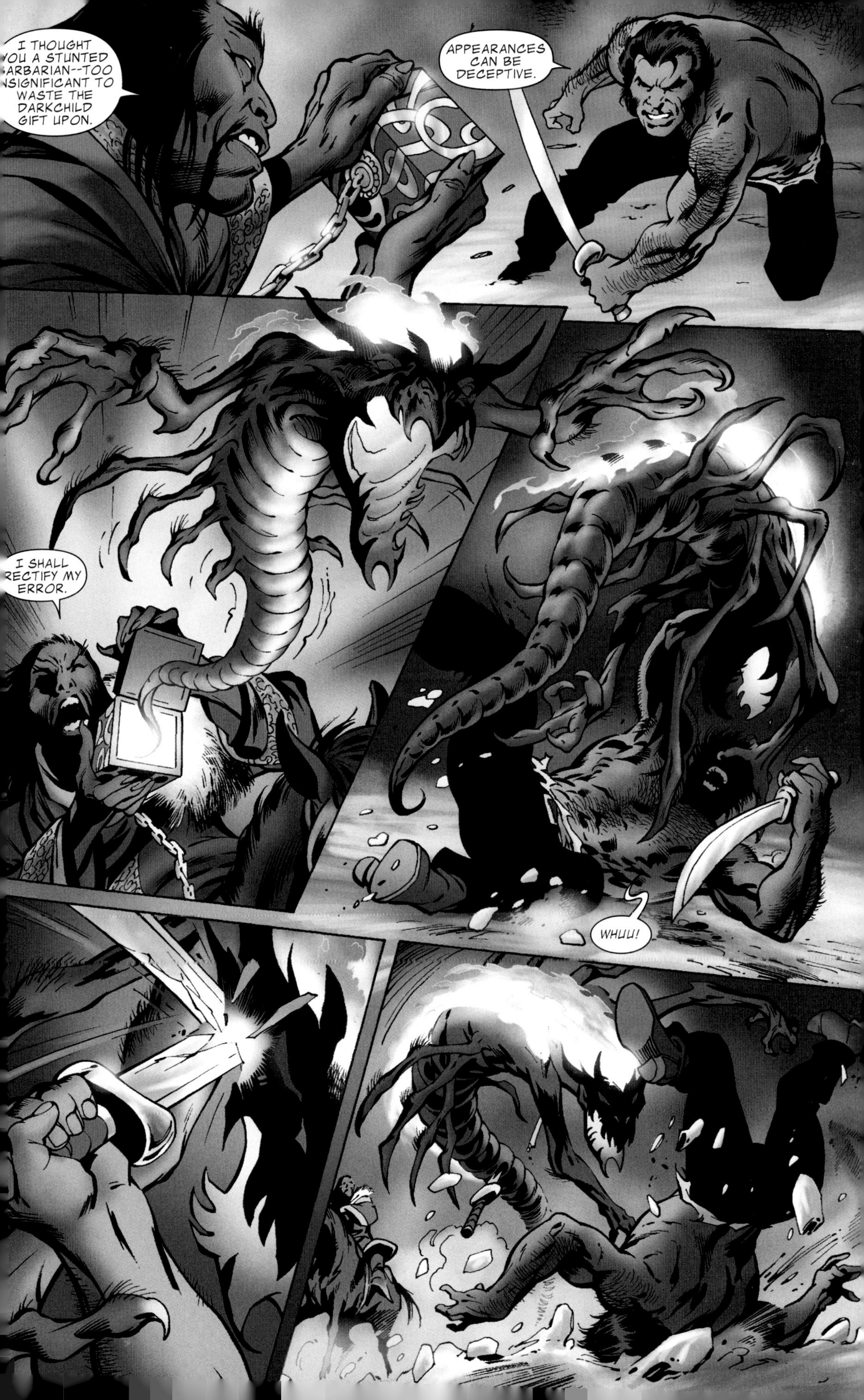
I THOUGHT YOU A STUNTED BARBARIAN--TOO INSIGNIFICANT TO WASTE THE DARKCHILD GIFT UPON.
APPEARANCES CAN BE DECEPTIVE.
I SHALL RECTIFY MY ERROR.
WHUU!

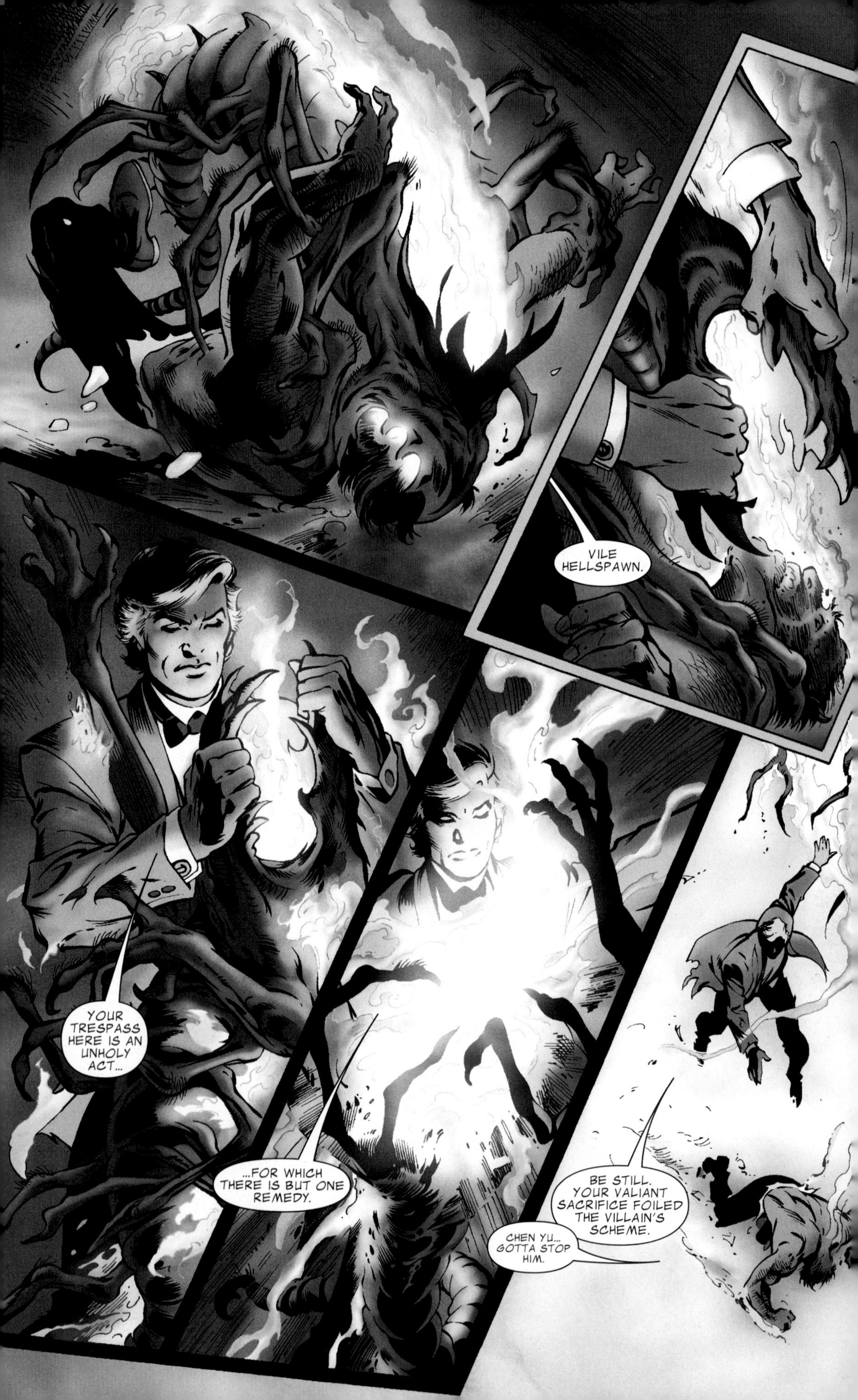
VILE HELLSPAWN.
YOUR TRESPASS HERE IS AN UNHOLY ACT...
...FOR WHICH THERE IS BUT ONE REMEDY.
BE STILL. YOUR VALIANT SACRIFICE FOILED THE VILLAIN'S SCHEME.
CHEN YU... GOTTA STOP HIM.

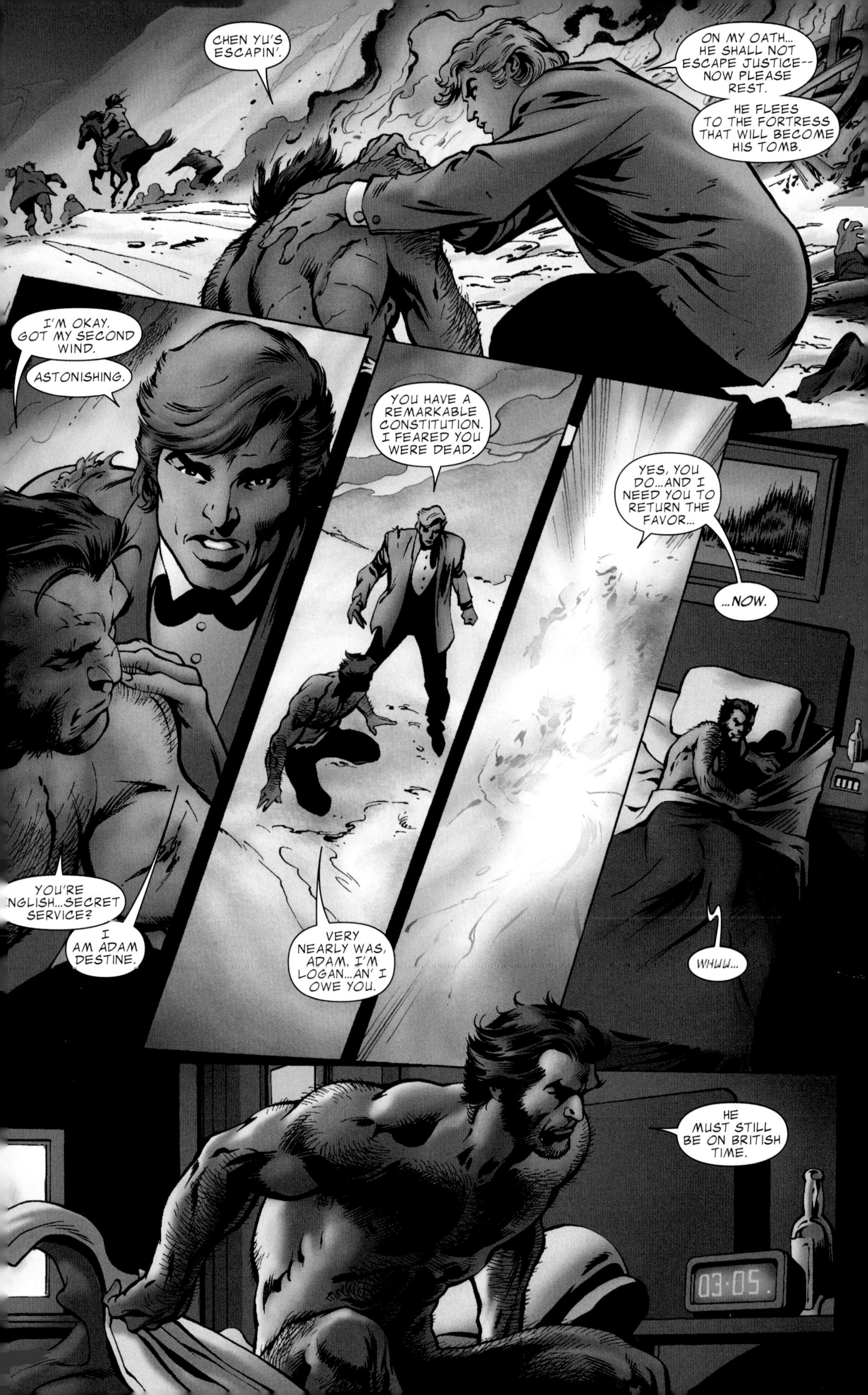

CHEN YU'S ESCAPIN'.
ON MY OATH... HE SHALL NOT ESCAPE JUSTICE-- NOW PLEASE REST.
HE FLEES TO THE FORTRESS THAT WILL BECOME HIS TOMB.
I'M OKAY. GOT MY SECOND WIND.
ASTONISHING.
YOU'RE ENGLISH...SECRET SERVICE?
I AM ADAM DESTINE.
YOU HAVE A REMARKABLE CONSTITUTION. I FEARED YOU WERE DEAD.
VERY NEARLY WAS, ADAM. I'M LOGAN...AN' I OWE YOU.
YES, YOU DO...AND I NEED YOU TO RETURN THE FAVOR...
...NOW.
WHUU...
HE MUST STILL BE ON BRITISH TIME.
03:05

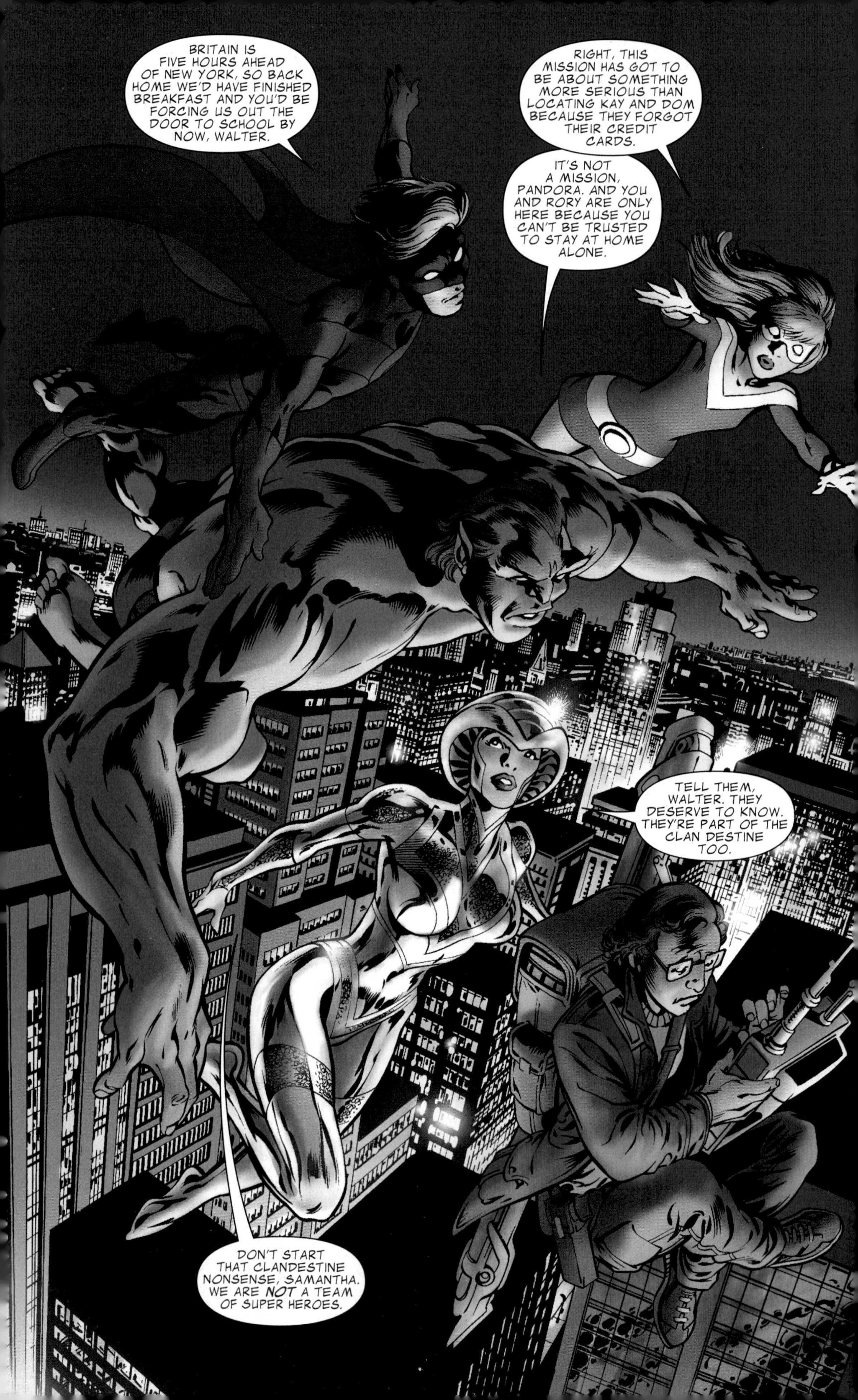
BRITAIN IS FIVE HOURS AHEAD OF NEW YORK, SO BACK HOME WE'D HAVE FINISHED BREAKFAST AND YOU'D BE FORCING US OUT THE DOOR TO SCHOOL BY NOW, WALTER.
RIGHT, THIS MISSION HAS GOT TO BE ABOUT SOMETHING MORE SERIOUS THAN LOCATING KAY AND DOM BECAUSE THEY FORGOT THEIR CREDIT CARDS.
IT'S NOT A MISSION, PANDORA. AND YOU AND RORY ARE ONLY HERE BECAUSE YOU CAN'T BE TRUSTED TO STAY AT HOME ALONE.
TELL THEM, WALTER. THEY DESERVE TO KNOW. THEY'RE PART OF THE CLAN DESTINE TOO.
DON'T START THAT CLANDESTINE NONSENSE, SAMANTHA. WE ARE *NOT* A TEAM OF SUPER HEROES.

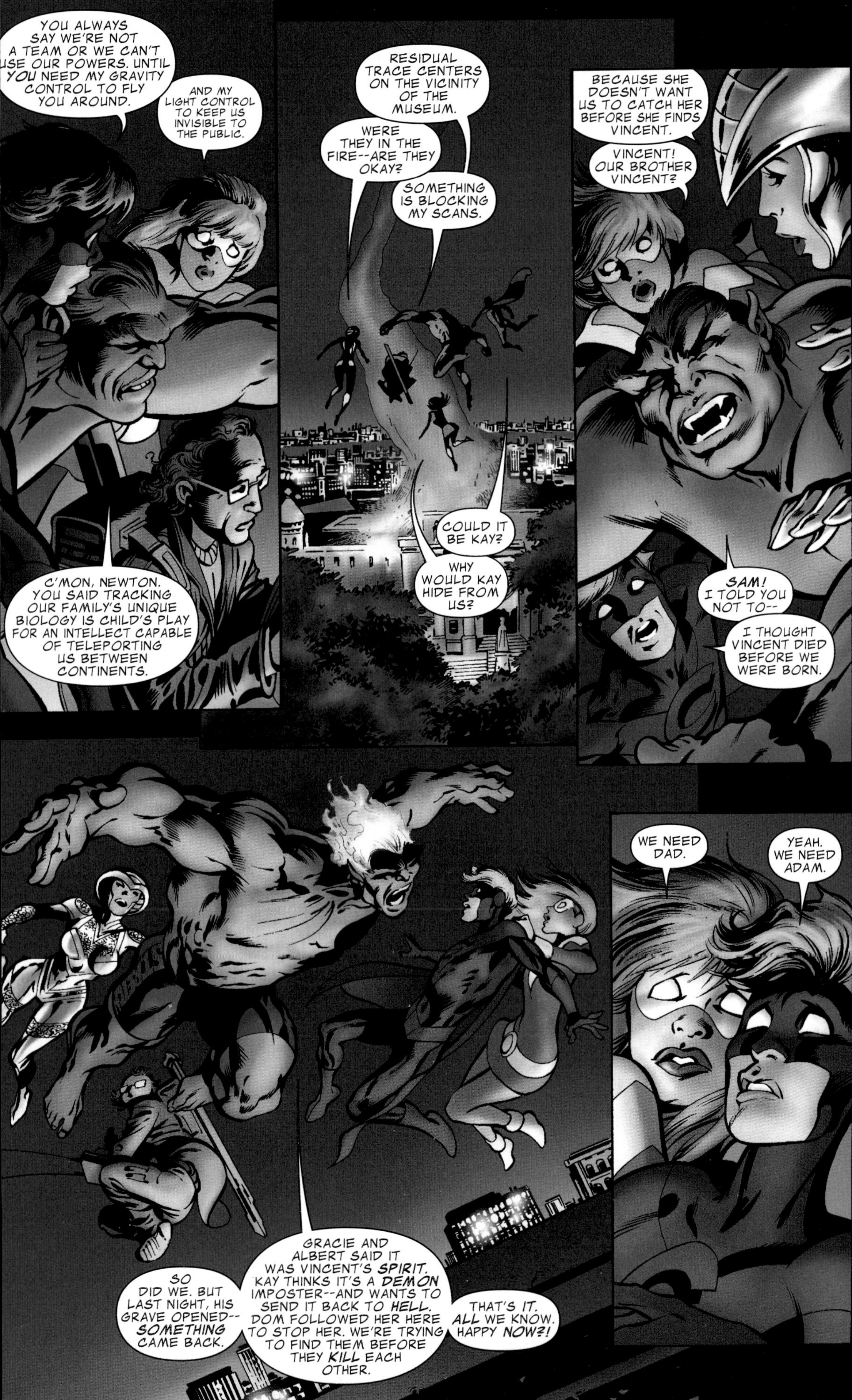
YOU ALWAYS SAY WE'RE NOT A TEAM OR WE CAN'T USE OUR POWERS. UNTIL YOU NEED MY GRAVITY CONTROL TO FLY YOU AROUND.
AND MY LIGHT CONTROL TO KEEP US INVISIBLE TO THE PUBLIC.
C'MON, NEWTON. YOU SAID TRACKING OUR FAMILY'S UNIQUE BIOLOGY IS CHILD'S PLAY FOR AN INTELLECT CAPABLE OF TELEPORTING US BETWEEN CONTINENTS.
RESIDUAL TRACE CENTERS ON THE VICINITY OF THE MUSEUM.
WERE THEY IN THE FIRE--ARE THEY OKAY?
SOMETHING IS BLOCKING MY SCANS.
COULD IT BE KAY?
WHY WOULD KAY HIDE FROM US?
BECAUSE SHE DOESN'T WANT US TO CATCH HER BEFORE SHE FINDS VINCENT.
VINCENT! OUR BROTHER VINCENT?
SAM! I TOLD YOU NOT TO--
I THOUGHT VINCENT DIED BEFORE WE WERE BORN.
SO DID WE. BUT LAST NIGHT, HIS GRAVE OPENED-- SOMETHING CAME BACK.
GRACIE AND ALBERT SAID IT WAS VINCENT'S SPIRIT. KAY THINKS IT'S A DEMON IMPOSTER--AND WANTS TO SEND IT BACK TO HELL. DOM FOLLOWED HER HERE TO STOP HER. WE'RE TRYING TO FIND THEM BEFORE THEY KILL EACH OTHER.
THAT'S IT. ALL WE KNOW. HAPPY NOW?!
WE NEED DAD.
YEAH. WE NEED ADAM.

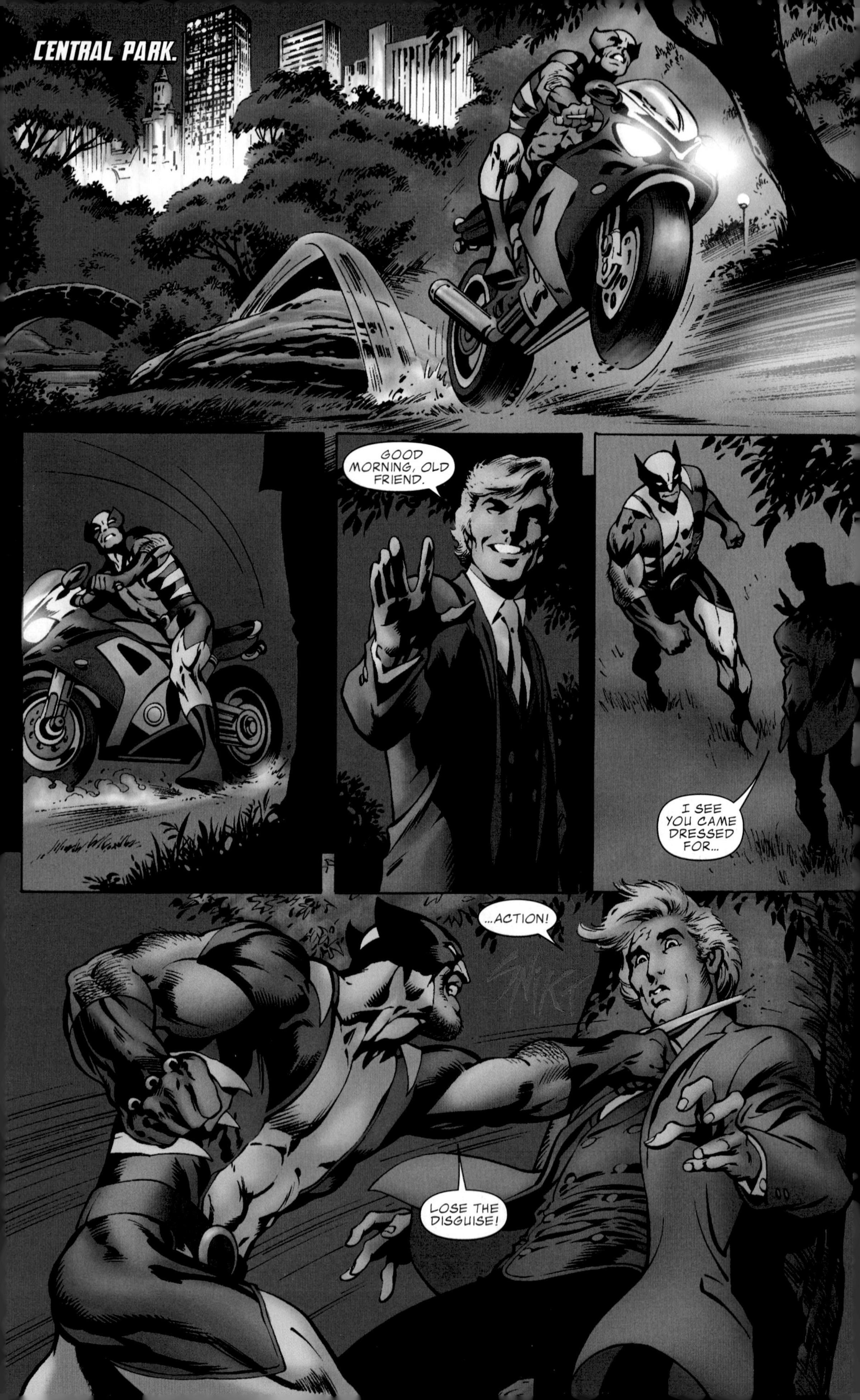
CENTRAL PARK.
GOOD MORNING, OLD FRIEND.
I SEE YOU CAME DRESSED FOR...
...ACTION!
SNIKT
LOSE THE DISGUISE!

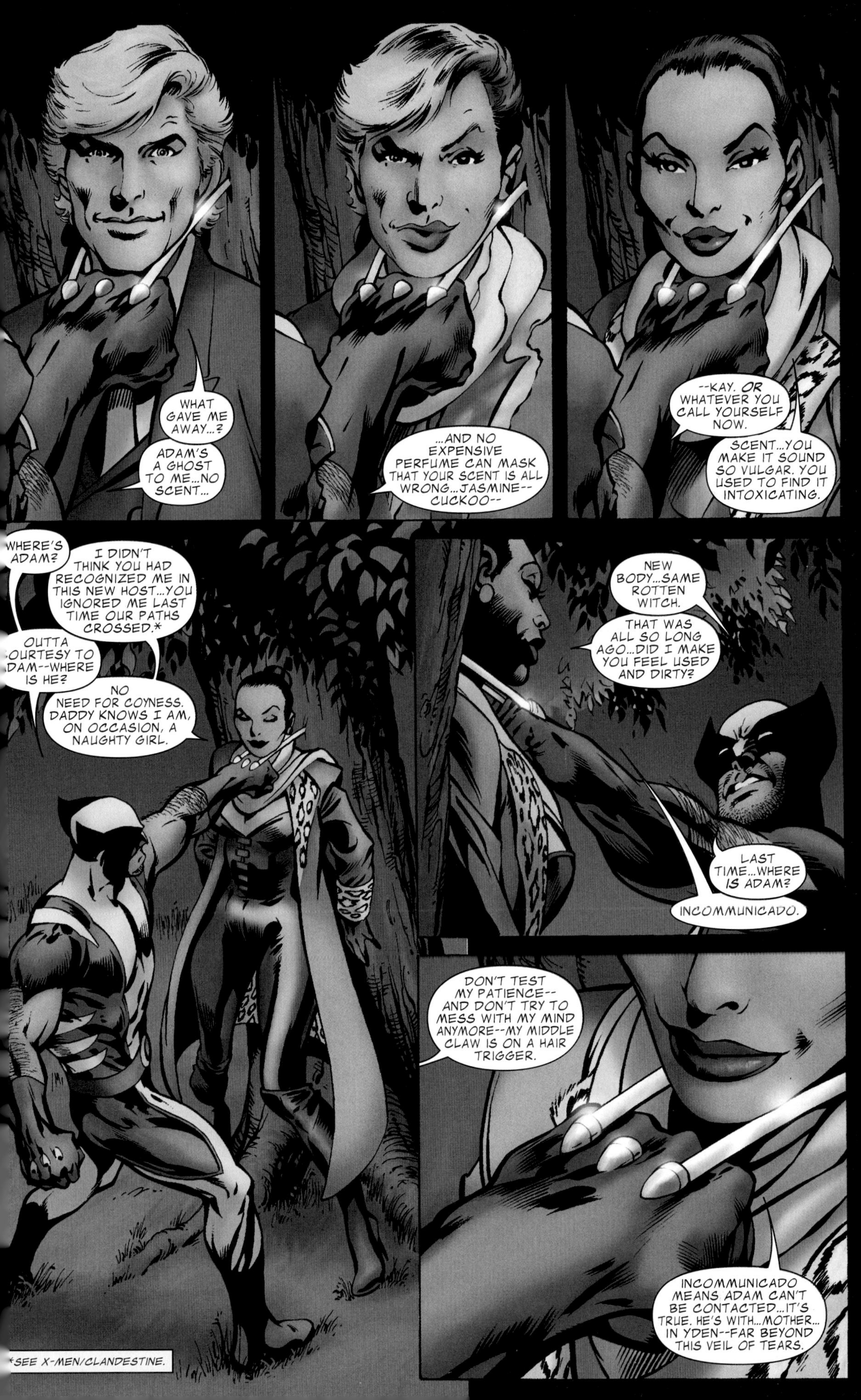
WHAT GAVE ME AWAY...?
ADAM'S A GHOST TO ME...NO SCENT...
...AND NO EXPENSIVE PERFUME CAN MASK THAT YOUR SCENT IS ALL WRONG...JASMINE-- CUCKOO--
--KAY. OR WHATEVER YOU CALL YOURSELF NOW.
SCENT...YOU MAKE IT SOUND SO VULGAR. YOU USED TO FIND IT INTOXICATING.
WHERE'S ADAM?
I DIDN'T THINK YOU HAD RECOGNIZED ME IN THIS NEW HOST...YOU IGNORED ME LAST TIME OUR PATHS CROSSED.*
OUTTA COURTESY TO ADAM--WHERE IS HE?
NO NEED FOR COYNESS. DADDY KNOWS I AM, ON OCCASION, A NAUGHTY GIRL.
NEW BODY...SAME ROTTEN WITCH.
THAT WAS ALL SO LONG AGO...DID I MAKE YOU FEEL USED AND DIRTY?
LAST TIME...WHERE IS ADAM?
INCOMMUNICADO.
DON'T TEST MY PATIENCE-- AND DON'T TRY TO MESS WITH MY MIND ANYMORE--MY MIDDLE CLAW IS ON A HAIR TRIGGER.
INCOMMUNICADO MEANS ADAM CAN'T BE CONTACTED...IT'S TRUE. HE'S WITH...MOTHER... IN YDEN--FAR BEYOND THIS VEIL OF TEARS.
*SEE X-MEN/CLANDESTINE.

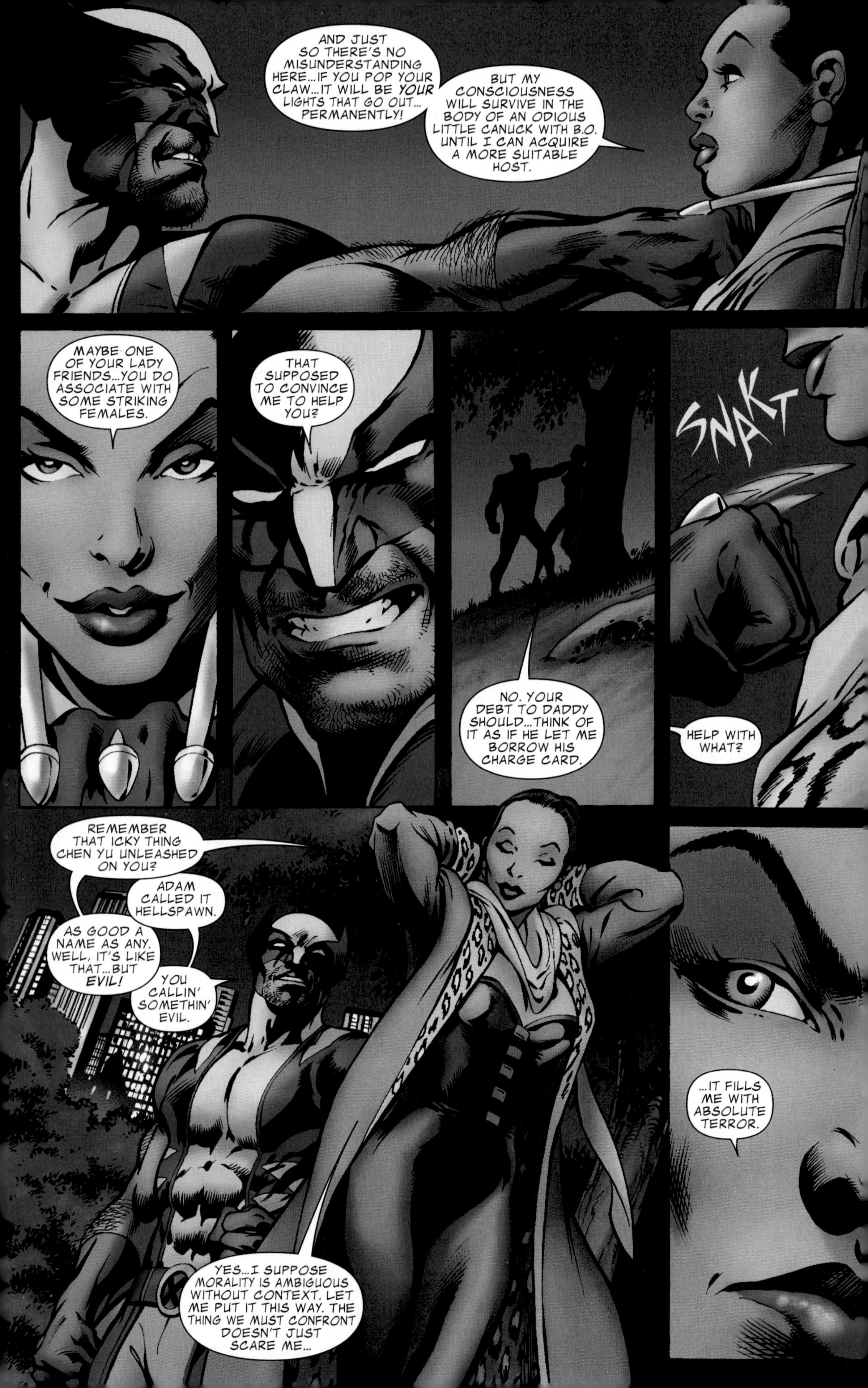
AND JUST SO THERE'S NO MISUNDERSTANDING HERE...IF YOU POP YOUR CLAW...IT WILL BE YOUR LIGHTS THAT GO OUT... PERMANENTLY!
BUT MY CONSCIOUSNESS WILL SURVIVE IN THE BODY OF AN ODIOUS LITTLE CANUCK WITH B.O. UNTIL I CAN ACQUIRE A MORE SUITABLE HOST.
MAYBE ONE OF YOUR LADY FRIENDS...YOU DO ASSOCIATE WITH SOME STRIKING FEMALES.
THAT SUPPOSED TO CONVINCE ME TO HELP YOU?
NO. YOUR DEBT TO DADDY SHOULD...THINK OF IT AS IF HE LET ME BORROW HIS CHARGE CARD.
SNAKT
HELP WITH WHAT?
REMEMBER THAT ICKY THING CHEN YU UNLEASHED ON YOU?
ADAM CALLED IT HELLSPAWN.
AS GOOD A NAME AS ANY. WELL, IT'S LIKE THAT...BUT EVIL!
YOU CALLIN' SOMETHIN' EVIL.
YES...I SUPPOSE MORALITY IS AMBIGUOUS WITHOUT CONTEXT. LET ME PUT IT THIS WAY. THE THING WE MUST CONFRONT DOESN'T JUST SCARE ME...
...IT FILLS ME WITH ABSOLUTE TERROR.

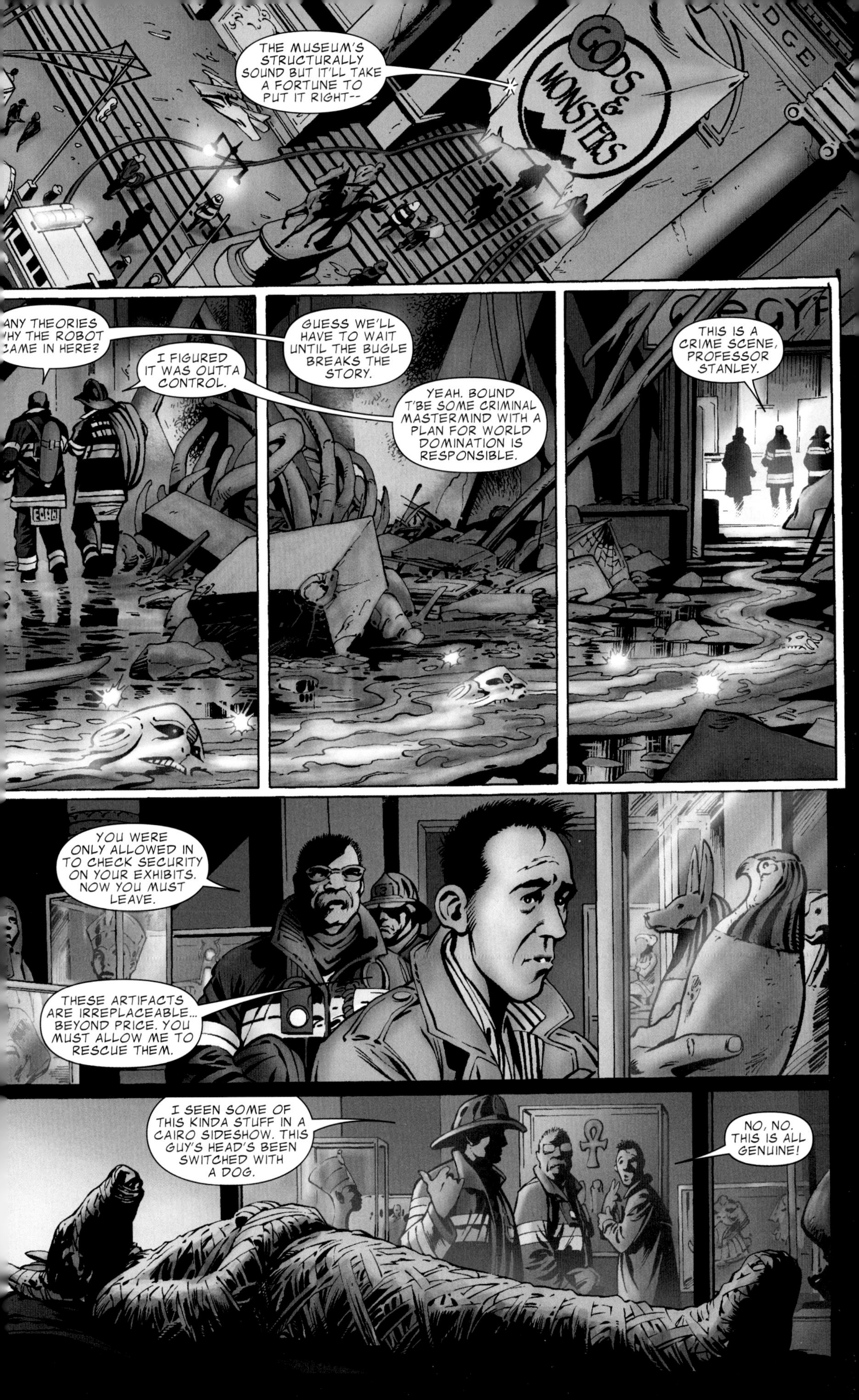
THE MUSEUM'S STRUCTURALLY SOUND BUT IT'LL TAKE A FORTUNE TO PUT IT RIGHT--
GODS & MONSTERS
ANY THEORIES WHY THE ROBOT CAME IN HERE?
I FIGURED IT WAS OUTTA CONTROL.
GUESS WE'LL HAVE TO WAIT UNTIL THE BUGLE BREAKS THE STORY.
YEAH. BOUND T'BE SOME CRIMINAL MASTERMIND WITH A PLAN FOR WORLD DOMINATION IS RESPONSIBLE.
THIS IS A CRIME SCENE, PROFESSOR STANLEY.
YOU WERE ONLY ALLOWED IN TO CHECK SECURITY ON YOUR EXHIBITS. NOW YOU MUST LEAVE.
THESE ARTIFACTS ARE IRREPLACEABLE... BEYOND PRICE. YOU MUST ALLOW ME TO RESCUE THEM.
I SEEN SOME OF THIS KINDA STUFF IN A CAIRO SIDESHOW. THIS GUY'S HEAD'S BEEN SWITCHED WITH A DOG.
NO, NO. THIS IS ALL GENUINE!

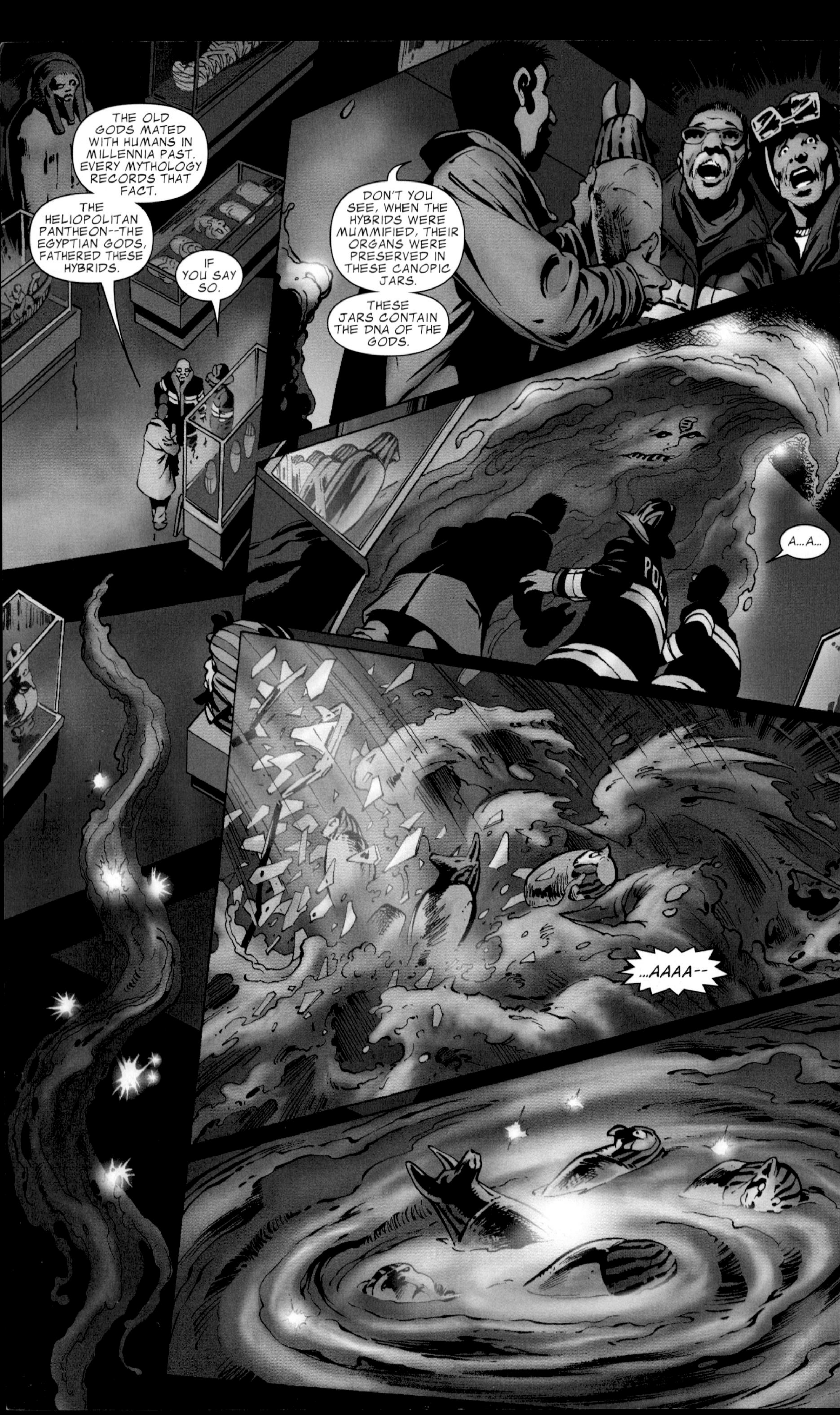
THE OLD GODS MATED WITH HUMANS IN MILLENNIA PAST. EVERY MYTHOLOGY RECORDS THAT FACT.
THE HELIOPOLITAN PANTHEON--THE EGYPTIAN GODS, FATHERED THESE HYBRIDS.
IF YOU SAY SO.
DON'T YOU SEE, WHEN THE HYBRIDS WERE MUMMIFIED, THEIR ORGANS WERE PRESERVED IN THESE CANOPIC JARS.
THESE JARS CONTAIN THE DNA OF THE GODS.
A...A...
...AAAA--

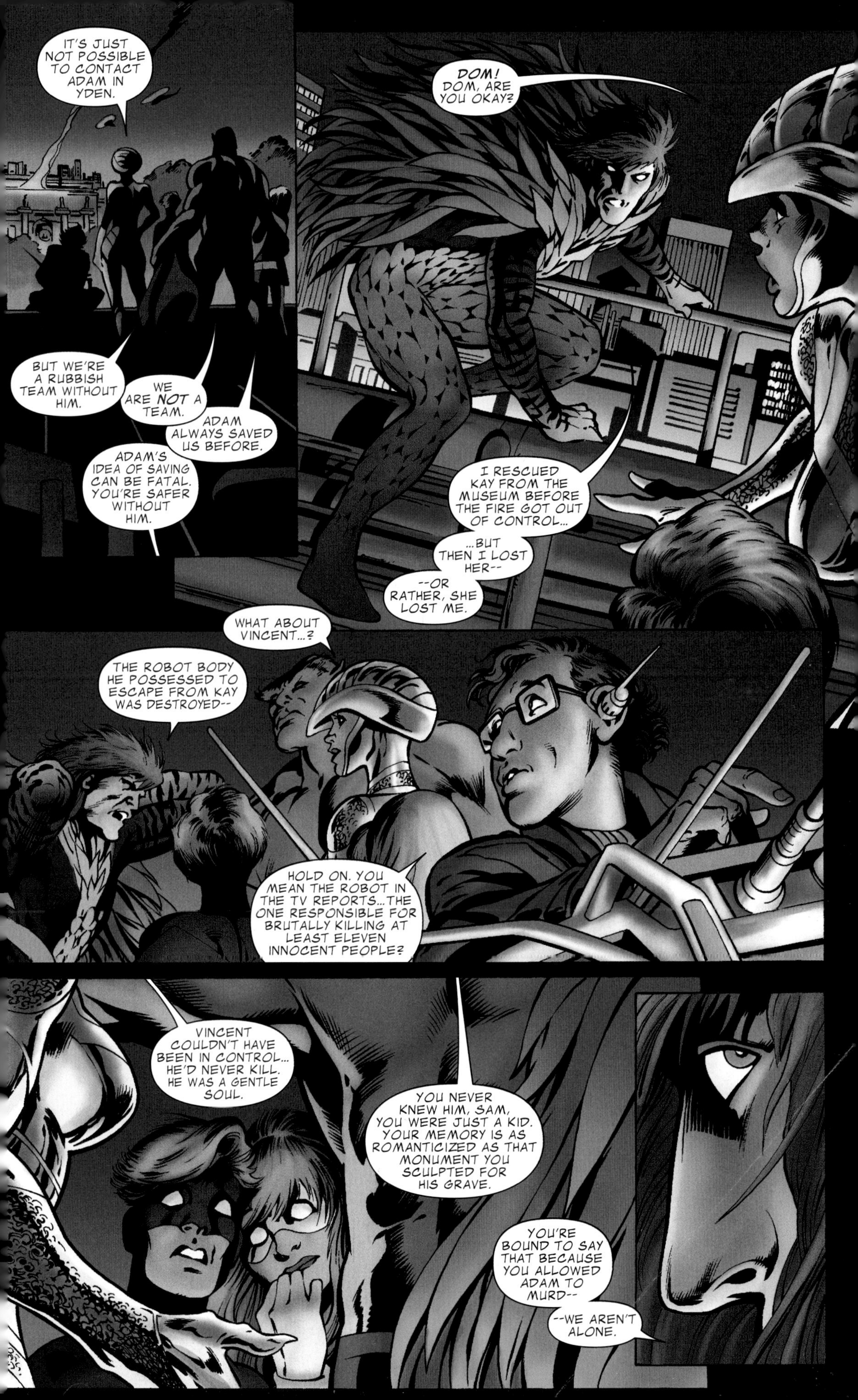
IT'S JUST NOT POSSIBLE TO CONTACT ADAM IN YDEN.
BUT WE'RE A RUBBISH TEAM WITHOUT HIM.
WE ARE NOT A TEAM.
ADAM ALWAYS SAVED US BEFORE.
ADAM'S IDEA OF SAVING CAN BE FATAL. YOU'RE SAFER WITHOUT HIM.
DOM! DOM, ARE YOU OKAY?
I RESCUED KAY FROM THE MUSEUM BEFORE THE FIRE GOT OUT OF CONTROL...
...BUT THEN I LOST HER--
--OR RATHER, SHE LOST ME.
WHAT ABOUT VINCENT...?
THE ROBOT BODY HE POSSESSED TO ESCAPE FROM KAY WAS DESTROYED--
HOLD ON. YOU MEAN THE ROBOT IN THE TV REPORTS...THE ONE RESPONSIBLE FOR BRUTALLY KILLING AT LEAST ELEVEN INNOCENT PEOPLE?
VINCENT COULDN'T HAVE BEEN IN CONTROL... HE'D NEVER KILL. HE WAS A GENTLE SOUL.
YOU NEVER KNEW HIM, SAM, YOU WERE JUST A KID. YOUR MEMORY IS AS ROMANTICIZED AS THAT MONUMENT YOU SCULPTED FOR HIS GRAVE.
YOU'RE BOUND TO SAY THAT BECAUSE YOU ALLOWED ADAM TO MURD--
--WE AREN'T ALONE.

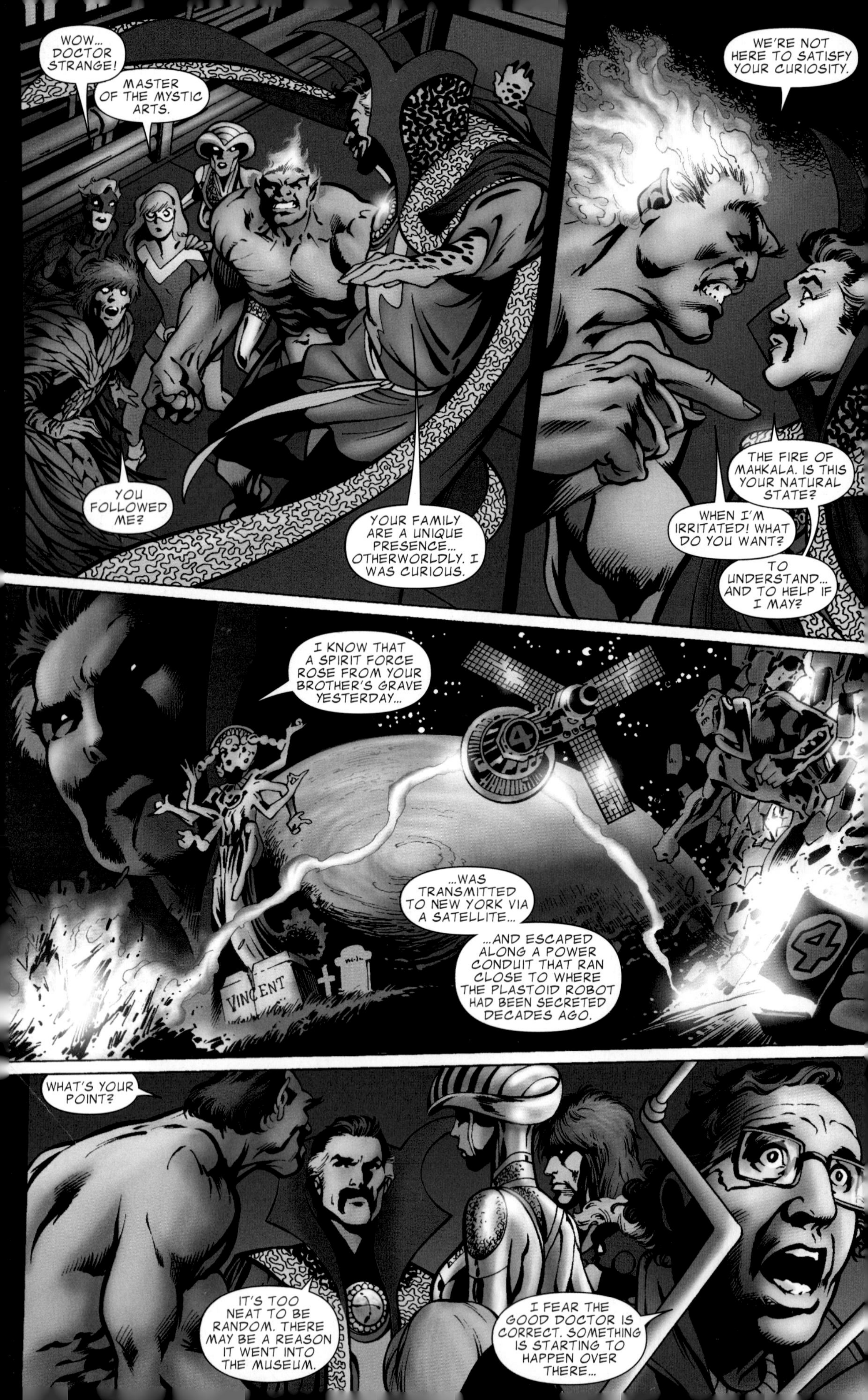
WOW... DOCTOR STRANGE!
MASTER OF THE MYSTIC ARTS.
YOU FOLLOWED ME?
YOUR FAMILY ARE A UNIQUE PRESENCE... OTHERWORLDLY. I WAS CURIOUS.
WE'RE NOT HERE TO SATISFY YOUR CURIOSITY.
THE FIRE OF MAHKALA. IS THIS YOUR NATURAL STATE?
WHEN I'M IRRITATED! WHAT DO YOU WANT?
TO UNDERSTAND... AND TO HELP IF I MAY?
I KNOW THAT A SPIRIT FORCE ROSE FROM YOUR BROTHER'S GRAVE YESTERDAY...
VINCENT
...WAS TRANSMITTED TO NEW YORK VIA A SATELLITE...
...AND ESCAPED ALONG A POWER CONDUIT THAT RAN CLOSE TO WHERE THE PLASTOID ROBOT HAD BEEN SECRETED DECADES AGO.
WHAT'S YOUR POINT?
IT'S TOO NEAT TO BE RANDOM. THERE MAY BE A REASON IT WENT INTO THE MUSEUM.
I FEAR THE GOOD DOCTOR IS CORRECT. SOMETHING IS STARTING TO HAPPEN OVER THERE...

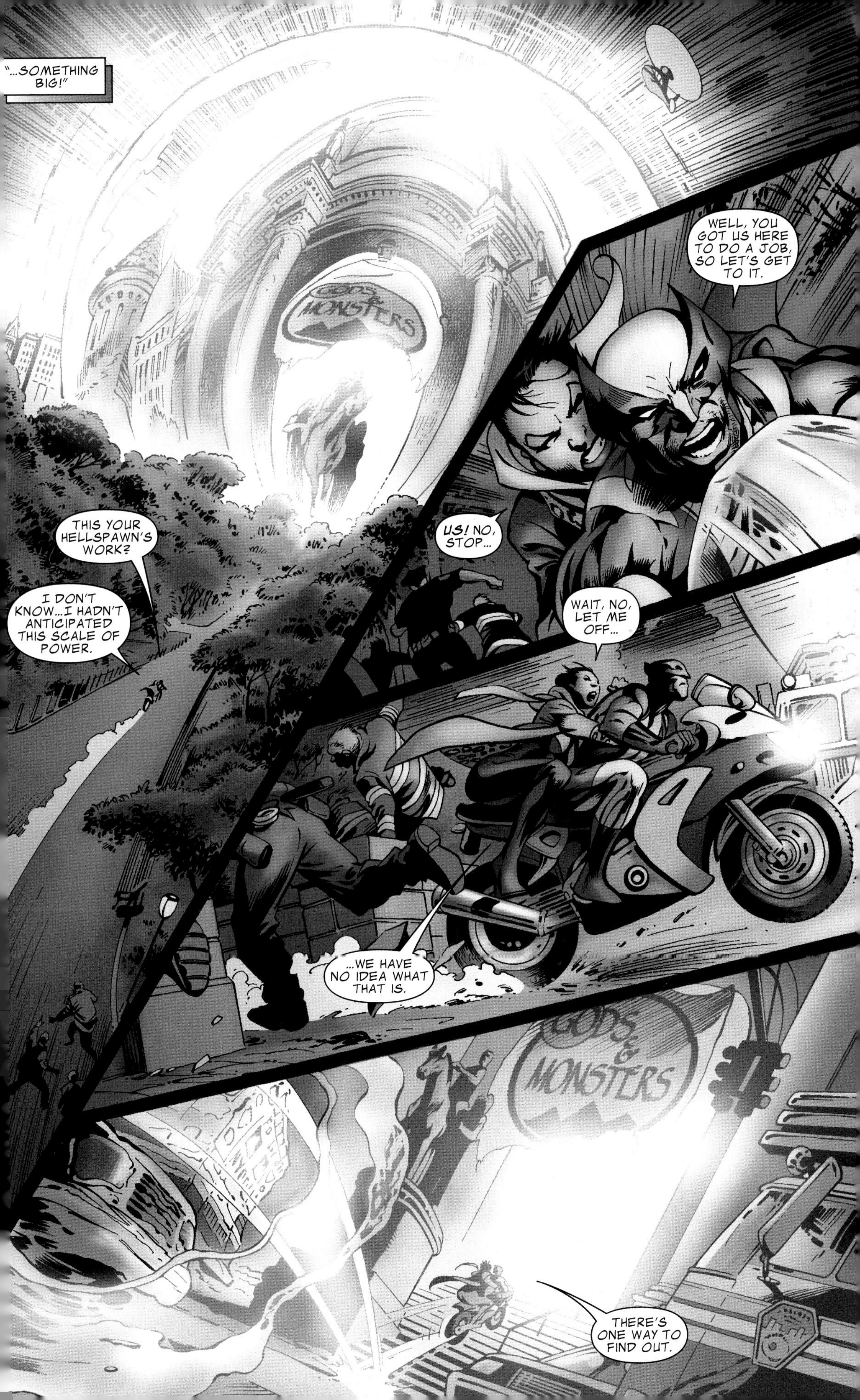
"...SOMETHING BIG!"
WELL, YOU GOT US HERE TO DO A JOB, SO LET'S GET TO IT.
THIS YOUR HELLSPAWN'S WORK?
I DON'T KNOW...I HADN'T ANTICIPATED THIS SCALE OF POWER.
US! NO, STOP...
WAIT, NO, LET ME OFF...
...WE HAVE NO IDEA WHAT THAT IS.
GODS & MONSTERS
THERE'S ONE WAY TO FIND OUT.

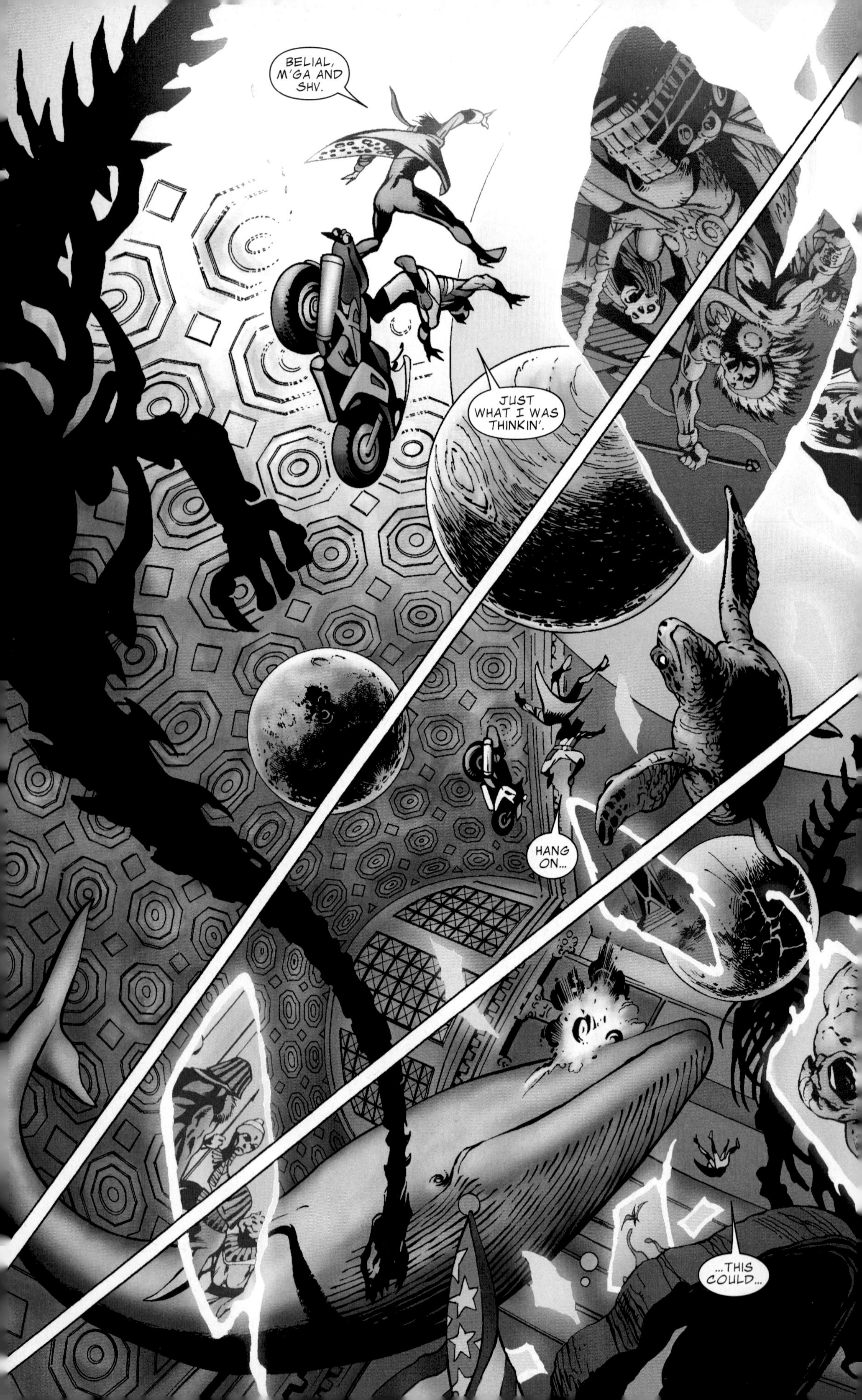
BELIAL, M'GA AND SHV.
JUST WHAT I WAS THINKIN'.
HANG ON...
...THIS COULD...

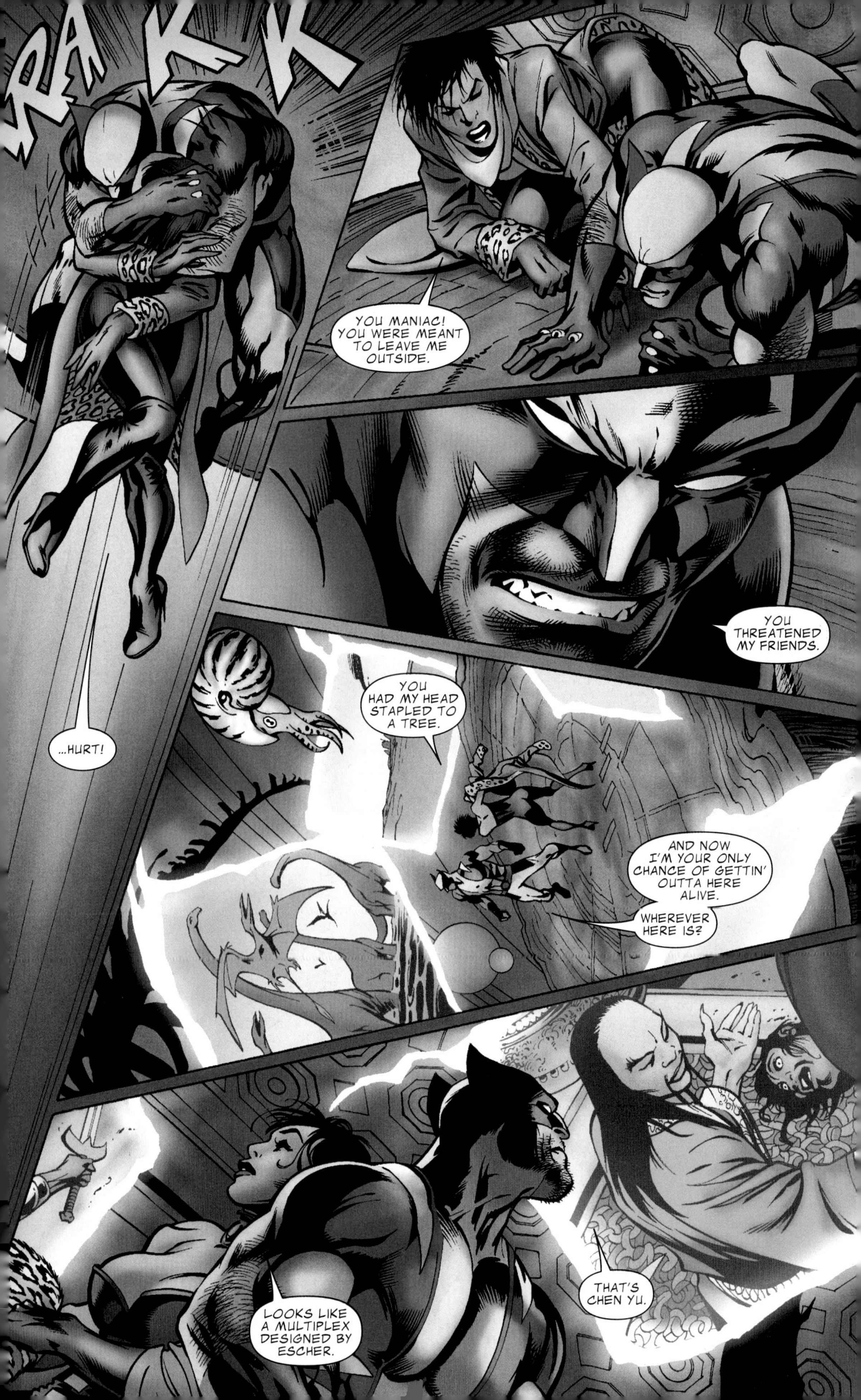
RAKK
YOU MANIAC! YOU WERE MEANT TO LEAVE ME OUTSIDE.
...HURT!
YOU THREATENED MY FRIENDS.
YOU HAD MY HEAD STAPLED TO A TREE.
AND NOW I'M YOUR ONLY CHANCE OF GETTIN' OUTTA HERE ALIVE.
WHEREVER HERE IS?
LOOKS LIKE A MULTIPLEX DESIGNED BY ESCHER.
THAT'S CHEN YU.

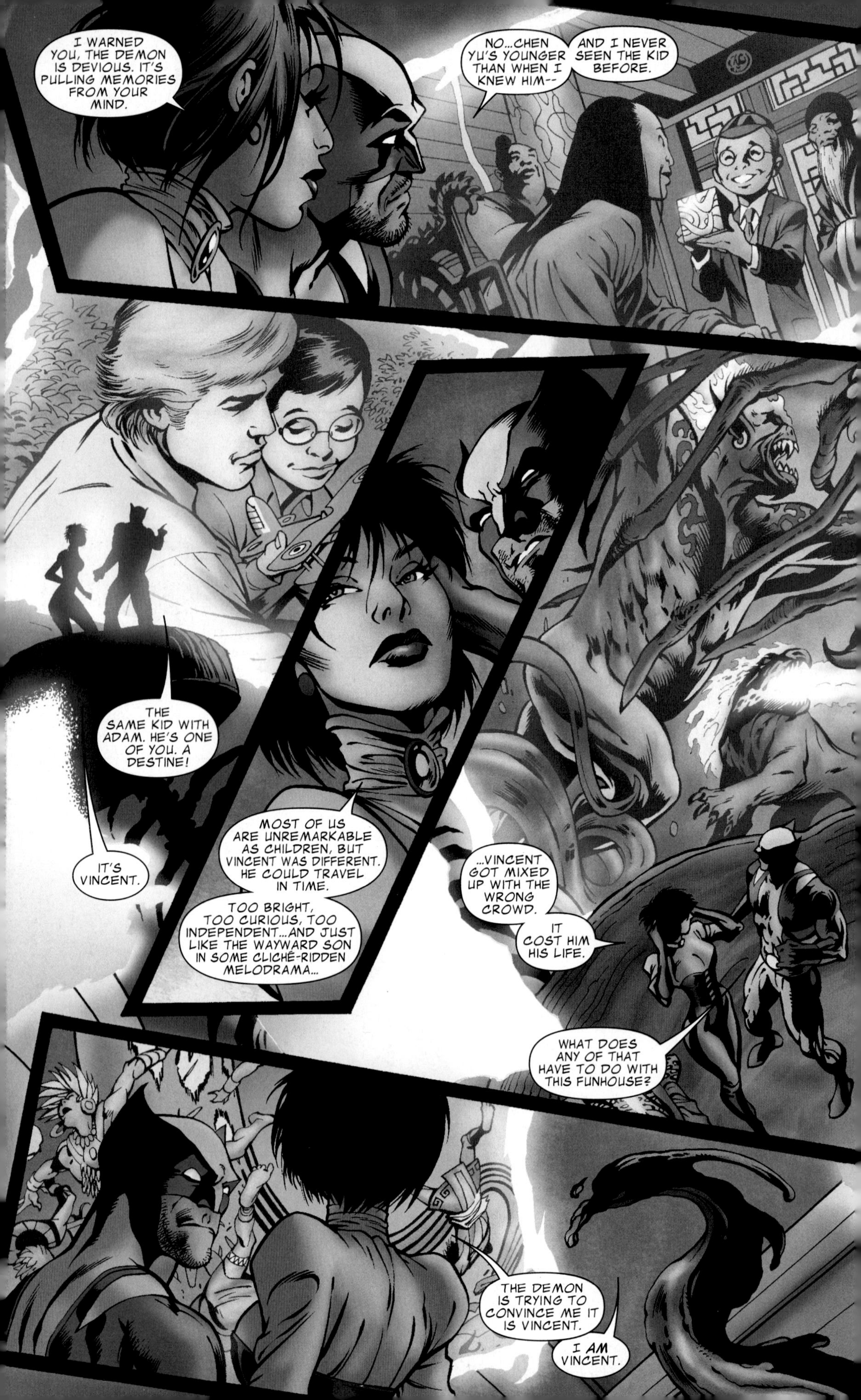
I WARNED YOU, THE DEMON IS DEVIOUS. IT'S PULLING MEMORIES FROM YOUR MIND.
NO...CHEN YU'S YOUNGER THAN WHEN I KNEW HIM--
AND I NEVER SEEN THE KID BEFORE.
THE SAME KID WITH ADAM. HE'S ONE OF YOU. A DESTINE!
IT'S VINCENT.
MOST OF US ARE UNREMARKABLE AS CHILDREN, BUT VINCENT WAS DIFFERENT. HE COULD TRAVEL IN TIME.
TOO BRIGHT, TOO CURIOUS, TOO INDEPENDENT...AND JUST LIKE THE WAYWARD SON IN SOME CLICHÉ-RIDDEN MELODRAMA...
...VINCENT GOT MIXED UP WITH THE WRONG CROWD.
IT COST HIM HIS LIFE.
WHAT DOES ANY OF THAT HAVE TO DO WITH THIS FUNHOUSE?
THE DEMON IS TRYING TO CONVINCE ME IT IS VINCENT.
I *AM* VINCENT.

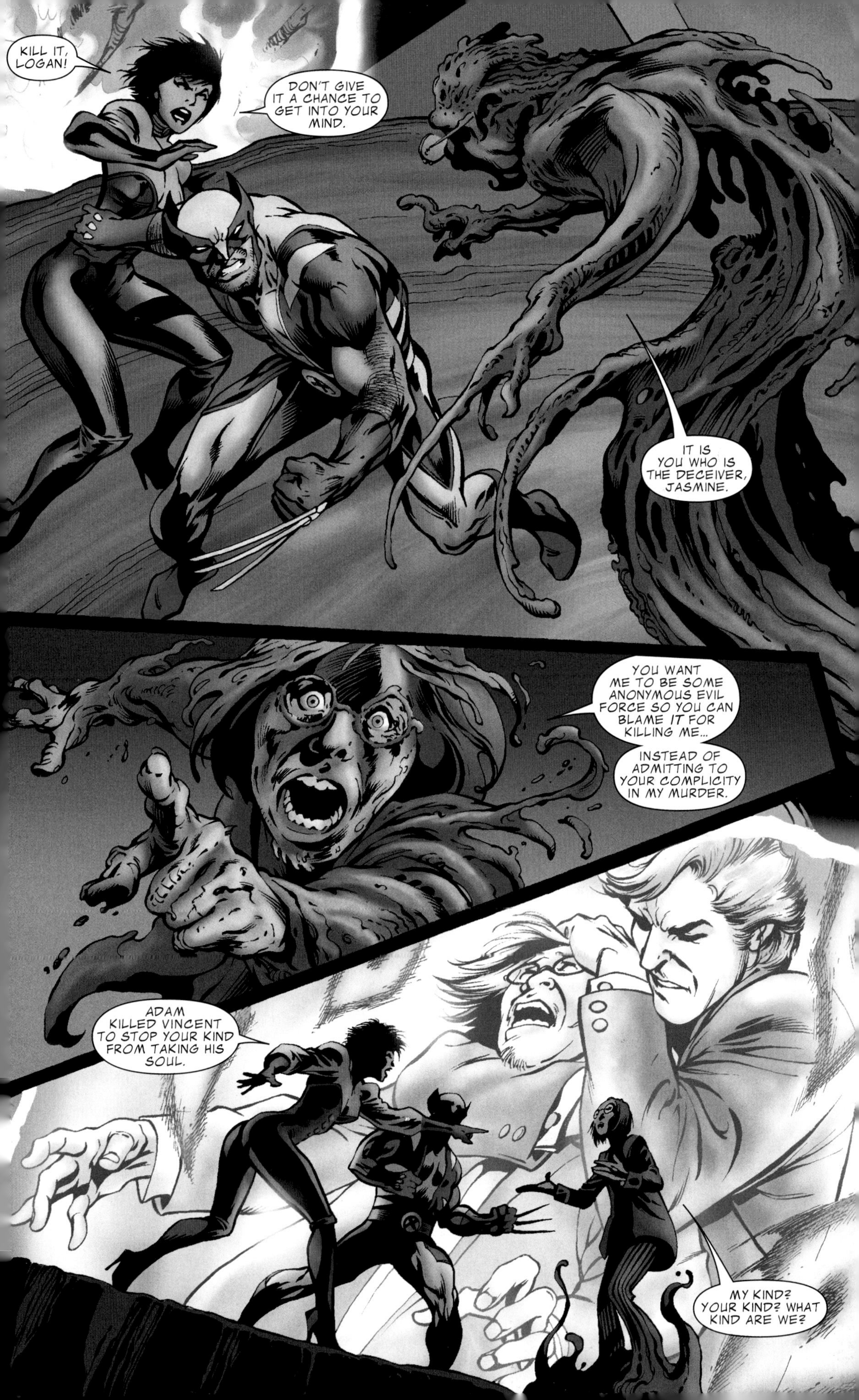
KILL IT, LOGAN!
DON'T GIVE IT A CHANCE TO GET INTO YOUR MIND.
IT IS YOU WHO IS THE DECEIVER, JASMINE.
YOU WANT ME TO BE SOME ANONYMOUS EVIL FORCE SO YOU CAN BLAME IT FOR KILLING ME...
INSTEAD OF ADMITTING TO YOUR COMPLICITY IN MY MURDER.
ADAM KILLED VINCENT TO STOP YOUR KIND FROM TAKING HIS SOUL.
MY KIND? YOUR KIND? WHAT KIND ARE WE?

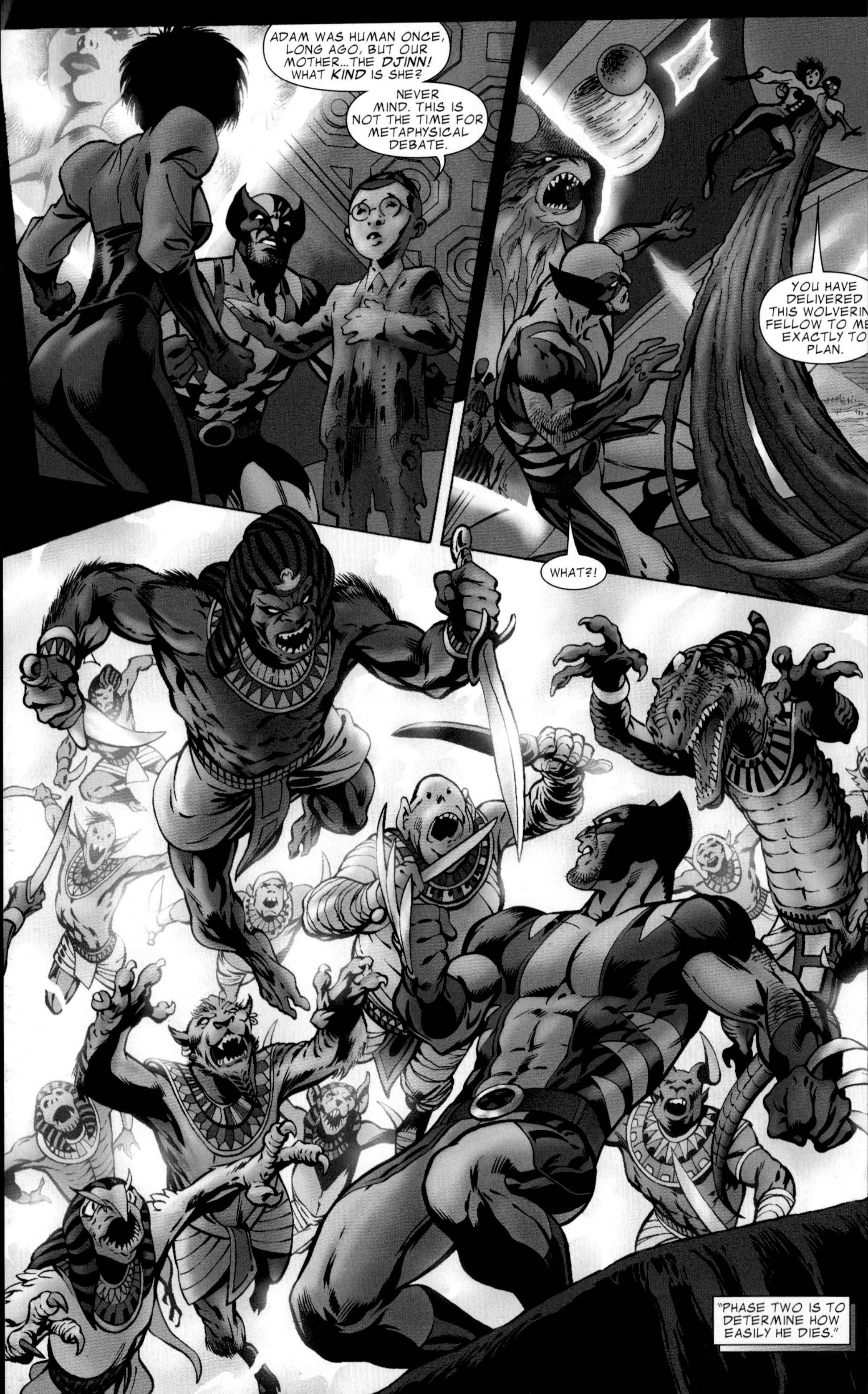
ADAM WAS HUMAN ONCE, LONG AGO, BUT OUR MOTHER... THE DJINN! WHAT KIND IS SHE?
NEVER MIND. THIS IS NOT THE TIME FOR METAPHYSICAL DEBATE.
YOU HAVE DELIVERED THIS WOLVERIN FELLOW TO ME EXACTLY TO PLAN.
WHAT?!
"PHASE TWO IS TO DETERMINE HOW EASILY HE DIES."

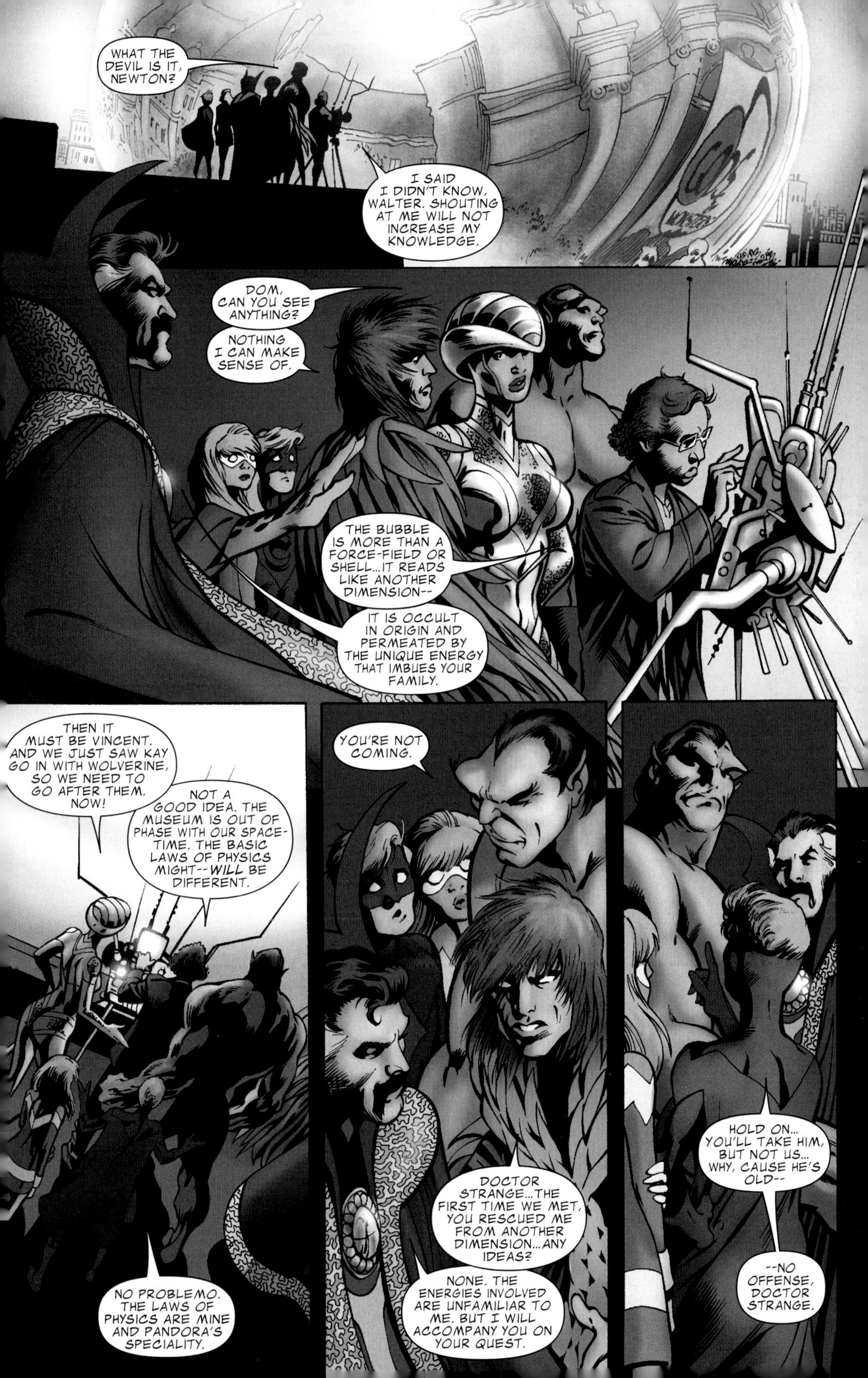
WHAT THE DEVIL IS IT, NEWTON?
I SAID I DIDN'T KNOW, WALTER. SHOUTING AT ME WILL NOT INCREASE MY KNOWLEDGE.
DOM, CAN YOU SEE ANYTHING?
NOTHING I CAN MAKE SENSE OF.
THE BUBBLE IS MORE THAN A FORCE-FIELD OR SHELL...IT READS LIKE ANOTHER DIMENSION--
IT IS OCCULT IN ORIGIN AND PERMEATED BY THE UNIQUE ENERGY THAT IMBUES YOUR FAMILY.
THEN IT MUST BE VINCENT. AND WE JUST SAW KAY GO IN WITH WOLVERINE, SO WE NEED TO GO AFTER THEM. NOW!
NOT A GOOD IDEA. THE MUSEUM IS OUT OF PHASE WITH OUR SPACE-TIME. THE BASIC LAWS OF PHYSICS MIGHT--WILL BE DIFFERENT.
NO PROBLEMO. THE LAWS OF PHYSICS ARE MINE AND PANDORA'S SPECIALITY.
YOU'RE NOT COMING.
DOCTOR STRANGE...THE FIRST TIME WE MET, YOU RESCUED ME FROM ANOTHER DIMENSION...ANY IDEAS?
NONE. THE ENERGIES INVOLVED ARE UNFAMILIAR TO ME. BUT I WILL ACCOMPANY YOU ON YOUR QUEST.
HOLD ON... YOU'LL TAKE HIM, BUT NOT US... WHY, CAUSE HE'S OLD--
--NO OFFENSE, DOCTOR STRANGE.

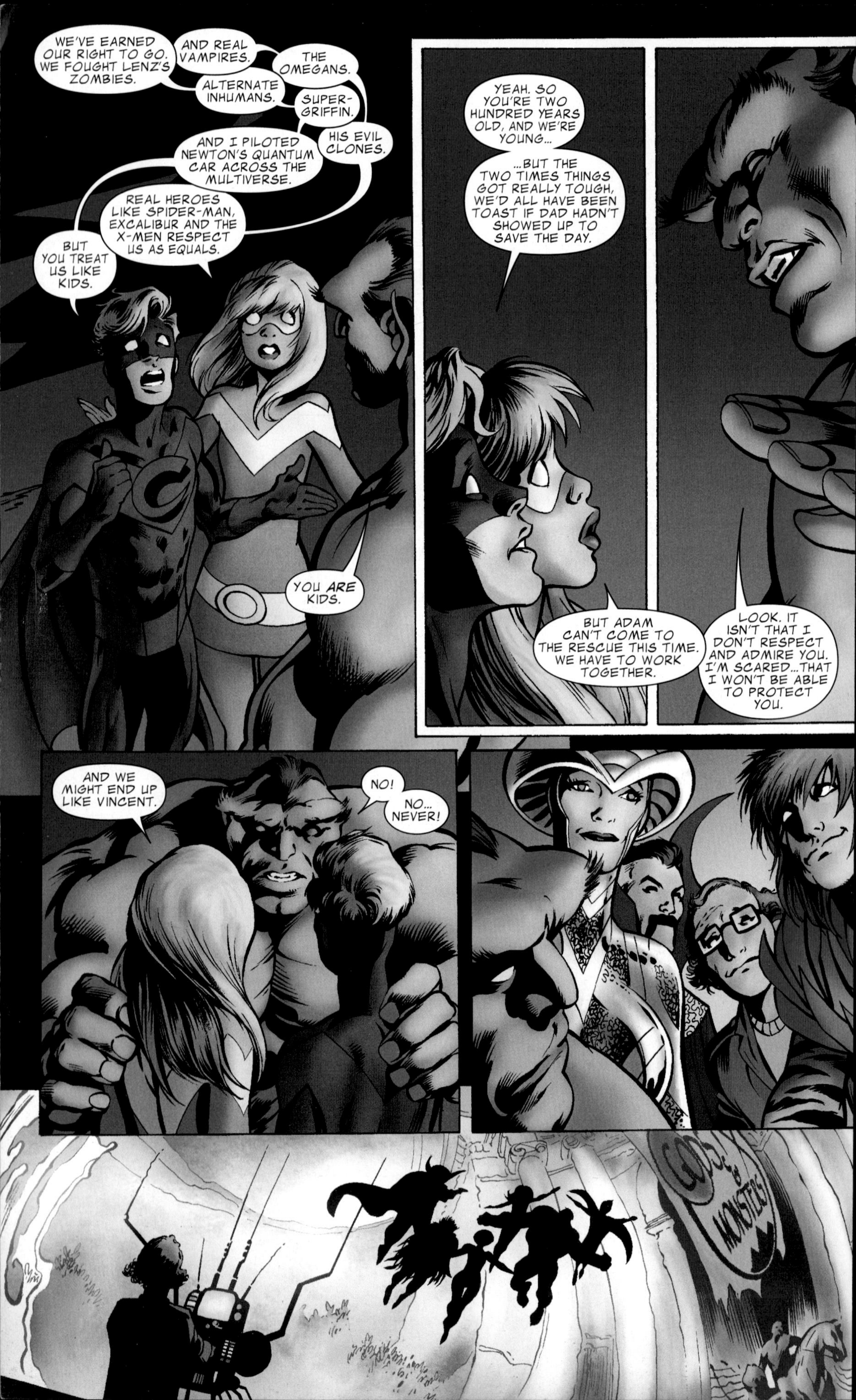
WE'VE EARNED OUR RIGHT TO GO. WE FOUGHT LENZ'S ZOMBIES.
AND REAL VAMPIRES.
THE OMEGANS.
ALTERNATE INHUMANS.
SUPER-GRIFFIN.
HIS EVIL CLONES.
AND I PILOTED NEWTON'S QUANTUM CAR ACROSS THE MULTIVERSE.
REAL HEROES LIKE SPIDER-MAN, EXCALIBUR AND THE X-MEN RESPECT US AS EQUALS.
BUT YOU TREAT US LIKE KIDS.
YOU ARE KIDS.
YEAH. SO YOU'RE TWO HUNDRED YEARS OLD, AND WE'RE YOUNG...
...BUT THE TWO TIMES THINGS GOT REALLY TOUGH, WE'D ALL HAVE BEEN TOAST IF DAD HADN'T SHOWED UP TO SAVE THE DAY.
BUT ADAM CAN'T COME TO THE RESCUE THIS TIME. WE HAVE TO WORK TOGETHER.
LOOK. IT ISN'T THAT I DON'T RESPECT AND ADMIRE YOU. I'M SCARED...THAT I WON'T BE ABLE TO PROTECT YOU.
AND WE MIGHT END UP LIKE VINCENT.
NO!
NO... NEVER!
MONSTERS

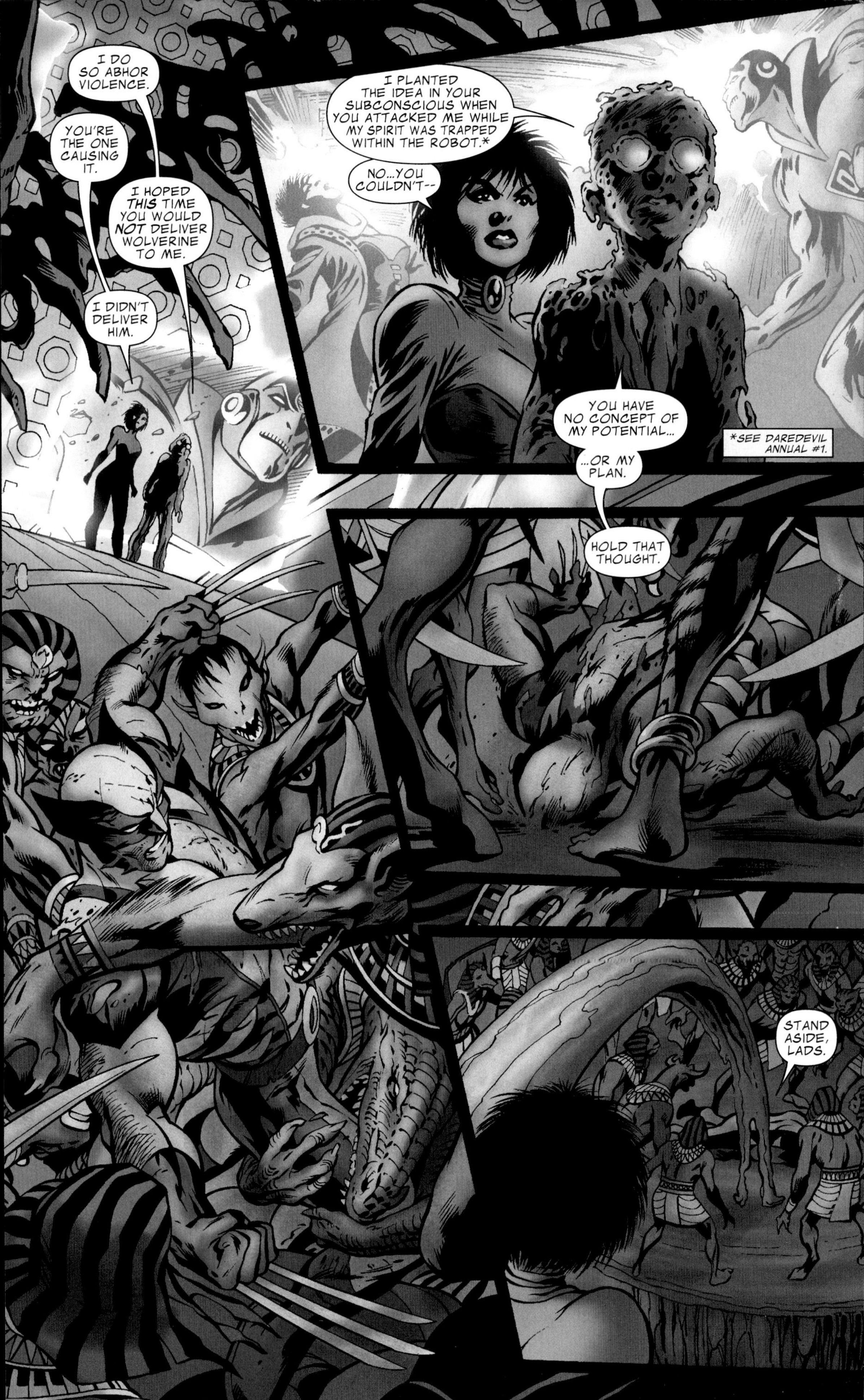
I DO SO ABHOR VIOLENCE.
YOU'RE THE ONE CAUSING IT.
I HOPED **THIS** TIME YOU WOULD **NOT** DELIVER WOLVERINE TO ME.
I DIDN'T DELIVER HIM.
I PLANTED THE IDEA IN YOUR SUBCONSCIOUS WHEN YOU ATTACKED ME WHILE MY SPIRIT WAS TRAPPED WITHIN THE ROBOT.*
NO...YOU COULDN'T--
YOU HAVE NO CONCEPT OF MY POTENTIAL...
...OR MY PLAN.
*SEE DAREDEVIL ANNUAL #1.
HOLD THAT THOUGHT.
STAND ASIDE, LADS.

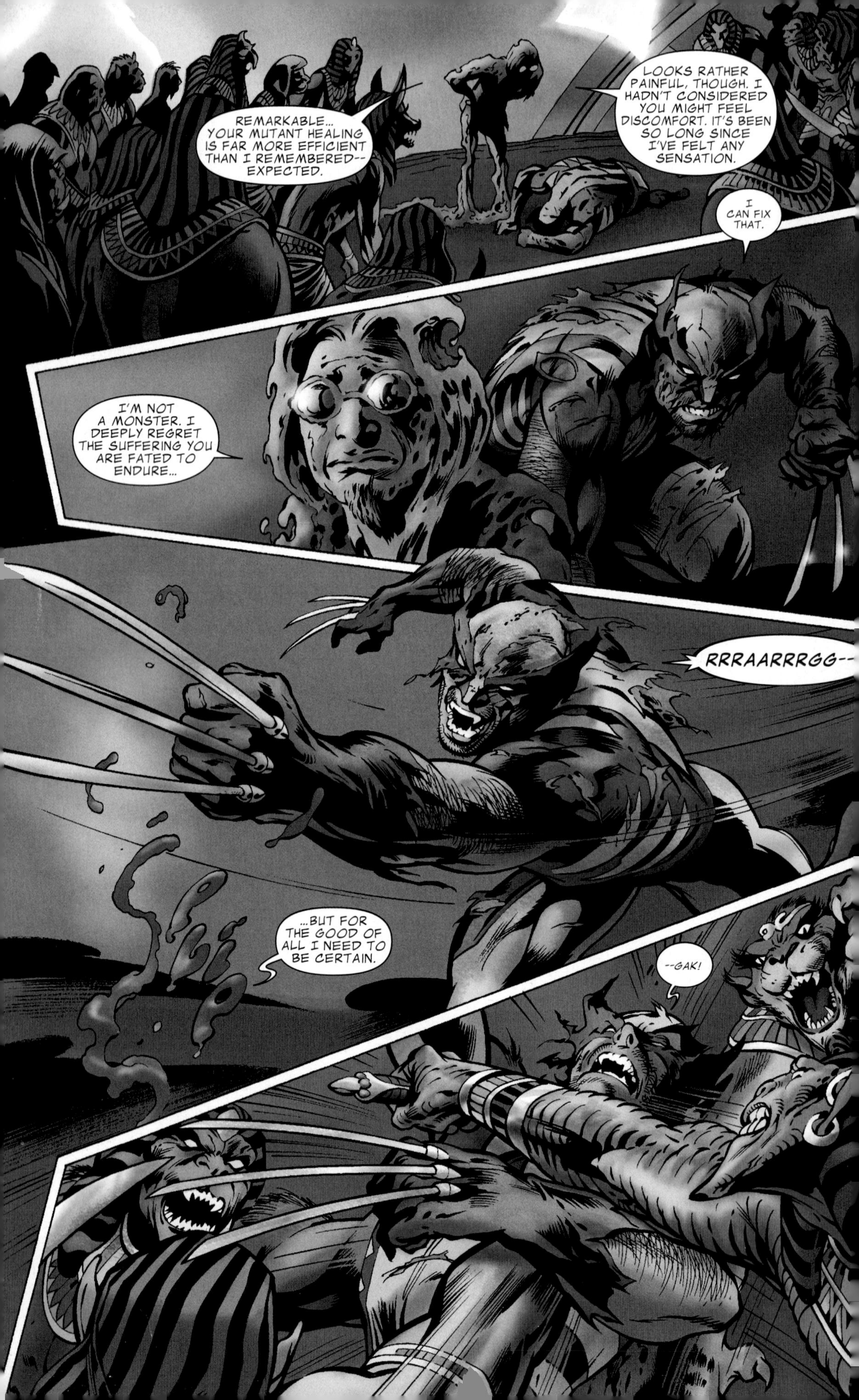
REMARKABLE... YOUR MUTANT HEALING IS FAR MORE EFFICIENT THAN I REMEMBERED-- EXPECTED.
LOOKS RATHER PAINFUL, THOUGH. I HADN'T CONSIDERED YOU MIGHT FEEL DISCOMFORT. IT'S BEEN SO LONG SINCE I'VE FELT ANY SENSATION.
I CAN FIX THAT.
I'M NOT A MONSTER. I DEEPLY REGRET THE SUFFERING YOU ARE FATED TO ENDURE...
RRRAARRRGG--
...BUT FOR THE GOOD OF ALL I NEED TO BE CERTAIN.
--GAK!

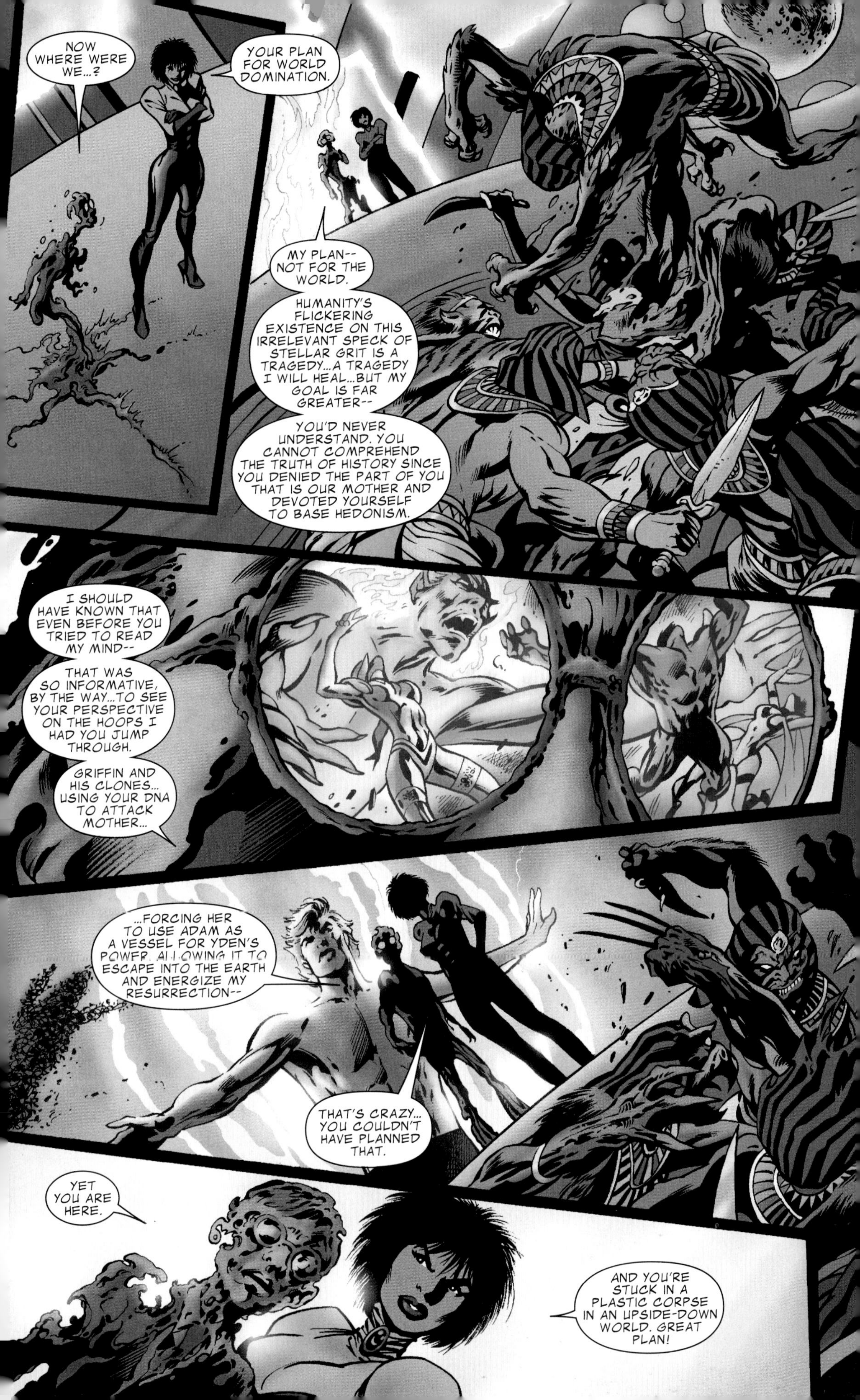
NOW WHERE WERE WE...?
YOUR PLAN FOR WORLD DOMINATION.
MY PLAN-- NOT FOR THE WORLD.
HUMANITY'S FLICKERING EXISTENCE ON THIS IRRELEVANT SPECK OF STELLAR GRIT IS A TRAGEDY...A TRAGEDY I WILL HEAL...BUT MY GOAL IS FAR GREATER--
YOU'D NEVER UNDERSTAND. YOU CANNOT COMPREHEND THE TRUTH OF HISTORY SINCE YOU DENIED THE PART OF YOU THAT IS OUR MOTHER AND DEVOTED YOURSELF TO BASE HEDONISM.
I SHOULD HAVE KNOWN THAT EVEN BEFORE YOU TRIED TO READ MY MIND--
THAT WAS SO INFORMATIVE, BY THE WAY...TO SEE YOUR PERSPECTIVE ON THE HOOPS I HAD YOU JUMP THROUGH.
GRIFFIN AND HIS CLONES... USING YOUR DNA TO ATTACK MOTHER...
...FORCING HER TO USE ADAM AS A VESSEL FOR YDEN'S POWER, ALLOWING IT TO ESCAPE INTO THE EARTH AND ENERGIZE MY RESURRECTION--
THAT'S CRAZY... YOU COULDN'T HAVE PLANNED THAT.
YET YOU ARE HERE.
AND YOU'RE STUCK IN A PLASTIC CORPSE IN AN UPSIDE-DOWN WORLD. GREAT PLAN!

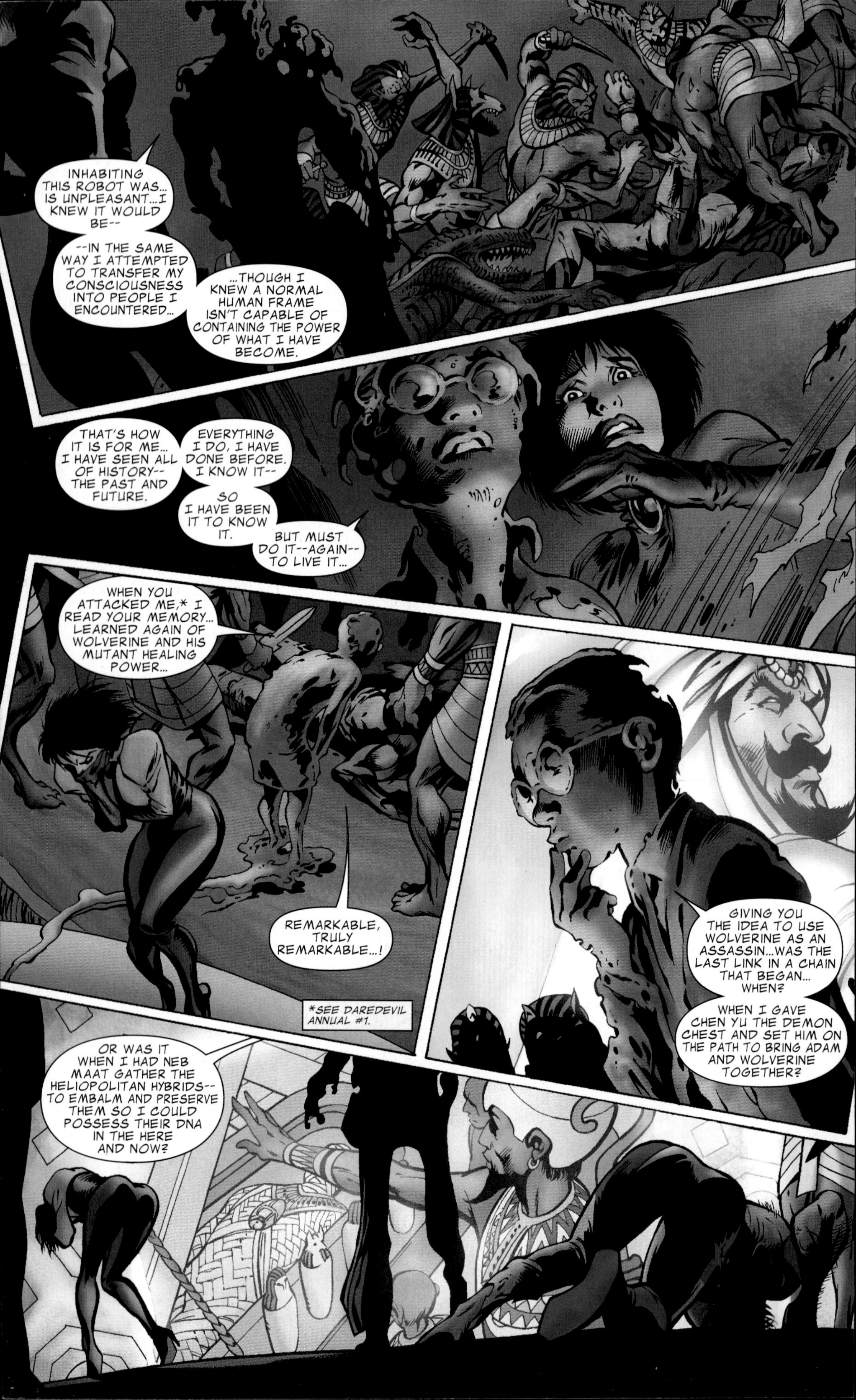
INHABITING THIS ROBOT WAS... IS UNPLEASANT...I KNEW IT WOULD BE--
--IN THE SAME WAY I ATTEMPTED TO TRANSFER MY CONSCIOUSNESS INTO PEOPLE I ENCOUNTERED...
...THOUGH I KNEW A NORMAL HUMAN FRAME ISN'T CAPABLE OF CONTAINING THE POWER OF WHAT I HAVE BECOME.
THAT'S HOW IT IS FOR ME... I HAVE SEEN ALL OF HISTORY-- THE PAST AND FUTURE.
EVERYTHING I DO, I HAVE DONE BEFORE. I KNOW IT--
SO I HAVE BEEN IT TO KNOW IT.
BUT MUST DO IT--AGAIN-- TO LIVE IT...
WHEN YOU ATTACKED ME,* I READ YOUR MEMORY... LEARNED AGAIN OF WOLVERINE AND HIS MUTANT HEALING POWER...
REMARKABLE, TRULY REMARKABLE...!
*SEE DAREDEVIL ANNUAL #1.
GIVING YOU THE IDEA TO USE WOLVERINE AS AN ASSASSIN...WAS THE LAST LINK IN A CHAIN THAT BEGAN... WHEN?
WHEN I GAVE CHEN YU THE DEMON CHEST AND SET HIM ON THE PATH TO BRING ADAM AND WOLVERINE TOGETHER?
OR WAS IT WHEN I HAD NEB MAAT GATHER THE HELIOPOLITAN HYBRIDS-- TO EMBALM AND PRESERVE THEM SO I COULD POSSESS THEIR DNA IN THE HERE AND NOW?

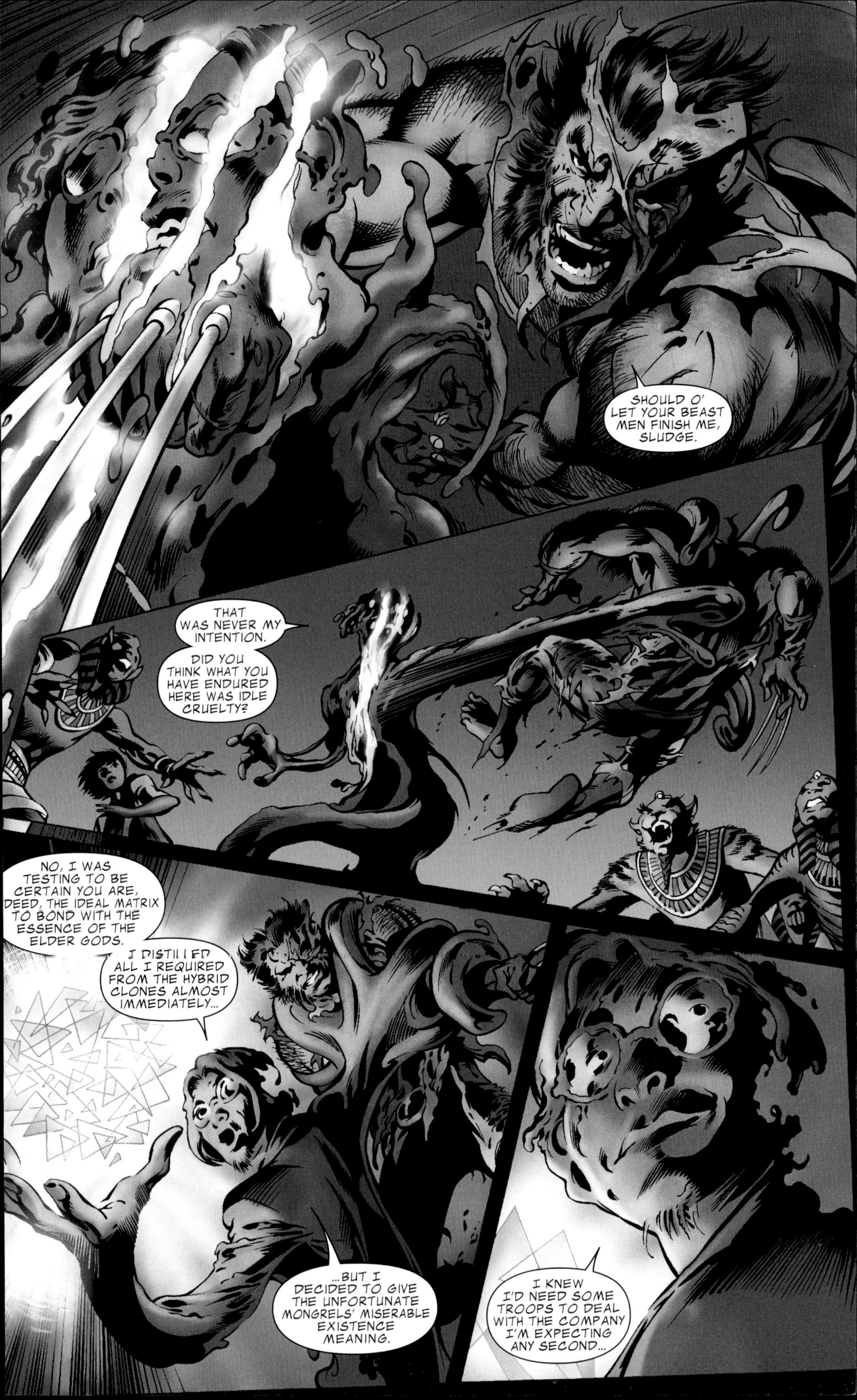

SHOULD O' LET YOUR BEAST MEN FINISH ME, SLUDGE.
THAT WAS NEVER MY INTENTION.
DID YOU THINK WHAT YOU HAVE ENDURED HERE WAS IDLE CRUELTY?
NO, I WAS TESTING TO BE CERTAIN YOU ARE, DEED, THE IDEAL MATRIX TO BOND WITH THE ESSENCE OF THE ELDER GODS.
I DISTILLED ALL I REQUIRED FROM THE HYBRID CLONES ALMOST IMMEDIATELY...
...BUT I DECIDED TO GIVE THE UNFORTUNATE MONGRELS' MISERABLE EXISTENCE MEANING.
I KNEW I'D NEED SOME TROOPS TO DEAL WITH THE COMPANY I'M EXPECTING ANY SECOND...

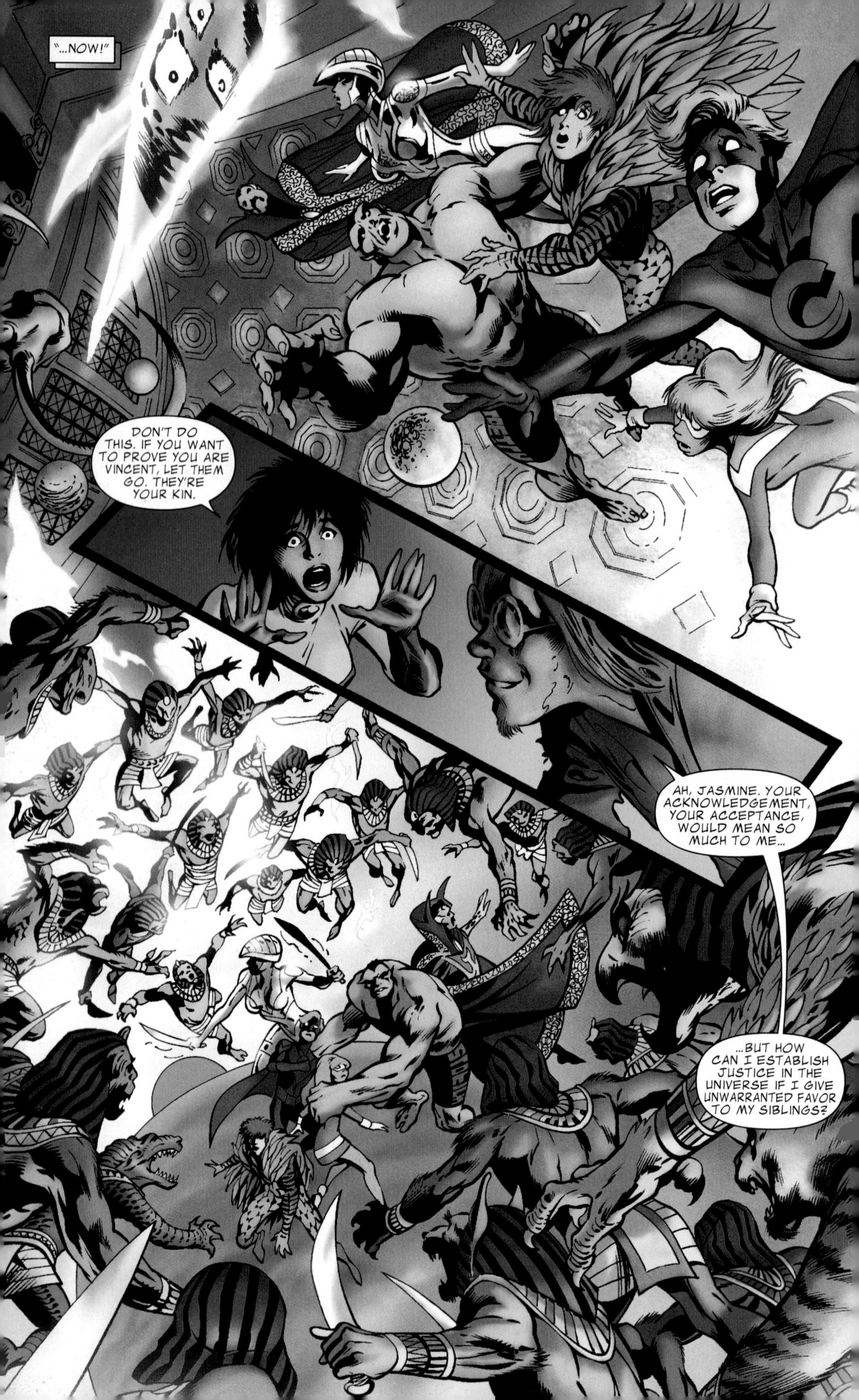
"...NOW!"
DON'T DO THIS. IF YOU WANT TO PROVE YOU ARE VINCENT, LET THEM GO. THEY'RE YOUR KIN.
AH, JASMINE. YOUR ACKNOWLEDGEMENT, YOUR ACCEPTANCE, WOULD MEAN SO MUCH TO ME...
...BUT HOW CAN I ESTABLISH JUSTICE IN THE UNIVERSE IF I GIVE UNWARRANTED FAVOR TO MY SIBLINGS?

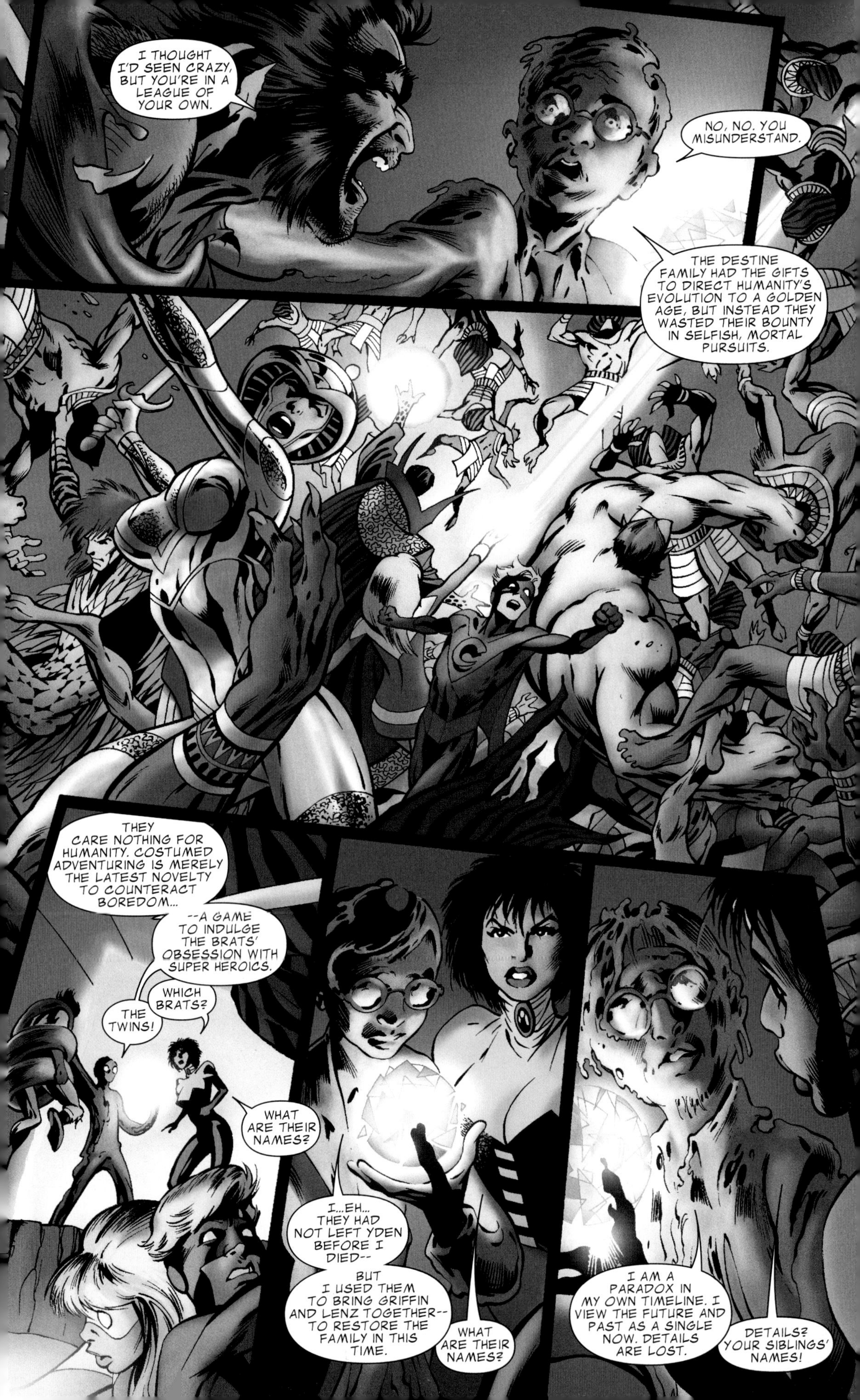
I THOUGHT I'D SEEN CRAZY, BUT YOU'RE IN A LEAGUE OF YOUR OWN.
NO, NO. YOU MISUNDERSTAND.
THE DESTINE FAMILY HAD THE GIFTS TO DIRECT HUMANITY'S EVOLUTION TO A GOLDEN AGE, BUT INSTEAD THEY WASTED THEIR BOUNTY IN SELFISH, MORTAL PURSUITS.
THEY CARE NOTHING FOR HUMANITY. COSTUMED ADVENTURING IS MERELY THE LATEST NOVELTY TO COUNTERACT BOREDOM...
--A GAME TO INDULGE THE BRATS' OBSESSION WITH SUPER HEROICS.
WHICH BRATS?
THE TWINS!
WHAT ARE THEIR NAMES?
I...EH... THEY HAD NOT LEFT YDEN BEFORE I DIED--
BUT I USED THEM TO BRING GRIFFIN AND LENZ TOGETHER-- TO RESTORE THE FAMILY IN THIS TIME.
WHAT ARE THEIR NAMES?
I AM A PARADOX IN MY OWN TIMELINE. I VIEW THE FUTURE AND PAST AS A SINGLE NOW. DETAILS ARE LOST.
DETAILS? YOUR SIBLINGS' NAMES!

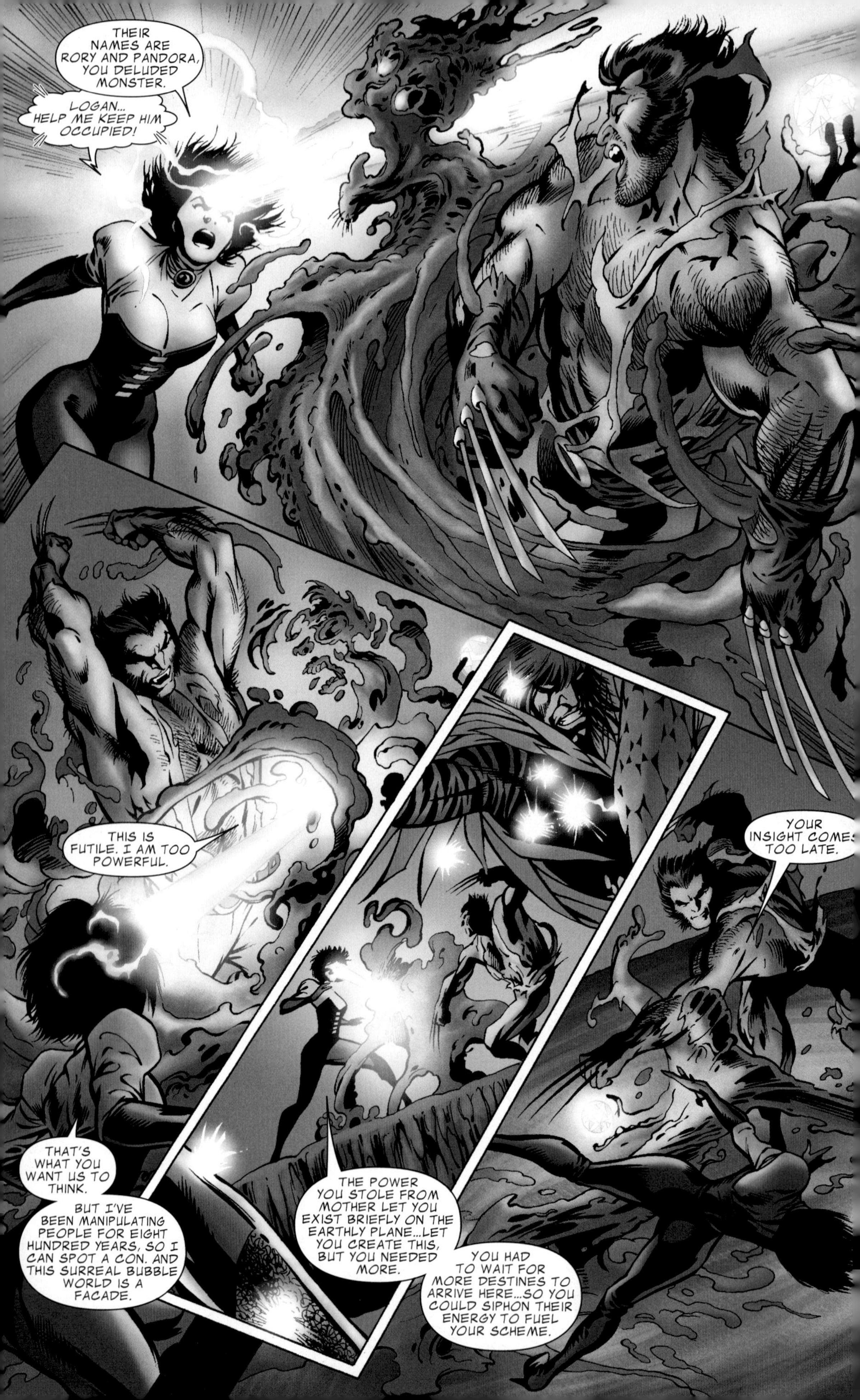
THEIR NAMES ARE RORY AND PANDORA, YOU DELUDED MONSTER.
LOGAN... HELP ME KEEP HIM OCCUPIED!
THIS IS FUTILE. I AM TOO POWERFUL.
YOUR INSIGHT COMES TOO LATE.
THAT'S WHAT YOU WANT US TO THINK.
BUT I'VE BEEN MANIPULATING PEOPLE FOR EIGHT HUNDRED YEARS, SO I CAN SPOT A CON. AND THIS SURREAL BUBBLE WORLD IS A FACADE.
THE POWER YOU STOLE FROM MOTHER LET YOU EXIST BRIEFLY ON THE EARTHLY PLANE...LET YOU CREATE THIS, BUT YOU NEEDED MORE.
YOU HAD TO WAIT FOR MORE DESTINES TO ARRIVE HERE...SO YOU COULD SIPHON THEIR ENERGY TO FUEL YOUR SCHEME.

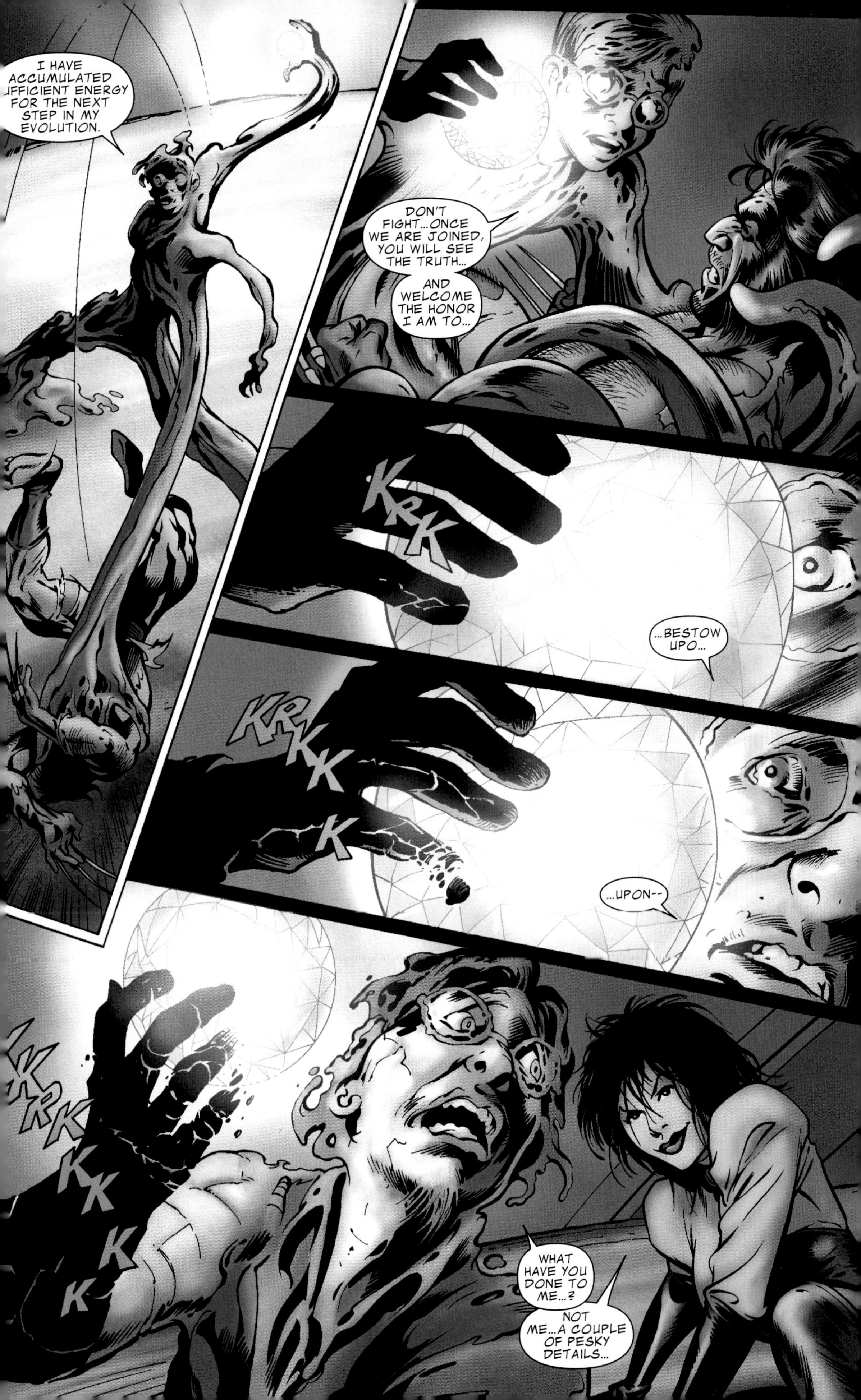
I HAVE ACCUMULATED UFFICIENT ENERGY FOR THE NEXT STEP IN MY EVOLUTION.
DON'T FIGHT...ONCE WE ARE JOINED, YOU WILL SEE THE TRUTH...
AND WELCOME THE HONOR I AM TO...
KRK
...BESTOW UPO...
KRKKK
...UPON--
KKKKK
WHAT HAVE YOU DONE TO ME...?
NOT ME...A COUPLE OF PESKY DETAILS...

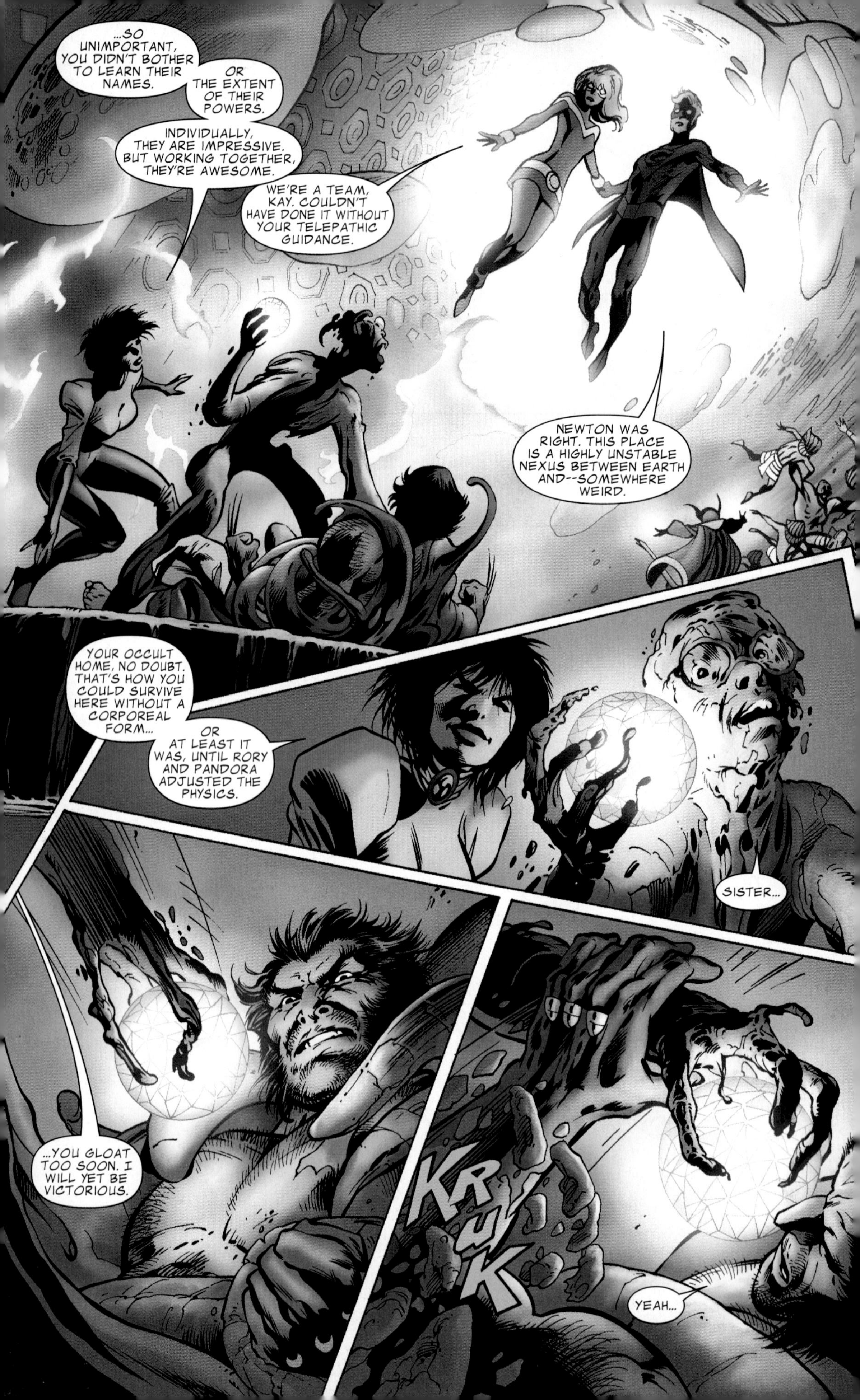
...SO UNIMPORTANT, YOU DIDN'T BOTHER TO LEARN THEIR NAMES.
OR THE EXTENT OF THEIR POWERS.
INDIVIDUALLY, THEY ARE IMPRESSIVE. BUT WORKING TOGETHER, THEY'RE AWESOME.
WE'RE A TEAM, KAY. COULDN'T HAVE DONE IT WITHOUT YOUR TELEPATHIC GUIDANCE.
NEWTON WAS RIGHT. THIS PLACE IS A HIGHLY UNSTABLE NEXUS BETWEEN EARTH AND--SOMEWHERE WEIRD.
YOUR OCCULT HOME, NO DOUBT. THAT'S HOW YOU COULD SURVIVE HERE WITHOUT A CORPOREAL FORM...
OR AT LEAST IT WAS, UNTIL RORY AND PANDORA ADJUSTED THE PHYSICS.
SISTER...
...YOU GLOAT TOO SOON. I WILL YET BE VICTORIOUS.
KRUK
YEAH...

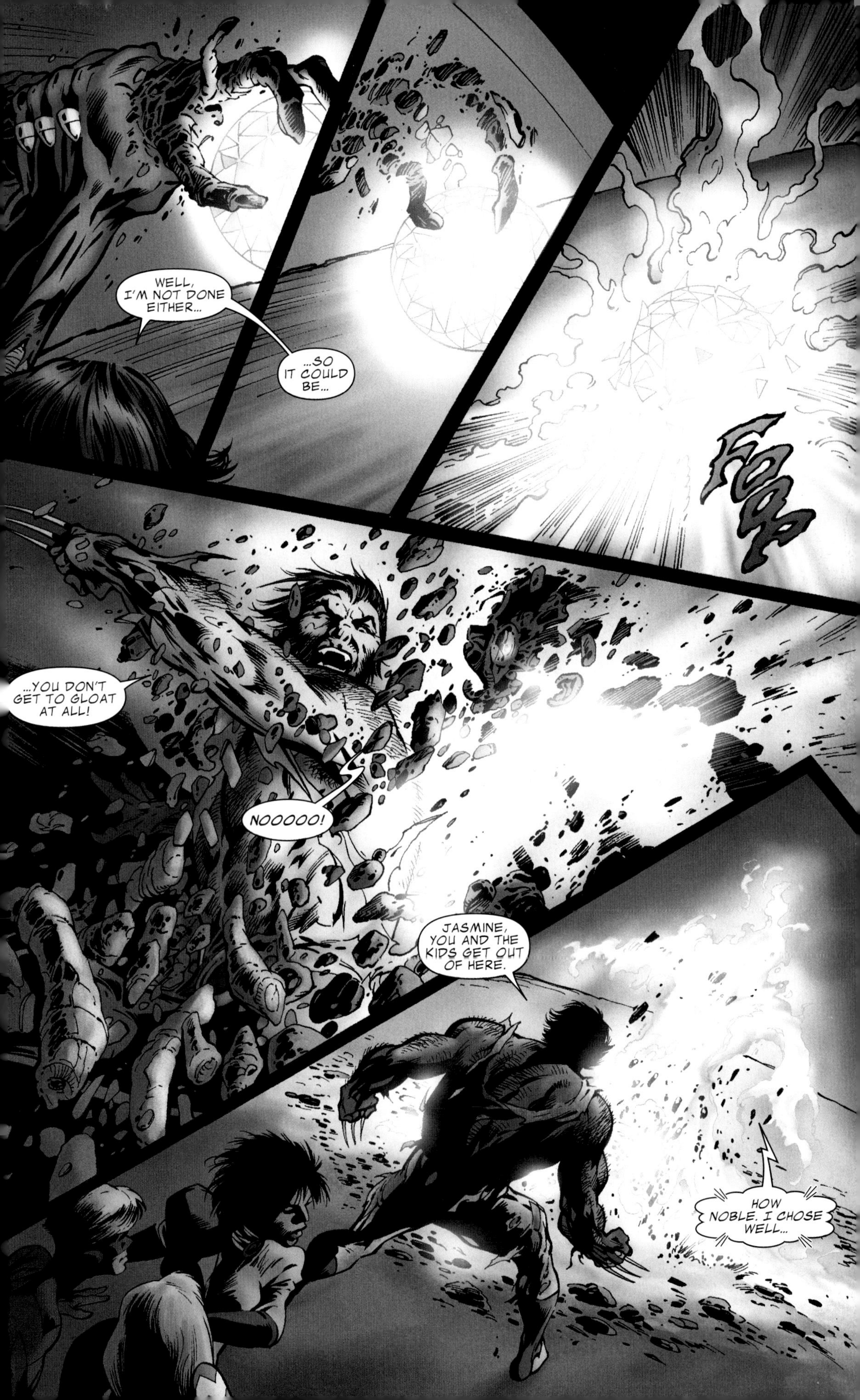
WELL, I'M NOT DONE EITHER...
...SO IT COULD BE...
FOOM
...YOU DON'T GET TO GLOAT AT ALL!
NOOOOO!
JASMINE, YOU AND THE KIDS GET OUT OF HERE.
HOW NOBLE. I CHOSE WELL...

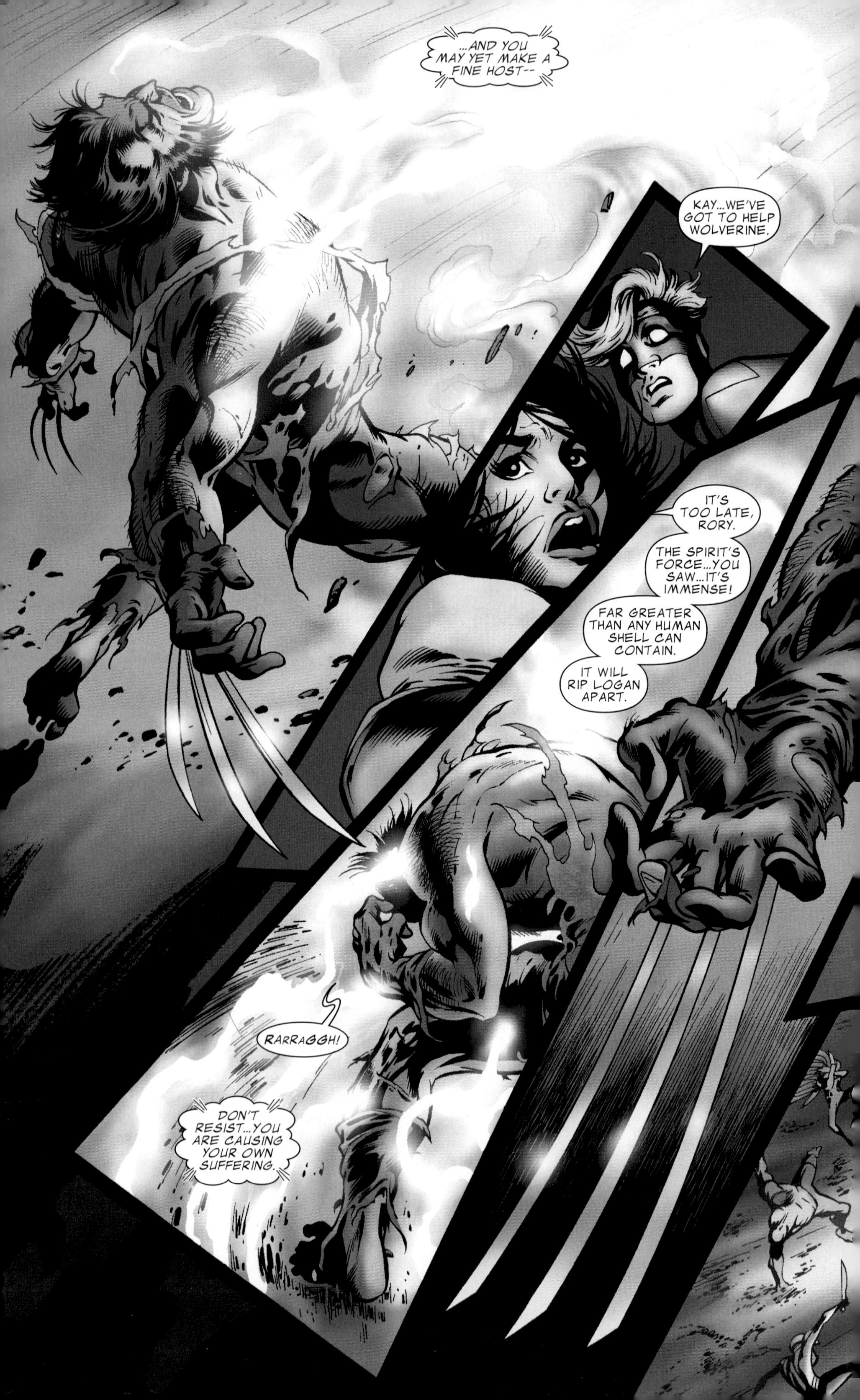
...AND YOU MAY YET MAKE A FINE HOST--
KAY...WE'VE GOT TO HELP WOLVERINE.
IT'S TOO LATE, RORY.
THE SPIRIT'S FORCE...YOU SAW...IT'S IMMENSE!
FAR GREATER THAN ANY HUMAN SHELL CAN CONTAIN.
IT WILL RIP LOGAN APART.
RARRAGGH!
DON'T RESIST...YOU ARE CAUSING YOUR OWN SUFFERING.

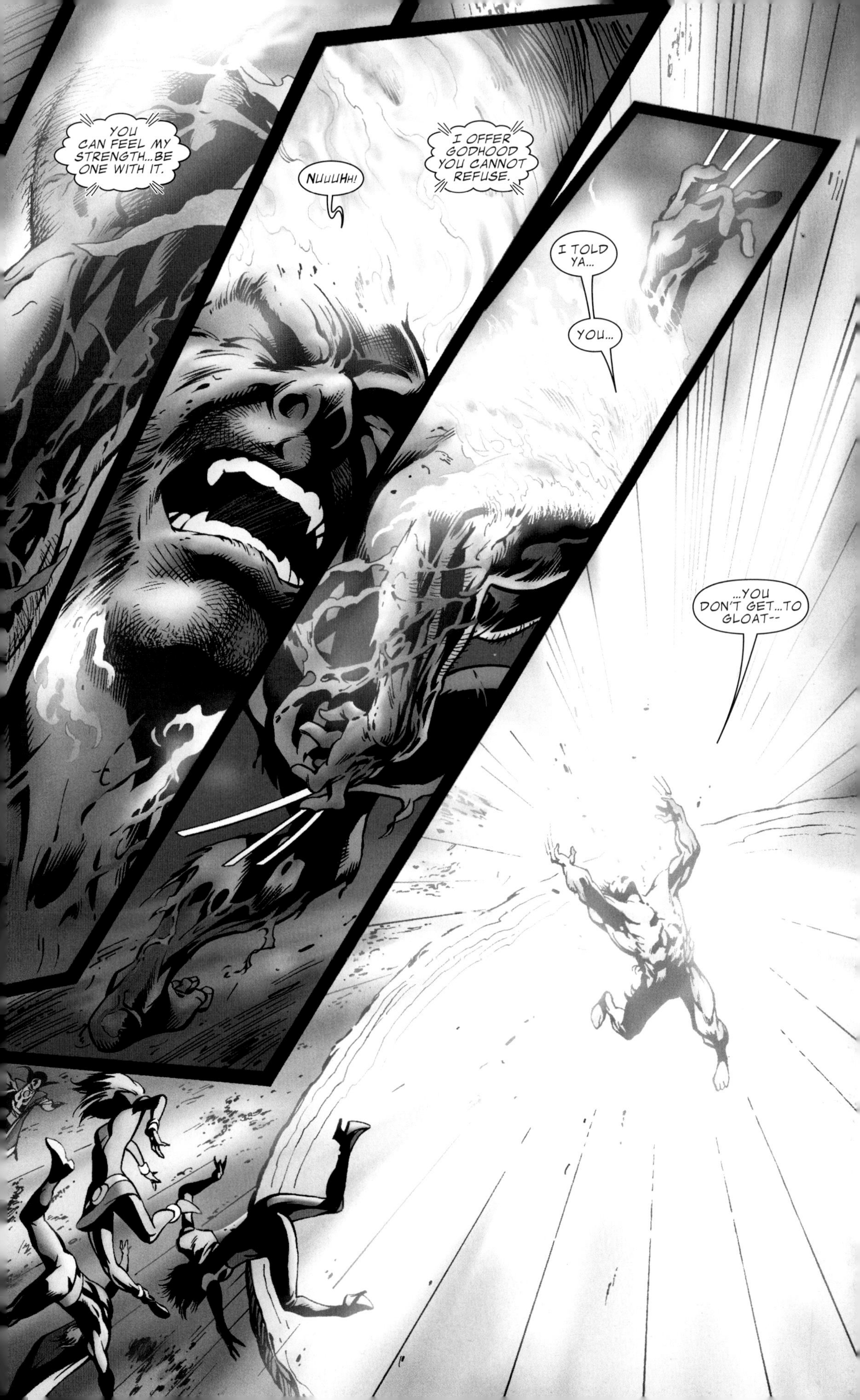
YOU CAN FEEL MY STRENGTH...BE ONE WITH IT.
NUUUHH!
I OFFER GODHOOD YOU CANNOT REFUSE.
I TOLD YA...
YOU...
...YOU DON'T GET...TO GLOAT--

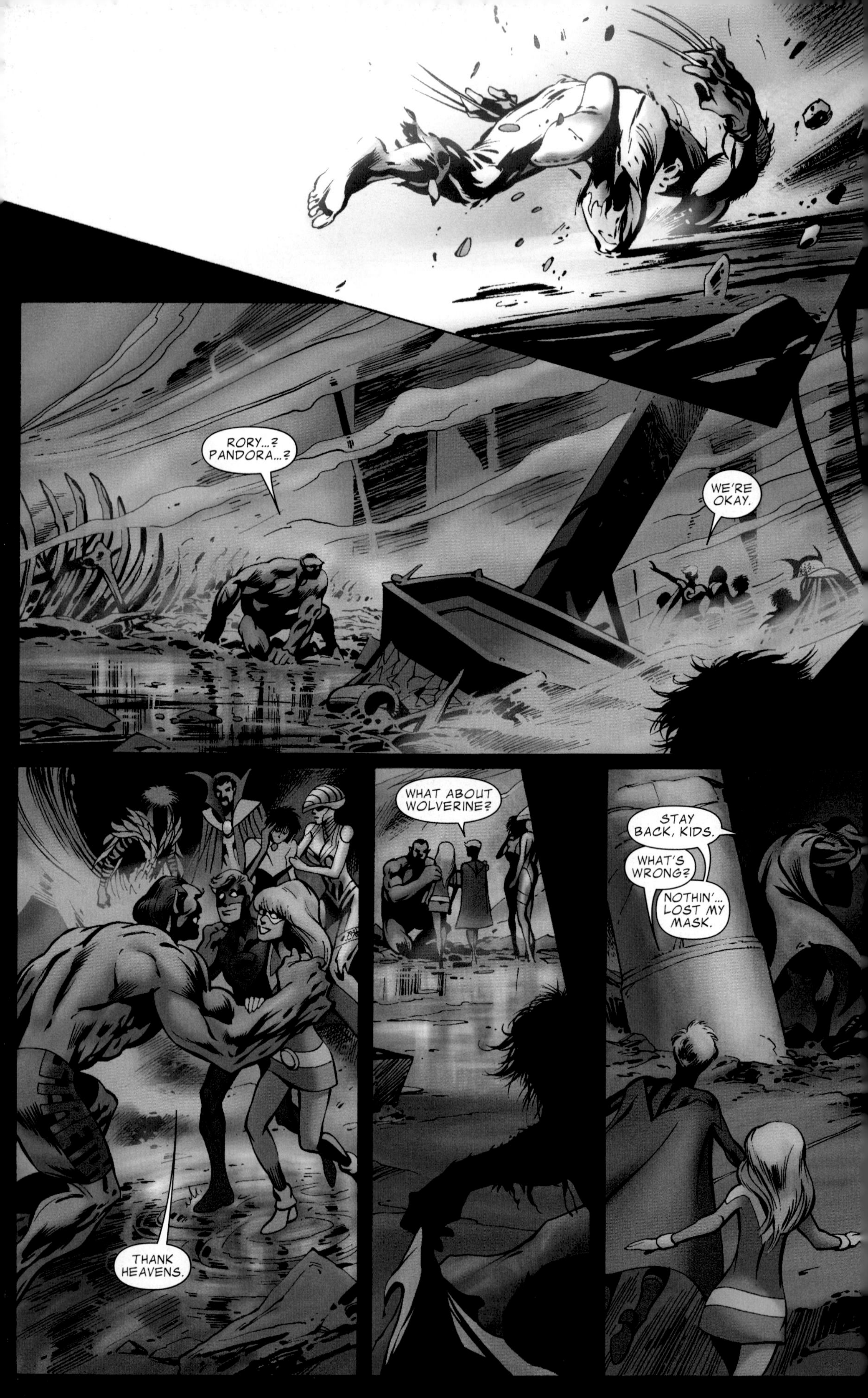
RORY...? PANDORA...?
WE'RE OKAY.
THANK HEAVENS.
WHAT ABOUT WOLVERINE?
STAY BACK, KIDS.
WHAT'S WRONG?
NOTHIN'... LOST MY MASK.

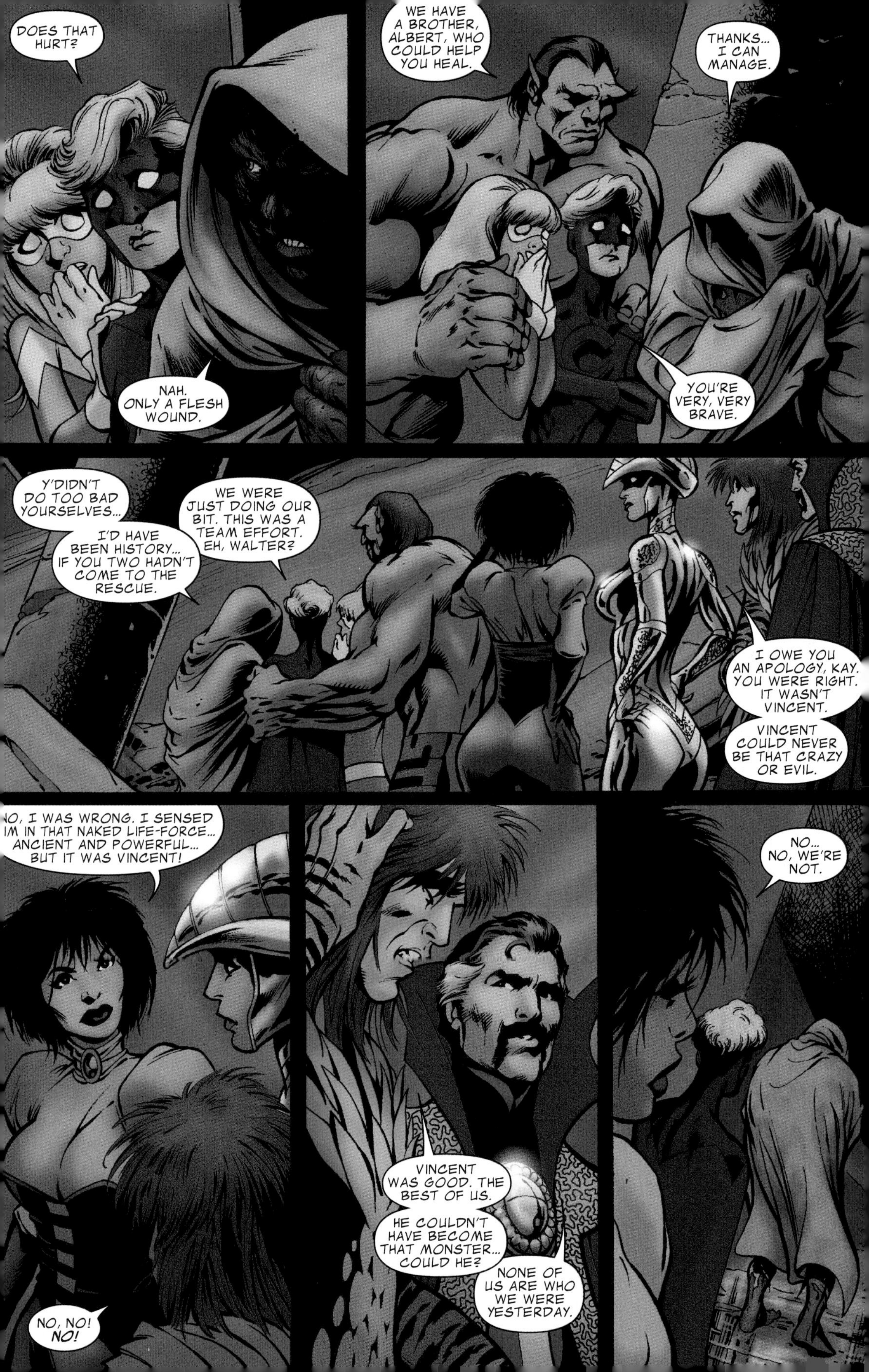
DOES THAT HURT?
NAH. ONLY A FLESH WOUND.
WE HAVE A BROTHER, ALBERT, WHO COULD HELP YOU HEAL.
THANKS... I CAN MANAGE.
YOU'RE VERY, VERY BRAVE.
Y'DIDN'T DO TOO BAD YOURSELVES...
I'D HAVE BEEN HISTORY... IF YOU TWO HADN'T COME TO THE RESCUE.
WE WERE JUST DOING OUR BIT. THIS WAS A TEAM EFFORT. EH, WALTER?
I OWE YOU AN APOLOGY, KAY. YOU WERE RIGHT. IT WASN'T VINCENT.
VINCENT COULD NEVER BE THAT CRAZY OR EVIL.
NO, I WAS WRONG. I SENSED IM IN THAT NAKED LIFE-FORCE... ANCIENT AND POWERFUL... BUT IT WAS VINCENT!
NO, NO! NO!
VINCENT WAS GOOD. THE BEST OF US.
HE COULDN'T HAVE BECOME THAT MONSTER... COULD HE?
NONE OF US ARE WHO WE WERE YESTERDAY.
NO... NO, WE'RE NOT.

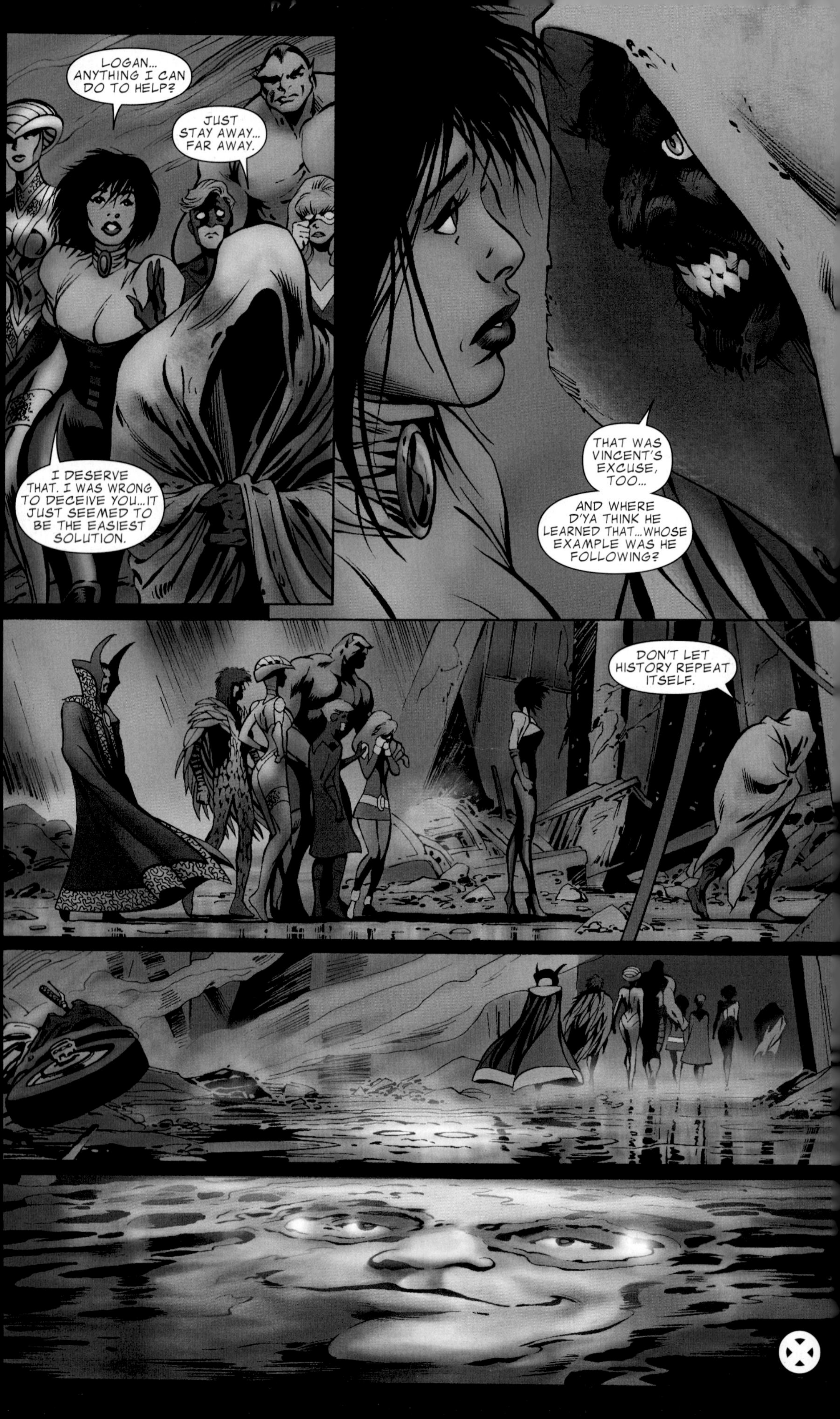
LOGAN... ANYTHING I CAN DO TO HELP?
JUST STAY AWAY... FAR AWAY.
I DESERVE THAT. I WAS WRONG TO DECEIVE YOU...IT JUST SEEMED TO BE THE EASIEST SOLUTION.
THAT WAS VINCENT'S EXCUSE, TOO...
AND WHERE D'YA THINK HE LEARNED THAT...WHOSE EXAMPLE WAS HE FOLLOWING?
DON'T LET HISTORY REPEAT ITSELF.

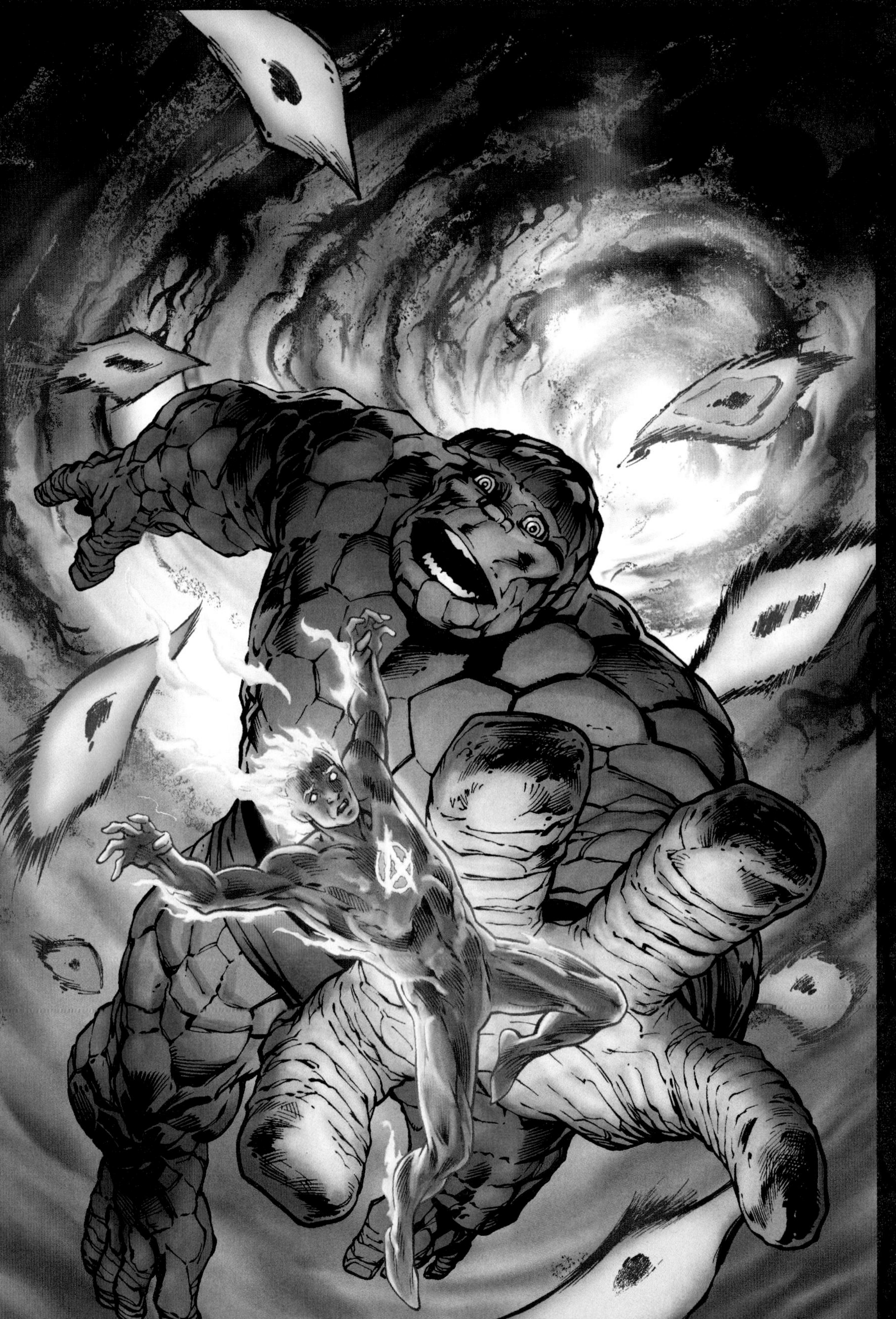

FANTASTIC FOUR ANNUAL #33 COVER

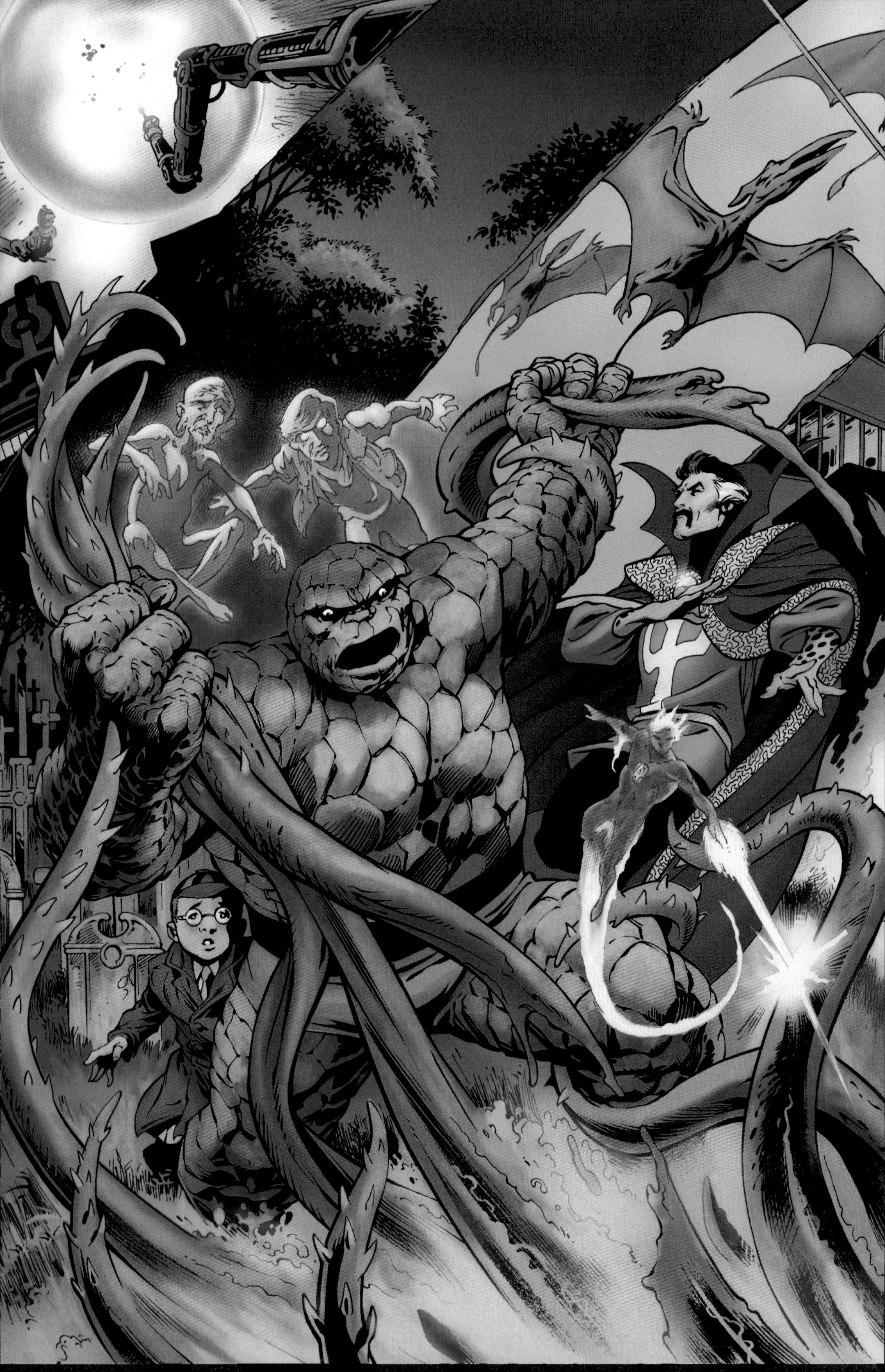

FANTASTIC FOUR ANNUAL #33 VARIANT COVER

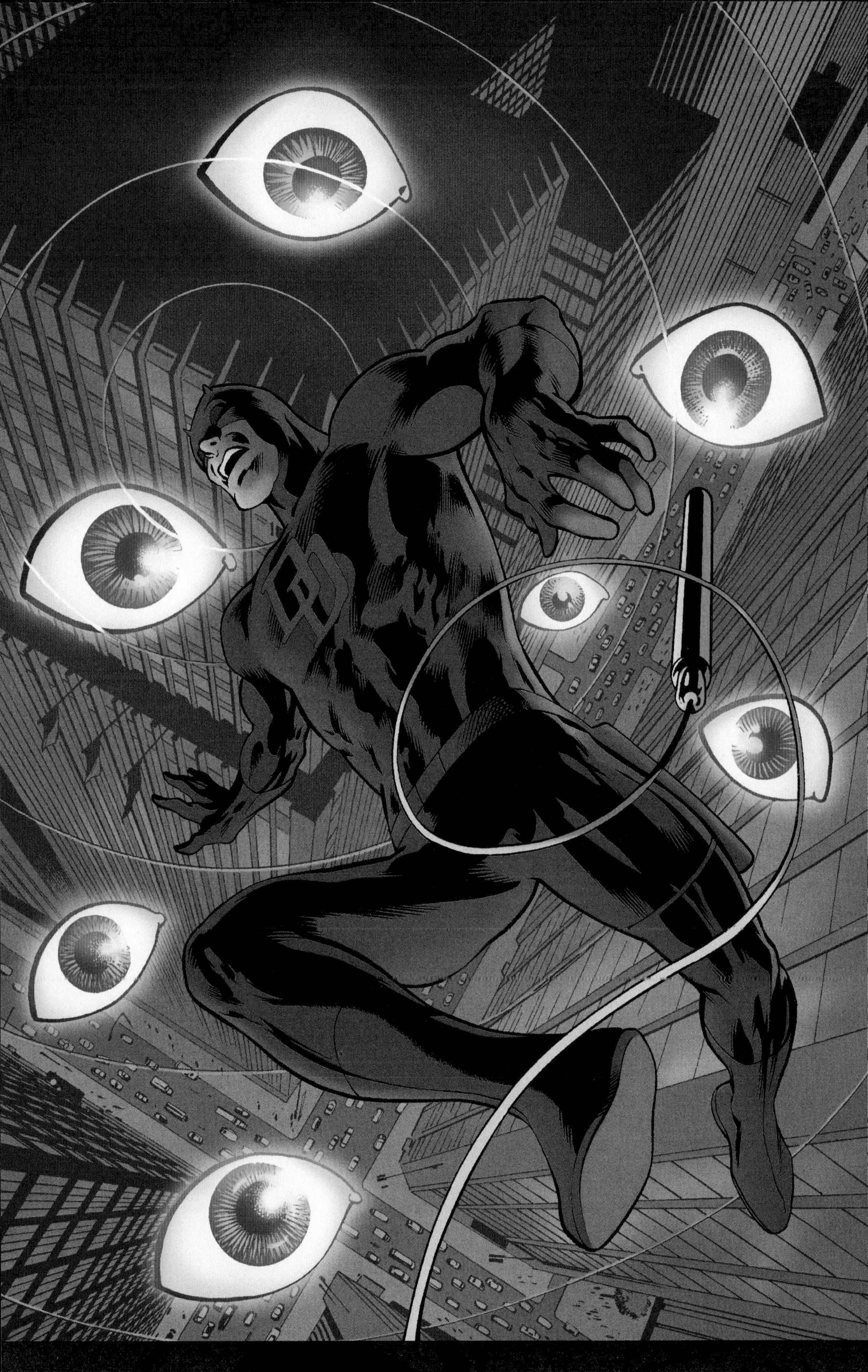

DAREDEVIL ANNUAL #1 COVER

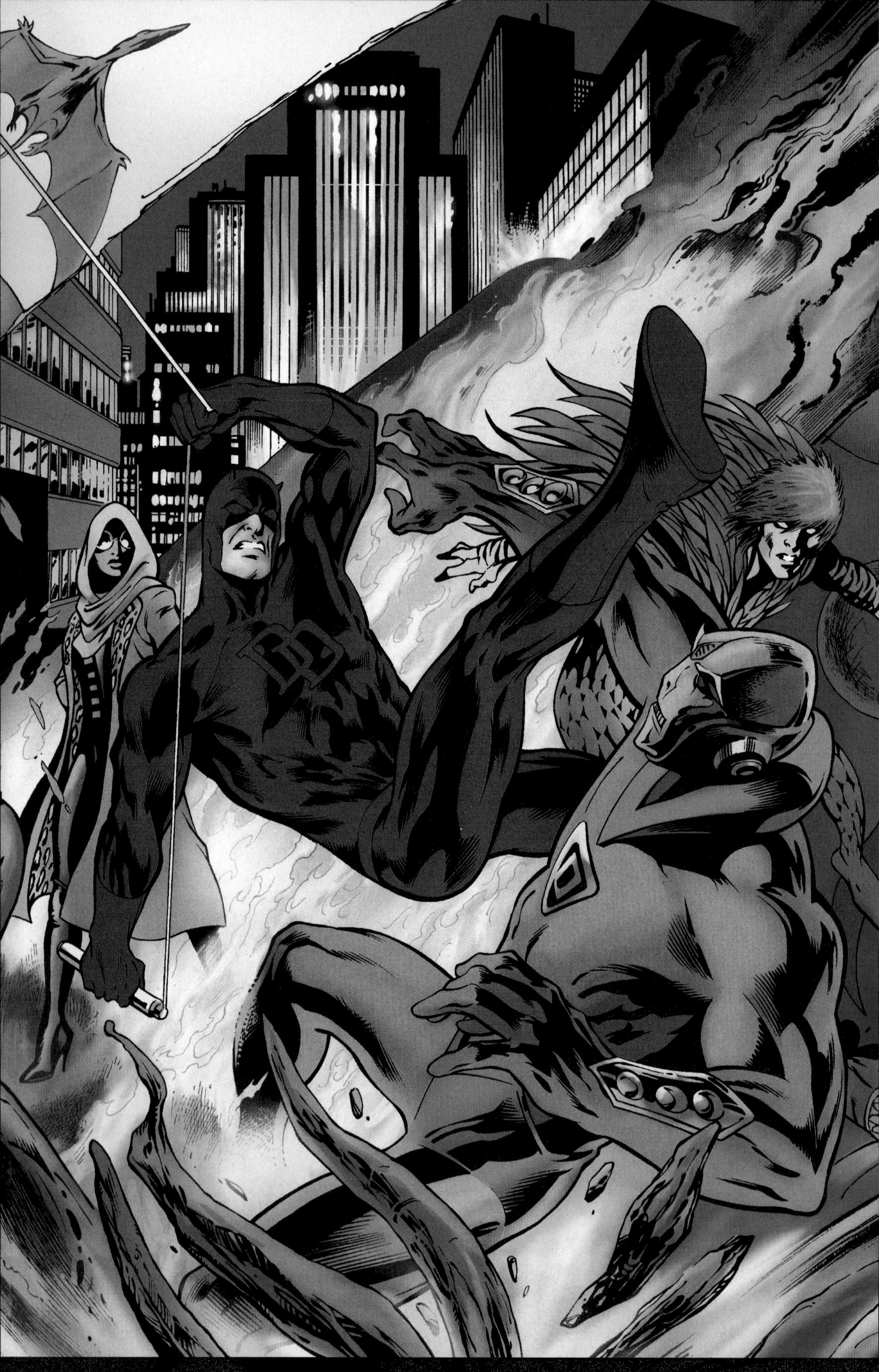

DAREDEVIL ANNUAL #1 VARIANT COVER

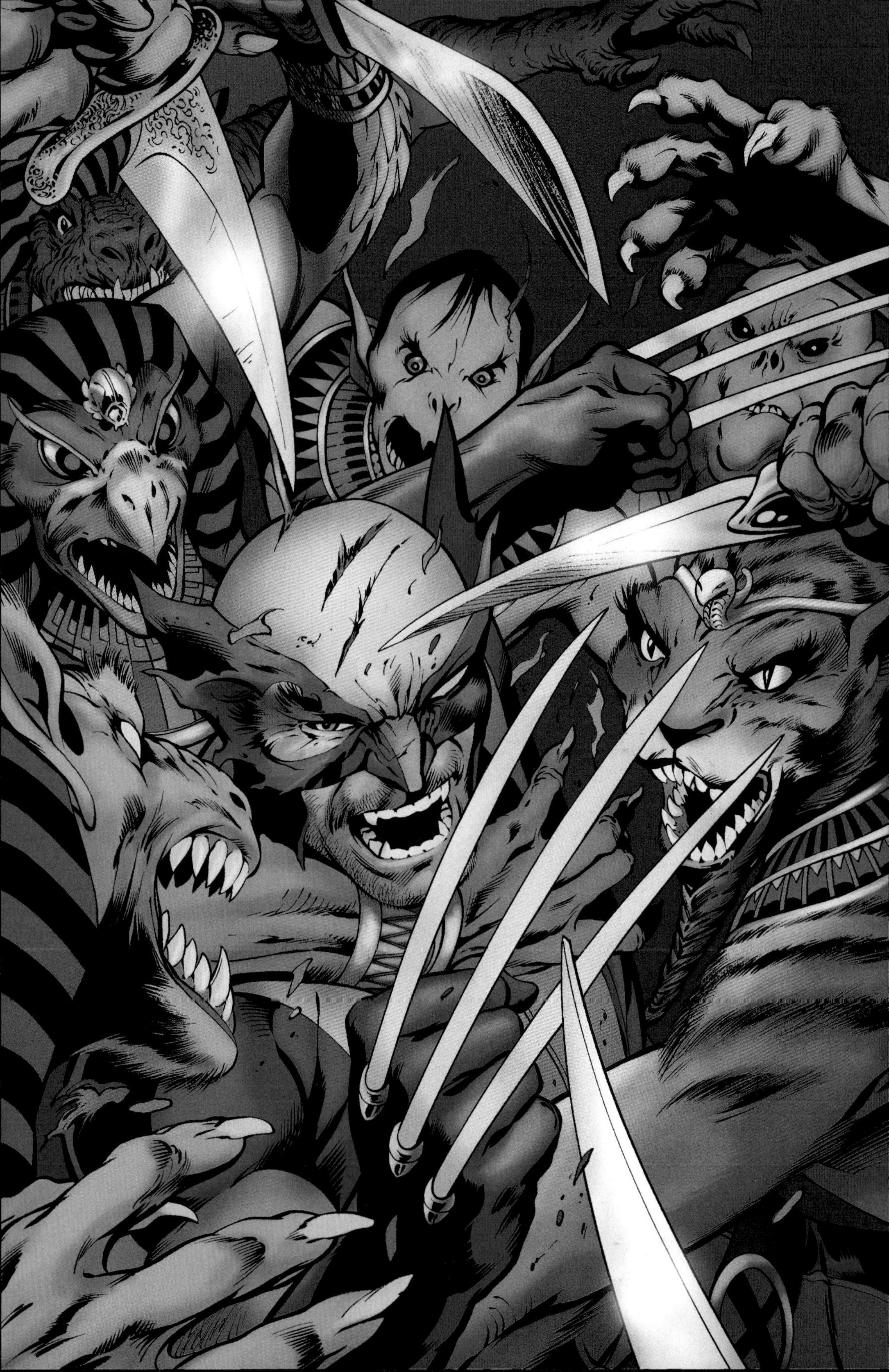

WOLVERINE ANNUAL #1 COVER

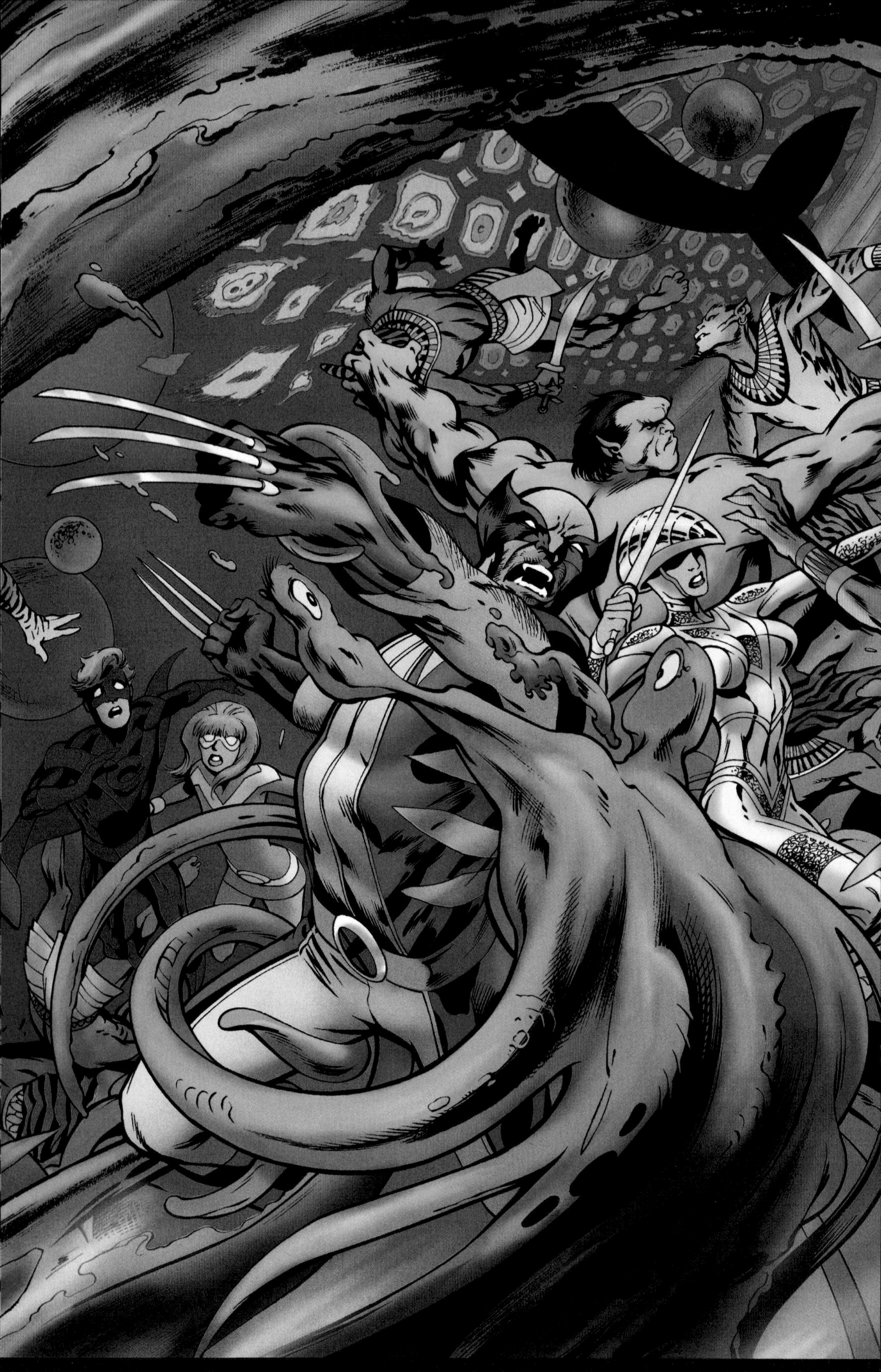

WOLVERINE ANNUAL #1 VARIANT COVER

# EPILOGUE

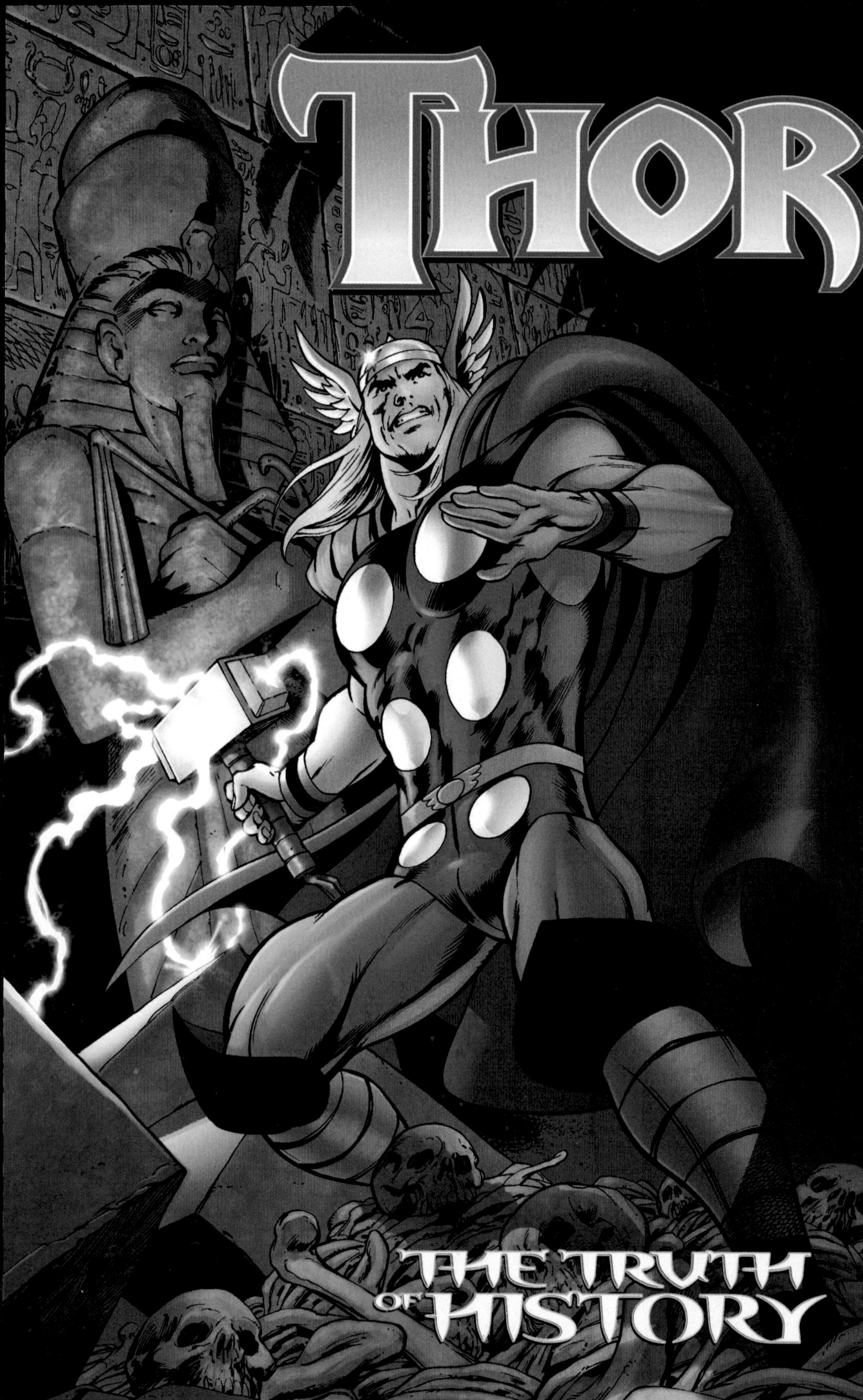
THOR
THE TRUTH OF HISTORY

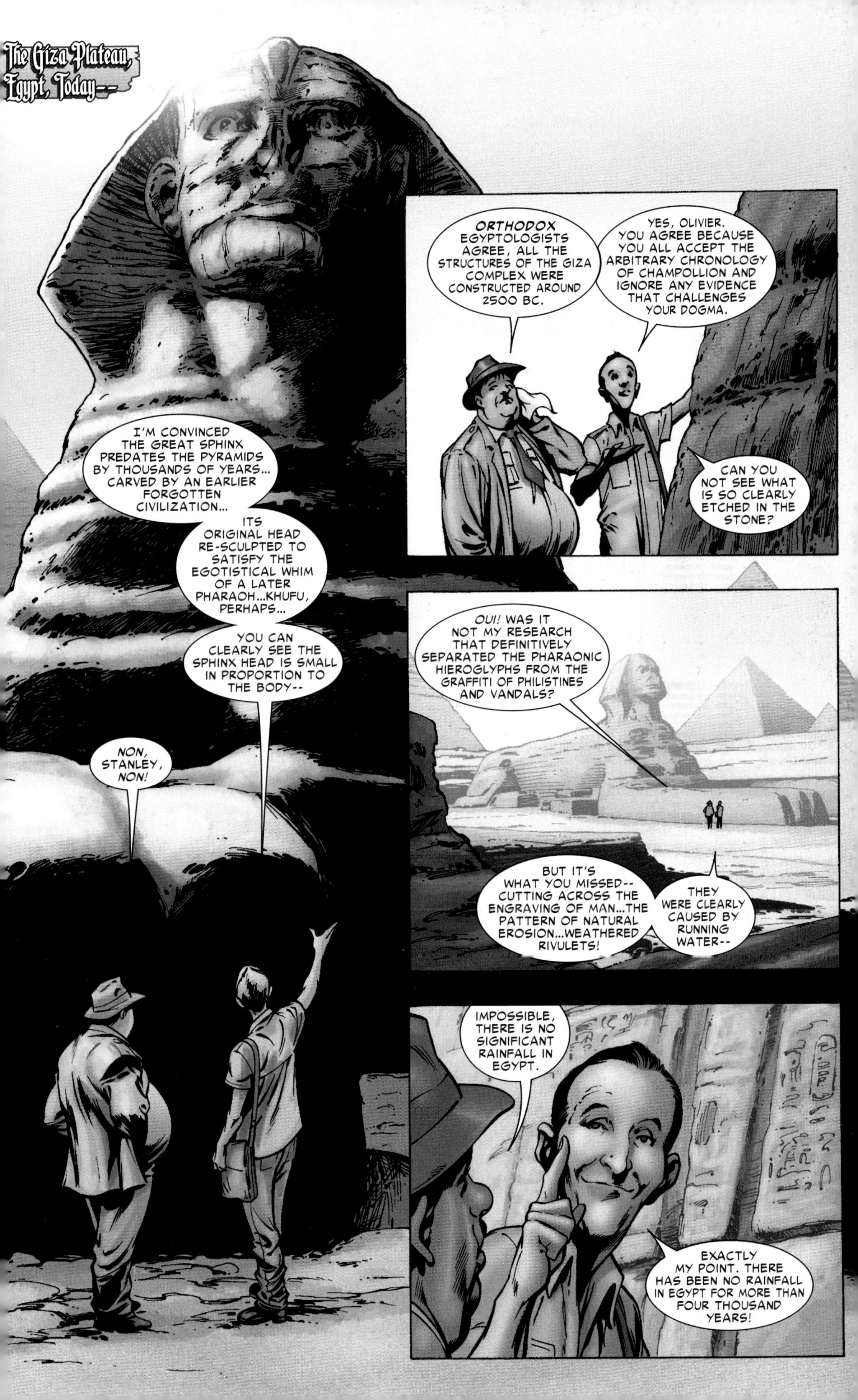
The Giza Plateau, Egypt, Today--
ORTHODOX EGYPTOLOGISTS AGREE, ALL THE STRUCTURES OF THE GIZA COMPLEX WERE CONSTRUCTED AROUND 2500 BC.
YES, OLIVIER. YOU AGREE BECAUSE YOU ALL ACCEPT THE ARBITRARY CHRONOLOGY OF CHAMPOLLION AND IGNORE ANY EVIDENCE THAT CHALLENGES YOUR DOGMA.
CAN YOU NOT SEE WHAT IS SO CLEARLY ETCHED IN THE STONE?
I'M CONVINCED THE GREAT SPHINX PREDATES THE PYRAMIDS BY THOUSANDS OF YEARS... CARVED BY AN EARLIER FORGOTTEN CIVILIZATION...
ITS ORIGINAL HEAD RE-SCULPTED TO SATISFY THE EGOTISTICAL WHIM OF A LATER PHARAOH...KHUFU, PERHAPS...
YOU CAN CLEARLY SEE THE SPHINX HEAD IS SMALL IN PROPORTION TO THE BODY--
NON, STANLEY, NON!
OUI! WAS IT NOT MY RESEARCH THAT DEFINITIVELY SEPARATED THE PHARAONIC HIEROGLYPHS FROM THE GRAFFITI OF PHILISTINES AND VANDALS?
BUT IT'S WHAT YOU MISSED-- CUTTING ACROSS THE ENGRAVING OF MAN...THE PATTERN OF NATURAL EROSION...WEATHERED RIVULETS!
THEY WERE CLEARLY CAUSED BY RUNNING WATER--
IMPOSSIBLE, THERE IS NO SIGNIFICANT RAINFALL IN EGYPT.
EXACTLY MY POINT. THERE HAS BEEN NO RAINFALL IN EGYPT FOR MORE THAN FOUR THOUSAND YEARS!

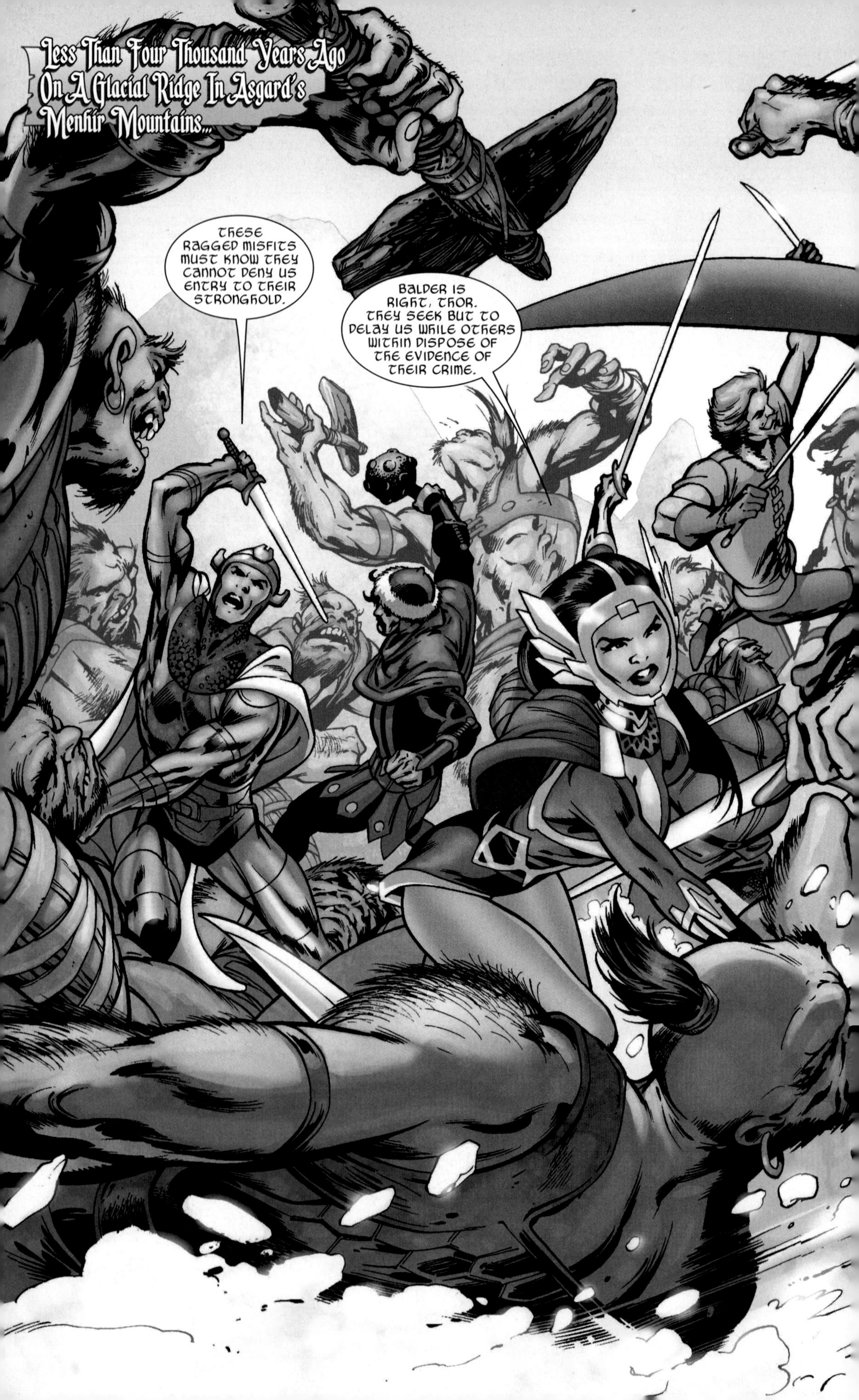
Less Than Four Thousand Years Ago On A Glacial Ridge In Asgard's Menhir Mountains...
THESE RAGGED MISFITS MUST KNOW THEY CANNOT DENY US ENTRY TO THEIR STRONGHOLD.
BALDER IS RIGHT, THOR. THEY SEEK BUT TO DELAY US WHILE OTHERS WITHIN DISPOSE OF THE EVIDENCE OF THEIR CRIME.

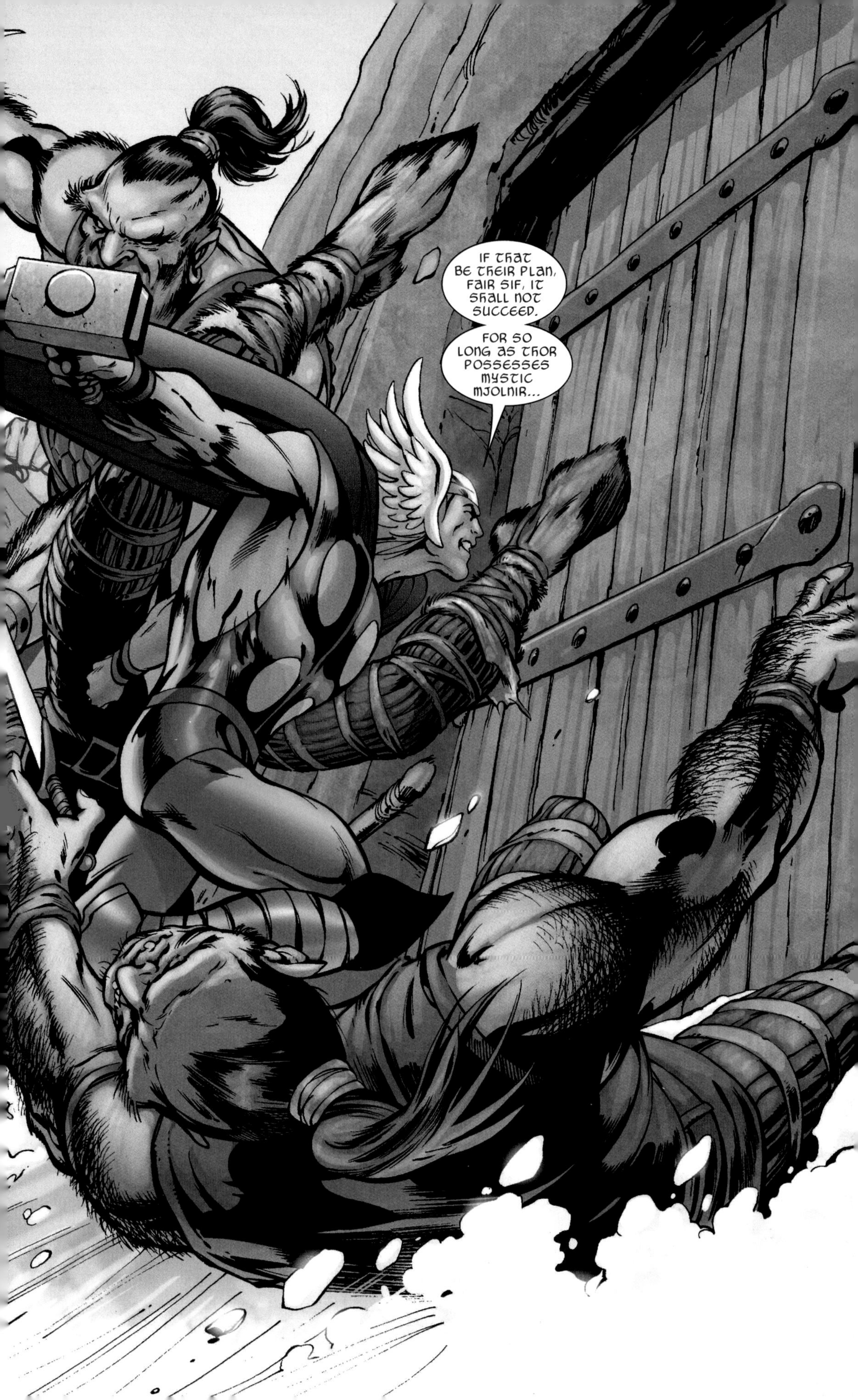
IF THAT BE THEIR PLAN, FAIR SIF, IT SHALL NOT SUCCEED.
FOR SO LONG AS THOR POSSESSES MYSTIC MJOLNIR...

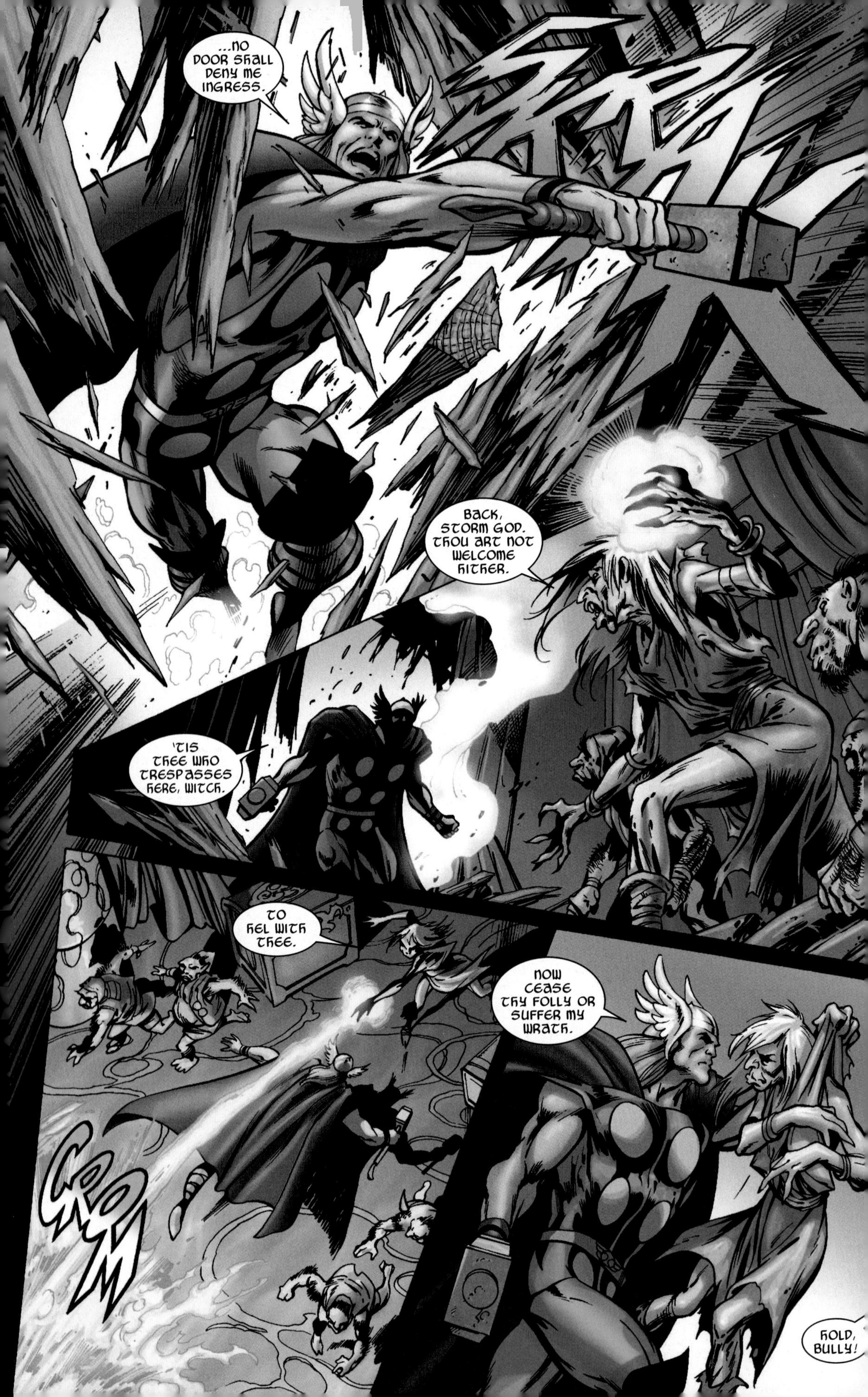
...NO DOOR SHALL DENY ME INGRESS.
BACK, STORM GOD. THOU ART NOT WELCOME HITHER.
'TIS THEE WHO TRESPASSES HERE, WITCH.
TO HEL WITH THEE.
NOW CEASE THY FOLLY OR SUFFER MY WRATH.
HOLD, BULLY!

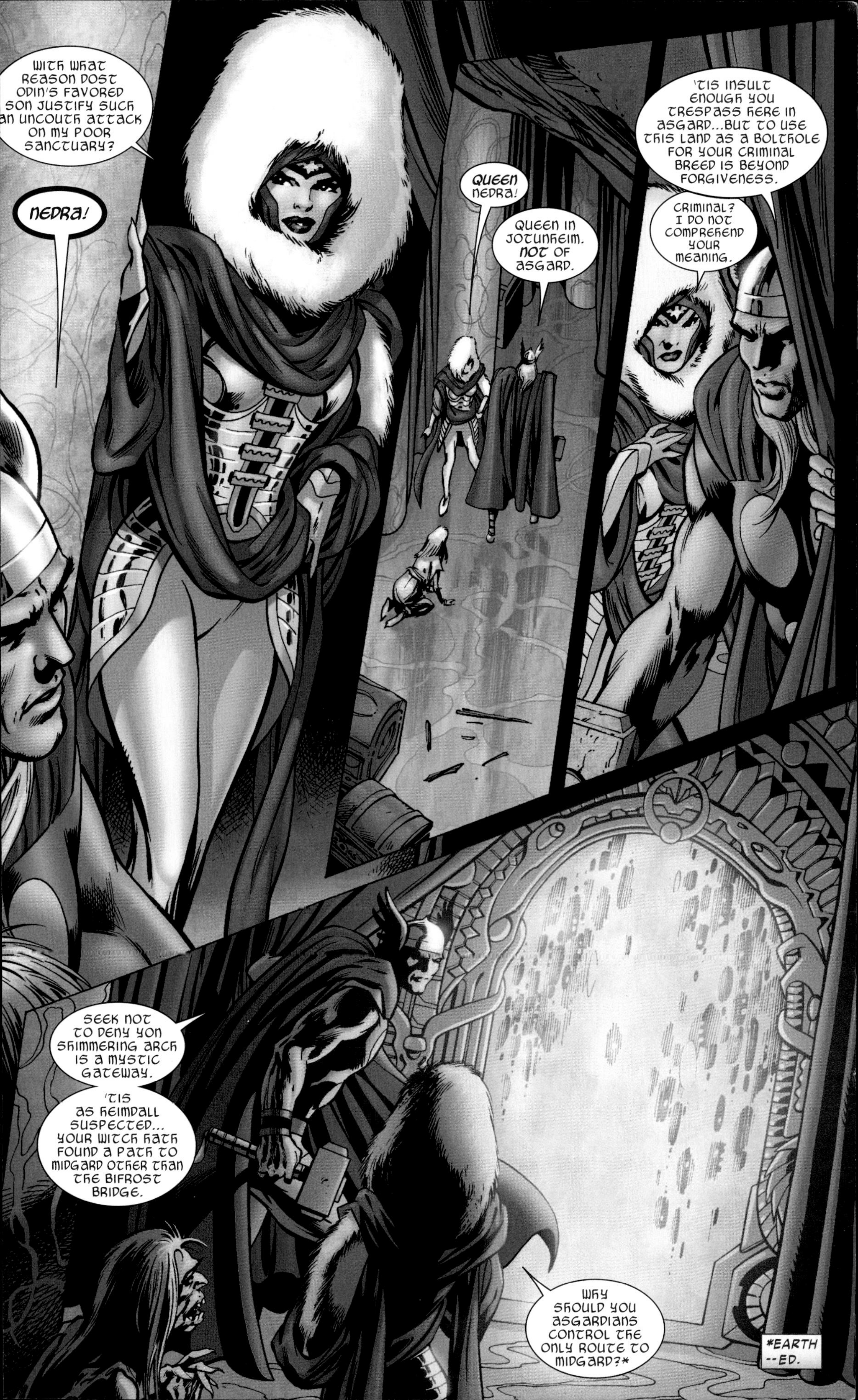
WITH WHAT REASON DOST ODIN'S FAVORED SON JUSTIFY SUCH AN UNCOUTH ATTACK ON MY POOR SANCTUARY?
NEDRA!
QUEEN NEDRA!
QUEEN IN JOTUNHEIM. NOT OF ASGARD.
'TIS INSULT ENOUGH YOU TRESPASS HERE IN ASGARD...BUT TO USE THIS LAND AS A BOLTHOLE FOR YOUR CRIMINAL BREED IS BEYOND FORGIVENESS.
CRIMINAL? I DO NOT COMPREHEND YOUR MEANING.
SEEK NOT TO DENY YON SHIMMERING ARCH IS A MYSTIC GATEWAY.
'TIS AS HEIMDALL SUSPECTED... YOUR WITCH HATH FOUND A PATH TO MIDGARD OTHER THAN THE BIFROST BRIDGE.
WHY SHOULD YOU ASGARDIANS CONTROL THE ONLY ROUTE TO MIDGARD?*
*EARTH --ED.

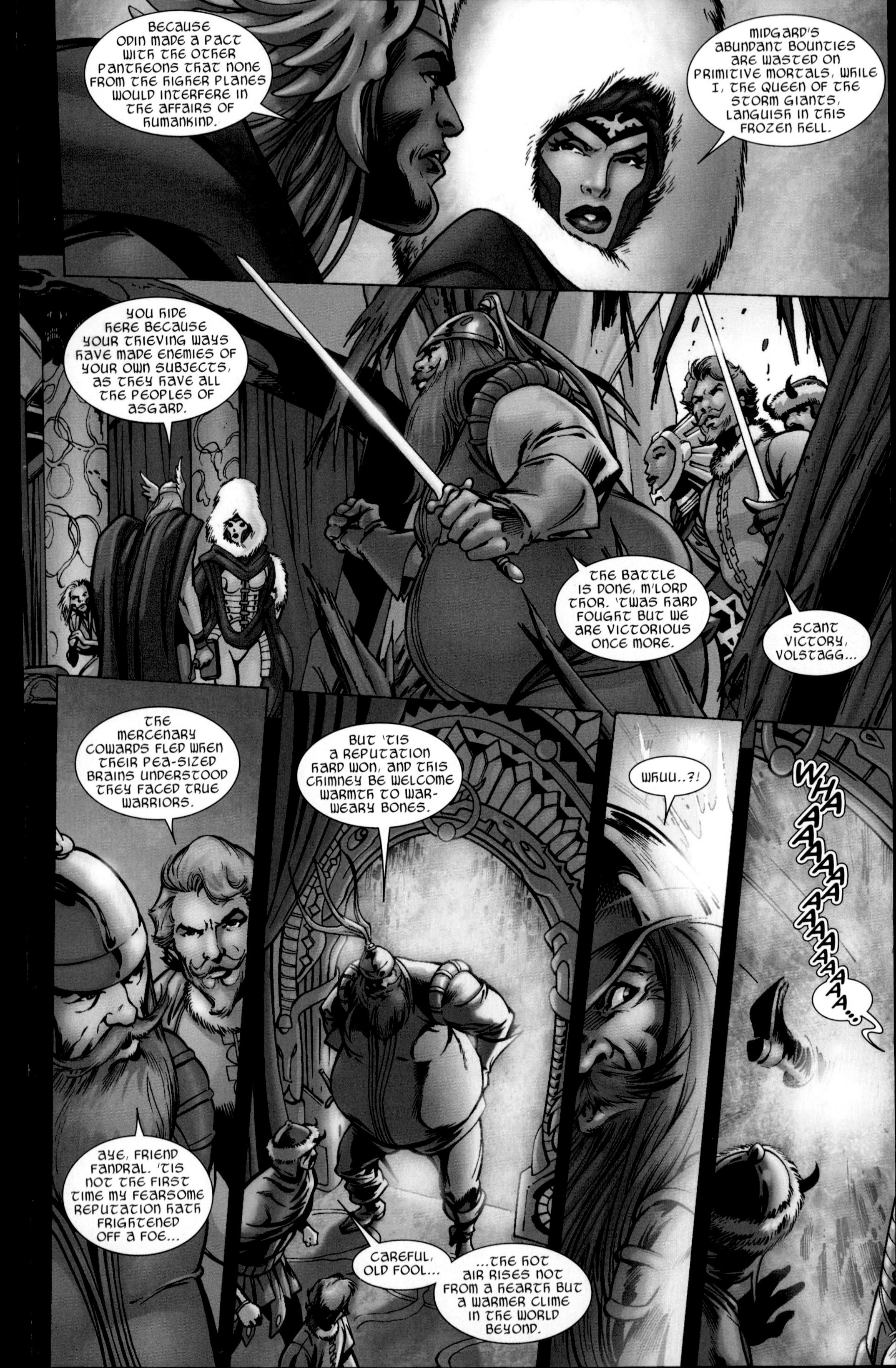
BECAUSE ODIN MADE A PACT WITH THE OTHER PANTHEONS THAT NONE FROM THE HIGHER PLANES WOULD INTERFERE IN THE AFFAIRS OF HUMANKIND.
MIDGARD'S ABUNDANT BOUNTIES ARE WASTED ON PRIMITIVE MORTALS, WHILE I, THE QUEEN OF THE STORM GIANTS, LANGUISH IN THIS FROZEN HELL.
YOU HIDE HERE BECAUSE YOUR THIEVING WAYS HAVE MADE ENEMIES OF YOUR OWN SUBJECTS, AS THEY HAVE ALL THE PEOPLES OF ASGARD.
THE BATTLE IS DONE, M'LORD THOR. 'TWAS HARD FOUGHT BUT WE ARE VICTORIOUS ONCE MORE.
SCANT VICTORY, VOLSTAGG...
THE MERCENARY COWARDS FLED WHEN THEIR PEA-SIZED BRAINS UNDERSTOOD THEY FACED TRUE WARRIORS.
AYE, FRIEND FANDRAL. 'TIS NOT THE FIRST TIME MY FEARSOME REPUTATION HATH FRIGHTENED OFF A FOE...
BUT 'TIS A REPUTATION HARD WON, AND THIS CHIMNEY BE WELCOME WARMTH TO WAR-WEARY BONES.
CAREFUL, OLD FOOL...
...THE HOT AIR RISES NOT FROM A HEARTH BUT A WARMER CLIME IN THE WORLD BEYOND.
WHUU..?!
WHAAAAAAAAAAAAAAA...

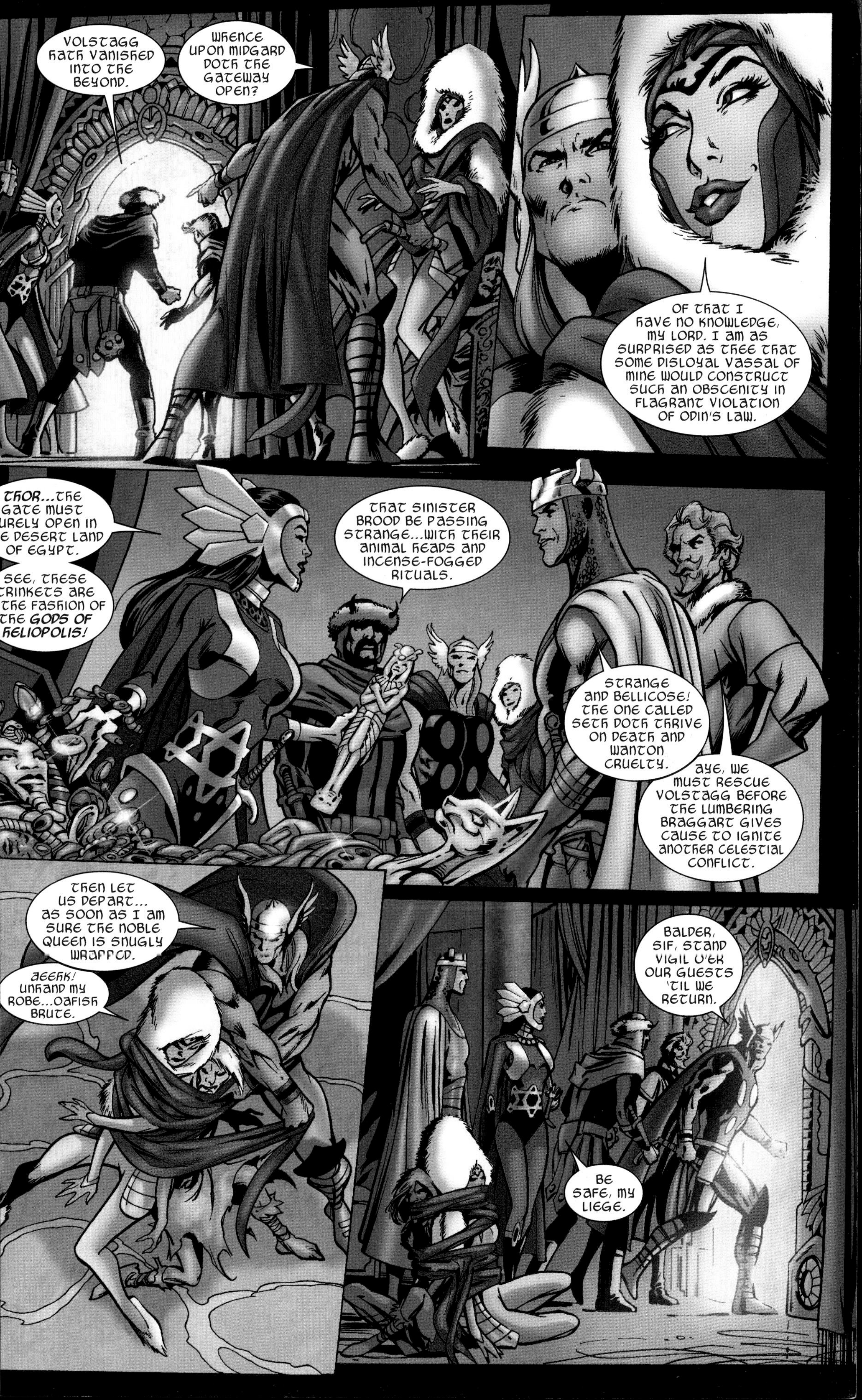
VOLSTAGG HATH VANISHED INTO THE BEYOND.
WHENCE UPON MIDGARD DOTH THE GATEWAY OPEN?
OF THAT I HAVE NO KNOWLEDGE, MY LORD. I AM AS SURPRISED AS THEE THAT SOME DISLOYAL VASSAL OF MINE WOULD CONSTRUCT SUCH AN OBSCENITY IN FLAGRANT VIOLATION OF ODIN'S LAW.
*THOR*...THE GATE MUST URELY OPEN IN E DESERT LAND OF EGYPT.
SEE, THESE TRINKETS ARE THE FASHION OF THE ***GODS OF HELIOPOLIS***!
THAT SINISTER BROOD BE PASSING STRANGE...WITH THEIR ANIMAL HEADS AND INCENSE-FOGGED RITUALS.
STRANGE AND BELLICOSE! THE ONE CALLED SETH DOTH THRIVE ON DEATH AND WANTON CRUELTY.
AYE, WE MUST RESCUE VOLSTAGG BEFORE THE LUMBERING BRAGGART GIVES CAUSE TO IGNITE ANOTHER CELESTIAL CONFLICT.
THEN LET US DEPART... AS SOON AS I AM SURE THE NOBLE QUEEN IS SNUGLY WRAPPED.
AEEHK! UNHAND MY ROBE...OAFISH BRUTE.
BALDER, SIF, STAND VIGIL O'ER OUR GUESTS 'TIL WE RETURN.
BE SAFE, MY LIEGE.

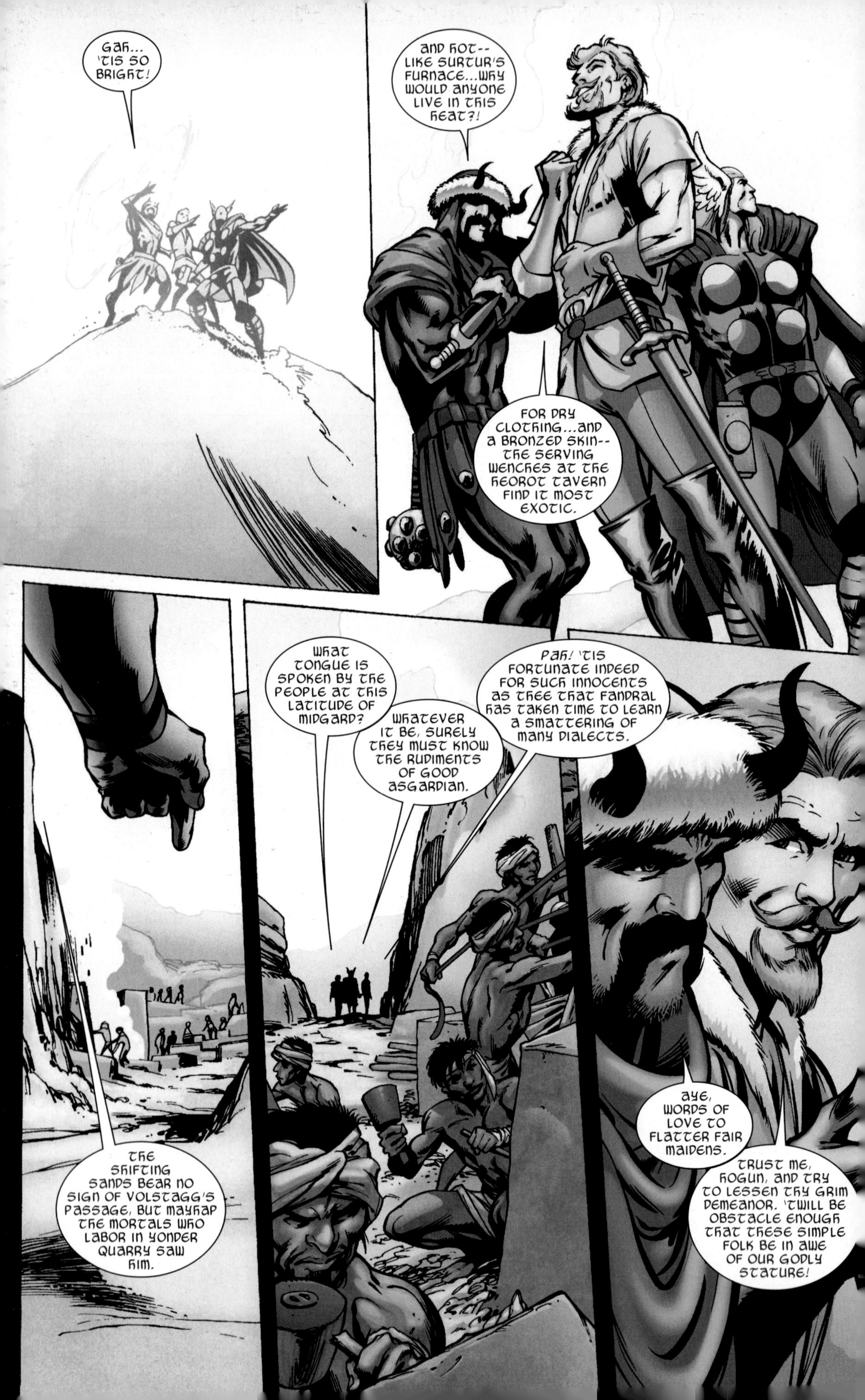
GAH... 'TIS SO BRIGHT!
AND HOT-- LIKE SURTUR'S FURNACE...WHY WOULD ANYONE LIVE IN THIS HEAT?!
FOR DRY CLOTHING...AND A BRONZED SKIN-- THE SERVING WENCHES AT THE HEOROT TAVERN FIND IT MOST EXOTIC.
THE SHIFTING SANDS BEAR NO SIGN OF VOLSTAGG'S PASSAGE, BUT MAYHAP THE MORTALS WHO LABOR IN YONDER QUARRY SAW HIM.
WHAT TONGUE IS SPOKEN BY THE PEOPLE AT THIS LATITUDE OF MIDGARD?
WHATEVER IT BE, SURELY THEY MUST KNOW THE RUDIMENTS OF GOOD ASGARDIAN.
PAH! 'TIS FORTUNATE INDEED FOR SUCH INNOCENTS AS THEE THAT FANDRAL HAS TAKEN TIME TO LEARN A SMATTERING OF MANY DIALECTS.
AYE, WORDS OF LOVE TO FLATTER FAIR MAIDENS.
TRUST ME, HOGUN, AND TRY TO LESSEN THY GRIM DEMEANOR. 'TWILL BE OBSTACLE ENOUGH THAT THESE SIMPLE FOLK BE IN AWE OF OUR GODLY STATURE!

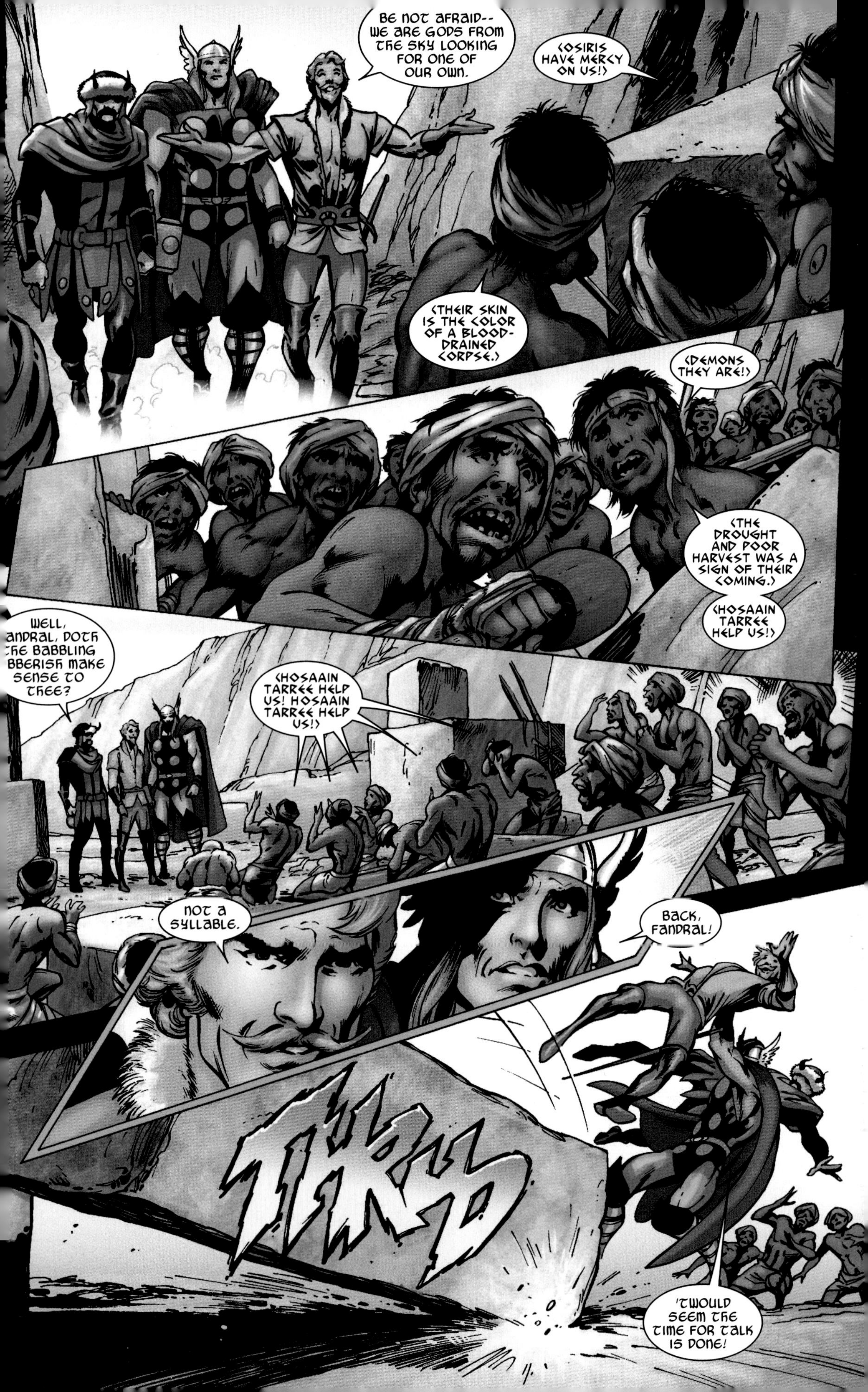
BE NOT AFRAID-- WE ARE GODS FROM THE SKY LOOKING FOR ONE OF OUR OWN.
<OSIRIS HAVE MERCY ON US!>
<THEIR SKIN IS THE COLOR OF A BLOOD-DRAINED CORPSE.>
<DEMONS THEY ARE!>
<THE DROUGHT AND POOR HARVEST WAS A SIGN OF THEIR COMING.>
<HOSAAIN TARREE HELP US!>
WELL, ANDRAL, DOTH THE BABBLING BBERISH MAKE SENSE TO THEE?
<HOSAAIN TARREE HELP US! HOSAAIN TARREE HELP US!>
NOT A SYLLABLE.
BACK, FANDRAL!
'TWOULD SEEM THE TIME FOR TALK IS DONE!

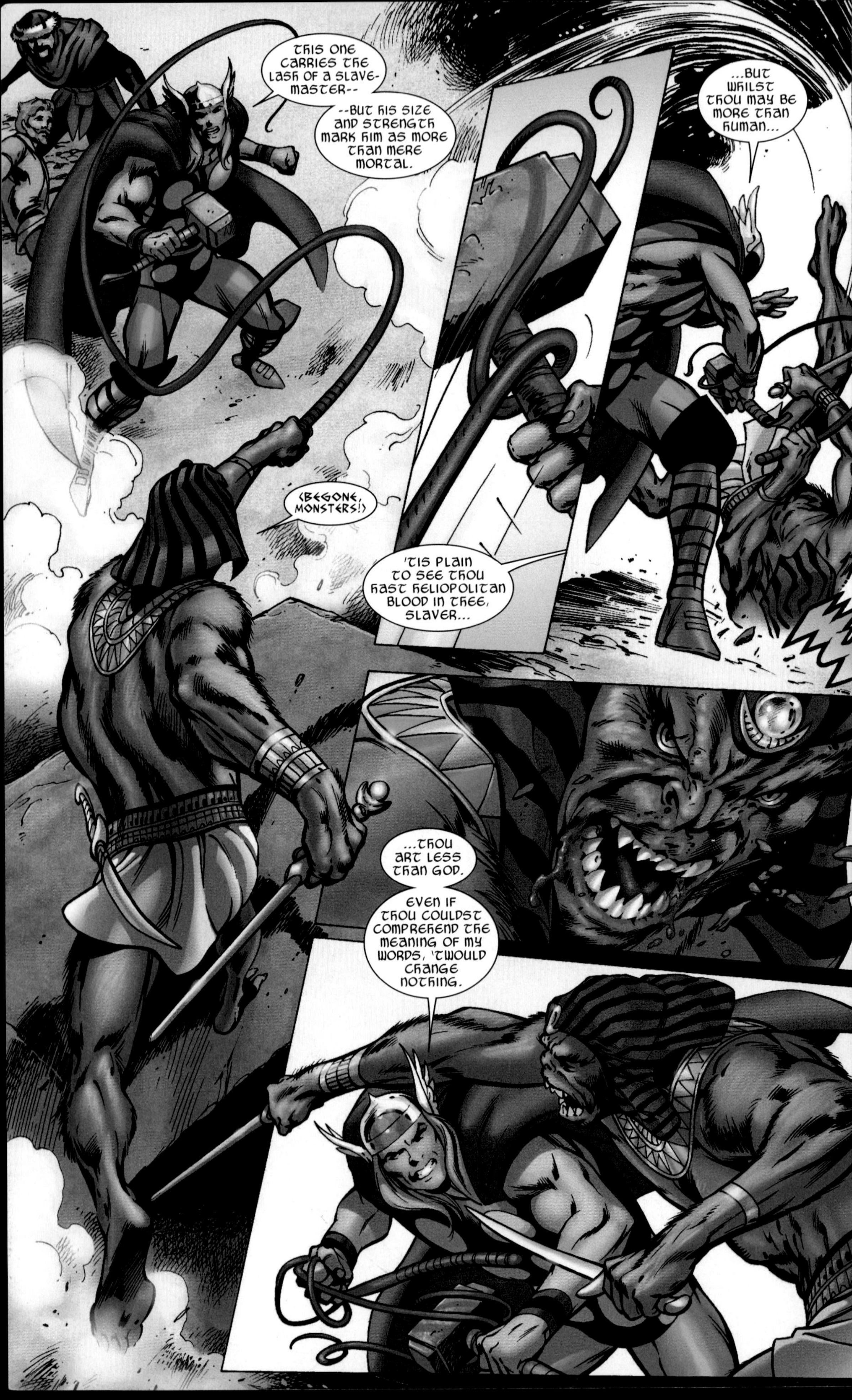
THIS ONE CARRIES THE LASH OF A SLAVE-MASTER--
--BUT HIS SIZE AND STRENGTH MARK HIM AS MORE THAN MERE MORTAL.
...BUT WHILST THOU MAY BE MORE THAN HUMAN...
‹BEGONE, MONSTERS!›
'TIS PLAIN TO SEE THOU HAST HELIOPOLITAN BLOOD IN THEE, SLAVER...
...THOU ART LESS THAN GOD.
EVEN IF THOU COULDST COMPREHEND THE MEANING OF MY WORDS, 'TWOULD CHANGE NOTHING.

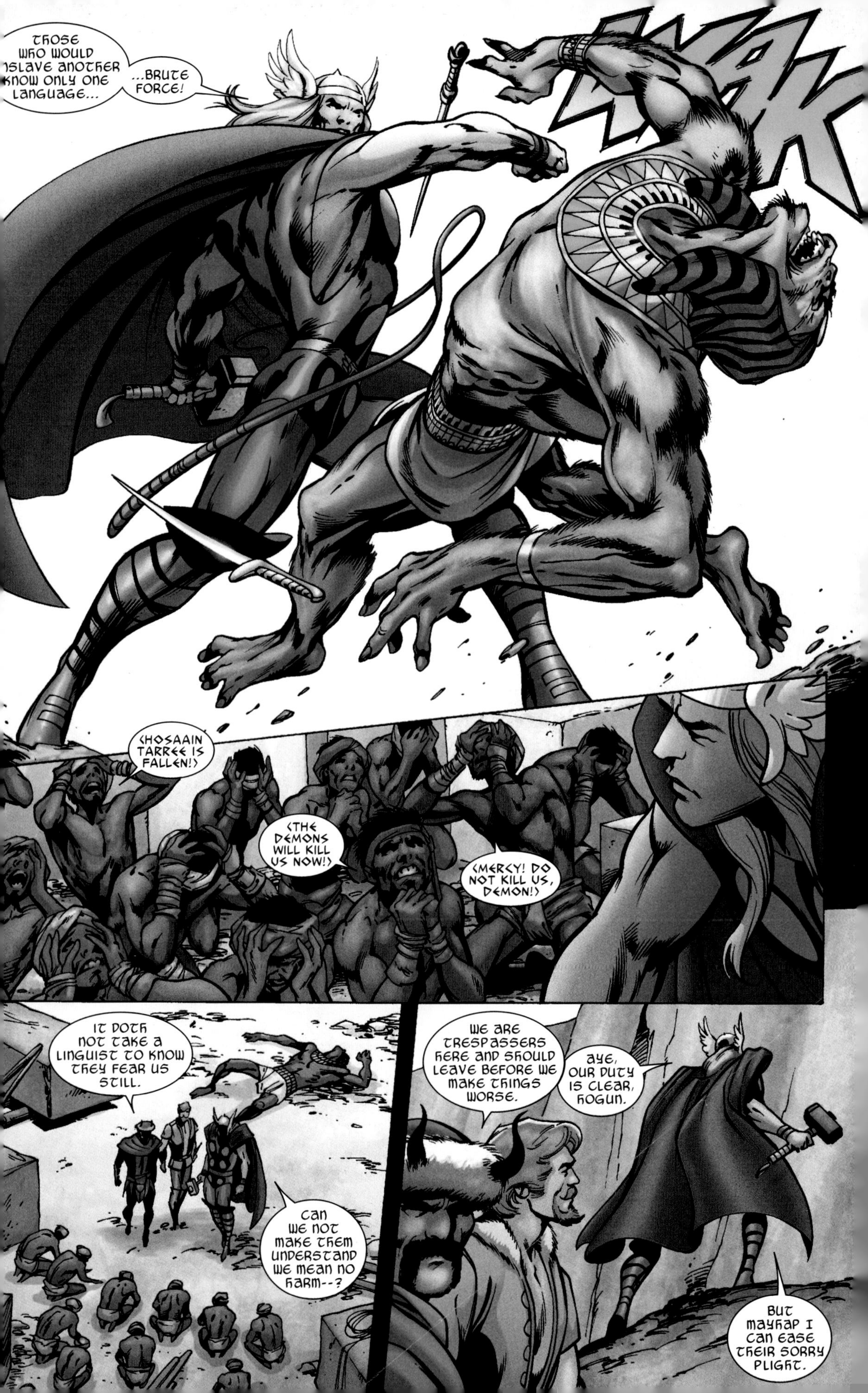
THOSE WHO WOULD ENSLAVE ANOTHER KNOW ONLY ONE LANGUAGE...
...BRUTE FORCE!
<HOSAAIN TARREE IS FALLEN!>
<THE DEMONS WILL KILL US NOW!>
<MERCY! DO NOT KILL US, DEMON!>
IT DOTH NOT TAKE A LINGUIST TO KNOW THEY FEAR US STILL.
CAN WE NOT MAKE THEM UNDERSTAND WE MEAN NO HARM--?
WE ARE TRESPASSERS HERE AND SHOULD LEAVE BEFORE WE MAKE THINGS WORSE.
AYE, OUR DUTY IS CLEAR, HOGUN.
BUT MAYHAP I CAN EASE THEIR SORRY PLIGHT.

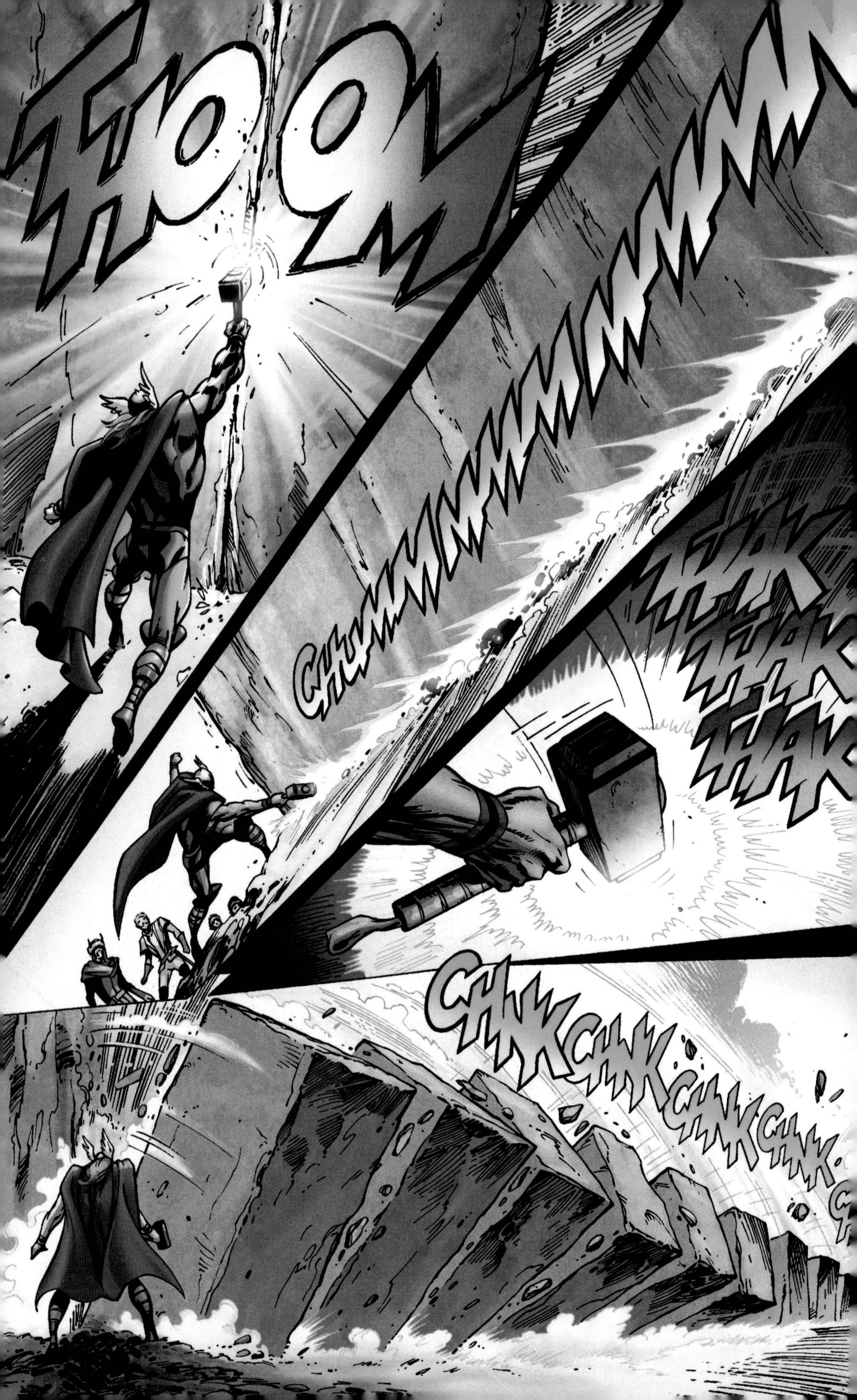
THAK THAK THAK
CHNK CHNK CHNK CHNK

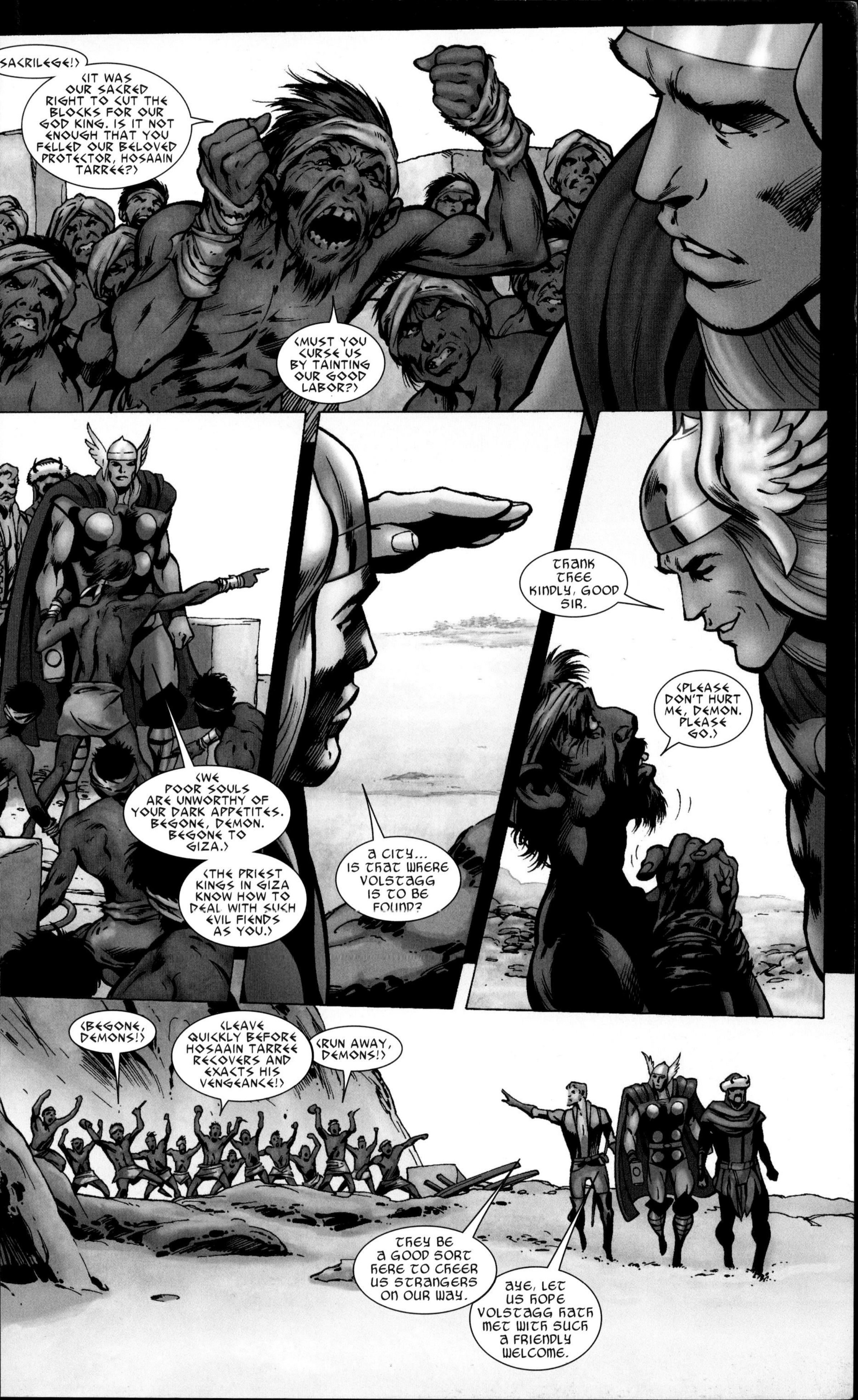

‹SACRILEGE!›
‹IT WAS OUR SACRED RIGHT TO CUT THE BLOCKS FOR OUR GOD KING. IS IT NOT ENOUGH THAT YOU FELLED OUR BELOVED PROTECTOR, HOSAAIN TARREE?›
‹MUST YOU CURSE US BY TAINTING OUR GOOD LABOR?›
‹WE POOR SOULS ARE UNWORTHY OF YOUR DARK APPETITES. BEGONE, DEMON. BEGONE TO GIZA.›
‹THE PRIEST KINGS IN GIZA KNOW HOW TO DEAL WITH SUCH EVIL FIENDS AS YOU.›
A CITY... IS THAT WHERE VOLSTAGG IS TO BE FOUND?
THANK THEE KINDLY, GOOD SIR.
‹PLEASE DON'T HURT ME, DEMON. PLEASE GO.›
‹BEGONE, DEMONS!›
‹LEAVE QUICKLY BEFORE HOSAAIN TARREE RECOVERS AND EXACTS HIS VENGEANCE!›
‹RUN AWAY, DEMONS!›
THEY BE A GOOD SORT HERE TO CHEER US STRANGERS ON OUR WAY.
AYE, LET US HOPE VOLSTAGG HATH MET WITH SUCH A FRIENDLY WELCOME.

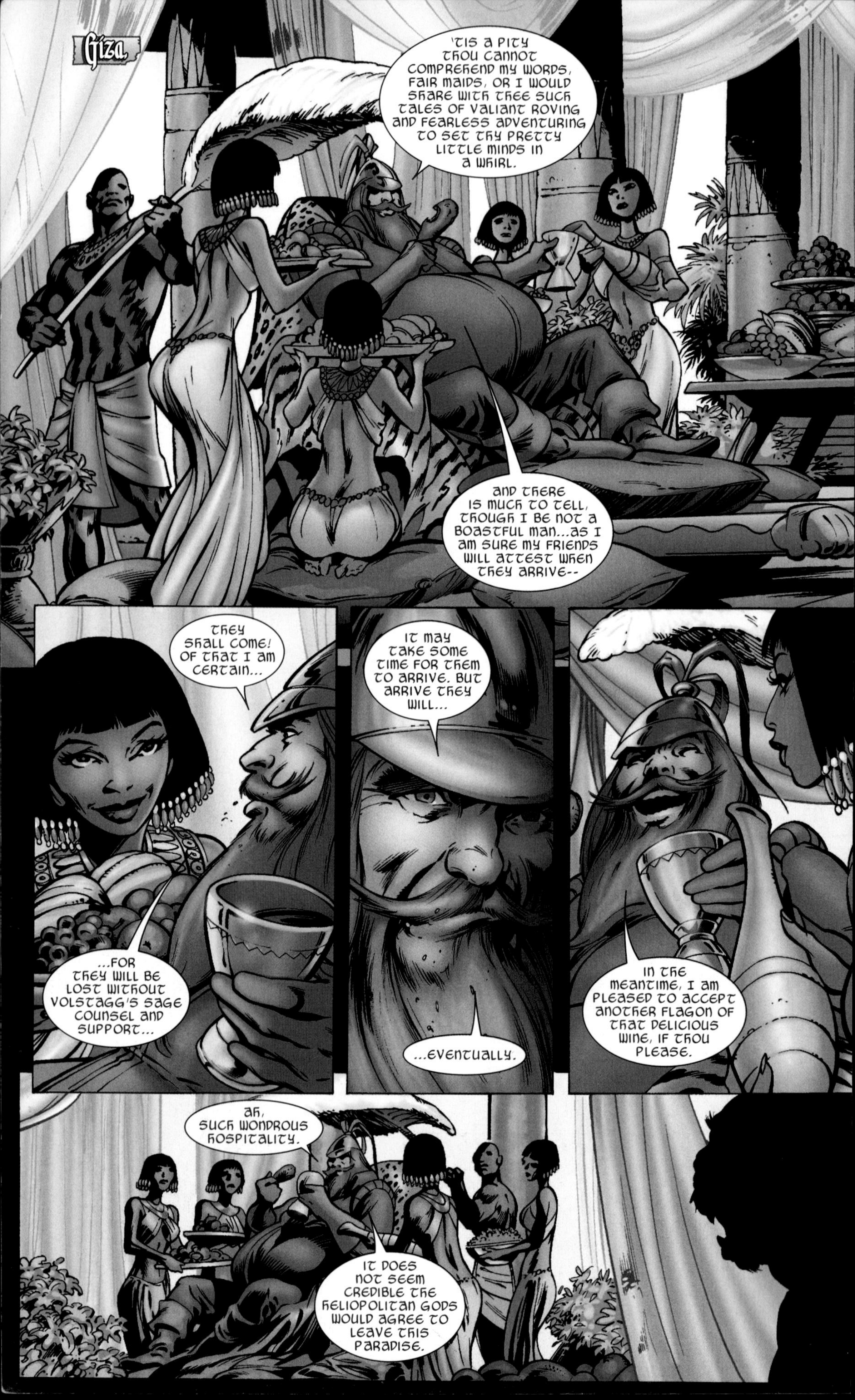
Giza
'TIS A PITY THOU CANNOT COMPREHEND MY WORDS, FAIR MAIDS, OR I WOULD SHARE WITH THEE SUCH TALES OF VALIANT ROVING AND FEARLESS ADVENTURING TO SET THY PRETTY LITTLE MINDS IN A WHIRL.
AND THERE IS MUCH TO TELL, THOUGH I BE NOT A BOASTFUL MAN...AS I AM SURE MY FRIENDS WILL ATTEST WHEN THEY ARRIVE--
THEY SHALL COME! OF THAT I AM CERTAIN...
...FOR THEY WILL BE LOST WITHOUT VOLSTAGG'S SAGE COUNSEL AND SUPPORT...
IT MAY TAKE SOME TIME FOR THEM TO ARRIVE. BUT ARRIVE THEY WILL...
...EVENTUALLY.
IN THE MEANTIME, I AM PLEASED TO ACCEPT ANOTHER FLAGON OF THAT DELICIOUS WINE, IF THOU PLEASE.
AH, SUCH WONDROUS HOSPITALITY.
IT DOES NOT SEEM CREDIBLE THE HELIOPOLITAN GODS WOULD AGREE TO LEAVE THIS PARADISE.

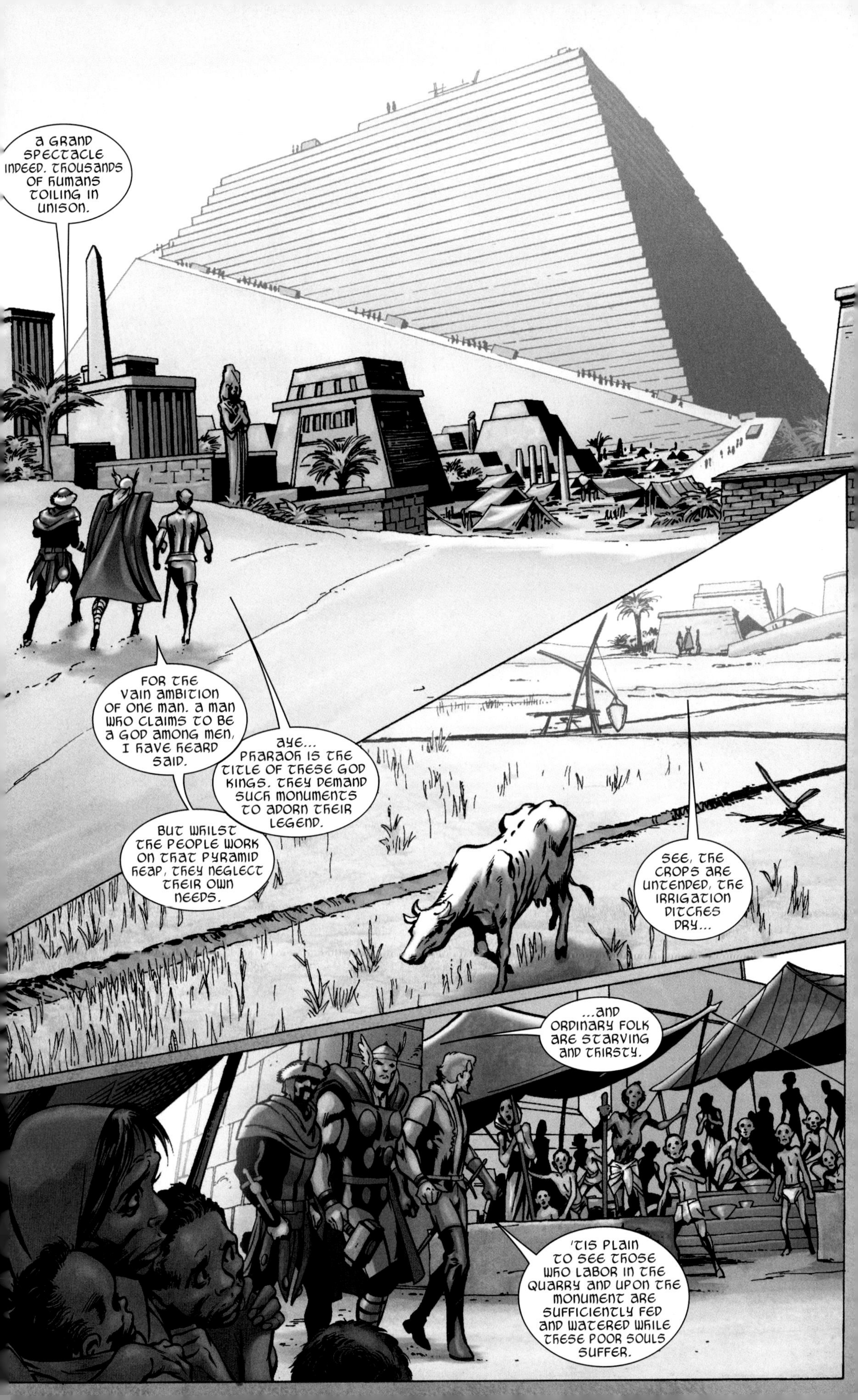
A GRAND SPECTACLE INDEED. THOUSANDS OF HUMANS TOILING IN UNISON.
FOR THE VAIN AMBITION OF ONE MAN. A MAN WHO CLAIMS TO BE A GOD AMONG MEN, I HAVE HEARD SAID.
AYE... PHARAOH IS THE TITLE OF THESE GOD KINGS. THEY DEMAND SUCH MONUMENTS TO ADORN THEIR LEGEND.
BUT WHILST THE PEOPLE WORK ON THAT PYRAMID HEAP, THEY NEGLECT THEIR OWN NEEDS.
SEE, THE CROPS ARE UNTENDED, THE IRRIGATION DITCHES DRY...
...AND ORDINARY FOLK ARE STARVING AND THIRSTY.
'TIS PLAIN TO SEE THOSE WHO LABOR IN THE QUARRY AND UPON THE MONUMENT ARE SUFFICIENTLY FED AND WATERED WHILE THESE POOR SOULS SUFFER.

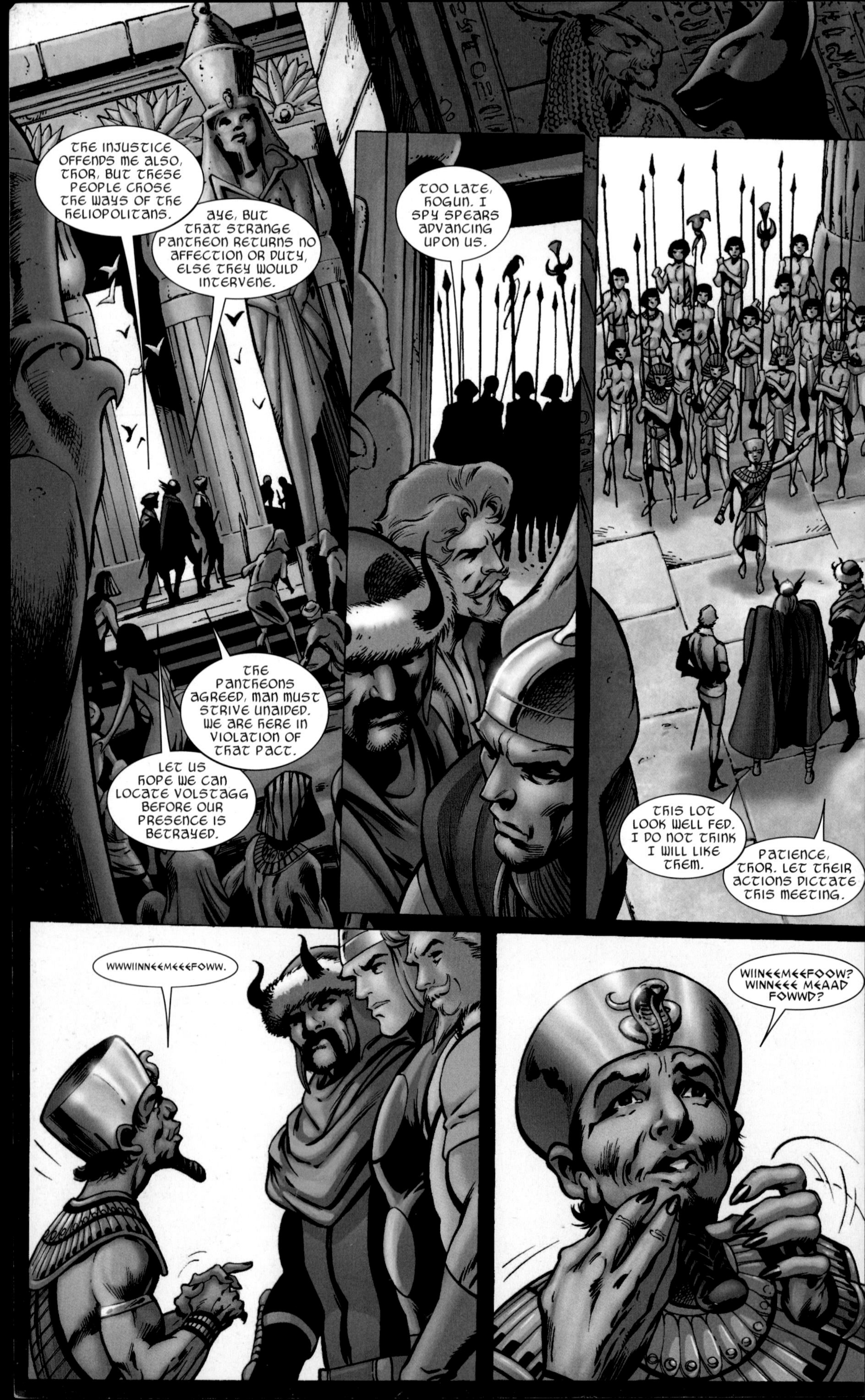

THE INJUSTICE OFFENDS ME ALSO, THOR, BUT THESE PEOPLE CHOSE THE WAYS OF THE HELIOPOLITANS.
AYE, BUT THAT STRANGE PANTHEON RETURNS NO AFFECTION OR DUTY, ELSE THEY WOULD INTERVENE.
THE PANTHEONS AGREED, MAN MUST STRIVE UNAIDED. WE ARE HERE IN VIOLATION OF THAT PACT.
LET US HOPE WE CAN LOCATE VOLSTAGG BEFORE OUR PRESENCE IS BETRAYED.
TOO LATE, HOGUN. I SPY SPEARS ADVANCING UPON US.
THIS LOT LOOK WELL FED. I DO NOT THINK I WILL LIKE THEM.
PATIENCE, THOR. LET THEIR ACTIONS DICTATE THIS MEETING.
WWWIINNEEMEEEFOWW.
WIINEEMEEFOOW? WINNEEE MEAAD FOWWD?

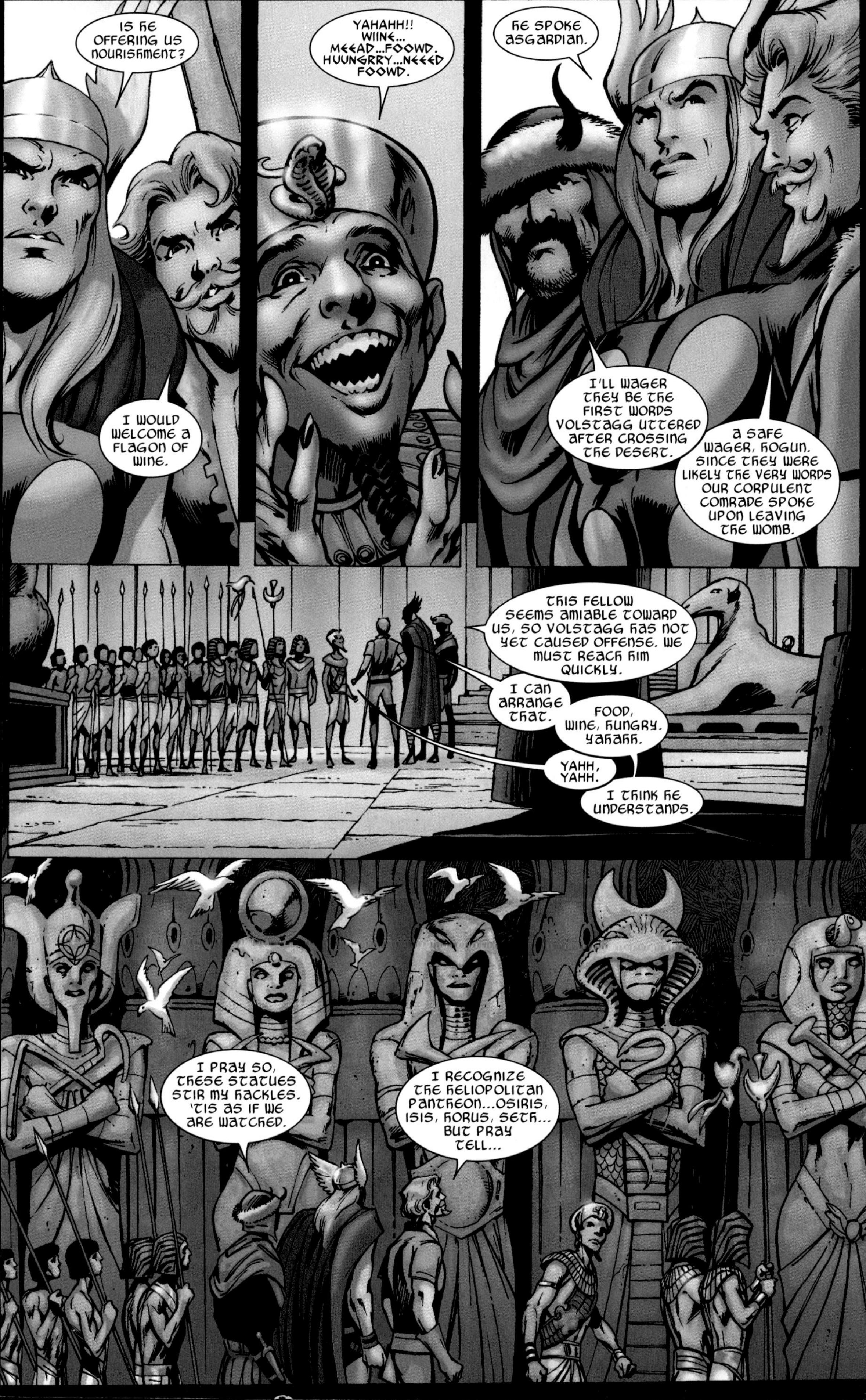
IS HE OFFERING US NOURISHMENT?
I WOULD WELCOME A FLAGON OF WINE.
YAHAHH!! WIINE... MEEAD...FOOWD. HUUNGRRY...NEEED FOOWD.
HE SPOKE ASGARDIAN.
I'LL WAGER THEY BE THE FIRST WORDS VOLSTAGG UTTERED AFTER CROSSING THE DESERT.
A SAFE WAGER, HOGUN. SINCE THEY WERE LIKELY THE VERY WORDS OUR CORPULENT COMRADE SPOKE UPON LEAVING THE WOMB.
THIS FELLOW SEEMS AMIABLE TOWARD US, SO VOLSTAGG HAS NOT YET CAUSED OFFENSE. WE MUST REACH HIM QUICKLY.
I CAN ARRANGE THAT.
FOOD, WINE, HUNGRY. YAHAHH.
YAHH, YAHH.
I THINK HE UNDERSTANDS.
I PRAY SO, THESE STATUES STIR MY HACKLES. 'TIS AS IF WE ARE WATCHED.
I RECOGNIZE THE HELIOPOLITAN PANTHEON...OSIRIS, ISIS, HORUS, SETH... BUT PRAY TELL...

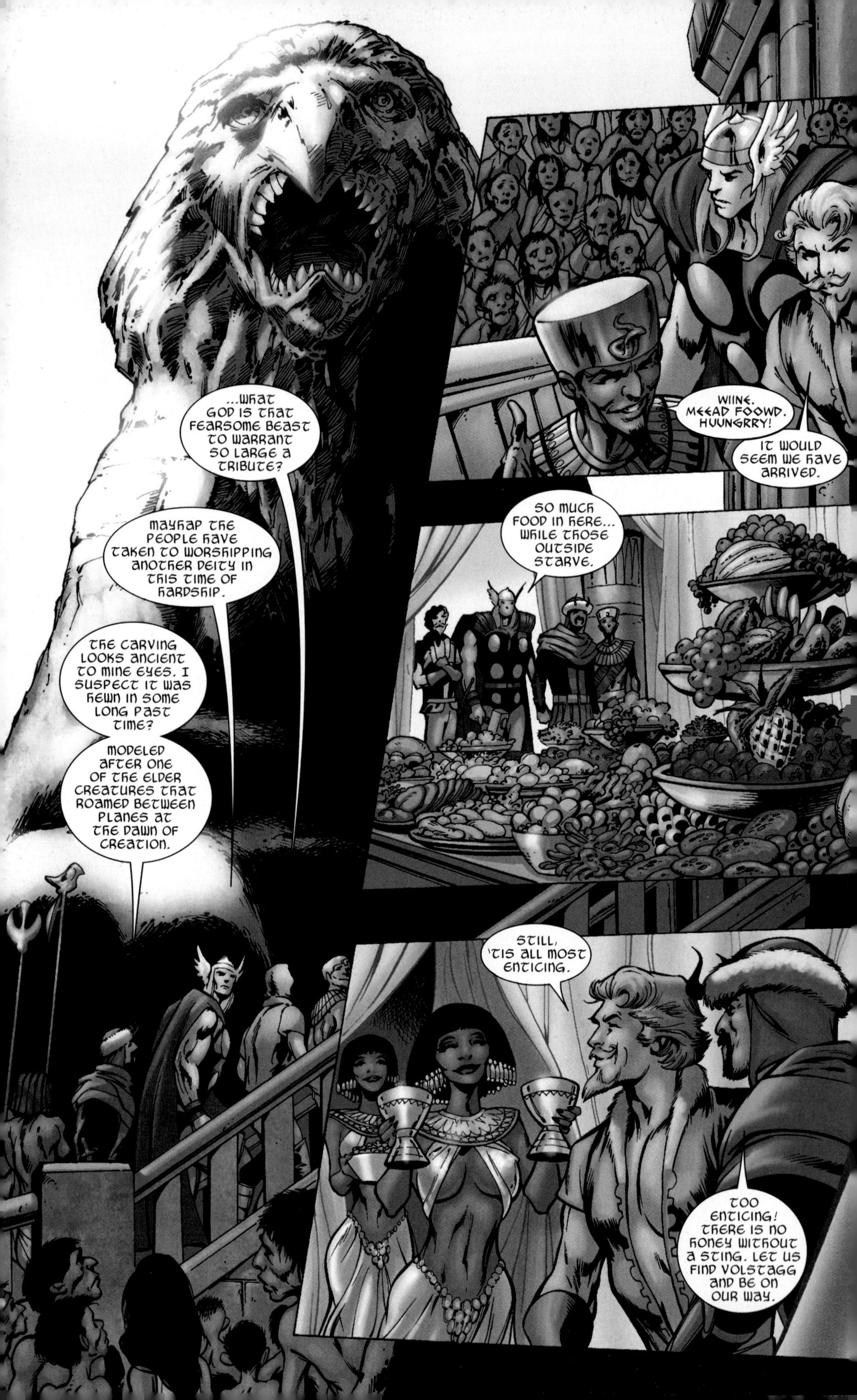
...WHAT GOD IS THAT FEARSOME BEAST TO WARRANT SO LARGE A TRIBUTE?
MAYHAP THE PEOPLE HAVE TAKEN TO WORSHIPPING ANOTHER DEITY IN THIS TIME OF HARDSHIP.
THE CARVING LOOKS ANCIENT TO MINE EYES. I SUSPECT IT WAS HEWN IN SOME LONG PAST TIME?
MODELED AFTER ONE OF THE ELDER CREATURES THAT ROAMED BETWEEN PLANES AT THE DAWN OF CREATION.
WIINE. MEEAD FOOWD. HUUNGRRY!
IT WOULD SEEM WE HAVE ARRIVED.
SO MUCH FOOD IN HERE... WHILE THOSE OUTSIDE STARVE.
STILL, 'TIS ALL MOST ENTICING.
TOO ENTICING! THERE IS NO HONEY WITHOUT A STING. LET US FIND VOLSTAGG AND BE ON OUR WAY.

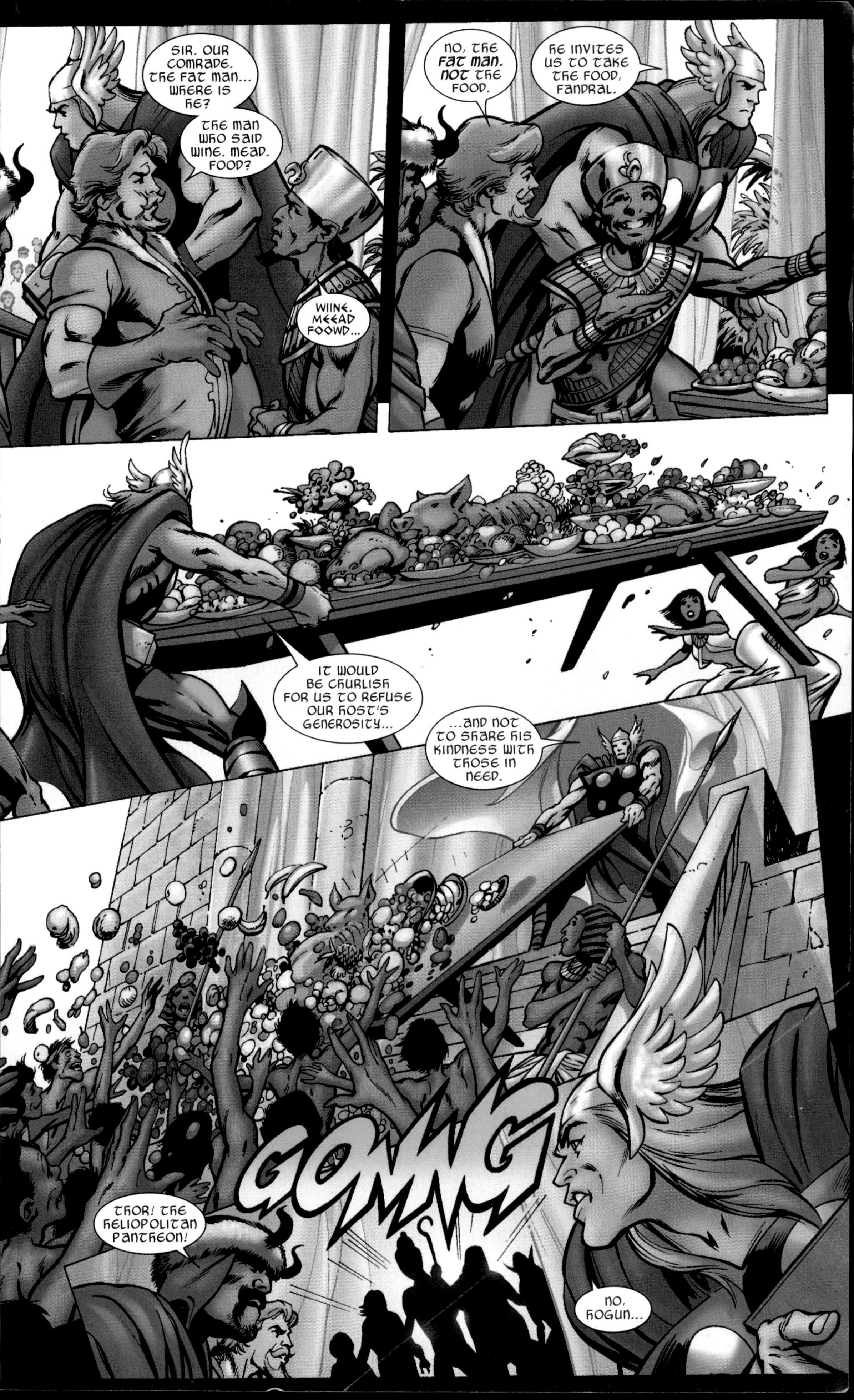
SIR. OUR COMRADE. THE FAT MAN... WHERE IS HE?
THE MAN WHO SAID WINE. MEAD. FOOD?
WIINE. MEEAD FOOWD...
NO, THE FAT MAN. NOT THE FOOD.
HE INVITES US TO TAKE THE FOOD, FANDRAL.
IT WOULD BE CHURLISH FOR US TO REFUSE OUR HOST'S GENEROSITY...
...AND NOT TO SHARE HIS KINDNESS WITH THOSE IN NEED.
GONNG
THOR! THE HELIOPOLITAN PANTHEON!
NO, HOGUN...

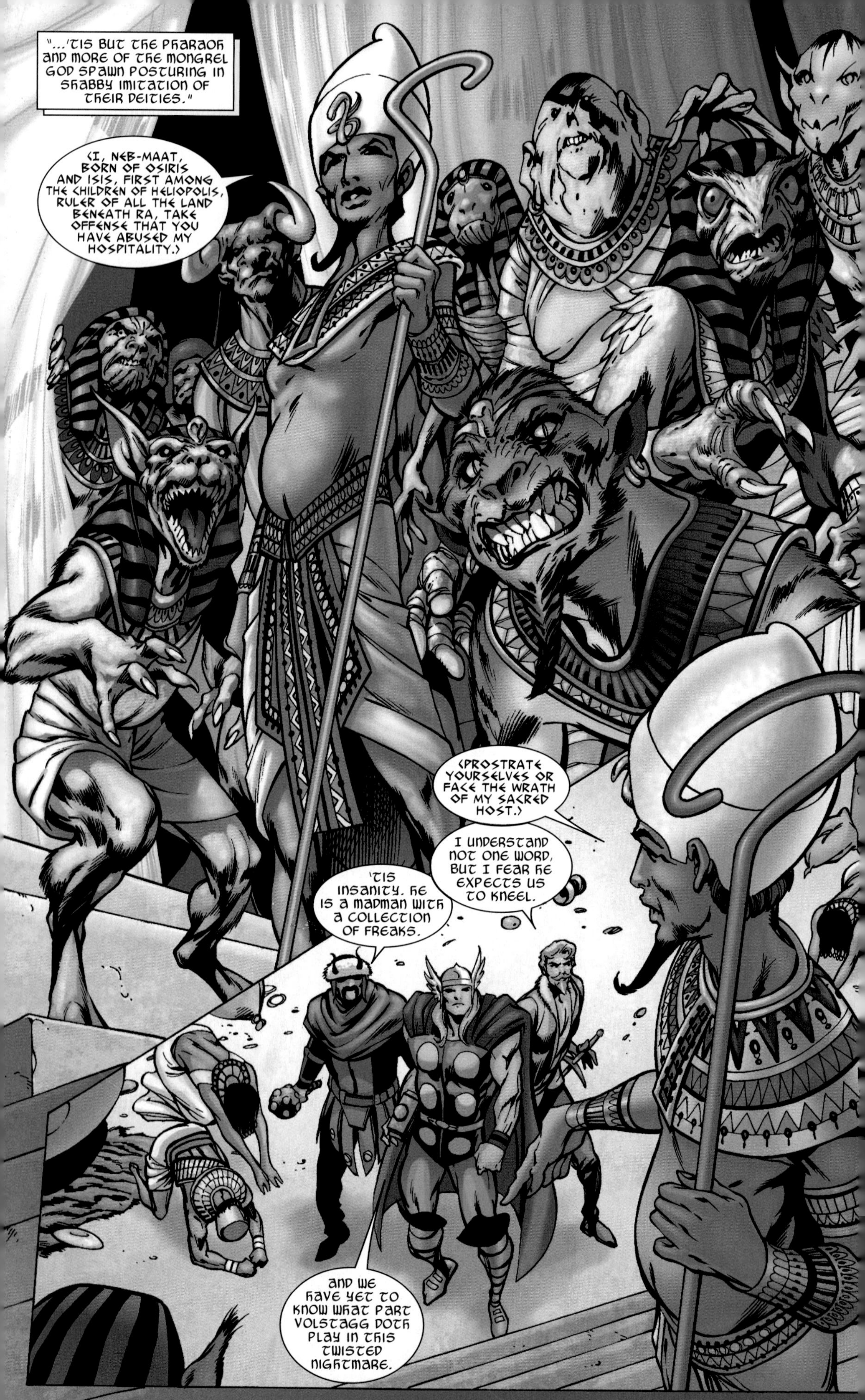
"...'TIS BUT THE PHARAOH AND MORE OF THE MONGREL GOD SPAWN POSTURING IN SHABBY IMITATION OF THEIR DEITIES."
‹I, NEB-MAAT, BORN OF OSIRIS AND ISIS, FIRST AMONG THE CHILDREN OF HELIOPOLIS, RULER OF ALL THE LAND BENEATH RA, TAKE OFFENSE THAT YOU HAVE ABUSED MY HOSPITALITY.›
‹PROSTRATE YOURSELVES OR FACE THE WRATH OF MY SACRED HOST.›
I UNDERSTAND NOT ONE WORD, BUT I FEAR HE EXPECTS US TO KNEEL.
'TIS INSANITY. HE IS A MADMAN WITH A COLLECTION OF FREAKS.
AND WE HAVE YET TO KNOW WHAT PART VOLSTAGG DOTH PLAY IN THIS TWISTED NIGHTMARE.

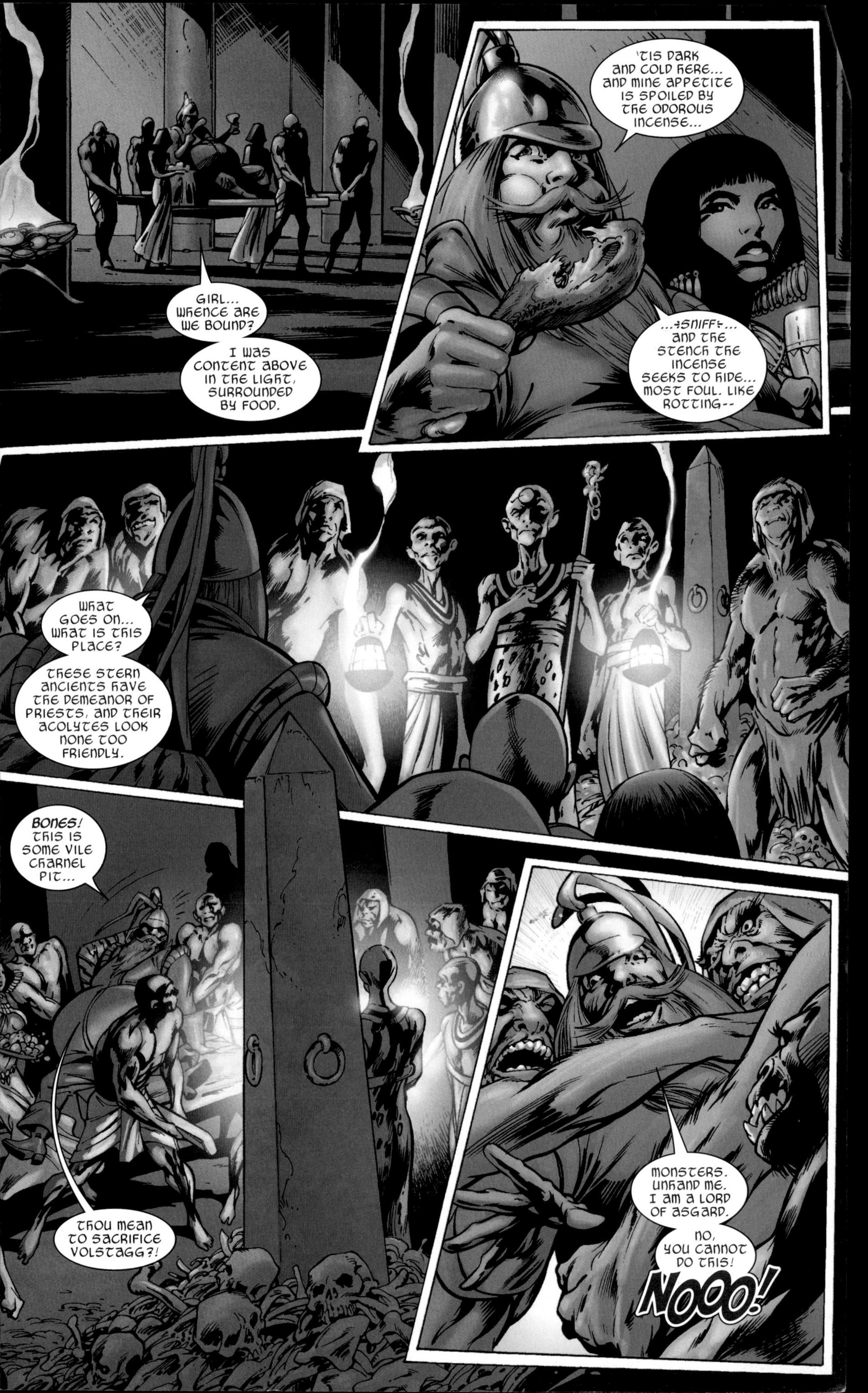

GIRL... WHENCE ARE WE BOUND?
I WAS CONTENT ABOVE IN THE LIGHT, SURROUNDED BY FOOD.
'TIS DARK AND COLD HERE... AND MINE APPETITE IS SPOILED BY THE ODOROUS INCENSE...
...*SNIFF*... AND THE STENCH THE INCENSE SEEKS TO HIDE... MOST FOUL. LIKE ROTTING--
WHAT GOES ON... WHAT IS THIS PLACE?
THESE STERN ANCIENTS HAVE THE DEMEANOR OF PRIESTS, AND THEIR ACOLYTES LOOK NONE TOO FRIENDLY.
BONES! THIS IS SOME VILE CHARNEL PIT...
THOU MEAN TO SACRIFICE VOLSTAGG?!
MONSTERS. UNHAND ME. I AM A LORD OF ASGARD.
NO, YOU CANNOT DO THIS!
NOOO!

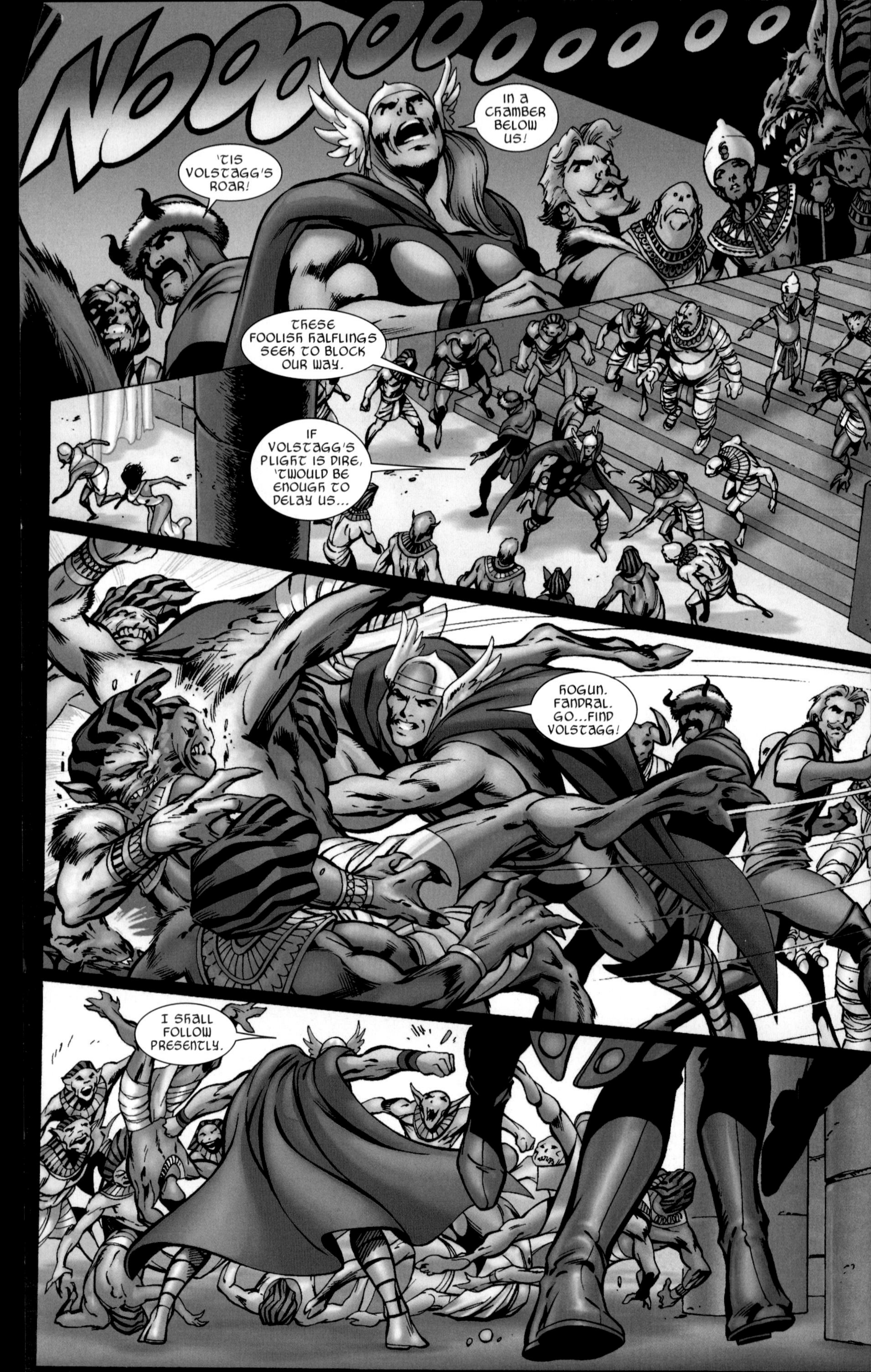
NOOOOOOOOOOOOO
'TIS VOLSTAGG'S ROAR!
IN A CHAMBER BELOW US!
THESE FOOLISH HALFLINGS SEEK TO BLOCK OUR WAY.
IF VOLSTAGG'S PLIGHT IS DIRE, 'TWOULD BE ENOUGH TO DELAY US...
HOGUN. FANDRAL. GO...FIND VOLSTAGG!
I SHALL FOLLOW PRESENTLY.

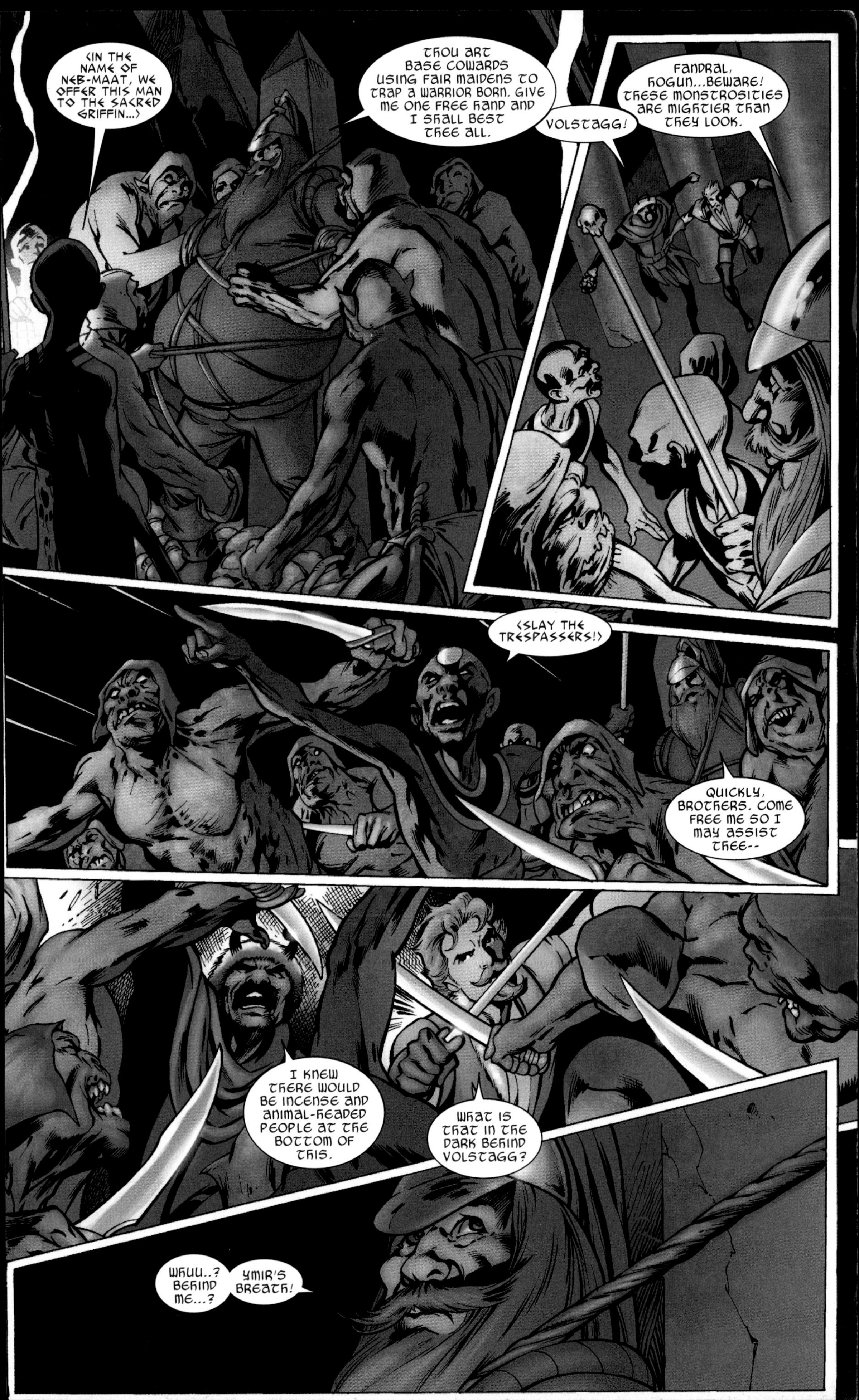
‹IN THE NAME OF NEB-MAAT, WE OFFER THIS MAN TO THE SACRED GRIFFIN...›
THOU ART BASE COWARDS USING FAIR MAIDENS TO TRAP A WARRIOR BORN. GIVE ME ONE FREE HAND AND I SHALL BEST THEE ALL.
VOLSTAGG!
FANDRAL, HOGUN...BEWARE! THESE MONSTROSITIES ARE MIGHTIER THAN THEY LOOK.
‹SLAY THE TRESPASSERS!›
QUICKLY, BROTHERS. COME FREE ME SO I MAY ASSIST THEE--
I KNEW THERE WOULD BE INCENSE AND ANIMAL-HEADED PEOPLE AT THE BOTTOM OF THIS.
WHAT IS THAT IN THE DARK BEHIND VOLSTAGG?
WHUU..? BEHIND ME...?
YMIR'S BREATH!

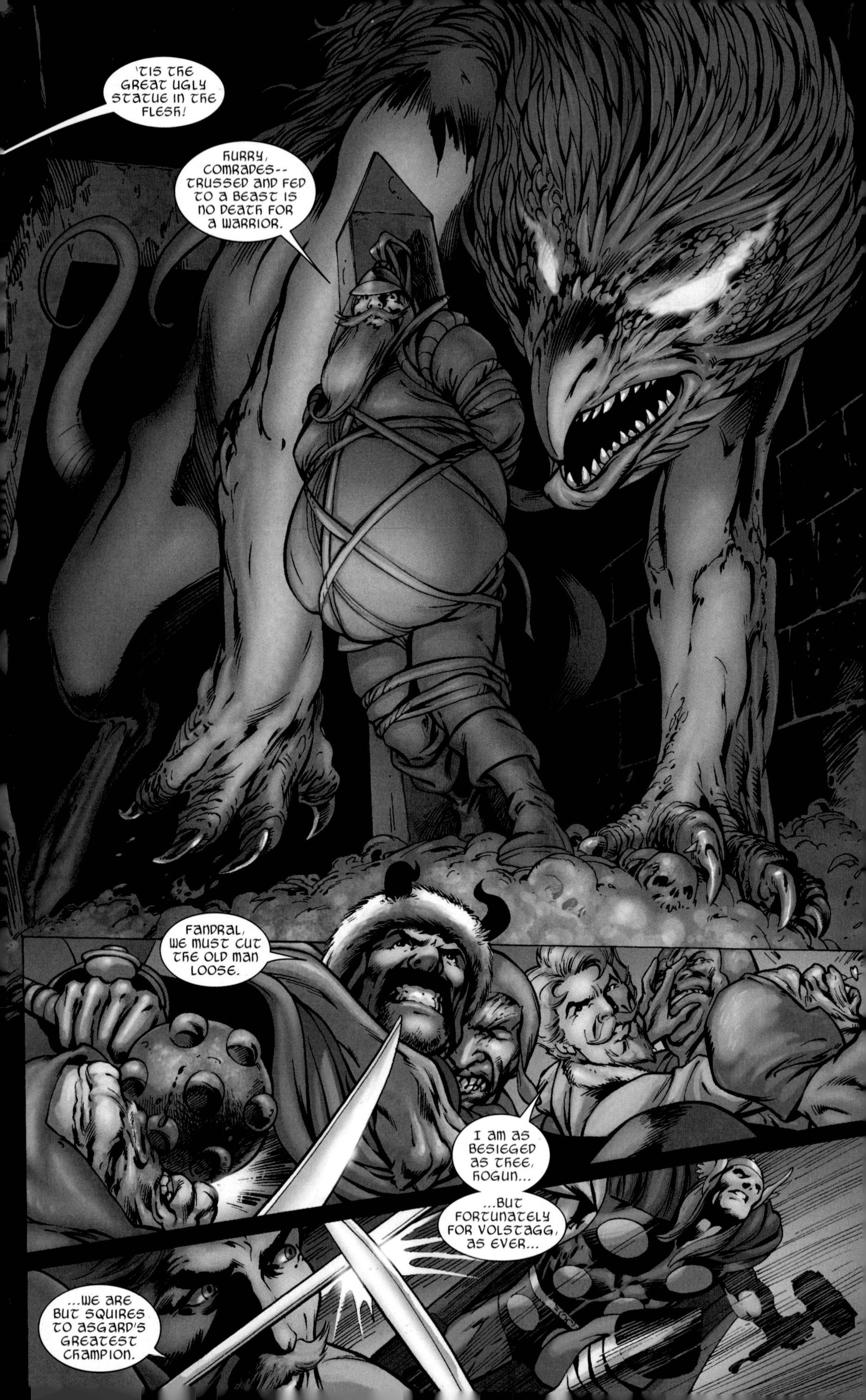
'TIS THE GREAT UGLY STATUE IN THE FLESH!
HURRY, COMRADES-- TRUSSED AND FED TO A BEAST IS NO DEATH FOR A WARRIOR.
FANDRAL, WE MUST CUT THE OLD MAN LOOSE.
I AM AS BESIEGED AS THEE, HOGUN...
...BUT FORTUNATELY FOR VOLSTAGG, AS EVER...
...WE ARE BUT SQUIRES TO ASGARD'S GREATEST CHAMPION.

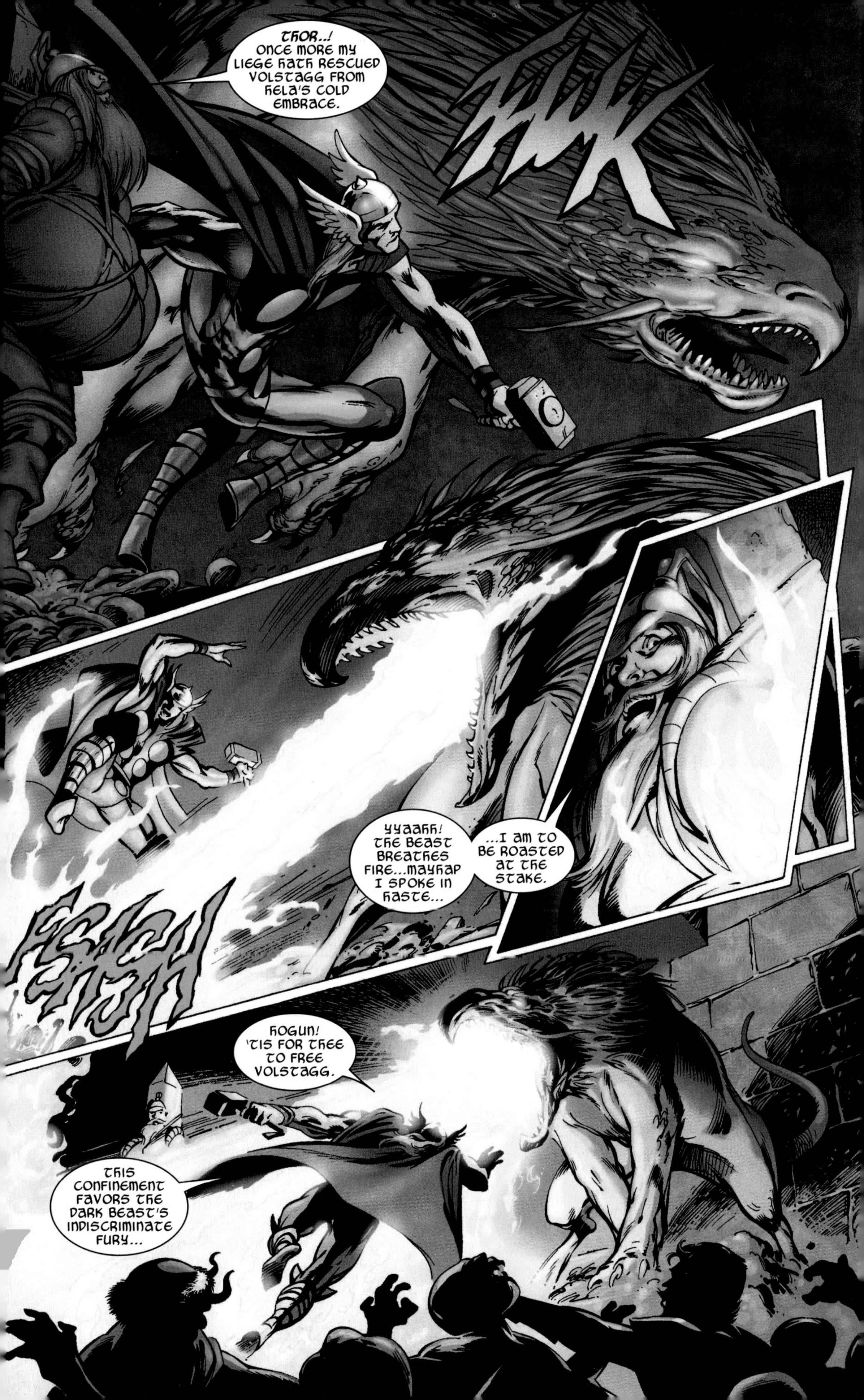
THOR..! ONCE MORE MY LIEGE HATH RESCUED VOLSTAGG FROM HELA'S COLD EMBRACE.
YYAAHH! THE BEAST BREATHES FIRE...MAYHAP I SPOKE IN HASTE...
...I AM TO BE ROASTED AT THE STAKE.
HOGUN! 'TIS FOR THEE TO FREE VOLSTAGG.
THIS CONFINEMENT FAVORS THE DARK BEAST'S INDISCRIMINATE FURY...

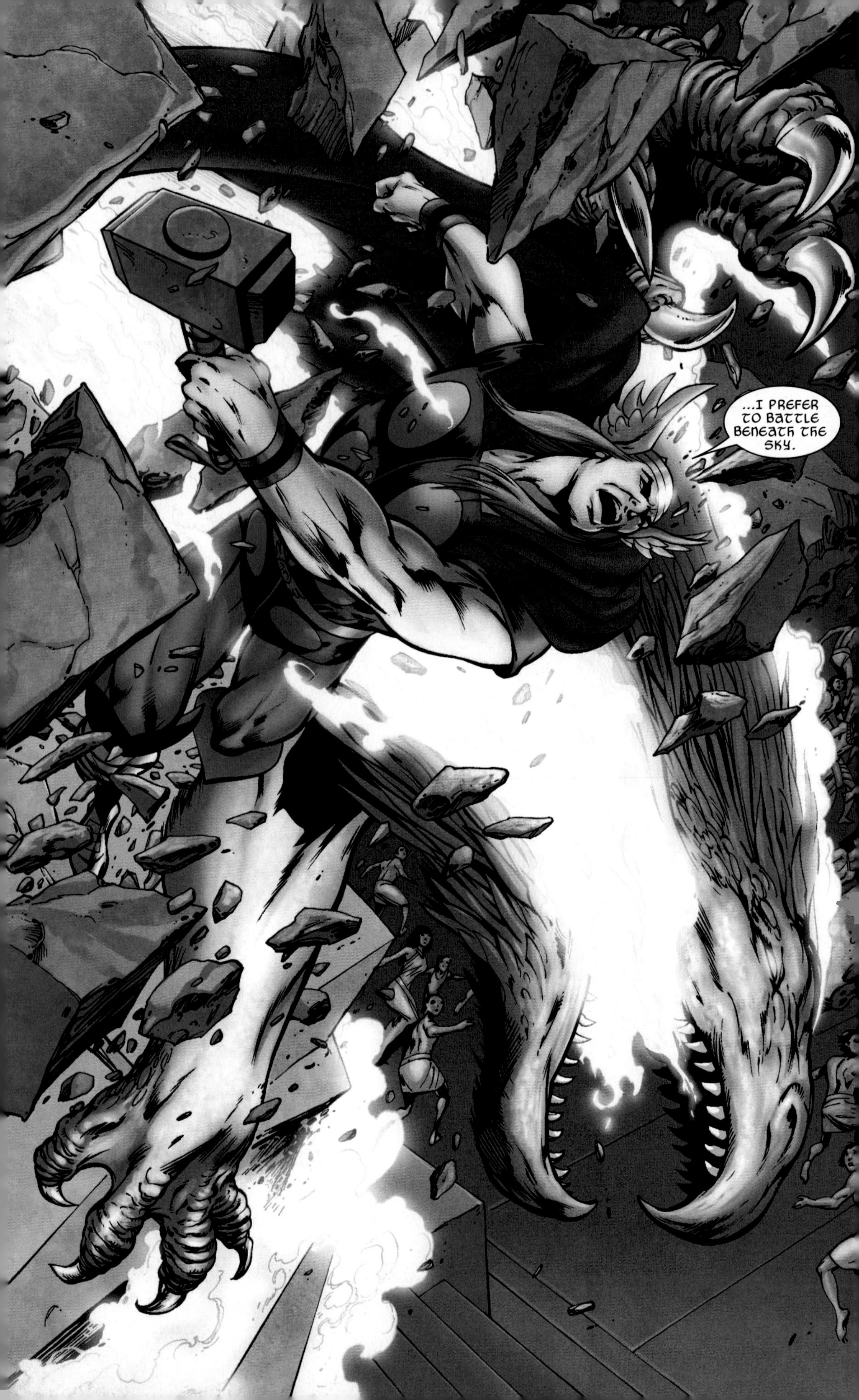
...I PREFER TO BATTLE BENEATH THE SKY.

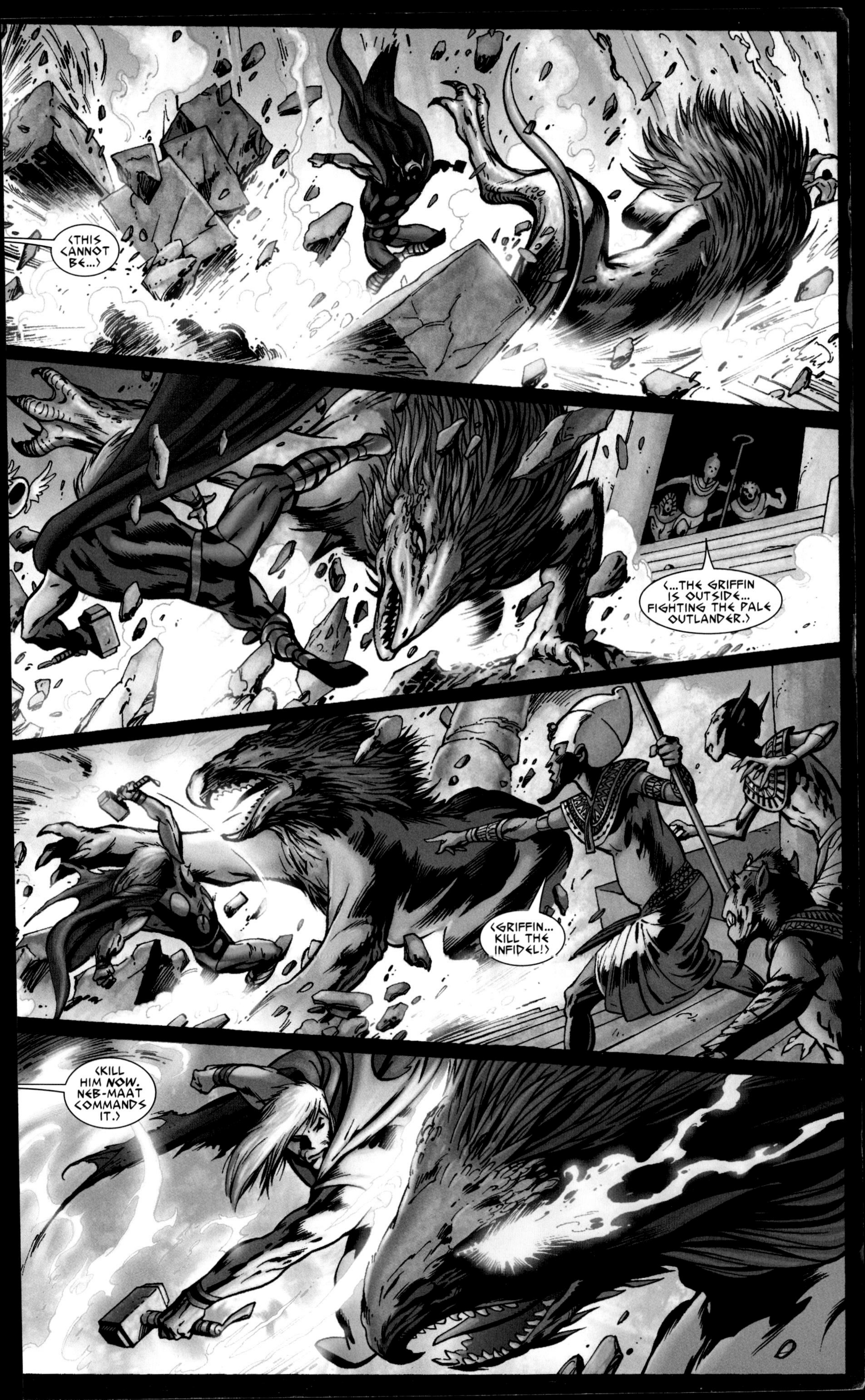

<THIS <CANNOT BE...>
<...THE GRIFFIN IS OUTSIDE... FIGHTING THE PALE OUTLANDER.>
<GRIFFIN... KILL THE INFIDEL!>
<KILL HIM NOW. NEB-MAAT COMMANDS IT.>

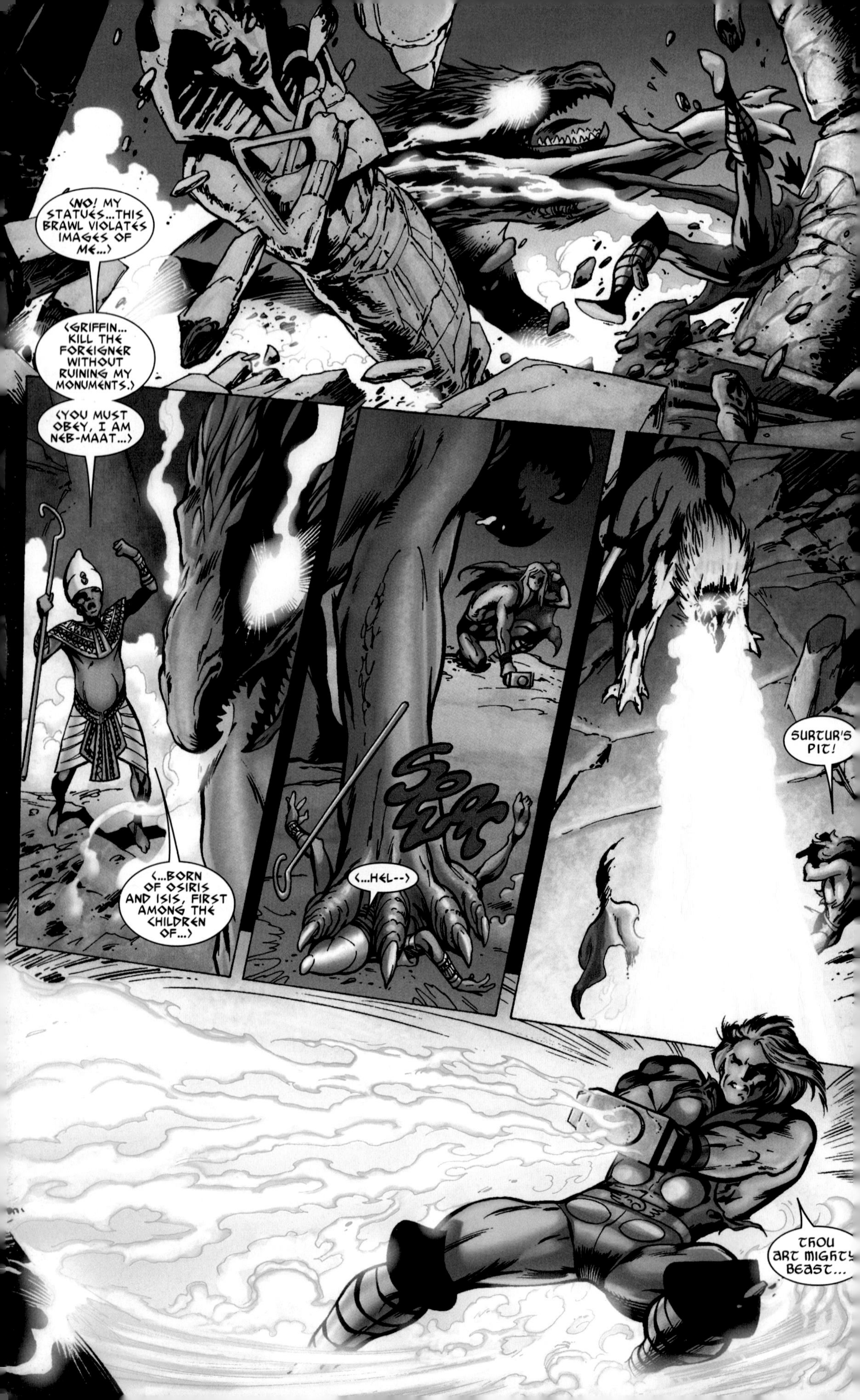

‹NO! MY STATUES...THIS BRAWL VIOLATES IMAGES OF ME...›
‹GRIFFIN... KILL THE FOREIGNER WITHOUT RUINING MY MONUMENTS.›
‹YOU MUST OBEY, I AM NEB-MAAT...›
‹...BORN OF OSIRIS AND ISIS, FIRST AMONG THE CHILDREN OF...›
‹...HEL--›
SURTUR'S PIT!
THOU ART MIGHTY BEAST...

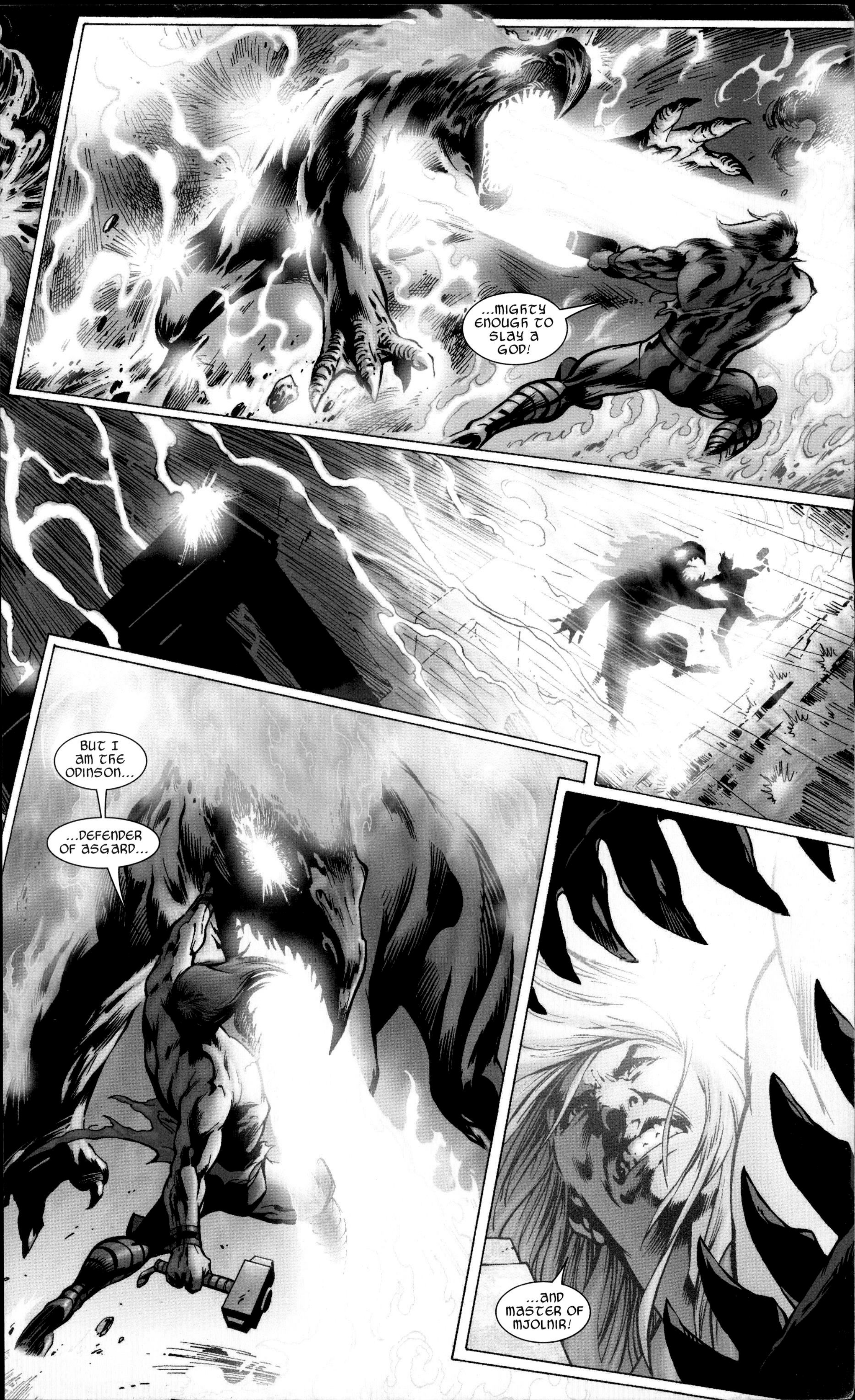
...MIGHTY ENOUGH TO SLAY A GOD!
BUT I AM THE ODINSON...
...DEFENDER OF ASGARD...
...AND MASTER OF MJOLNIR!

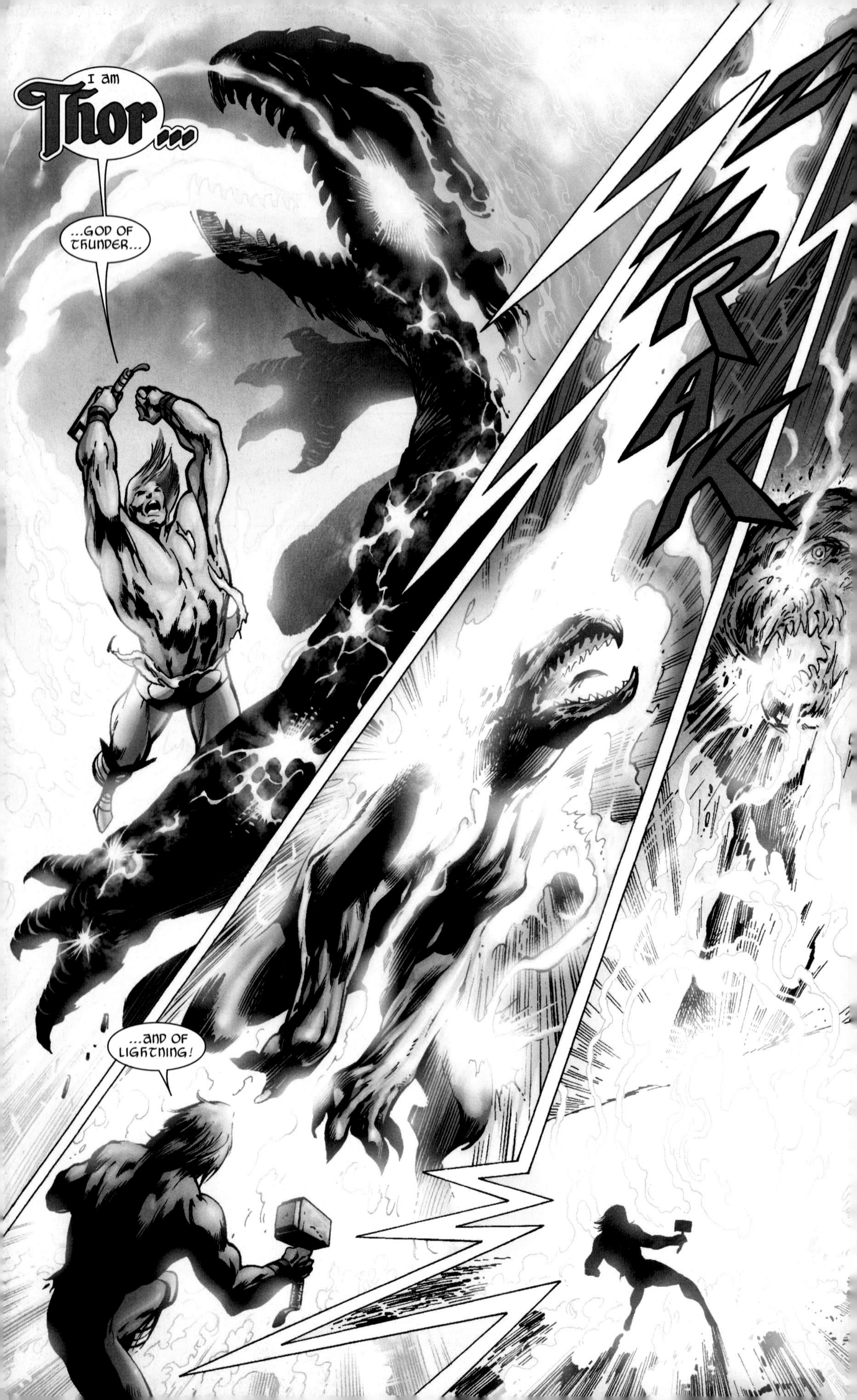
I am Thor...
...GOD OF THUNDER...
...AND OF LIGHTNING!
KRAAAK

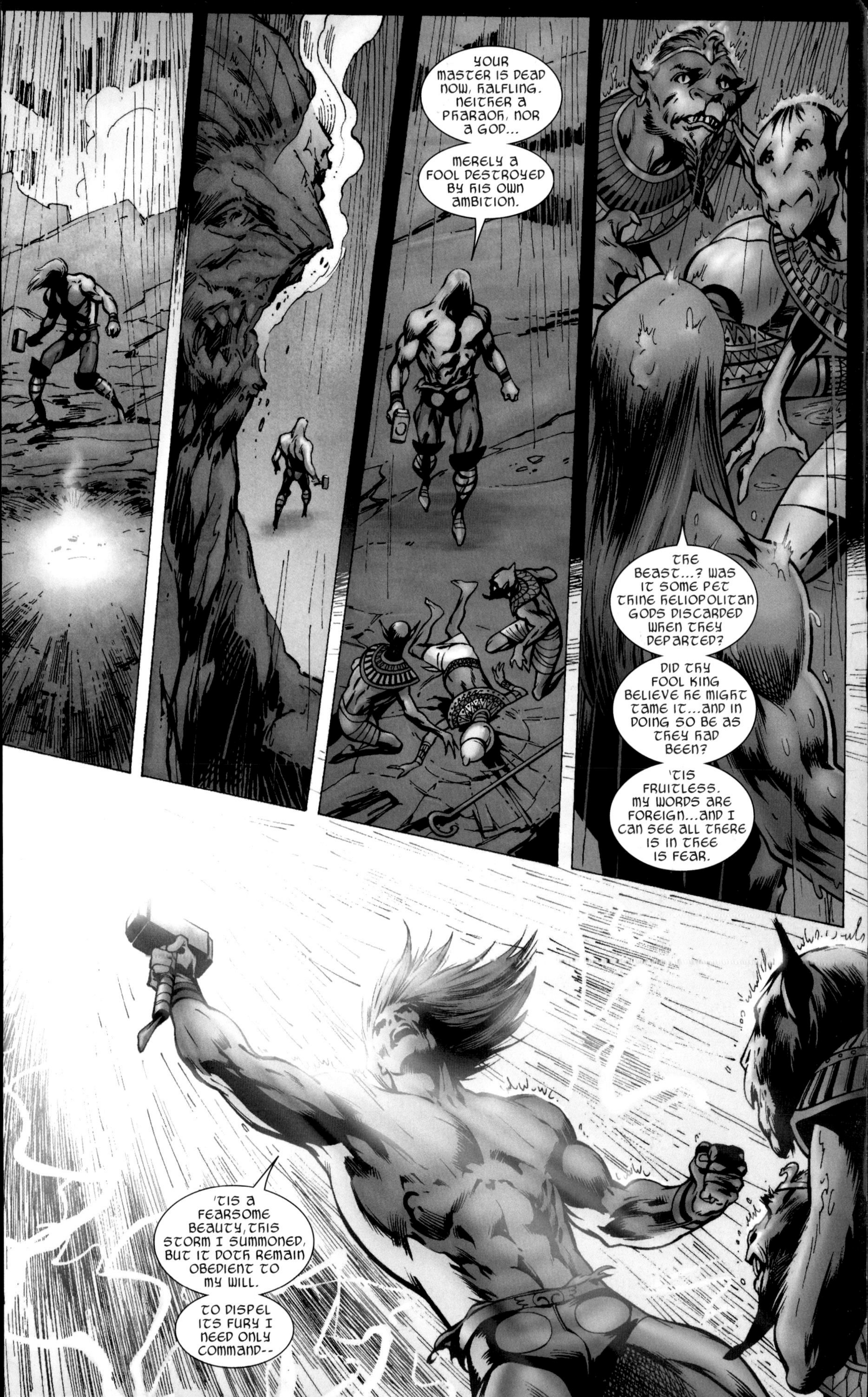
YOUR MASTER IS DEAD NOW, HALFLING. NEITHER A PHARAOH, NOR A GOD...
MERELY A FOOL DESTROYED BY HIS OWN AMBITION.
THE BEAST...? WAS IT SOME PET THINE HELIOPOLITAN GODS DISCARDED WHEN THEY DEPARTED?
DID THY FOOL KING BELIEVE HE MIGHT TAME IT...AND IN DOING SO BE AS THEY HAD BEEN?
'TIS FRUITLESS. MY WORDS ARE FOREIGN...AND I CAN SEE ALL THERE IS IN THEE IS FEAR.
'TIS A FEARSOME BEAUTY, THIS STORM I SUMMONED, BUT IT DOTH REMAIN OBEDIENT TO MY WILL.
TO DISPEL ITS FURY I NEED ONLY COMMAND--

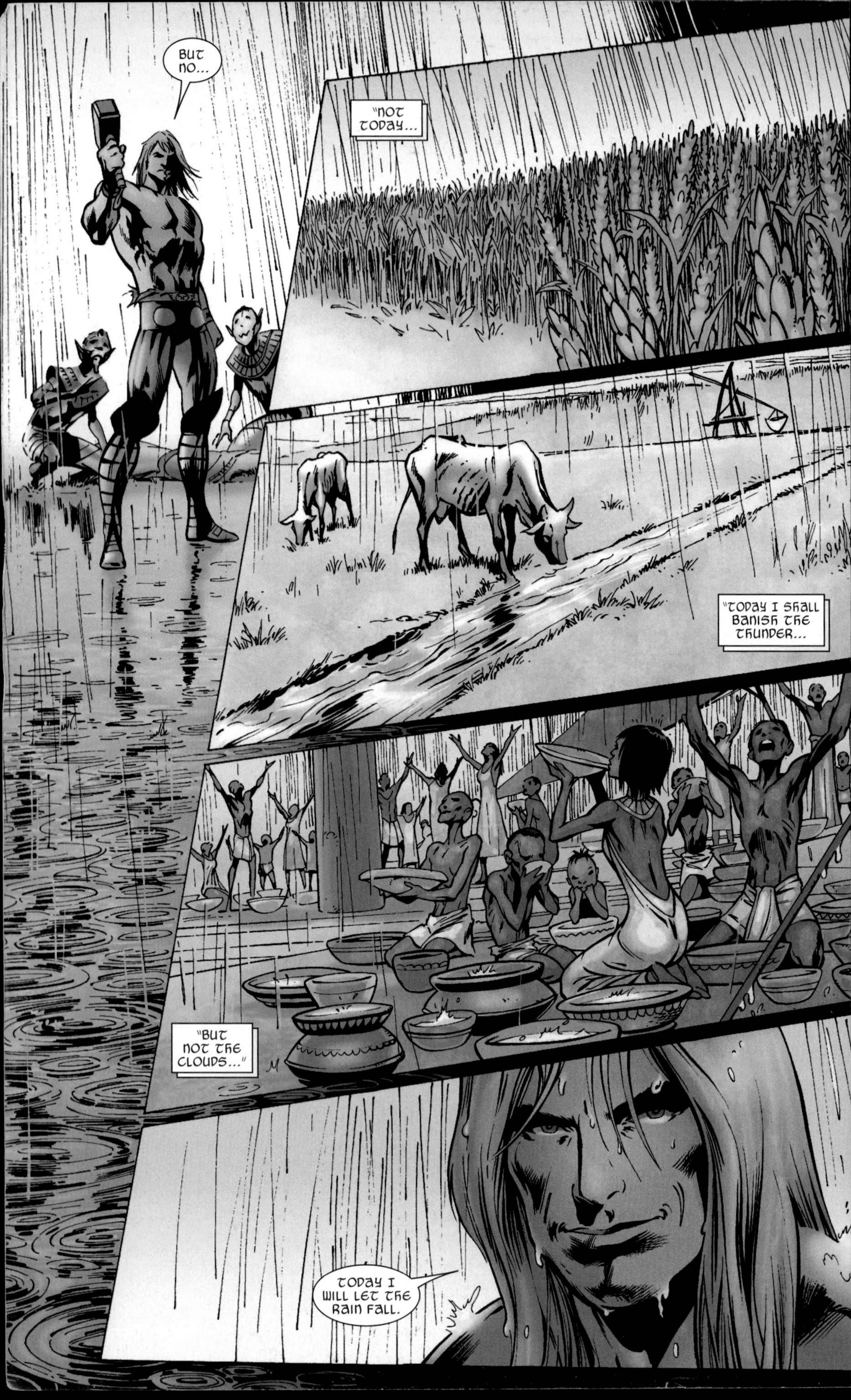
BUT NO...
"NOT TODAY...
"TODAY I SHALL BANISH THE THUNDER...
"BUT NOT THE CLOUDS..."
TODAY I WILL LET THE RAIN FALL.

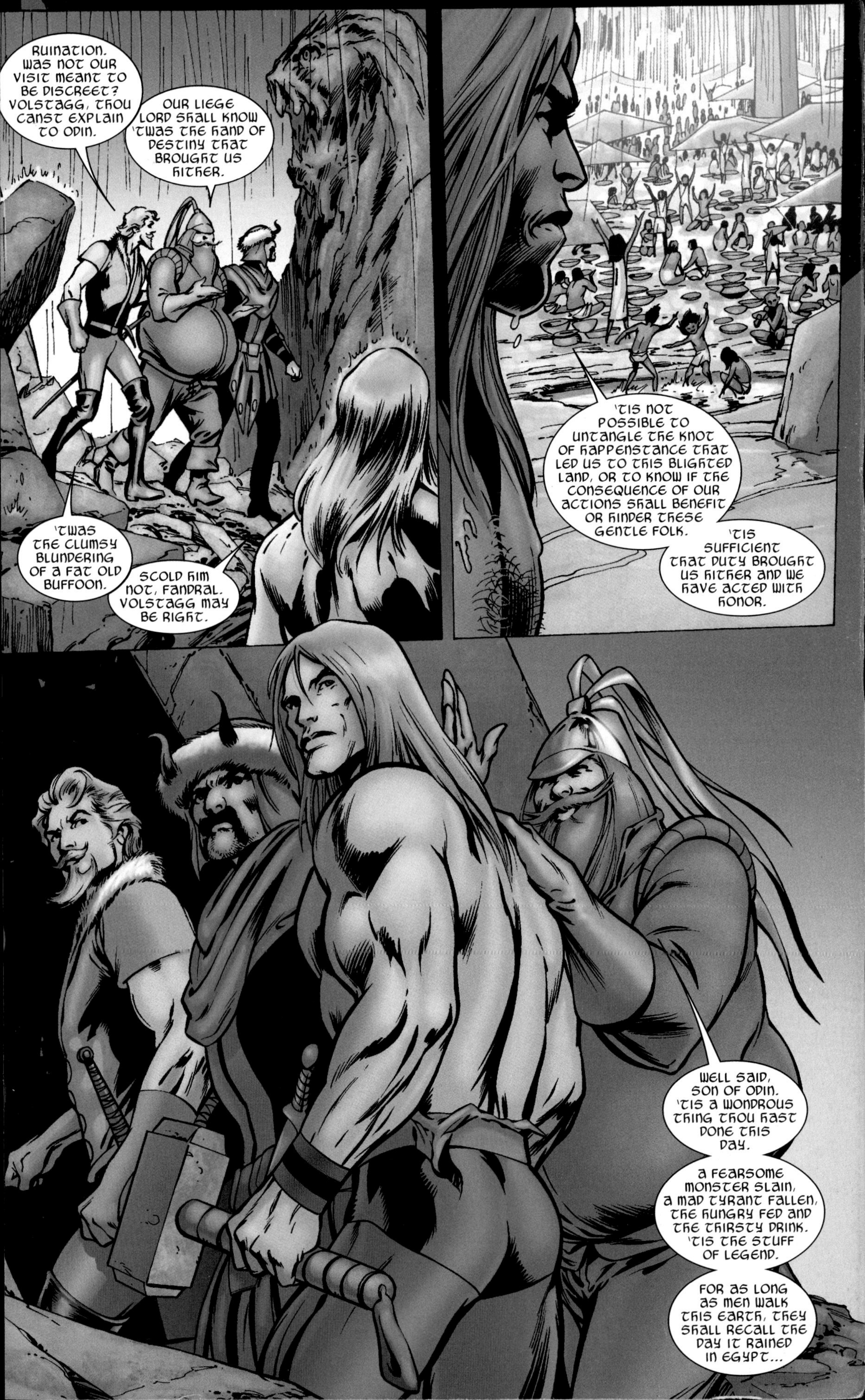
RUINATION. WAS NOT OUR VISIT MEANT TO BE DISCREET? VOLSTAGG, THOU CANST EXPLAIN TO ODIN.
OUR LIEGE LORD SHALL KNOW 'TWAS THE HAND OF DESTINY THAT BROUGHT US HITHER.
'TWAS THE CLUMSY BLUNDERING OF A FAT OLD BUFFOON.
SCOLD HIM NOT, FANDRAL. VOLSTAGG MAY BE RIGHT.
'TIS NOT POSSIBLE TO UNTANGLE THE KNOT OF HAPPENSTANCE THAT LED US TO THIS BLIGHTED LAND, OR TO KNOW IF THE CONSEQUENCE OF OUR ACTIONS SHALL BENEFIT OR HINDER THESE GENTLE FOLK.
'TIS SUFFICIENT THAT DUTY BROUGHT US HITHER AND WE HAVE ACTED WITH HONOR.
WELL SAID, SON OF ODIN. 'TIS A WONDROUS THING THOU HAST DONE THIS DAY.
A FEARSOME MONSTER SLAIN, A MAD TYRANT FALLEN, THE HUNGRY FED AND THE THIRSTY DRINK. 'TIS THE STUFF OF LEGEND.
FOR AS LONG AS MEN WALK THIS EARTH, THEY SHALL RECALL THE DAY IT RAINED IN EGYPT...

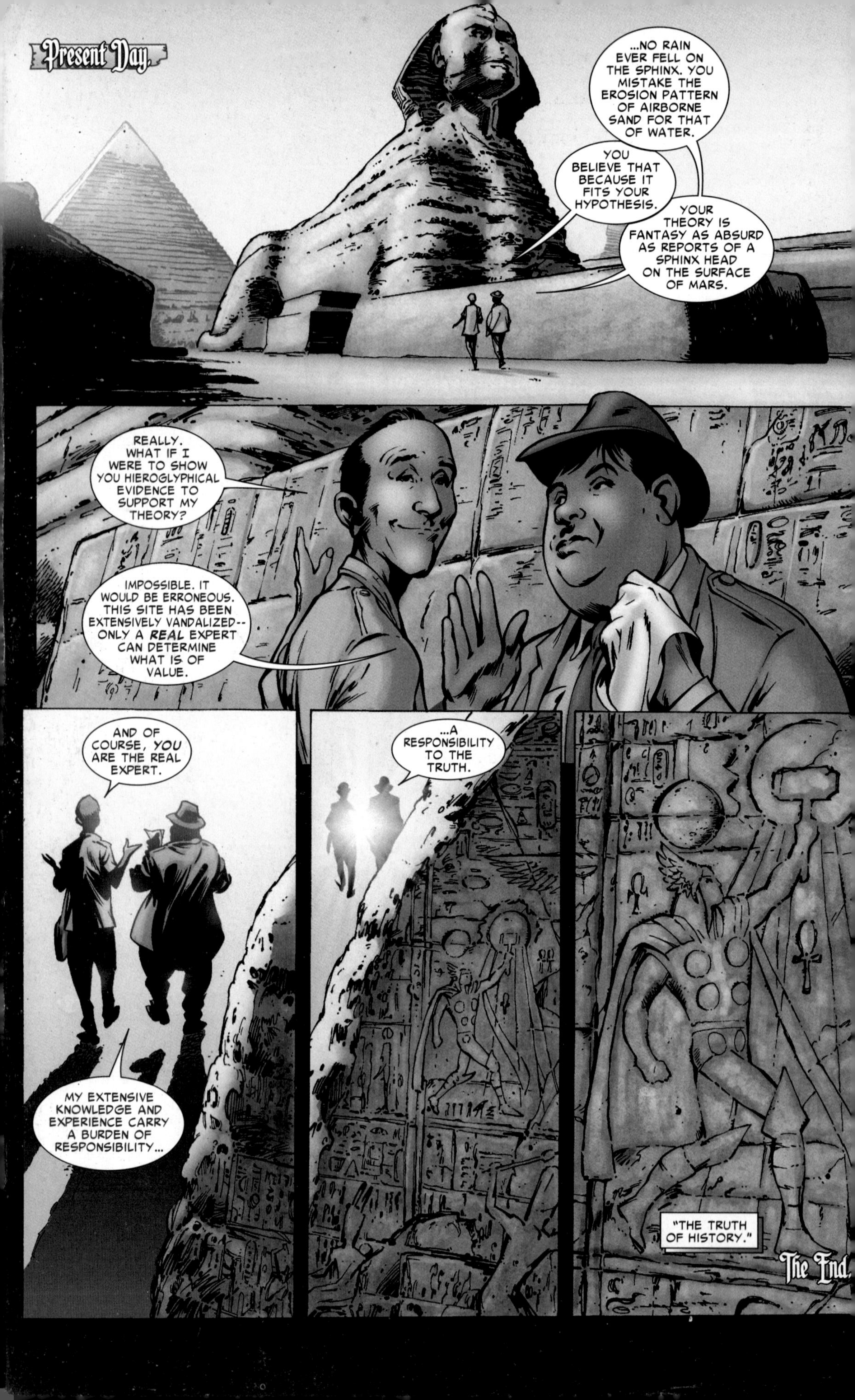
Present Day.
...NO RAIN EVER FELL ON THE SPHINX. YOU MISTAKE THE EROSION PATTERN OF AIRBORNE SAND FOR THAT OF WATER.
YOU BELIEVE THAT BECAUSE IT FITS YOUR HYPOTHESIS.
YOUR THEORY IS FANTASY AS ABSURD AS REPORTS OF A SPHINX HEAD ON THE SURFACE OF MARS.
REALLY. WHAT IF I WERE TO SHOW YOU HIEROGLYPHICAL EVIDENCE TO SUPPORT MY THEORY?
IMPOSSIBLE. IT WOULD BE ERRONEOUS. THIS SITE HAS BEEN EXTENSIVELY VANDALIZED--ONLY A *REAL* EXPERT CAN DETERMINE WHAT IS OF VALUE.
AND OF COURSE, *YOU* ARE THE REAL EXPERT.
MY EXTENSIVE KNOWLEDGE AND EXPERIENCE CARRY A BURDEN OF RESPONSIBILITY...
...A RESPONSIBILITY TO THE TRUTH.
"THE TRUTH OF HISTORY."
The End.